NATIONAL FOUNDATION FOR EDUCATIONAL
RESEARCH IN ENGLAND AND WALES

RESEARCH REPORTS

Streaming
in the
Primary School

Streaming in the Primary School

A Longitudinal Study of Children in Streamed and Non-Streamed Junior Schools

by

JOAN C. BARKER LUNN
Streaming Research Project, NFER

With the assistance of
ELSA FERRI

NATIONAL FOUNDATION FOR EDUCATIONAL
RESEARCH IN ENGLAND AND WALES
THE MERE, UPTON PARK, SLOUGH, BUCKS

Published by the National Foundation for Educational Research
in England and Wales

The Mere, Upton Park, Slough, Bucks
and at 79 Wimpole Street, London, W1M 8EA

First Published 1970

© *National Foundation for Educational Research*
in England and Wales, 1970

Printed in Great Britain by
KING, THORNE & STACE LTD., SCHOOL ROAD, HOVE, SUSSEX

Acknowledgements

M Y thanks are due to the heads and teachers concerned for their patience and generous co-operation; to the children who were involved; to Dr. W. D. Wall, Mr. D. A. Pidgeon, Professor B. Morris and Dr. K. Miller for their helpful advice and encouragement; to Dr. S. Wiseman, Mr. Alfred Yates, Professor F. Warburton, Miss M. Proctor, Mrs. E. Britton, Mr. A. E. Sanderson and Miss M. Cox for reading and commenting on the book. I also gratefully acknowledge the assistance of Mrs. Elsa Ferri, Mr. Chris. Tuppen, Mr. Peter Healey, Mrs. Janet Bouri, Miss Lois Wilson and Miss Rebecca Samad, past and present members of the research team; and also of Miss Jill Tarryer for her statistical advice. Also my thanks are due to Rothamstead Experimental Station who allowed us valuable computer facilities.

The research was supported by a grant from the Department of Education and Science.

v

Acknowledgements

Contents

Contents

Contents

Contents

APPENDICES

Contents

List of Tables

List of Tables

APPENDIX 4

A4.1	Test reliabilities (calculated by the Kuder-Richardson Formula 20)	312
A4.2	Inter-correlations between the six markers	313
A4.3	Inter-correlations between the chosen markers	314
A4.4	Inter-correlations of items (phi coefficient)	316
A4.5	Inter-correlations of items (phi coefficient) 1967	317
A4.6	Reproducibilities of Guttman Scales for teachers' attitudes (Questionnaire S.3)	326

APPENDIX 5

A5.1	Type of school	329
A5.2	Fathers' occupational group	330
A5.3	Details of the 28 school sample	331
A5.4	Details of the Cohort 1 children involved in the study of attitude change in the 28 schools	332
A5.5	Details of the Cohorts 1 and 2 children involved in the study of attitude (scores) in the 28 schools	333

APPENDIX 6: TABLES NOT IN THE TEXT

3.2	Number of years' teaching experience	334
3.3	Age of head teachers in streamed and non-streamed schools	335
3.4	Frequency of tests and of different types of arithmetic lessons in streamed and non-streamed schools over the four years	336
3.5	Frequency of writing stories and of comprehension exercises and punctuation lessons in streamed and non-streamed schools at 9+ and 10+	337
4.5	Method used for teaching English	338
4.6	Method used for teaching Maths.	339
4.7	Method used for teaching Reading	340
4.8	Method used for teaching other subjects, e.g. History, Social Studies	341
4.9	Criteria used for assigning children to seats	342
4.10	Sex of Type 1 and Type 2 teachers in streamed and non-streamed schools	343

xv

List of Tables

List of Tables

List of Tables

List of Tables

APPENDIX 7A

APPENDIX 7B

APPENDIX 8

List of Graphs

List of Figures

INTRODUCTION

THE favoured method of organizing classes in large junior schools for the last thirty years or more in England has been 'streaming', otherwise known, particularly in the United States, as 'homogeneous ability grouping'. Under this system, children within each year group are sub-divided into 'streams' according to their ability or attainments, which may be assessed either by objective standardized tests, by school examinations or by head's or teachers' reports.

After the Hadow Report of 1926 which recommended that all-age elementary schools should be divided into primary and senior schools, the question of the internal organization of these schools was raised. 'Streaming' was recommended in the *Primary School Report* of 1931, which said:

> 'The break at the age of eleven has rendered possible a more thorough classification of children. . . . One great advantage of the self-contained primary school is that the teachers have special opportunities for making a suitable classification of the children according to their natural gifts and abilities. On the one hand, immediate treatment of an appropriate character can be provided for retarded children and on the other hand, suitable arrangements may be made for specially bright children.'

It was suggested that, where possible, there should be a 'triple track' or streamed system of organization comprising A-, B- and C-streams. The A classes would be for the bright pupils, the B classes for average children and the C classes, made up of a smaller number of pupils, would provide for the 'retarded' children.

Research on streaming and non-streaming

In the early 1950s, articles criticizing streaming began to appear and research on the subject began to be published in the late nineteen-fifties.

Within the last few years, a movement has grown up whose members have questioned the need for streaming. A number of heads have unstreamed their junior schools and have reported benefits from doing so. The journal *Forum*, in particular, has published many articles on the topic and suggested methods of running a non-streamed school; a number of these articles have been

1

published in book form (Simon, 1964). Also in 1964, Jackson's *Streaming: An Education System in Miniature* was published. This book, by a believer in non-streaming, gave personal impressions of visits to a number of streamed and non-streamed schools as well as the results of a questionnaire survey of a large number of schools.

The effects of streaming upon pupil attainments have been studied in small scale inquiries by Daniels (1961), Blandford (1958) and Rudd (1958). These pioneering studies have been valuable but they cannot be considered conclusive. The findings of Daniels and Blandford favoured non-streaming and Rudd found no difference between the two types of school organization.

Blandford (1958) compared the scores obtained by pupils over three years in five streamed and six non-streamed schools. However, at the time of the research, most schools that were large enough to stream did so, and he had to take for his non-streamed schools those with only enough pupils for one class per age group and which had, in effect, mixed ability classes.

He found that the spread of scores in the attainment tests was greater in streamed schools, that is, the brighter children did better, and the slower children obtained lower test scores than their counterparts in 'non-streamed' schools.

Rudd, in 1958, published the results of a study comparing attainments of two groups of children in the same secondary school, one of which was streamed and the other not streamed. No difference in attainments or attitudes was found between the two groups. The big drawback of this study was that it was carried out in one school, making it impossible for either group to experience the 'true climate' of a 'streamed' or 'non-streamed' school. This also applies to the 'non-streamed' schools in Blandford's study.

Daniels (1961) compared the progress of pupils over a four-year period in two pairs of junior schools. One member of each pair was a three-stream school and the other was non-streamed. The schools were matched for amenities, buildings, staffing ratio, teacher experience and ability, although there was no indication of how the latter was assessed. The teachers in the non-streamed schools, it was reported, 'tended to be keener and more interested in their work'.

Initially, children whose test results were to be compared were matched by groups, so that each of the paired groups had the same mean and dispersion of test scores. This matching procedure was used for Reading, IQ, English and Arithmetic. The mean and standard deviations of the groups were compared between treatments. Daniels found that the average level of mental ability and attainment tended to be higher in non-streamed than streamed schools. He found some evidence that the higher average level of attainment in the non-streamed schools was accompanied by a closer bunching of scores around the mean. The standard deviations were significantly different for Reading and English but not for Intelligence or Arithmetic, although the latter two exhibited similar tendencies (that is, the standard deviations were smaller in the non-streamed schools).

Daniels concludes that the increase in ability and attainment in non-streamed schools 'is achieved without any noticeable holding back of brighter pupils, though it seems true that the main effect of non-streaming is a radical "pulling up" of the more backward children'. Actually the numbers of superior and slow pupils involved in Daniels' study were far too small for these generalizations to be made.

Besides studies investigating the effects of streaming on attainments, other research has looked at the effects on the social adjustment and attitudes of pupils. However, these studies, too, suffer from the use of small samples and are therefore inconclusive. Of the three best-known studies that examine the effects of streaming on non-cognitive aspects, each shows a different result: Willig's (1963) conclusions favour non-streaming, Finch's (1954) favour streaming and Rudd (1956) finds no difference between the two types of school organization.

It would seem that everyone can find evidence in previous research to support whichever side they take on this issue.

Most of the above studies have been too small in scale and also too short in duration. It has become increasingly apparent that the sample must be of a statistically respectable size, not only in terms of pupils, but also of teachers. Small scale studies will only show that Mr. X with streaming obtained result A while Mrs. Y with non-streaming obtained result B. One cannot generalize from such results.

The inconclusiveness of research in the United States

There has been a vast amount of research on streaming in the United States. Despite its abundance there is, however, no clear trend emerging which indicates the superiority of either streaming or non-streaming: different researchers have found contradictory results.

Ekstrom (1959), in her review of important grouping experiments from the 1920s to 1959, reported that the findings were generally inconclusive: 13 studies found differences favouring streaming, 15 found either no differences or results detrimental to streaming, and five studies gave mixed results.

Franseth (1966) reviewed research findings on the relative merits of different grouping methods for pupil learning and achievement. She also found results to be indefinite and inconclusive. Some studies showed achievement gains in favour of streaming, some in favour of mixed ability grouping, and others showed no significant difference between the two.

The American research does not lead to a general consensus and on the whole the standard of research has not been good.

Passow (1966) suggests seven reasons why studies differ in their conclusions:

1. They vary in scope, aim and purpose. Some studies deal with college students, others with elementary schools. Sometimes only one school subject is studied; at other times two or more school subjects are studied.

2. They differ in the number of pupils and groups, and in the size of classes involved. Very few studies have used an adequate sample, either in the United States or in Britain.

3. They differ in duration, varying from a few months to several years.

4. They differ in treatment—that is, in the similarity or differences in curricula and teaching method between experimental and control groups.

5. They differ with respect to the test instruments used. Non-cognitive aspects have been rather neglected and advantage has not been taken of recent developments in psychometric methods. Although arguments for and against grouping frequently refer to such changes as work study habits, social adjustments, attitudes towards self and school, few efforts have been made to evaluate the effects of grouping in these areas of development.

6. They have usually ignored the relative efficiency, enthusiasm and attitudes of teachers.

7. They differ in the adequacy of the selection bases and the means of matching experimental and control groups.

Two of the more recent large-scale studies of grouping which have been carried out in the United States are, however, worth considering. These are the studies of Borg and Goldberg.

Borg (1964) studied two adjacent and comparable districts in Utah. One district employed ability grouping, speeding or slowing down the presentation of materials to pupils, and the other used random grouping with enrichment. Pupils in grades 4, 6, 7, 8 and 9 were studied for four years. Initially the sample numbered 2,500 pupils but was increased in the second year to 4,000.

The ability grouping system used in District A employed the California Achievement Tests as a basis for grouping the pupils in three ability levels. The same tests were also administered to the randomly grouped sample but only in order to provide samples of pupils of comparable ability. The variables considered were achievement, study habits, sociometric status, pupil problems, self-concept, aspiration level, pupil attitudes, and personality.

In terms of achievement, Borg concluded that there was little to choose between ability grouping with acceleration and random grouping with enrichment; neither system had a consistent effect on achievement at any of the grade levels tested.

In comparing all five grade levels which were studied, a total of 47 between-treatment comparisons were made for each ability level. For *superior* pupils it was found that 15 comparisons favoured ability grouping, 3 favoured random grouping, and the remaining 29 showed no significant differences. The comparisons between achievement gains of *slow* pupils in the two districts revealed 4 favouring ability grouping and 7 favouring random grouping; the remaining 36 were not significant. For *average* pupils 13 of the comparisons favoured ability grouping, 6 random grouping and the others were found to show no significant differences.

Borg says: 'Therefore it is our conclusion that the decision to employ ability or random grouping must be based upon considerations other than achievement'.

In addition to achievement, Borg gathered data on other variables. A summary of these results is given in Table 0.1.

The most striking aspect of Borg's work is the number of comparisons made which were non-significant. In every case when numbers were reported which were significant, favouring either A (ability grouping) or R (random grouping), they were always much smaller than the number of comparisons which were not significant.

Random grouping appeared more favourable for slow pupils, except with regard to measures of sociometric status and attitudes to school and teacher.

There was a very slight tendency for *average* pupils to have lower attainments but more favourable non-cognitive scores with random grouping. *Superior* pupils appeared to have higher attainments with ability grouping, but the results on the non-cognitive tests had a tendency to favour random grouping.

TABLE 0.1: *Summary of results from Borg's study, showing the number of comparisons favouring District A and District R*

VARIABLES	SUPERIOR PUPILS	AVERAGE PUPILS	SLOW PUPILS
Attainments	15A, 3R, 29NS	13A, 6R, 28NS	4A, 7R, 36NS
Over and under achievers	More over and fewer under-achievers in District A than District R	Little or no difference	
Study habits	Pupils in random grouped classes (District R) developed better study habits than pupils in ability grouped classes		
Sociometry	Higher sociometric status in random grouped classes	Higher sociometric status in ability grouped classes	
Self and wanted self	District A pupils had higher emotional disturbance scores than District R on 'Thinking about yourself' questionnaire. Ability grouped pupils had a greater discrepancy between 'Self' and 'Wanted Self'.		
Pupil problems	20A, 2R, 28NS Favours A	17A, 25NS Favours A	6A, 44NS Favours A
Pupil attitudes: to teachers	More favourable attitudes in A	No difference	More favourable attitudes in A
to peers	No difference	No difference	No difference
to school	No difference	No difference	More favourable attitudes in A
Concept of self	Better self-concepts in District R 2A, 6R, 16NS	10R, 23NS	5R, 18NS
Acceptance of self	15 significantly favour R, 57NS		
Discrepancy scores	6A, 5R, 18NS	6R, 18NS	2R, 22NS
Ideal self	1A, 1R, 22NS	4R, 20NS	2R, 22NS

6

TABLE 0.1:—*continued*

VARIABLES	SUPERIOR PUPILS	AVERAGE PUPILS	SLOW PUPILS
Level of aspiration	No difference		
Feeling of belonging	Pupils in random grouped classes score higher; favours R		
Withdrawing tendencies	No difference		
Anti-social tendencies	Favours R		
Total adjustment	5 out of 6 comparisons favour R		
Inferiority and ascendancy	No difference		
Anxiety	No difference		

Note: Numbers refer to the number of comparisons favouring either A (ability grouping/streaming) or R (random grouping/non-streaming). NS= number of comparisons between A and R not significantly different.

Many of the instruments used in this study were confined to older age groups, since they were not suitable for use with children less than ten years old. Also there was no attempt to control teacher or home background variables which might have affected the results.

The other study is that by Goldberg *et al.* (1966). This was a comparative study of classes covering broad, medium and narrow ranges of ability. Approximately two thousand pupils in 45 elementary schools were classified according to five ability levels and the 86 classes involved were classified into three ability ranges.

The aim of the study was to test the hypothesis 'Neither the presence nor the absence of gifted or slow pupils, nor the range of abilities in any given classroom, nor the relative position of a particular ability level within the range will affect the attainment of elementary school pupils'. The classes remained intact for two years from the beginning to the end of the research. The pupils were tested at the beginning of the fifth grade and at the end of the sixth grade.

7

The testing programme included the following:

(1) Academic achievement in reading, arithmetic, language arts, and work study skills—Science Research Associates Achievement Series (grades 4–6).

(2) Academic achievement in science and social studies—Stanford achievement tests.

(3) Interests: 'What I like to do' inventory.

(4) Attitudes towards self: 'How I feel about myself' inventory.

(5) Attitudes towards more and less able pupils: 'Describing a pupil' check list.

(6) Attitude towards school: 'What I like to do' questionnaire.

(7) Teacher appraisal: Teacher rating form.

For all five ability levels taken together, the greatest achievement gains were consistently associated with the broad ability range classes. However, the differences were generally small and for no one group were they significant in more than two or three subjects tested. The authors concluded that 'simply narrowing the ability range in the classroom does not necessarily result in a greater differentiation of content or method and is not associated with greater academic achievement for any ability level'.

In general, ability grouping seemed to have a more significant and consistent effect on self-attitudes than on achievement. The presence of gifted children resulted in improved self-attitudes among the brighter pupils, and less positive appraisals for the slow ones, but had little effect on those of average ability.

Changes in expectations of academic success were significantly but not consistently affected by ability range. The slower pupils raised their expectations in narrow and medium ability range classes and lowered them in broad ability range classes. The reverse was true for brighter pupils.

Grouping seemed to have no consistent predictable effects on either pupils' interests or their attitudes towards school. Nor did it have any effect on pupil attitudes towards peers of varying levels of ability.

The general conclusion drawn by Goldberg *et al.* was that ability grouping in itself is unlikely to raise the academic attainments of pupils. 'In the absence of specific plans for changing the content and methods of teaching so as deliberately to provide the most needed and challenging learning situation for each group of pupils, ability grouping does not seem to make any appreciable difference.'

Introduction

In December 1964, a conference of research workers, representing the United States, the United Kingdom and countries of Western and Northern Europe, was held at the UNESCO Institute for Education, Hamburg. The aim of this was to discuss the basis, operation and effectiveness of the forms of grouping practised within these countries. The outcome was published in book form (Yates, 1966).

The conclusion of the Hamburg conference members concerning research into streaming within the school was the same as that reached by Ekstrom and Franseth earlier. They found research abundant but inconclusive. The reasons given for this were that many of the inquiries had involved inadequate samples and were conducted over too short a period of time. Others had failed to take account of important variables or had been too limited in scope.

The conference was impressed by the amount of available evidence that had shown a significant relationship between teachers' attitudes towards a particular form of grouping and the results in terms of their pupils' progress and attainments. These attitudes were claimed to be partly determined by the teacher's views about the status conferred upon him by employment within a particular kind of organization, and also by the extent to which he was or believed himself to be competent to teach the group for whose tuition he was made responsible. It was argued that grouping practices and methods of instruction were closely related: streaming facilitates a particular method of teaching; non-streaming permits or demands a different approach.

Implications of past studies and direction for this research

Why have research studies investigating streaming produced inconsistent and inconclusive results? The fact that sometimes the differences favour streaming and other times non-streaming would seem to indicate that factors other than particular grouping procedures must account for any differences in achievement gains that occur between children in streamed and non-streamed schools. What then really accounts for the results?

It would seem from this brief review of grouping that many researchers have failed to take account of important variables. Rarely, if at all, have teachers' attitudes or methods of working been considered.

One possible explanation for the inconsistent findings is that different teachers respond differently to the two forms of organization. Some teachers believe in the system, use suitable methods and

B

their pupils gain; others cannot accept the system or use inappropriate methods, and their pupils do relatively badly. When the results obtained are averaged, little overall difference between the two forms of groupings is obtained.

But attitudes and methods of working are part of the grouping situation and will interact with it. In the past these variables have not been represented and therefore there has been no opportunity of demonstrating their effects. It is useless to attempt to measure the effects of grouping without taking account of the interaction of these variables.

References

BLANDFORD, J. S. (1958). 'Standardized tests in junior schools with special reference to the effects of streaming on the constancy of results', *Brit. J. Educ. Psychol.*, 28, 170-3.

BOARD OF EDUCATION (GREAT BRITAIN). (1926). *The Education of the Adolescent*. (Chairman: Sir William H. Hadow). London: HM Stationery Office.

BOARD OF EDUCATION (GREAT BRITAIN). (1931). *The Primary School*. (Chairman: Sir William H. Hadow). London: HM Stationery Office.

BORG, W. R. (1964). *An Evaluation of Ability Grouping*. Co-op. Res. Proj. No. 577. Salt Lake City: Utah State University.

DANIELS, J. C. (1961). 'The effects of streaming in the primary school, I: What teachers believe; II: Comparison of streamed and unstreamed schools', *Brit. J. Educ. Psychol.*, 31, 69-78; 119-26.

EKSTROM, R. B. (1959). *Experimental Studies of Homogeneous Grouping: A Review of the Literature*. Princeton, NJ: Educational Testing Service.

FINCH, I. E. (1954). 'A study of the personal and social consequences for groups of secondary children of the experience of different methods of allocation within secondary courses'. M.A. thesis, University of London.

Forum. (1964). *Non-Streaming in the Junior School*. Edited by B. Simon. Leicester: PSW (Educational) Publications.

FRANSETH, J. and KOURY, R. (1966). *Survey of Research on Grouping as Related to Pupil Learning*. Washington, DC: US Department of Health, Education and Welfare.

GOLDBERG, M. L., PASSOW, A. H. and JUSTMAN, J. (1966). *The Effects of Ability Grouping*. New York: Teachers College Press, Columbia University.

JACKSON, B. (1964). *Streaming: An Education System in Miniature*. London: Routledge & Kegan Paul.

PASSOW, H. (1966). 'The maze of research on ability grouping'. In: YATES, A. ed. *Grouping in Education*. Hamburg: Unesco Institute for Education; New York: Wiley.

RUDD, W. G. A. (1956). 'The psychological effects of streaming by attainment with special reference to a group of selected children', *Brit. J. Educ. Psychol.*, 28, 47-60.

WILLIG, C. J. (1963). 'Social implication of streaming in junior schools'. Unpublished M.Ed. thesis, University of Leicester.

YATES, A. ed. (1966). *Grouping in Education*. Hamburg: Unesco Institute for Education; New York: Wiley.

CHAPTER 1

Background to the Study

IN 1963, in response to a request from the Ministry of Education, a research project was initiated by the NFER to investigate the effects of streaming and non-streaming in large junior schools; the study was financially supported by a grant from the Department of Education and Science. It was hoped that some of the preliminary results from this study would provide evidence for the Plowden Committee which was being set up to report on the primary school (Department of Education and Science, 1967).

Broadly the aim of the study was to examine the effects of streaming and non-streaming on the personality and social and intellectual development of pupils.

Some of the main questions which the research set out to answer are given below. However, a fuller list of all questions stated in hypothesis form can be found in Appendix 1.

(1) Is the average level of performance in the 3 Rs higher in streamed or non-streamed schools?

(2) Do bright children make greater progress in streamed or non-streamed schools?

(3) Do below average or slow children make greater progress in streamed or non-streamed schools?

(4) Does streaming handicap working class children or does type of school organization make no difference to their scholastic progress?

(5) Are there any personality, attitude or interest differences in children of the same ability level in the two types of school?

(6) Are the social relationships of children affected by streaming?

The definition of streaming and non-streaming

The usual definition of streaming, which is given in *The Primary School Report* of 1931, is used here. A 'streamed' school is one in which the allocation of each yearly intake to classes is on the basis of ability or attainment, so that the most able are assigned to the top or A-streams, the less able to other streams.

A non-streamed school is defined as one in which pupils within each year group are assigned to classes made up of children from all ability levels. This may be done either by assessing the pupils' abilities and forming parallel classes which have roughly the same mean and range of ability; or by allocating to classes randomly, based for example, on alphabetical order of the children's surnames; or by allocating on the basis of age.

The NFER sample included only those schools which had been practising streaming or non-streaming for at least four years; streaming or non-streaming also had to be practised consistently in all four junior year groups.[1]

Programme of research

The inquiry consisted of three main parts:

(i) It began with a survey of the existing methods of school organization in a stratified random sample of 2,000 junior schools (i.e. one in eight of all junior schools in England and Wales). This survey was carried out in 1963 and has already been reported (Barker Lunn, 1967a).

(ii) The second phase was a comparative study consisting of matched pairs of streamed and non-streamed schools. This was in two parts:

(*a*) The first part was a cross-sectional study which was carried out in 1964 and involved all four year groups of junior school pupils. Full details of this can be found in the *Primary School Report* (Department of Education and Science, 1967) and elsewhere (Barker Lunn, 1967b).

(*b*) The second part was a longitudinal study and was mainly concerned with those pupils (5,500) aged seven-plus in 1964 (Cohort 1) who were followed through their entire junior school course until 1967. A limited follow-up study was also made of those pupils who were in their second year (eight-plus) in 1964 (Cohort 2).

---

[1] During the period of research, three of the non-streamed schools created a remedial class for one or two years so that a small number of the longitudinal study pupils in these schools were, strictly speaking, streamed at some time. Since the numbers involved were small and so as not to reduce the sample schools further, they were retained.

Initially, there were 100 schools in the comparative study sample, consisting of 50 matched pairs of streamed and non-streamed schools, but during the research the number was reduced as schools dropped out due to changes in organization or to reductions in numbers of pupils or staff. For the cross-sectional study, data from 84 schools, and for the longitudinal study, data from 72 schools were analysed.

(iii) Thirdly, two intensive studies were carried out. One of these involved six schools, and the aim was to observe these schools at work, to obtain the opinions and attitudes of their teachers, and also to carry out a number of individual case-studies. Children selected for individual case-histories were those making unexpected scholastic advancements or whose performance had deteriorated during their time in the junior school (see Chapter 15).

The other intensive study was carried out in schools making an organizational change, from streaming to non-streaming or vice versa. Three schools were involved and the aim here was to investigate the method, the reasons for the change and problems involved in such a programme (see Chapter 16).

The main purpose of this report is to describe the results of the longitudinal and intensive studies. First, however, the method and some results of the cross-sectional study will be given.

Cross-sectional study

The aim of the cross-sectional study was to make an assessment of all junior school pupils in all four year groups who were in the matched pairs of streamed and non-streamed schools in 1964. The design of this part of the inquiry was controlled by the necessity for a strict time-table imposed by the Central Advisory Council so that some evidence on streaming could be given to the Plowden Committee for its consideration. Although the cross-sectional study was restricted in this way, it nevertheless proved to be invaluable, and its findings determined much of the design of the longitudinal study.

The criteria for assessing the effects of streaming and non-streaming in the cross-sectional study were mainly restricted to pupil attainments. This enabled certain comparisons to be made between the two types of organization, based upon samples of children in the four different years of the junior school. Cross-sectional data have, however, certain disadvantages, the most notable of these being that inferences about the growth of children based upon two groups, tested at the same time but of different ages, are less dependable than inferences about the same group of children tested or examined at intervals of time. Nor, in cross-sectional samples, can conclusions be drawn about the progress of children who initially were of similar ability. An examination of the long-term effects of streaming and non-streaming, however, was to be left to the longitudinal study.

One aim of the inquiry was to discover whether children tended to learn more in the basic school subjects under one system or the other. For this reason, tests of attainment were to be of major importance.

It was also clear that the social behaviour and attitudes of pupils should be studied, although it was not immediately clear what aspects should and could be assessed in a reasonably objective way. For example, in the literature, there was much mention of the 'atmosphere' or the 'morale' of the school. It was felt that such concepts, significant though they undoubtedly are to people in schools, could not readily be defined in a way that would permit different observers to make meaningful comparisons. A further problem was that the teacher's method and outlook could well support or undermine the school's policy of streaming or non-streaming. For these reasons, it was essential to carry out exploratory research in order to discover those aspects of the school, teacher and pupil which should be given particular attention.

It was decided to carry this out in two stages. Prior to the cross-sectional study there was a first exploratory stage consisting of visits to schools and interviews with heads and teachers. Questions for more systematic study were selected on the basis of this and some were incorporated into the design of the cross-sectional study while others had to wait for the longitudinal study (see Appendix 2). Secondly, there was an exploratory study consisting of interviews and discussions with children to establish which non-cognitive variables should be investigated. However, owing to time pressures, it was not possible to complete this stage and construct research instruments resulting from it in time for the cross-sectional study (see Appendix 3 and Chapter 9).

The interviews and visits to the schools suggested that streamed and non-streamed schools were not only different in organization but that the teaching staff held contrasting attitudes and used contrasting teaching methods. It also became clear that these differences might possibly outweigh the effects of streaming or non-streaming *per se.*

A good deal of attention was therefore given to the construction of questionnaires to assess the methods of teaching and attitudes of the teacher.

The questionnaires were administered to teachers in the cross-sectional (and later the longitudinal) study samples. The responses confirmed what had been indicated by the interviews and observed in the schools. Teachers in streamed schools tended to be more in favour of streaming, the eleven-plus selection test, and physical punishment; to be less tolerant of noise, to pay more attention to manners, tidiness, clean faces and hands; and to show a more favourable attitude towards the bright child. In addition, streamed schools tended to concentrate more on 'traditional' type lessons (i.e. learning lists of spellings, formal grammar, saying and learning by rote mathematical tables, writing class-prepared compositions); they made more use of tests, more use of formal computational arithmetic and less use of 'progressive' lessons (i.e. 'projects' in which a child does his own 'research', pupils working together in groups, practical arithmetic, free activities).

In non-streamed schools teachers tended to hold more 'permissive' views on such things as noise, cleanliness, manners; they disapproved of physical punishment and of eleven-plus selection and streaming. Their teaching tended to place more emphasis on self-expression, learning by discovery and practical experience. In short, the two types of school exhibited markedly contrasting features.

The second important finding was that a straight comparison between streamed and non-streamed schools indicated that pupils in streamed schools had slightly higher mean scores on the attainment tests. There were two possible reasons for this. One was that the tests were somewhat biased against the non-streamed schools. The more the test reflected 'traditional' educational practices, as emphasized by streamed schools, the greater the score differences. These were greatest in Mechanical Arithmetic and smallest in Reading. Thus it was possible that the results obtained were largely due to factors such as teaching method and the greater frequency of 'traditional' type lessons rather than the type of organization. Another reason could have been that, although the two groups of schools were matched as far as possible for social class, the streamed schools had slightly more pupils from a higher social background.[1]

[1] For a discussion of the need for caution in interpreting these results, see Barker Lunn (1967b).

Implications of cross-sectional study findings

The findings of the cross-sectional study indicated the complexity of the problem under review, but the study also drew attention to three areas which should be given careful consideration in the longitudinal study.

First, it was apparent that differences other than type of school organization were present between the sample of streamed and non-streamed schools. Some of these differences were not unexpected; for it is obvious that a change from streaming to non-streaming must be accompanied by a change in attitude, and must embody to some degree a different philosophy of education and a different teaching approach. However, differences in curricula (or rather, differences in the frequency of teaching certain types of lesson), however slight, make for difficulties in assessment and these could well mask the true effects of type of organization. Thus it became apparent that a straightforward comparison was likely to be misleading and a more sophisticated analysis was needed which would take into account other factors, such as the 'traditional lessons' score, which may be associated with progress in a particular subject. The need for the collection of this type of teacher data throughout the follow-up was confirmed by the results of the cross-sectional study.

This leads on to the second area. An important question raised by the above findings was: What criteria should be used to assess the outcome of streaming and non-streaming? As discussed earlier, the teaching methods and aims of the two types of school differed to some extent so that tests of the more conventional type, such as Mechanical Arithmetic, could favour the streamers just because the content of these tests was more frequently taught in streamed schools.

Tests of Reading, English, Problem Arithmetic and Mechanical Arithmetic were used in the cross-sectional study—these being considered a fair test of the pupil's performance in the 3 Rs. The content of these tests was of the kind usually demanded for juniors by teachers and education authorities. But, as such, the programme was perhaps more geared to the assessment of skills developed under 'traditional' teaching methods[1], and schools using a more 'progressive' approach[2] might be at a disadvantage. In order to correct any imbalance, measures of less conventional objectives of primary education were introduced into the longitudinal programme. A new

[1,2] For definitions, see Chapter 3.

arithmetic test, Number Concept, was constructed to assess the pupil's understanding of mathematical principles. Two other English tests were concerned with creative writing and the aim of these was to assess the child's flow of ideas, his imaginative powers, his originality and creative thinking.

Although these additional tests were devised to be in accord with the aims and philosophies expressed by many teachers in non-streamed schools and by some in streamed schools, there has been during the 1960s a gradual swing towards 'new' mathematics of the type proposed by the Nuffield Project, by Sealey, Cuisenaire, Dienes and others, and also towards free expression in writing, art, music and crafts (Department of Education and Science, 1967).

Ideally, to make a fair comparison, criteria should be chosen which assess common aims and objectives in the two types of school. Of the achievement tests, three can be held to be neutral, *vis-a-vis* the type of organization and teaching method. One is the Reading test; both types of school share the aim of teaching children to read and the test gives a measure of how far this has been achieved. Two other tests, completely independent of particular subject-teaching, are the reasoning tests, the Verbal and the Non-Verbal; these give a measure of general thinking qualities.

But in addition, in any comparison it would seem important to know as much as possible about the changes produced in pupils undergoing different treatments—how much is being sacrificed and how much is being gained? So that of the tests that might be biased towards one type of school or the other the question asked will be: To what extent are schools superior in the tests fundamental to their approach and how do they stand in those that are not? Here it must be emphasized that the aims and objectives of the two types of school did not lie poles apart, but that their differences were rather a matter of degree (see Chapter 3).

Another stated aim was to examine the effects of streaming and non-streaming on children's personality characteristics, attitudes and social adjustment. Very little attempt was made in the cross-sectional study to examine these non-cognitive factors; but as criteria they are fair to both sides. To those who judge the outcome of streaming or non-streaming solely in terms of scholastic progress, evidence of this kind is largely irrelevant. But if one is concerned with its more far-reaching implications then criteria other than scholastic progress and attainments must be taken into account. The non-cognitive criteria are discussed in detail in the next chapter.

17

Finally, the non-conforming teacher needed to be considered. Some teachers 'step out of line', with views and practices that are in conflict with the aims of the school. What happens when a teacher does not agree with his school's organizational policy? It is probable that such teachers have a counteracting effect—especially in a non-streamed school where a teacher, believing in streaming, probably streams within the class and possibly manages to annul everything that the head had hoped to achieve. This means that the teacher variable cannot be ignored, for teachers make or mar the success of the school organization.

The importance of the teacher variable

It is surprising to find that past research on streaming has taken little or no account of teachers' attitudes, personalities or their methods of working in the classroom. It may seem obvious enough that if the class teacher does not share the head's enthusiasm for some new scheme which is being tried, the method is not receiving a fair trial. But very rarely is the teacher's view known or any attempt made to measure the effect of the teacher's attitude on the final outcome.

It may well be that differences in pupils' achievement gains, sometimes attributed to particular grouping procedures, are due rather to particular teacher attitudes. There is sufficient evidence to indicate that the attitudes teachers hold make a difference to children's behaviour, their values and what they learn (Franseth, 1966). Thus it is surprising that teachers' attitudes are so often ignored in research of this type.

An important finding of the cross-sectional study was that 'any effect which may be shown to be associated with streaming or non-streaming is unlikely to be purely and simply due to the form of organization used. Teaching method, the ideas which underlie disciplinary systems, the views teachers hold about their children, in short the whole climate of relationships built up by what teachers say and do and what they appear to their pupils to imply may well be the critical factors' (Barker Lunn, 1967b).

So the problem was widened in scope to focus not only on forms of organization but also on the teacher. The aim of the longitudinal study was modified to an assessment of the effects of the different forms of school organization, taking into consideration the teachers, their attitudes and beliefs, their methods of teaching and their method of grouping within the class.

References

BARKER LUNN, J. C. (1967a). 'The effects of streaming and other forms of grouping in junior schools—Junior schools and their types of school organization', *New Research in Education*, 1, 4-45.

BARKER LUNN, J. C. (1967b). 'The effects of streaming and non-streaming in junior schools', *New Research in Education*, 1, 46-75.

BOARD OF EDUCATION (GREAT BRITAIN). (1931). *The Primary School.* (Chairman: Sir William H. Hadow). London: HM Stationery Office.

DEPARTMENT OF EDUCATION AND SCIENCE: CENTRAL ADVISORY COUNCIL FOR EDUCATION. (1967). *Children and their Primary Schools.* (Plowden Committee Primary School Report). London: HM Stationery Office.

FRANSETH, J. and KOURY, R. (1966). *Survey of Research on Grouping as Related to Pupil Learning.* Washington, DC: US Department of Health, Education and Welfare.

CHAPTER 2

The Design of the Research

A S a result of stage 1 of the survey a sufficient number of streamed but an inadequate number of non-streamed schools were found. LEAs therefore provided addresses of non-streamed schools in their areas and, after checking with heads that the schools met the requirements of the definition of a non-streamed school, the Foundation was able to locate about eighty non-streamed schools—probably all the schools in the country that could be classified as such at that particular time.

In order to obtain overall comparable samples of streamed and non-streamed schools, selection was based on 'match'. Each non-streamed school was matched with the most similar streamed one that could be found. For matching the following criteria were used:—

(a) Type of school: Junior or Junior with Infants, urban or rural.

(b) Number of classes in the school.

(c) Average number of pupils per class.

(d) Geographical region: North, Midlands, South.

(e) Percentage of children in LEA attending non-selective schools.

(f) Percentage of pupils' parents in professional, clerical and skilled occupations.

Initially there were 50 pairs of schools in the sample but unfortunately during the study this was reduced as schools dropped out due to changes in organization or to reductions in numbers of pupils or staff.

For the cross-sectional study (i.e. in 1964, the first year) data from 84 schools, 42 matched pairs, had been analysed (Barker Lunn, 1967b).

However this number was reduced further and, for the longitudinal analysis, only schools which had completed the full research programme were considered. These numbered 78. Owing to the loss of schools, the samples of streamed and non-streamed schools were no longer comparable and those remaining had to be re-matched. In the end, data from 72 schools, 36 matched pairs, were considered in the longitudinal study. Further details of the sample of schools can be found in Appendix 5.

Twenty-eight of these schools, 14 matched pairs of streamed and non-streamed schools were studied more intensively and the attitudes of their pupils and parents were assessed (see Appendix 5 and Table 2.1). They are referred to as 'the 28 school sample'.

Sample of pupils

In 1964, the first year of the research, all junior pupils in the 100 schools were assessed and tested for the cross-sectional study (see Barker Lunn, 1967). The longitudinal study, however, was concerned with those children who were in their first year in 1964 and who remained in the school throughout the whole of the junior course. These children are referred to as 'Cohort 1'. A limited follow-up study was also made of children who were in their second year in 1964 (Cohort 2) but this was restricted to the 28 school sample.

At seven-plus, over 7,000 Cohort 1 children in the 72 schools were initially involved. However, during the research some pupils left the school and in the fourth junior year and final year of the study only 5,521 of the original 7,000 pupils remained. The longitudinal study is mainly concerned with these pupils.

Dependent variables

(*a*) *Achievement Tests*

Considerable attention has already been paid to the achievement tests (see Chapter 1). Table 2.1 indicates the battery of tests that was used in the longitudinal study.

Tests of Reading, English, Mechanical Arithmetic and Problem Arithmetic were given at the end of each of the four junior school years. These tests were specially constructed for this research project. Each test was devised to be suitable for all ages from seven to ten-plus in order that measures of gain in achievement could be made during the longitudinal study (see Appendix 4). There were two parallel versions of each test and half the matched pairs of schools worked the A-version (sample A) and the others the B-version (sample B). This had a number of advantages. Firstly, in effect, two independent studies were carried out simultaneously, each

21

acting as a check on the other. Secondly, use was made of the two versions to reduce the effects of cumulative test practice, the alternate parallel form being used in the third year.

TABLE 2.1: *Details of instruments used each year in the longitudinal study*

	1964	1965	1966	1967

COHORT 1
 	
All Schools
	7+
	Reading†
	English†
	Problem†
	Mechanical†
	Sociometric†
	School
	  activities†
		8+
		Reading
		English
		Problem
		Mechanical
		Concept†
		Verbal†
			9+
			Reading
			English
			Problem
			Mechanical
			Concept
			Verbal/Non-
			  verbal†
			Free Writing
			  SA1 & SB1†
			Interests†
			Sociometric
			Aspirations†
				10+
				Reading
				English
				Problem
				Mechanical
				Concept
				Verbal/Non-
				  verbal
				Free Writing
				  SA2 & SB2
				Interests
				Sociometric
				School
				  activities
				Aspirations

COHORT 1
In addition
  to above in
  28 Schools
			9+
			Pupils'
			  Attitudes†
			Parents'
			  Attitudes†
				10+
				Pupils'
				  Attitudes

COHORT 2
(28 School
  Sample
  only)
	8+
	Same as
	Cohort 1†
		9+	10+
			English
			Problem
			Pupils'
			  Attitudes†
			Parents'
			  Attitudes†	

Note: † indicates initial measurement.

In the second year, Number Concept and Verbal Reasoning tests were included and thereafter used annually (see Appendix 4). The former test was introduced as a result of the cross-sectional study findings. A verbal reasoning test had been planned for each year, but of the available commercial tests none was sufficiently reliable for children aged seven-plus.[1] In year two, the NFER Primary Verbal I test was used, being suitable for children of this age; while in years three and four, use was made of a 'closed' test covering verbal and non-verbal reasoning. This had formerly been constructed by the NFER for use by J. W. B. Douglas (1964) in his Population Investigation Study.

A Free Writing assessment, in the form of two tests, was introduced in the third year and a similar version repeated in the fourth year. One of these, the Free Writing SA, consisted of two essay items, both designed to stimulate the child's imagination and creative thinking. These were marked for originality of ideas rather than for a grammatically well-written but 'stereotyped' essay. Each was marked by a panel of three experienced teachers.

The second Free Writing Test, SB, was concerned with 'creative' thinking. In constructing this test, material from American tests, notably tests devised by Torrance (1962) and Guilford (1950), was drawn on; also similar items were constructed by the NFER[2] (see Chapter 6 and Appendix 4).

(b) Non-cognitive Dependent Variables

One aim of the research was to examine achievement, another was to look at the effects of streaming and non-streaming on children's personality, attitudes and social adjustment.

Educators and teachers alike make claims that the type of school organization, whether it is streamed or non-streamed, influences the 'ethos' or atmosphere of a school, as well as the children's behaviour and 'morale'. In order to make meaningful assessments of these concepts, attitude scales, defined in operational terms, were constructed.[3]

There is evidence that a pupil's attitude to school is related to his scholastic performance (Barker Lunn, 1969), and an attempt has been made to measure the effects of school organization on attitudes. Several attitude scales were constructed, including measures of *attitude to school, interest in school work, relationship with the teacher,*

---

[1] Time and budgetary conditions were a restriction, and available verbal reasoning tests had to be used.

[2] Discussions were held with Miss Anne Coghill, post-graduate student, Birkbeck College, University of London, and some of the items used in her test of 'creativity' were modified for use.

[3] The study of attitudes was restricted to a 1 in 2 sample of pupils in the 28-school sample. For full details, see Chapter 9 and Appendix 3.

and *importance of doing well at school.* Two others dealt with *attitude to class* and '*other*' *image of class;* the aim of these was to assess whether, as many opponents of streaming would hold, lower stream pupils feel less satisfaction with their class and develop a sense of inferiority.

Also it has been held that the social-adjustment of pupils, particularly of less able ones, is closely associated with the type of school organization. So, by sociometric techniques and a self-report social adjustment scale, assessments were made of the *pupil's ability to get on with his classmates.*

A pupil's self-esteem could be influenced by the type of organization of his school—whether it is streamed or non-streamed. If this is so it is important, for a pupil's self-concept has been shown by numerous research studies to be related to academic performance (Brookover and Thomas, 1964; Bledsoe, 1964). Some supporters of streaming claim that the presence of bright pupils in a class gives to the less able daily reminders of their inadequacies, thereby destroying their confidence and having disastrous effects on their self-image. Others, however, suggest that streaming lowers the aspirational level of children in all streams below the top stream, and that these pupils underrate their own abilities and develop poor self-concepts. A measure of *self-image,* in terms of school work, was devised, and the question of the effects of type of school organization on it was examined.

Anxiety has been shown to have a damaging effect on achievement; level of anxiety could well be affected by the form of school organization. This, too, was investigated.

Other personality variables studied were related to maladjustment. Frequency of fighting, bullying, social-withdrawal, disobedience, baiting or teasing, were assessed by teachers who rated their pupils on these traits. Also, the pupils themselves indicated on an attitude scale the desirability of *conforming versus non-conforming behaviour.*

In years three and four, a limited study was made of the interests of children in the two types of school and also of their intended occupation on leaving school.

In addition to the dependent variables discussed above, measurement was also made of factors which could influence or be associated with the dependent variables such as academic progress, attitudes, and interests. These background variables were of three types— those associated with the pupil, his teacher and his home.

The chief background or independent variables were assumed to be the pupil's sex, age, social class, school attendance, position in class, physical disabilities, attitude to school work, and pleasurability in class—the latter two characteristics as perceived by the teacher.

The findings of the cross-sectional study suggested that teachers' attitudes and classroom practices might be associated with the progress, personality and attitudes of pupils. Two questionnaires were used to assess these variables. In addition, in a personal data questionnaire, teachers gave information about themselves: their sex, age, qualifications, and number of years teaching experience (see Chapter 3 and Appendix 4).

A study, limited to 28 schools, was also made of some of the home variables which could affect a child's progress, attitudes, social adjustment, etc. and in 1966 a short questionnaire dealing with parents' interest in and aspirations for their children's educational and vocational careers was sent out to all parents involved in the research.[1]

References

BARKER LUNN, J. C. (1967). 'The effects of streaming and non-streaming in junior schools', *New Research in Education*, 1, 46-75.

BARKER LUNN, J. C. (1969). 'The development of scales to measure junior school children's attitudes', *Brit. J. Educ. Psychol.*, vol. 39, pt. 1, 64-71.

BLEDSOE, J. C. (1964). 'Self-concepts of children and their intelligence, achievement, interests and anxiety', *J. Individ. Psychol.*, 20, 55-8.

BROOKOVER, W. B. and THOMAS, S. (1964). 'Self-concept of ability and school achievement', *Sociol. Educ.*, 37, 3.

DOUGLAS, J. M. (1964). *Home and School.* London: MacGibbon & Kee.

GUILFORD, J. P. (1950). 'Creativity', *Amer. Psychologist*, 5, 444-54.

TORRANCE, E. P. (1962). *Administration and Scoring Manual for Abbreviated Form VII Minnesota Tests of Creative Thinking.* Bureau of Educational Research, University of Minnesota.

---

[1] Full details of the dependent and background variables can be found in Appendix 4.

CHAPTER 3

Characteristics of the Teachers

IT will be remembered from Chapter 1 that the cross-sectional study revealed differences in the attitudes and teaching methods of teachers in streamed and non-streamed schools (see Appendix 2). The crucial point of this finding was that any trend of this type might outweigh the effects of streaming or non-streaming *per se.* It was important, therefore, that information concerned with teaching methods and attitudes should be obtained each year from teachers involved in the longitudinal study.

The responses of the teachers are shown in Table 3.1, which brings out clearly the differences between the two types of school in terms of the attitudes, methods and experience of the teachers.

The climate in the non-streamed school was more 'permissive' and tolerant, and its teachers placed less emphasis on 'traditional' and more on 'progressive' methods of teaching than those in streamed schools.

It must be emphasized, however, that although different patterns emerged for streamed and non-streamed schools, not all teachers in each type conformed to the predominant pattern. A substantial proportion of teachers believed in streaming and made use of the teaching methods usually accompanying this form of organization, although they were actually teaching in a non-streamed school.

From the material recorded at the interviews with teachers, three questionnaires were devised. The first was concerned with biographical information such as sex, age, and teaching experience. The second was concerned with information about the methods of teaching used and the way in which children were organized for learning. The purpose of the third questionnaire was to obtain the opinions of teachers on such matters as streaming, and eleven-plus selection.

Amount of teaching experience

On the whole, teachers in non-streamed schools had had less experience as teachers than those in streamed schools. However, the difference was more pronounced when the children were in the

TABLE 3.1 *Differences between streamed and non-streamed schools*

	TEACHERS† IN STREAMED SCHOOLS	TEACHERS IN NON-STREAMED SCHOOLS	CHI-SQUARE TEST AND INFERENCE
No. of years' experience as a teacher	More years' experience	Fewer years' experience	$\chi^2=24\cdot82$ df$=5$ $P<0\cdot001$ difference significant
'Traditional' lessons	More use made of 'traditional' lessons	Less use made of 'traditional' lessons	$\chi^2=34\cdot52$ df$=6$ $P<0\cdot001$ difference significant
'Progressive' lessons	Less use made of 'progressive' lessons	More use made of 'progressive' lessons	$\chi^2=46\cdot21$ df$=6$ $P<0\cdot001$ difference significant
Frequency of formal sums	More frequent	Less frequent	$\chi^2=22\cdot08$ df$=5$ $P<0\cdot001$ difference significant
Frequency of tests	More frequent	Less frequent	$\chi^2=29\cdot15$ df$=5$ $P<0\cdot001$ difference significant
'Permissive' versus 'non-permissive' attitude to children's behaviour	Less 'permissive'	More 'permissive'	$\chi^2=17\cdot51$ df$=5$ $P<0\cdot01$ difference significant
Attitude to physical punishment	More pro punishment	Less pro punishment	$\chi^2=24\cdot34$ df$=6$ $P<0\cdot001$ difference significant
Attitude to talking and noise in the classroom	Lower tolerance of noise	Higher tolerance of noise	$\chi^2=31\cdot97$ df$=6$ $P<0\cdot001$ difference significant
Attitude to A-stream children	Pro A-stream children	Less pro A-stream children	$\chi^2=56\cdot91$ df$=6$ $P<0\cdot001$ difference significant
Attitude to eleven-plus selection	Pro eleven-plus	Anti eleven-plus	$\chi^2=25\cdot25$ df$=5$ $P<0\cdot001$ difference significant
Attitude to streaming	Pro streaming	Pro non-streaming	$\chi^2=186\cdot01$ df$=7$ $P<0\cdot001$ difference significant

†The sample of teachers includes those teaching the follow-up children, Cohort 1, in any of the four junior years.

lower half of the junior school: 21 per cent of teachers in non-streamed schools and 10 per cent of teachers in streamed schools who were teaching the sample of seven-year-olds, had had less than two years' experience; with eight-year-olds, the corresponding figures were 27 per cent and 17 per cent. The differences at nine and ten-plus were not significant (see Table 3.2, Appendix 6).

It is interesting to note that the ages of the heads in the two types of school were also different, and that those in the non-streamed schools tended to be younger than those in streamed schools. A third of the heads in non-streamed schools compared with six per cent in streamed schools were less than 50 years of age (see Appendix 6, Table 3.3).

Teaching methods used

The questionnaire on teaching methods fell into three sections:

(*a*) Teachers were asked to indicate how often they used various types of lesson. From the responses made two scores were derived: a 'traditional lessons' score, indicating how often the teacher used lessons of the more 'traditional' type, and a complementary 'progressive lessons' score. (See Appendix 4). The two scales contained the following items: 'Traditional'—writing class-prepared compositions; learning lists of spellings; formal grammar—e.g. understanding parts of speech, punctuation; saying and learning tables by rote. 'Progressive'—projects in which the child did his own 'research'; pupils working or helping each other in groups; practical arithmetic, e.g. measuring, apparatus work; free activities.

This questionnaire was completed each year by teachers who also supplied information on the frequency of formal sums, problem sums and tests, and, in the third and fourth years, on the frequency of writing stories and of comprehension and punctuation exercises.

(*b*) A section on the use of class teaching, mixed ability group teaching and ability grouping within the class. (See Chapter 4).

(*c*) A section concerned with seating arrangements and the criteria used for allocating children to their seats. (See Chapter 4).

Teachers in streamed schools, on average, tended to make more frequent use of 'traditional' lessons and less frequent use of 'progressive' lessons than teachers in non-streamed schools. However, the use made of 'traditional' lessons, and, to a lesser extent, 'progressive' lessons seemed to depend on three factors: the age of the children being taught; their achievement level, and the philosophy or attitudes of the teacher.

'Traditional' lessons were not only more frequently used in streamed schools, but were more common in both types of school when the children were seven or eight-plus than when they were nine or ten years old. Similarly, they were more frequently used by teachers of the lower ability streams than the higher ability streams.

Graphs Ia and Ib illustrate the greater emphasis on 'traditional' lessons in streamed schools and also the shift in both schools toward the non-traditional end of the scale at 10+.[1]

Similarly the frequency of 'progressive' lessons was related to the age of the children; the older they were, the greater the emphasis on these lessons. The greater frequency of 'progressive' lessons in non-streamed schools was thus more pronounced when the children were ten than when they were seven years old.

The explanation of the differences at different ages probably lies in the definition of 'traditional' and 'progressive' lessons as used in this study. The lesson that is considered appropriate at seven-plus or ten-plus is not necessarily considered so at the other age. A high 'traditional lessons' score could be interpreted as an indication of formal learning of the basic skills, and by the time a child reached the fourth year of the junior school, fewer teachers believed in the necessity for daily recitation of tables or the daily blackboard of formal sums. The teacher who made frequent use of 'traditional' lessons at ten-plus, tended to be 'non-permissive' in outlook[2] (the correlation between the use of 'traditional' lessons and 'non-permissive' scale, which was 0·33, was higher than with any of the other attitude scales).

Similarly, there was a relationship between the frequency of using 'progressive' lessons and the attitudes of teachers of ten-year-olds, but this was less strong in teachers of younger children. The more 'progressive' tended to express more 'permissive' views, to be more tolerant of noise in the classroom, to be less approving of physical punishment and so on[3] (see correlation matrix, Appendix 7A).

[1] Evidence that this is not a change of emphasis occurring in schools is obtained from the cross-sectional data. In 1964 information was obtained from teachers in *all* four year groups and the difference between teachers of different year groups was observed then (see Barker Lunn, 1967).

[2] 'Non-permissive' describes those teachers who were most prone to object to children fidgeting, to demand clean hands and good manners, to rate the 3 Rs more highly than self-expression, see page 34.

[3] For description of attitude scales, see page 33.

A possible explanation of the weaker relationship between the 'progressive' lessons score and the attitudes of teachers of younger children is that the use of apparatus (e.g. Dienes, Cuisenaire) and consequent group work is becoming increasingly popular with younger juniors and is introduced by the school rather than being *chosen* by the individual teacher. So teachers who are not really interested in this approach, make use of the apparatus, unwillingly perhaps, and blur any natural relationship between attitude and choice of method.

GRAPH Ia: *Scores obtained on the 'traditional lessons' scale by teachers when children seven years old*

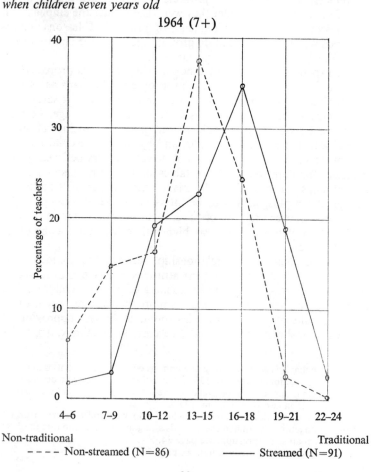

1964 (7+)

Non-traditional   Traditional

- - - - Non-streamed (N=86)   ——— Streamed (N=91)

In addition, other types of lessons which did not form part of the 'traditional or progressive lessons' scales were also investigated. Lessons in formal sums, such as mechanical computation, and tests in arithmetic and other subjects were more frequent over the four years in streamed than non-streamed schools, whereas practical arithmetic and the use of apparatus was more common in non-streamed schools. Problem arithmetic was the only form of teaching mathematics which was equally common to both (see Appendix 6, Table 3.4).

GRAPH Ib: *Scores obtained on the 'traditional lessons' scale by teachers when children ten years old*

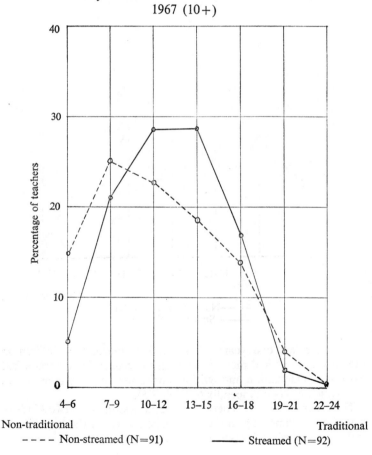

1967 (10+)

Non-traditional   Traditional

– – – – Non-streamed (N=91) ——— Streamed (N=92)

31

GRAPH IIa: *Scores obtained on the 'progressive lessons' scale by teachers when children seven years old*

1964 (7+)

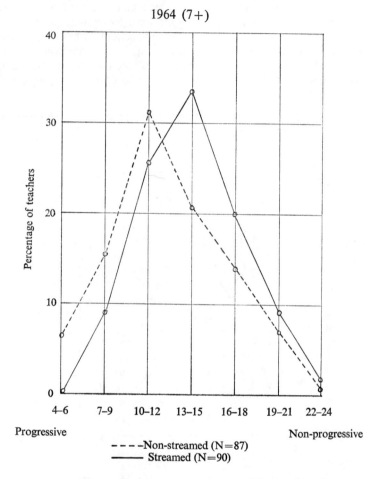

Progressive

Non-progressive

- - - - Non-streamed (N=87)
———— Streamed (N=90)

Over the last two years of the junior course, the children in streamed schools had more practice in comprehension exercises, but lessons in punctuation and writing stories were equally common in the two schools (see Appendix 6, Table 3.5).

The general differences between types of lesson in the two kinds of school are summed up in the composite scores on the 'traditional' and 'progressive' scales (see Table 3.1).

GRAPH IIb: *Scores obtained on the 'progressive lessons' scale by teachers when children ten years old*

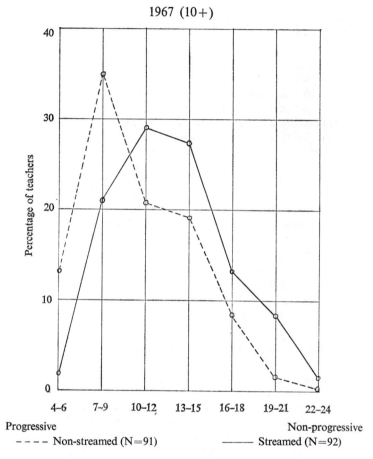

1967 (10+)

Progressive   Non-progressive

– – – – Non-streamed (N=91)   ———— Streamed (N=92)

Attitudes of teachers

The exploratory research had indicated a number of fundamental attitude areas that were relevant to the inquiry. The questionnaire measuring these attitudes was in the form of a number of statements of opinion which had actually been made by other teachers in the exploratory interviews. In responding, the teacher was asked to indicate his degree of agreement or disagreement with each statement, using a five-point scale ranging from 'strongly agree' to 'strongly

33

disagree'. Thus each attitude area could be represented as a dimension along which teachers could be placed according to their score.

Seven attitude areas in the form of scales were investigated, all except (*f*) constructed by Guttman's method of scalogram analysis (see Appendix 4)[1]. These were:

(*a*) 'Permissive' versus 'non-permissive'.
(*b*) Attitude towards physical punishment.
(*c*) Attitude towards noise in the classroom.
(*d*) Attitude towards eleven-plus selection.
(*e*) Attitude towards A-stream children.
(*f*) Attitude towards backward children.[2]
(*g*) Attitude towards streaming.

The titles of the scales are self-explanatory, with the possible exception of (*a*), of which more details are given below. It will be noticed, too, that three of these attitudes (*a*, *b* and *c* scales) are of a fairly specific kind and may give some indication of the way in which teachers are likely to react to their pupils and of the kind of climate they will create in the classroom. The remaining four concern views of a socio-policital nature and may be said to form part of a more general system of values.

It is proposed to give the results in terms of those teachers who taught the longitudinal study children in their first, second, third and fourth junior years. Attitudes were measured in 1964 and again in 1966[3] (see Appendix 4 for Attitudes questionnaire).

(*a*) 'Permissive' versus 'Non-Permissive'

This scale ranked teachers in terms of the 'permissiveness' of their attitudes towards junior school children. It must not, of course, be interpreted too literally. It is convenient to use some title to describe those teachers who were most prone to object to children fidgeting, to demand clean hands and good manners, who rated the 3 Rs more highly than self-expression, and vice versa. There was a significant tendency (P <0.01) for teachers in non-streamed schools

---

[1] The scales, with the exception of (*f*) were constructed by C. J. Tuppen, a member of the research team, and formed the basis of his M.A. thesis (Tuppen, 1965).

[2] This scale was not available for use in 1964 and was only used in later years. It was constructed on a correlational basis by means of Cronbach's alpha coefficient (see Appendix 4).

[3] *All* teachers in the sample schools completed the questionnaire in 1964 and those not in the school in 1964 or not teaching the longitudinal study children in 1966, completed it in the following year, i.e. in 1965 or 1967.

to be more 'permissive' in this sense than those in streamed schools (see Table 3.1). (For the content of this scale see Appendix 4: items 6, 14, 17, 20, 23.)

GRAPH III: *Permissiveness*   (4 years combined)

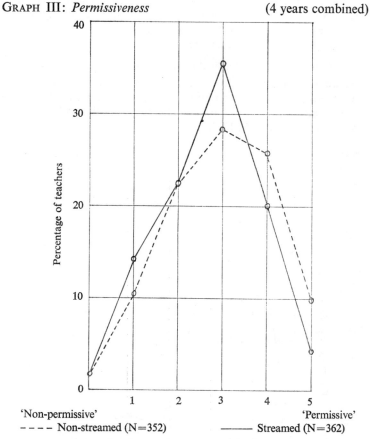

'Non-permissive'   'Permissive'
- - - - Non-streamed (N=352)   ———— Streamed (N=362)

It will be seen from the graph that the distribution of scores for the two groups of teachers is very similar and in fact that modal score[1] was the same. The difference arises at the 'permissive' end of the scale and here teachers in non-streamed schools were more frequently represented. However, the difference between the schools was less in 1966 than it was in 1964-65; some evidence for this is obtained from a comparison with the cross-sectional results

[1] Modal score refers to that obtained by the majority of teachers.

(Barker Lunn, 1967) but a more valid confirmation is obtained by comparing the attitudes expressed by the same group of teachers in 1964 and again in 1966. These results suggest a change of attitude in a more 'permissive' direction, particularly for teachers in streamed schools (Sign test $P<0{\cdot}01$) and less so (not statistically significant) for teachers in non-streamed schools, bringing the attitudes of the two groups of teachers closer together.

(*b*) *Attitude towards Physical Punishment*

There was, too, a general tendency ($P<0{\cdot}001$) for the teachers in streamed schools to favour physical punishment more than those in non-streamed schools. (The items forming this scale can be found in Appendix 4: items 4, 11, 13, 22, 25, 30.)

GRAPH IV: *Attitude to physical punishment*   (4 years combined)

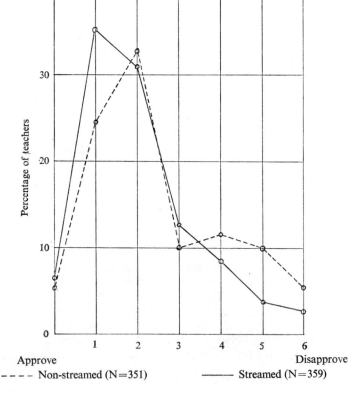

Approve   Disapprove

- - - - Non-streamed (N=351)   ———— Streamed (N=359)

It will be seen from the graph that the difference arises chiefly from a small group of teachers in non-streamed schools who disapproved of physical punishment. The majority of teachers, however, in both types of school believed in using physical punishment. Only 19 per cent of non-streamers and 7 per cent of streamers disagreed with the statement: 'I think a good slap in the right place at the right time does an awful lot of good', and 60 per cent of non-streamers and 70 per cent of streamers believed that 'an occasional hard slap does children no harm'. However, as with 'permissiveness', there was a tendency towards a slight change in attitude for those teachers who were in the study in 1964 and still there in 1966.

GRAPH V: *Attitude to noise*   (4 years combined)

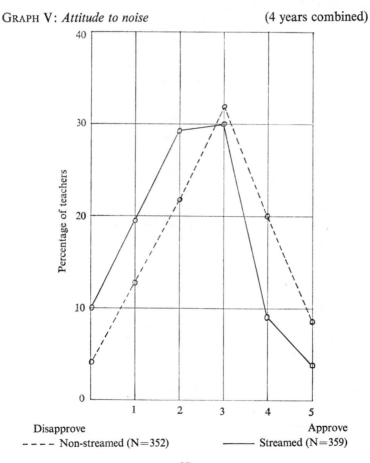

Disapprove   Approve

– – – – Non-streamed (N=352)   ——— Streamed (N=359)

Teachers in streamed schools expressed a slightly less approving attitude towards physical punishment (Sign test $P<0·05$), and there was a tendency in non-streamed schools for a slight move in the opposite direction (Sign test $P<0·05$).

(c) *Attitude towards Noise in the Classroom*

Teachers in non-streamed schools were slightly more tolerant of noise in the classroom than those in streamed schools (P $<0·001$) (see Table 3.1). (The items forming this scale were 2, 7, 18, 27, 31: see Appendix 4.)

The majority (59%) of non-streamers obtained a score of 3 or more and the majority (57%) of streamers a score of 2 or less. Put in more concrete terms 59 per cent of non-streamers were uncertain or disagreed with the statement: 'A quiet atmosphere is the one best suited to all school work', whereas 57 per cent of teachers in streamed schools agreed with it. Over the three years of the longitudinal study no significant change in attitude was noted in this area.

(d) *Attitude towards Eleven-plus Selection*

The differences in attitude towards eleven-plus selection between teachers in streamed and non-streamed schools were highly significant (P $<0·001$): teachers in streamed schools tended to approve of eleven-plus selection while their counterparts in non-streamed schools disapproved. (The items forming this scale were 10, 14, 19, 26, 35: see Appendix 4.)

The most discriminating statement in this scale concerned the justice of the eleven-plus. Sixty-nine per cent of teachers in non-streamed schools had doubts about the eleven-plus exam as an entirely fair method of assessing a child's abilities, compared with only 54 per cent of teachers in streamed schools. No change in attitude towards eleven-plus selection was recorded between 1964 and 1966.

(e) *Attitude to A-stream Children*

This scale contains items suggesting that A-stream children have wider interests, tend to become conceited, are too competitive, etc. (see Appendix 4: items 3, 5, 8, 10, 26). Teachers in streamed schools had a more favourable attitude to A-stream children (presumably believing in the value of A-streams for brighter children) than teachers in non-streamed schools. The difference was highly statistically significant (P $<0·001$). (See graph VIIc, p. 42).

38

Characteristics of the Teachers

The graph shows a clear division of opinion in the two schools, but it is important to note that substantial proportions in both types of school disapproved *and* approved of the A-stream child.

What, perhaps, is a most interesting trend is the change of attitude that occurred during the years of the longitudinal study. Graph VIIa shows the attitudes expressed in 1964 and Graph VIIb the attitudes expressed by the same teachers in 1966. It can be seen that there has been a shift in attitude for both groups of teachers: the streamers disapproving more of A-streams, and non-streamers becoming more approving.

GRAPH VI: *Attitude to 11+*   (4 years combined)

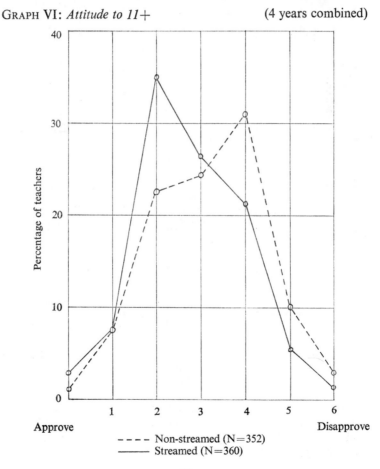

Approve   Disapprove

    - - - Non-streamed (N=352)
    ——— Streamed (N=360)

At present, non-streaming is in vogue and there is more likely to be a changeover to non-streaming than to streaming. One of the main reasons given for changing to non-streaming is a moral one, centring around the average and dull child. Those teachers in

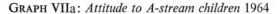
GRAPH VIIa: *Attitude to A-stream children* 1964

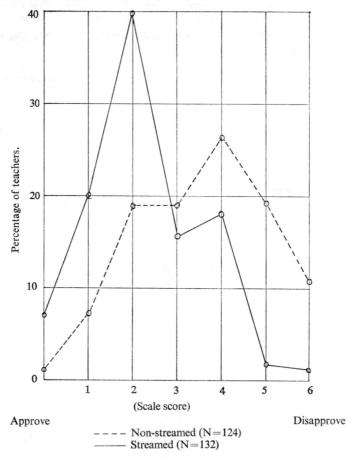

(Scale score)

Approve   Disapprove

- - - - Non-streamed (N=124)
———— Streamed (N=132)

streamed schools whose attitudes changed between 1964 and 1966 are not so sure about streaming, particularly for A-stream children, and it is suggested, are beginning to question whether it is a good thing to separate them from their contemporaries.

40

Characteristics of the Teachers

On the other hand, the teachers in non-streamed schools who approved more of the A-stream child than they did earlier in the study, have obviously become more concerned about the bright child in the non-streamed class and wonder whether his needs are being fulfilled.

GRAPH VIIb: *Attitude to A-stream children* 1966

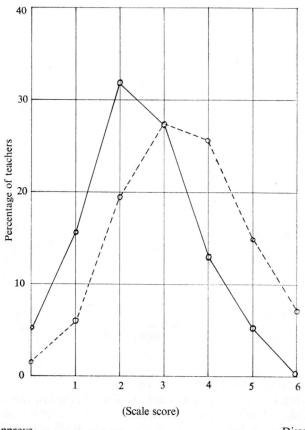

(Scale score)

Approve   Disapprove

---- Non-streamed (N=124)
——— Streamed (N=132)

GRAPH VIIc: *Attitude to A-stream children*   (4 years combined)

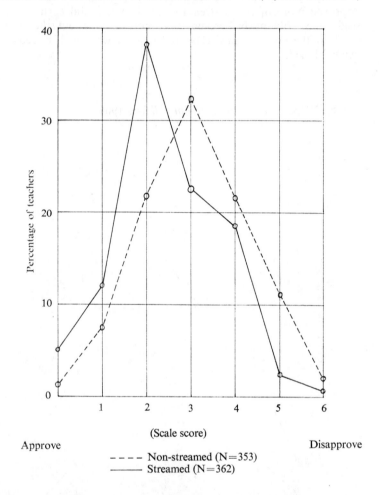

(Scale score)

Approve   Disapprove

- - - - Non-streamed (N=353)
——— Streamed (N=362)

(f) *Attitude to Backward Children*

Unfortunately this scale was only available in the last two years of the study.   Unlike the other attitude areas there was no difference between the teachers in streamed and non-streamed schools in their attitude to the backward child. The items forming this scale were: 6, 12, 18, 23, 25, 31: see Appendix 4.

It can be seen from the graph that the modal score was the same in both schools, and, if anything, there was a slightly greater spread of scores in streamed schools.

GRAPH VIII: *Attitude to backward children*

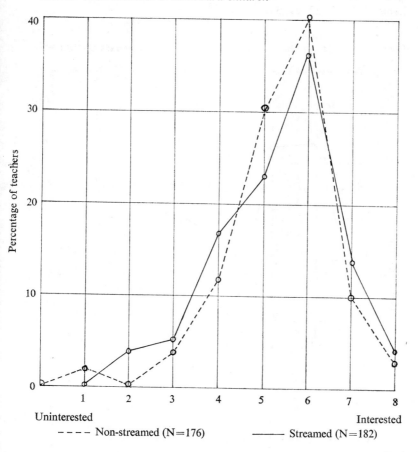

Uninterested   Interested

- - - - Non-streamed (N=176)   ———— Streamed (N=182)

(g) Attitudes towards Streaming

This attitude scale was perhaps the most important of all for this research project. It could be used as a means of identifying teachers who were committed to one point of view or the other. It was found that in streamed schools there were some teachers who favoured non-streaming; that in non-streamed schools there were teachers who

43

favoured streaming; and that in both types of school there were teachers who were uncommitted either way. However, the differences between teachers in the two schools were very significant (P <0·001) —teachers in streamed schools generally believing in streaming and teachers in non-streamed schools in non-streaming (see Appendix 4, items: 1, 9, 17, 22, 29, 34, 38).

GRAPH IX: *Attitude to streaming*   (4 years combined)

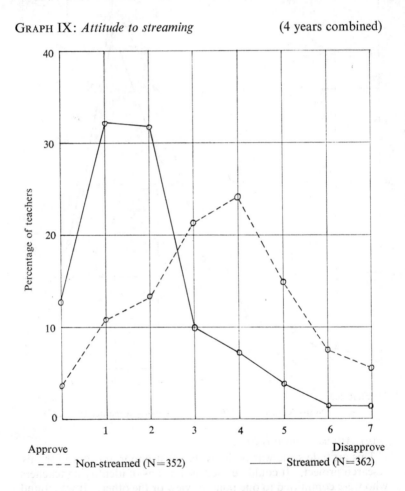

Approve   Disapprove

- - - - Non-streamed (N=352)   ——— Streamed (N=362)

Graph IX shows a different pattern of responses in the two groups. Clearly the majority conformed to the appropriate norm but in both types of school there were teachers whose views were in conflict with the practice of their school. It is also clear that there was more variation in the attitudes held in non-streamed schools, and that here there were more non-conformists.

The views of teachers who had been in the school in 1964 (or 1965 follow-up group) and were still there for the second assessment of attitudes in 1966 were compared. No consistent trend indicating a change in attitude to streaming emerged for either teachers in non-streamed or streamed schools.

Streamed and non-streamed schools embody different philosophies

It seems apparent from the foregoing that schools using streaming or non-streaming did not merely differ in organization. The streamed school seemed to be more systematic in its approach, concentrated more on 'traditional' lessons, gave more emphasis to the 3 Rs and was, at least overtly, more authoritarian. Its staff was likely to approve of bright children, of eleven-plus selection and of streaming as a means of adapting to individual differences. The non-streamed school presented an apparent contrast. Its teachers held more 'permissive' views on such things as cleanliness and manners, were more tolerant of noise and talking in the classroom, and disapproved of the differentiation implicit in streaming and the eleven-plus procedures. Their teaching tended to place more emphasis on self-expression, learning by discovery and practical experience. In short, the aims and practices of the two kinds of school seemed to embody different views about children and different philosophies of education.

In practice, however, the contrast is not as marked as this dichotomy might seem to imply, although of course specific schools, where staff and head share firm convictions, may represent quite thorough-going, even doctrinaire embodiments of these contrasting approaches.

What is clear from the findings of this chapter is that any effect which may be shown to be associated with streaming or non-streaming is unlikely to be purely and simply due to the form of organization used. Indeed, the strictly organizational aspects may be the least important in their bearing upon the development of pupils. The contrasting attitudes and values of teachers associated with the two types of school organization are taken into account in the comparisons that follow. In many schools of both types, however, there were teachers whose views and practices were in conflict with those of their colleagues. One might expect the influence of such teachers to mask any differences that might result from the differences in organization. The method used to overcome this problem is dealt with in Chapter 4.

References

BARKER LUNN, J. C. (1967). 'The effects of streaming and non-streaming in junior schools', *New Research in Education*, 1, 46-75.

TUPPEN, C. J. (1965). 'A study of the expressed attitudes of junior school teachers towards aspects of teaching, using a Guttman scaling method'. Unpublished M.A. thesis, University of London.

Different Types of Teacher

Non-conforming teachers

The previous chapter brings out clearly the differences between streamed and non-streamed schools. These were based on central or average tendencies, and little attention has been paid so far to the overlap in attitudes and methods of teachers in the two types of school.

An examination of Graphs I and II, showing scores on the 'traditional' and 'progressive' lessons scales (see Chapter 3) reveals many similarities as well as differences between teachers in the two types of school. Taking the modal score in each school (i.e. that obtained by the majority of teachers) to be the 'typical' teacher's score, consider Graph Ia, based on seven-plus, the age at which there was the greatest difference between the schools. The 'typical' teacher of seven-year-olds in streamed schools obtained a 'traditional lessons' score in the range of 16 to 18, while his counterpart in non-streamed schools obtained a score of 13 to 15. Teachers in streamed schools were *generally* more 'traditional' but 4 per cent of teachers in non-streamed schools were more 'traditional' than the typical 'streamed' teacher and 22 per cent of teachers in streamed schools were less 'traditional' than the typical 'non-streamed' teacher. A similar exercise can be carried out with Graph IIb—12 per cent of teachers of ten-year-old children in streamed schools were more 'progressive' than the 'typical non-streamer' and 30 per cent of non-streamers were less 'progressive' than the 'typical streamer'. Although there were general differences, substantial proportions in each type of school did not conform to the predominant pattern.

Similarly, and perhaps more remarkably, Graph IX (see Chapter 3) reveals that considerable proportions of teachers in both types of school were uncertain about or did not support their school's policy of streaming or non-streaming.

Who were the teachers who did not conform to the pattern of their type of school? An answer to this was partly obtained from the results of a factor analysis (see Appendix 7A) which revealed

47

that the attitudes of a teacher and selected teaching method were closely related. A teacher, for example, favouring non-streaming, *whether in a streamed or non-streamed school,* held similar attitudes to others favouring this approach and contrasting attitudes to those believing in streaming. Such a teacher would tend to score highly on the attitude scales indicating a 'permissive' attitude, disapproval of physical punishment and of eleven-plus selection, a higher tolerance of noise in the classroom and a less favourable attitude to A-stream children. He would also tend to make frequent use of 'progressive' lessons and less of 'traditional' ones.

To illustrate the relationship between attitudes and methods, let us consider classroom organization. The results obtained in the two types of school will be briefly discussed, and the chosen types of classroom organization in the non-streamed school will then be examined in relation to the teacher's attitudes.

Classroom organization

It will be remembered that each year teachers were asked to provide information on the way in which they organized their classes for instruction in each of the 3 Rs and other subjects. Four methods could be distinguished: whole class teaching, similar ability grouping, mixed ability grouping and the individual approach. Since streaming and non-streaming produce very different types of class composition in terms of the pupils' level and range of ability, one would expect a different teaching approach in the two types of school. This was indeed the case, and different patterns emerged.

In streamed schools, whole class teaching was most commonly used but similar ability grouping was also frequent, particularly for Maths and Reading. Teachers in non-streamed schools, on the other hand, had to cope with a wide range of ability and here, teaching children in groups of similar ability and individually were methods more commonly used. There were in both schools, however, slight variations from the average for the different school subjects and, of course, for individual teachers (see Appendix 6, Tables 4.5—4.8).

Teachers were also asked what criterion they used for assigning children to seats; and although the composition of classes in terms of ability range was so different in the two types of school, the responses were not dissimilar. When the children were eight and nine-plus they were usually seated according to achievement for *part of the time*, but at ten-plus nearly half the teachers allowed free choice or assigned children to seats on a basis other than academic performance.

These were the common patterns, but some teachers in both stream-ed and non-streamed schools 'streamed' within the class by seating children in fixed places according to their achievement level (see Table 4.9 in Appendix 6).

Classroom organization in the non-streamed school

The attitudes to streaming of individual teachers were examined in an effort to discover what kind of teacher 'streamed' within the class in *non-streamed schools*.[1]

Classroom organization was found to be related to teachers' attitudes, but this relationship did not hold for older teachers who, on the whole, probably tended to use the more conventional or familiar methods, whatever their views. Among the younger teachers, those of forty-five years and under, those 'streaming' by seating within the class were the ones who believed in streaming. The table below shows that the more a teacher believed in streaming, as

TABLE 4.1: *Attitudes of younger teachers (45 years and under) in non-streamed schools to streaming and their degree of streaming within the class through seating arrangements*

Seating	ATTITUDE OF TEACHER	
	Anti-Streaming (scored 4567)	*Undecided or Pro-Streaming (scored 0123)*
Based on free choice	39% (4)†	21% (7)
'Streamed' part of time	58% (12)	57% (19)
'Streamed' all the time	3% (10)	22% (15)
	100%	100%
No. of teachers giving information	108 (26)	86 (41)
Chi-square test	$\chi^2 = 20 \cdot 76, P < 0 \cdot 001$	

†Responses of older teachers shown in brackets.

[1] There was no relationship between attitudes to streaming and seating arrangements or ability grouping in streamed schools.

indicated by his attitude score, the more likely he was to 'stream within the class' through seating arrangements. No pattern emerged for the older teachers.

The teacher's attitude to the A-stream child also seemed to be related to seating arrangements: a favourable attitude was associated with streaming within the class and an unfavourable one with free choice ($r = 0.26$). Also teachers interested in the backward child were less likely to stream all of the time.

What about similar ability grouping? Is this a form of streaming within the class? The answer probably depends on how the members of the group are selected and placed, on the teachers' motivations, and on the children's feelings about the situation. Unfortunately information of this kind was not available. But choice of method of instruction did tend to reflect the teachers' views, although to a lesser extent than seating arrangements, and it was found that teachers believing in streaming tended to use similar ability grouping as their main method of instruction (i.e. method used most of the time) for *more* subjects than those holding opposing views. This tendency was found among all age groups of teacher. However, as stated above, the social and emotional aspects of grouping probably depend on the attitudes of the teacher and on the flexibility of the approach.

TABLE 4.2: *Attitude of teachers in non-streamed schools to streaming and their use of similar ability grouping*

Number of subjects in which similar ability grouping was the main method of instruction	ATTITUDE OF TEACHER	
	Anti-Streaming (scored 4567)	*Undecided or Pro-Streaming (scored 0123)*
None	52%	40%
One	31%	27%
Two or more	17%	33%
	100%	100%
Number of teachers giving information	136	129
Chi-square test	$\chi^2 = 8.95, P < 0.05$	

These findings illustrate the relationship between attitudes and choice of classroom organization or teaching method. They suggest that, although a school may change to non-streaming, there is likely to be streaming within the class if teachers cannot accept or are undecided about the approach and believe in streaming. They also suggest that teachers not accepting the school's policy of streaming or non-streaming moulded their environment to the one they found most congenial. For example, teachers believing in streaming in non-streamed schools, treated their class as a streamed one. Their teaching method, their lessons and their attitudes tended to reflect the pattern found in streamed schools. They even streamed their children into geographically located ability groups. To this extent, it could be misleading to regard these as non-streamed classes.

Classification of teachers

Since teachers in conflict with the school policy could well mask the true effect of organization, it was decided to classify teachers according to their attitudes and teaching methods. The classification procedure was based on ten variables and included those which best discriminated[1] between streamed and non-streamed schools (see Table 4.3).

The procedure employed was a cluster or profile analysis (see Appendix 7B). The principal objective here was 'to aid in the understanding of complex subject matter, by grouping the population into discrete, relatively homogeneous classes which can be visualised in terms of a typical member'.[2] In other words, teachers who had similar response patterns were grouped together. Two analyses were carried out, one for teachers of third and fourth year juniors and one for teachers of second year children, since it was known that the age of the children taught was related to the score obtained on some of the variables, such as the 'traditional' and 'progressive' lessons scales.

A number of different teacher-types were identified but, in order to have a reasonable sample size of each type, it was decided to analyse in terms of the two major types only (see Appendix 7B). One type of teacher was identified as typical of the non-streamed school (Type 1)

---

[1] Scores on the 'attitude to backward child' scale did not discriminate between streamed and non-streamed schools but did discriminate between teachers holding contrasting views on streaming in non-streamed schools.

[2] See *Users Guide to the Cluster Analysis Program*, Scientific Control Systems Ltd., July 1968.

and the other as typical of the streamed school (Type 2). The characteristics of the two types of teacher are shown in Table 4.3.

TABLE 4.3: *Attitudes and classroom practices of Type* 1 *and Type* 2 *teachers*

Type 1	Type 2
Believed in non-streaming	Believed in streaming
No streaming by seating	Some streaming by seating
More favourable attitude to slow child	Less interested in slow child
'Permissive'	'Non-permissive'
Tolerant of noise and talking in the classroom	Less tolerant of noise and talking in the classroom
Less favourable attitude to physical punishment	Favourable attitude to physical punishment
Made less use of 'traditional' lessons	Frequent use of 'traditional' lessons
Frequent use of 'progressive' lessons	Made less use of 'progressive' lessons
Tests at least once a month†	Tests at least once a month†
Formal sums about once a week	Formal sums every 2-3 days

†Frequency of tests did not discriminate between the two teacher-types.

Fifty-two per cent of teachers in non-streamed schools were classified as Type 1 and conformed to the pattern of the non-streamed school; the other 48 per cent were identified as Type 2. Eighty-three per cent of teachers in streamed schools were Type 2 and the remaining 17 per cent were Type 1.

Certain characteristics, such as age, sex and number of years' experience, discriminated Type 1 from Type 2 teachers.

Characteristics of Type 1 and Type 2 teachers in non-streamed schools

There was no sex difference in non-streamed schools for the proportions of Type 1 and Type 2 men and women teachers were approximately equal. There were, however, age differences, which were particularly marked among the older teachers. Forty-three per cent of teachers under thirty were in the Type 1 group, compared with 39 per cent in the Type 2 group. Forty per cent of Type 1 teachers were between thirty-one and forty-five compared with only 30 per cent of Type 2 teachers, but only 17 per cent of Type 1 teachers were over forty-six, compared with 31 per cent of Type 2 teachers.

As would be expected, the same relationship occurred between type of teacher and number of years' experience; there was a tendency for Type 1 teachers to have had less experience, and Type 2 more experience: 12 per cent of Type 1 had had more than twenty years' experience compared with 17 per cent identified as Type 2, and if those with eleven to twenty years' experience are also included, the percentages increase to 41 per cent and 53 per cent respectively (see Tables 4.11 and 4.12 in Appendix 6).

The next point of interest concerned the attitude to streaming of Type 2 teachers in non-streamed schools. One would expect them to favour streaming, since this was the group-trend, but it was found that 21 per cent of them believed in non-streaming. Why, then, had they been categorized as Type 2? It will be remembered that teachers were classified on the basis of their scores on ten factors; if they were more like Type 2 on the majority of these, then they would be allocated to that group. Thus, it would seem that the 21 per cent identified as Type 2 had intellectually accepted the philosophy of non-streaming but had not put into practice the methods and attitudes associated with it. Moreover these teachers tended to be older and to have had more teaching experience.

Thirty-three per cent of Type 2 teachers with more than twenty years' experience were of the type discussed above, that is, they accepted non-streaming as measured by their attitude score, but were not in reality putting it into practice, compared with 28 per cent of those with 'eleven to twenty years' experience' and 12 per cent of those with 'ten years' experience and under'.

Earlier it was noted that the attitudes of *older* teachers to streaming were not always related to their method of classroom organization; this lack of relationship was also found for other practices. For example, the frequency of having formal sums, tests and 'progressive' lessons was related to a teacher's attitude to streaming. Different trends in the expected direction were found on all these variables for younger teachers and, with the exception of 'progressive' lessons, none were found for older teachers.[1]

These results suggest that teachers, particularly the older ones, may accept and approve of non-streaming but be unable to put it into practice in the classroom. Changes to non-streaming imply both changes in approach and teaching method, and those who have been teaching for twenty years or more probably find it more difficult to

---

[1] See Tables 4.13-4.16 in Appendix 6.

adjust than those who have been teaching for, say, only five years. Older teachers will probably resist changes in method and will stick to their more familiar and routine methods, whatever their views.

Characteristics of Type 1 and Type 2 teachers in streamed schools

It will be remembered that 17 per cent of teachers in streamed schools were identified as Type 1 but 83 per cent were Type 2. What discriminated Type 1 from Type 2 teachers in streamed schools? This time there was a sex difference and there was a slight tendency for Type 1 teachers to be male.

Again the Type 1 teachers tended to be younger and had fewer years' teaching experience than Type 2, but the major differences again occurred among the older age groups. Nine per cent of Type 1 teachers, compared with 29 per cent of Type 2 teachers, had had more than twenty years' experience and similarly 17 per cent of Type 1 teachers and 33 per cent of Type 2 teachers were over forty-five years of age (see Tables 4.10–4.12 in Appendix 6).

The school as a whole

So far, teachers as individuals have been discussed, but what about the school as a whole? What are the chances of a child in a non-streamed school being taught by a Type 1 teacher throughout his entire junior school course?

The findings revealed that only about half the teachers in non-streamed schools were Type 1, and from this one might assume that a child would be taught by equal numbers of Type 1 and Type 2 teachers. However, the proportions in each school varied enormously. Nine of the thirty-six *non-streamed* schools had equal proportions of Type 1 and Type 2 teachers but in thirteen of the schools there was a preponderance of Type 2 and in fourteen, a preponderance of Type 1 teachers. Out of the thirteen schools staffed by predominantly Type 2, two of the schools had only *one* Type 1 teacher. Of the other fourteen schools, predominantly Type 1, half of them had all, or all except one, Type 1 teachers.

It must be remembered, however, that the above refers to a longitudinal section of teachers (i.e. each year's teachers of the follow-up children) rather than all those in the school at any one time. In 1964, the first year, information of the latter kind was collected but a classification of the teachers was not carried out. However, it was

54

then noted, using attitude to streaming as the criterion, that 'in a few schools less than half the staff were in agreement with the head's policy, while in others all were in accord' (Barker Lunn, 1967b).

It was possible to analyse the type of teacher the child had in the second, third and fourth year, and it was found that in non-streamed schools only 24 per cent of pupils were taught in these three years by Type 1 teachers, and 52 per cent had had at least two Type 2 teachers (see Table 4.4 below).

TABLE 4.4: *Percentage of children having various teacher-types in their second, third and fourth junior years*

Type of school:	Non-Streamed	Streamed
ALL TYPE 1 (i.e. taught by *Type 1* in second, third and fourth year)	24%	1%
MAJORITY OF TYPE 1 (i.e. taught by *Type 1* in two out of the three years)	24%	5%
MAJORITY OF TYPE 2 (i.e. taught by *Type 2* in two out of the three years)	35%	34%
ALL TYPE 2 (i.e. taught by *Type 2* in second, third and fourth year)	17%	60%
Number of pupils	100% 2705	100% 2797

Since only 17 per cent of teachers in streamed schools were identified as Type 1, the situation of a large proportion of teachers in the school being in conflict with the aims of its particular system, as in the non-streamed school, did not arise, and the Type 1 teachers teaching in streamed schools were well scattered throughout the thirty-six sample schools. Four schools only had as many as three Type 1 teachers.

It can be seen from Table 4.4 that only six per cent of pupils in streamed schools were taught by a majority of Type 1 teachers; for most pupils their class-teacher throughout was a Type 2.

The problem of ideological conflicts among staff is not one that teachers are likely to bring before the public, though undoubtedly it is important to know what factors cause the staff in one school to become committed to the school policy and in another to oppose it;

why some heads can make policy changes and carry staff opinion with them, while others achieve less than whole-hearted enthusiasm (see Chapter 16, Dynamics of Change). It is clear enough that a parent who deliberately chooses a school of one type rather than another, may later find that the outlook of the staff does not reflect the organization of the school.

Conclusions

The findings of this chapter make it quite clear that the problem of streaming versus non-streaming is not simply an organizational one. Where schools have changed to non-streaming, some are non-streamed in name only, for their staff have retained their former streaming views, classroom practices and teaching methods. The greater conformity among streamed school teachers in their attitudes and beliefs would be expected, since the organizational policy of the schools is the conventional one. The changeover to non-streaming is fairly new and at the time of the research, this form of organization was a comparative rarity. Since of all junior schools in the country which were large enough to do so, 65 per cent streamed (3 or 4 year groups) and only six per cent did not stream (any year group) (Barker Lunn, 1967a), it seems reasonable to suppose that most junior school teachers were in favour of streaming and that relatively few were firmly committed to non-streaming. Since attitudes for or against streaming seem to form part of a whole syndrome of views, practices and beliefs, the opinions of Type 2 teachers on teaching methods and other educational matters seem to represent the majority viewpoint. This makes it difficult for schools attempting to practice non-streaming. And it is clear that a mere change in organization, such as the abandonment of streaming, unaccompanied by a serious attempt to change teachers' attitudes, beliefs and methods of teaching, is unlikely to make much difference; in fact it is likely to result in a change from streaming between classes to streaming within classes.

References

BARKER LUNN, J. C. (1967a). 'The effects of streaming and other forms of grouping in junior schools—Junior schools and their types of school organization', *New Research in Education*, 1, 4-45.

BARKER LUNN, J. C. (1967b). 'The effects of streaming and non-streaming in junior schools', *New Research in Education*, 1, 46-75.

Users Guide to the Cluster Analysis Programme. (1968). London: Scientific Control Systems, Ltd.

CHAPTER 5

Attainments in Streamed and Non-Streamed Schools

MANY teachers ask if children do as well academically in non-streamed as in streamed schools. Teachers favouring streaming believe that 'it ensures brighter children make maximum progress'; that 'backward children receive special attention'; and that 'teaching is more efficient'. On the other hand, those in favour of non-streaming claim that average and slow or below average pupils do better in a non-streamed class, benefiting from the presence of bright pupils (see Appendix 2 and Chapter 14).

What really does happen? Does either form of organization produce better academic results? Do particular types of children, either of a certain ability level or social class, do better under one form of organization than under the other?

In order to assess attainments in the two types of school, tests of Reading, English, Mechanical Arithmetic and Problem Arithmetic were administered in the summer term of 1964 to all children included in the cross-sectional study (Barker Lunn, 1967b), i.e. all pupils aged 7+, 8+, 9+, 10+ in the sample schools. For the purposes of the longitudinal study, the pupils aged 7+ (Cohort 1) in 1964 were retested at 8+, 9+ and 10+. In their second year (8+) they were given the above four attainment tests and also Number Concept and Verbal Reasoning tests which were thereafter used annually; in their third year a Non-Verbal reasoning test was added to the battery. The same or similar tests were given each year so that measures of gain or progress could be made (see Chapter 2 and Appendix 4).

The objective in analysing the data was to determine whether pupils of comparable ability made greater academic progress in streamed or in non-streamed schools. Not only were gains examined over the entire junior course, but gains from year to year were also analysed.

It will be recalled that a random half of the schools (Sample A) worked one set of attainment tests and the other schools (Sample B) worked a parallel set (see Chapter 2). This meant that in effect two studies were carried out simultaneously and thus extensive cross-checking of results was possible.

Assessment was made of the attainment gains of children who were initially of similar measured ability in the first junior school year. Ability was defined in terms of reading score at seven-plus, and on this basis three groups of equal size were formed: (i) above average, (ii) average, and (iii) below average. It had been intended that the ability groups should be based on scores obtained from the four tests used in the first year (English, Problem, Mechanical, Reading). But data obtained from the cross-sectional study indicated that this could well bias the results in favour of non-streamed schools (see Chapter 1). It had been found that pupils in streamed schools had slightly higher mean scores on the attainment tests, possibly because their curriculum had covered the test-content more fully. For example, Mechanical Arithmetic or computational practice was emphasized in streamed schools, whereas in non-streamed schools the tendency was for a greater concentration on practical arithmetic, and in some of these latter schools computational practice was non-existent in the first junior school year. The more the test reflected traditional educational practices, as emphasized by streamed schools, the greater the score differences. It was considered, therefore, that any division of children into 'ability groups' on the basis of tests containing 'traditional items' would result in spuriously few children from non-streamed schools being allocated to the above average group. If this were the case, the bright children in non-streamed schools, having been allocated to too low an ability category, might make greater attainment gains than children of supposedly comparable ability in streamed schools, particularly in the later years when test-content became less important. Since the Reading test was the one most free from curriculum-bias, 'ability' was defined in terms of initial reading score corrected for age, and pupils were allocated to one of the three ability groups on this basis.[1]

[1] There were two main reasons for not allocating children to groups on the basis of intelligence. Firstly, there was no group test available which was sufficiently reliable for use with children aged seven-plus. Secondly, it is doubtful whether tests of intelligence measure something different from attainment tests. Educational opinion is not nearly so sure now that the former actually measure a child's potential (Vernon, 1960; Pidgeon, 1969). The work of Hebb (1949), Piaget (1952) and Bloom (1964) has shown that intelligence is not fixed but grows and develops and this is partly dependent on environmental stimulation. It can be regarded as a fluid collection of skills which are to a considerable extent developed by early experience, and subsequently affected by the quality and length of formal schooling that an individual undergoes.

Besides allocating pupils to an ability group, it was found necessary to take social class into account (see Appendix 8) and three groups were formed: (i) middle class (social classes 1 and 2), (ii) upper working class (social class 3), and (iii) lower working class (social classes 4 and 5). (For details of social class definitions, see Appendix 4.) The sex of the pupil was also considered as a factor which might affect progress scores and consequently data for boys and girls were analysed separately.

Influence of school organization on pupil progress

A comparison was made between the attainment gains of comparable children in the two types of school on each of the seven tests. Separate analyses were carried out for each test and, to be included, a pupil had to have a score for each year the test was given. Information concerning his social class and his initial Reading test score also had to be available so that he could be allocated to an ability group.[1] The results for approximately 5,500 pupils were analysed.

Attainment gains made by pupils of comparable sex, social class and 'ability' in the two types of school were compared. Using analysis of covariance (see Statistical Appendix 8) comparisons were made of gains from year to year and the overall gains between the first and fourth year.

Table 5.1 gives a summary of the results. When results were in favour of non-streamed schools asterisks (*) indicating level of statistical significance have been used and when in favour of streamed schools daggers (†) have been adopted. First, it is quite clear from Table 5.1 that in Sample A, pupils in non-streamed schools made better progress than those in streamed schools—44 of the comparisons favoured non-streamed schools and only 6 favoured streamed schools. But in Sample B, pupils in streamed schools made better progress and here 52 of the comparisons were in favour of streamed schools and only 9 in favour of non-streamed schools. Table 5.1 shows to a startling degree the consistency of the results; the asterisks predominate in sample A with just a scattering of daggers, and in sample B daggers predominate with just a few asterisks.

It is interesting to examine the Sample A and Sample B schools. In the first place, schools were assigned to one or other of the samples on a random basis—matched pairs of schools from the total sample list were allocated alternately to become A or B. Schools were ordered according to socio-economic background and by taking

[1] When initial reading score was not available teachers' estimate of general ability was taken—this involved only a small percentage of pupils.

TABLE 5.1: *A comparison of the attainment gains made by pupils in streamed and non-streamed schools*

SAMPLE A

	READING				ENGLISH				MECHANICAL				PROBLEM				CONCEPT			VERBAL			NON-VERBAL
	1–2	2–3	3–4	1–4	1–2	2–3	3–4	1–4	1–2	2–3	3–4	1–4	1–2	2–3	3–4	1–4	2–3	3–4	2–4	2–3	3–4	2–4	3–4
BOYS																							
Above average social class 1, 2	–	–	–	–	–	–	–	–	–	–	***	*	–	–	–	–	–	–	–	–	–	–	–
Above average social class 3	–	–	–	–	–	–	–	–	–	–	*	–	–	–	–	–	–	–	–	(*)	(*)	(**)	–
Above average social class 4, 5	–	–	–	–	–	**	–	–	–	–	–	–	–	–	*	–	–	–	–	–	–	–	–
Average social class 1, 2	–	*	–	–	–	–	–	–	–	*	–	–	*	*	*	–	–	–	–	–	–	–	–
Average social class 3	–	–	–	–	–	–	–	–	†	–	–	–	–	–	–	††	–	†	–	–	*	–	–
Average social class 4, 5	–	–	–	–	–	–	–	–	–	–	–	–	–	–	–	–	–	–	**	–	–	–	–
Below average social class 1, 2	–	–	–	(*)	–	–	–	–	**	–	–	–	**	–	–	–	**	–	–	–	–	–	–
Below average social class 3	–	–	††	–	–	–	(†)	–	–	–	–	–	**	–	–	–	–	**	–	–	–	–	–
Below average social class 4, 5	–	–	–	–	–	–	–	–	–	**	–	–	–	–	–	–	–	–	–	–	–	–	–
GIRLS																							
Above average social class 1, 2	–	–	–	–	–	–	–	–	–	–	***	*	–	–	–	–	–	–	–	–	–	*	–
Above average social class 3	–	–	–	–	–	–	–	–	–	–	–	–	–	–	–	–	–	–	–	*	†	**	–
Above average social class 4, 5	–	–	–	–	–	–	–	–	–	**	***	**	–	**	**	–	–	*	–	*	**	–	–
Average social class 1, 2	–	–	–	–	–	–	–	–	–	–	–	–	–	–	–	–	–	–	–	*	*	–	–
Average social class 3	–	–	–	–	–	*	–	–	**	–	–	–	–	**	**	*	–	*	–	–	–	–	–
Average social class 4, 5	–	–	–	–	–	–	–	–	–	–	–	–	–	–	–	–	–	–	–	–	–	–	–
Below average social class 1, 2	–	–	–	–	–	–	–	–	–	–	–	–	–	–	–	–	–	–	–	–	–	–	–
Below average social class 3	–	–	–	–	**	–	–	–	–	–	–	–	***	–	–	–	–	–	–	–	–	–	–
Below average social class 4, 5	–	*	–	–	–	–	–	–	–	–	–	(*)	–	–	–	*	–	–	–	–	–	–	–

TABLE 5.1:—*continued*

SAMPLE B

	READING				ENGLISH				MECHANICAL				PROBLEM				CONCEPT			VERBAL			NON-VERBAL
	1-2	2-3	3-4	1-4	1-2	2-3	3-4	1-4	1-2	2-3	3-4	1-4	1-2	2-3	3-4	1-4	2-3	3-4	2-4	2-3	3-4	2-4	3-4
BOYS																							
Above average social class 1,2	–	–	–	–	–	–	–	–	††	–	–	–	–	††	–	–	–	–	–	–	–	–	–
Above average social class 3	–	†	–	·	–	–	–	–	+	–	–	–	+	–	–	–	–	–	–	–	–	–	–
Above average social class 4,5	–	–	–	–	–	–	–	††	†††	–	–	††	††	–	–	††	–	–	–	–	–	–	–
Average social class 1,2	+	–	–	–	–	–	(*)	–	–	–	–	–	–	–	–	–	–	(†)	–	–	–	–	–
Average social class 3	–	–	–	–	–	–	–	–	†††	–	–	–	+	–	–	–	–	–	–	–	+	–	–
Average social class 4,5	+	–	†	††	+	†	–	†	(†††)	–	–	†	–	††	–	†	+	–	†	–	–	†	–
Below average social class 1,2	–	–	–	–	–	–	–	–	–	–	–	–	–	–	+	–	–	–	–	–	–	–	–
Below average social class 3	–	–	–	–	–	–	–	–	+	–	†	–	–	–	†	–	†	–	††	–	*	–	–
Below average social class 4,5	–	–	–	–	–	–	–	–	+	–	*	–	–	*	–	–	–	–	*	–	–	–	–
GIRLS																							
Above average social class 1,2	–	–	–	–	–	–	*	–	–	††	–	–	††	–	–	–	–	–	–	–	–	††	–
Above average social class 3	–	–	–	–	–	–	–	–	†††	–	–	–	+	–	–	–	†	–	+	–	+	††	–
Above average social class 4,5	–	–	–	–	–	–	–	–	–	–	–	–	(††)	–	–	–	–	–	–	–	–	–	–
Average social class 1,2	–	–	–	–	–	†	–	+	†††	–	–	–	+	–	–	–	–	–	–	–	–	–	–
Average social class 3	–	–	–	–	†	–	–	–	††	–	–	–	††	–	–	(†)	–	–	–	–	+	†	·
Average social class 4,5	–	–	–	–	–	–	–	–	(†††)	–	–	–	–	–	+	–	†	–	–	–	–	–	–
Below average social class 1,2	–	††	–	–	(*)	–	–	–	–	–	–	–	–	–	–	–	–	–	–	*	–	–	–
Below average social class 3	–	–	–	–	–	–	–	–	–	–	–	–	–	–	–	–	–	–	–	–	–	–	–
Below average social class 4,5	–	–	–	†	–	†	–	–	††	–	–	–	(†)	–	–	–	–	*	–	–	–	*	–

† = significant difference favours streamed schools
* = significant difference favours non-streamed schools
*, † = difference significant at 5% level
– = non-significant

**, †† = difference significant at 1% level
***, ††† = difference significant at 0·1% level
(*), (†) = signs in brackets indicate significant difference in means were accompanied by a significant difference in regression relationships—see cautionary note in Appendix 8.

For details of initial and final mean score see Table 5.5 in Appendix 6.

alternate pairs from the list the two samples were kept similar in terms of social background. It will be remembered that two parallel versions were available for four of the tests: Reading, English, Mechanical and Problem Arithmetic. Those schools designated 'A', worked the A-version of these tests in the first, second and fourth years but the B-version in the third year, while the Sample B schools worked the B-version in the first, second and fourth years, but changed to the A-version in the third year. Both Samples A and B used the same Number Concept, Verbal and Non-Verbal tests.

How can one account for the different results obtained by Samples A and B? There would seem to be two possible explanations: firstly, that the different results obtained by the two samples were due to sample differences; or secondly, that they were due to differences in the tests used. This latter explanation was, however, rejected since both samples in their third year used the other test, and, as can be seen from Table 5.1, there was no change in the pattern of results at this time. Also, of course, both samples used the same Number Concept, Verbal and Non-Verbal tests and the results obtained from these were consistent with the others. So it can be concluded that the different results obtained by the two samples were due to sample differences. What this means is that the better results obtained by the non-streamed Sample A schools and the better results obtained by the streamed Sample B schools had nothing whatsoever to do with their type of school organization. The statistically significant differences were due to some other unknown factor.

It is worth commenting here on the dangers of non-replication—had only Sample A or Sample B been used, very different conclusions might have been drawn. In this particular study, however, the sample was large enough to cope with extraneous factors. If the sample had not been divided into two, the results would have indicated no significant differences between school types since Sample A results would have cancelled out those of Sample B.

From the results obtained it can be concluded that there was no difference in the average attainment gains of children of comparable ability in streamed and non-streamed schools.[1]

---

[1] It was suggested in Chapter 1 that some of the attainment tests used in this study might favour streamed schools simply because their content had been given more emphasis. The test considered most likely to give such results was the Mechanical Arithmetic test. Practice in this type of activity was more common in streamed schools, particularly in the first three years, than in non-streamed schools (see Table 3.4, Appendix 6 and Chapter 3) and a possible

Influence of teacher-type on pupil progress

A possible explanation for the inconclusive findings produced by research studies investigating streaming, suggested in the Introduction, was that teachers respond differently to the two forms of organization. Some teachers believe in a particular system, use methods appropriate to it and their pupils benefit accordingly; others cannot accept the system or use inappropriate methods and their pupils tend to make less favourable progress. When the results obtained are averaged, it was suggested that little overall difference between the two forms of grouping is obtained.

In Chapter 3, it was found that many teachers were undecided about or opposed to their school's organizational policy. It was also found that teachers believing in non-streaming tended to hold certain attitudes and to favour particular teaching methods and classroom practices, while opposite or opposing views and practices were associated with those supporting streaming. Since teachers in conflict with the school's organizational policy could well frustrate its major aims, it was considered desirable to investigate this aspect. Two types of teacher were identified: Type 1 teachers held attitudes and used teaching methods typical of the non-streamed school; Type 2 teachers were in the same way typical of the streamed school (see Chapter 4).

Type of teacher was relatively unimportant in streamed schools since the majority were Type 2. On the other hand in non-streamed schools the two teacher types were equally common and, while pupils' academic progress was apparently unaffected by type of school organization, it was predicted that it would be influenced by teacher-type.

In order to examine the effects of teacher-type, three groups were formed: pupils who were taught by Type 1 teachers in non-streamed schools; pupils who were taught by Type 2 teachers in non-streamed

---

outcome might be greater facility in this test among pupils in the former schools. Table 5.1 reveals an interesting pattern of results; it can be seen that between the first and second years greater progress was made in Mechanical Arithmetic by pupils from streamed schools, whereas for non-streamed pupils progress came at a later stage between the third and fourth years. Even though there were sample differences, note the complete absence of significant gains favouring non-streamed schools between the first and second years and for streamed schools between the third and fourth years. Less emphasis on formal (computational) arithmetic in the early years in non-streamed schools is reflected in these results, but it appears that although their pupils make a slower start, they catch up by the end of the primary school. On the other hand, there was no pattern favouring either type of school on any of the other tests.

schools; and pupils in streamed schools. A covariance analysis was used as before, except that, instead of comparing attainment gains of two groups of comparable pupils, the gains of the above three groups were compared. Pupils were grouped according to social class and ability as in the previous analysis but, since the numbers were smaller as there were three rather than two groups, the analysis was carried out for boys and girls combined (see Appendix 8).

As was indicated earlier in Chapter 4, children in non-streamed schools were by no means taught by the same type of teacher each year, and it was not uncommon to find pupils having had a Type 1 teacher one year and a Type 2 the next year. When analysing attainment gains over consecutive years, the pupil's teacher in the second year of comparison was the 'type' considered. For example, if attainment gains between the end of the third and fourth years were being examined, the type of teacher the child had had in the fourth year was the one taken. In examining the attainment gains between the first and fourth year, teacher-type was defined in terms of the type who had taught the children most often over the three years (i.e. 1964-65; 1965-66; 1966-67) so that pupils allocated to a Type 1 group were those taught by at least *two* Type 1 teachers— but not necessarily in consecutive years. It can be seen that analysis of attainment gains by teacher-type was difficult, particularly over a number of years, since teacher-type did not remain constant.

Attainment gains in four tests were examined in the teacher-type analysis. These were English, Problem Arithmetic, Number Concept and Verbal Reasoning. Achievement gains over consecutive years were examined over the three-year period.[1]

Table 5.2 gives the results. It can be seen that similar results to those obtained in the first analysis (see Table 5.1) were found, and that there was no distinct pattern favouring streamed schools or children taught by Type 1 or Type 2 teachers. In Sample A the results favoured non-streamed schools, with significant results distributed among Type 1 and Type 2 teachers. On the other hand, the majority of significant differences in Sample B favoured streamed schools. The same version of the Number Concept and Verbal Reasoning tests was used by both Samples A and B and, as Table 5.2 shows, there was no pattern favouring either one or other type of school or teacher.

[1] The reason for not using all of the tests and examining progress gains over all four years was a lack of sufficient financial resources.

TABLE 5.2: *A comparison of the attainment gains of pupils in streamed schools and those taught by Type 1 and Type 2 teachers in non-streamed schools*

	ENGLISH				PROBLEM				CONCEPT	VERBAL
	1-2	2-3	3-4	1-4	1-2	2-3	3-4	1-4	3-4	3-4
SAMPLE A (*Boys and Girls*)										
Above average social class 1, 2	—	—	—	—	—	—	—	*ᵒ	—	—
Above average social class 3	—	***	—	—	—	—	—	—	—	—
Above average social class 4, 5	—	—	*ᵘ	—	—	—	—	*ᵘᵒ	—	—
Average social class 1, 2	—	*ᵒ	—	—	—	**ᵒ	—	**ᵒ	—	—
Average social class 3	—	—	—	—	—	—	(*)	—	—	—
Average social class 4, 5	—	—	—	—	—	—	—	—	—	—
Below average social class 1, 2	—	—	—	—	***	—	—	—	—	—
Below average social class 3	—	—	—	—	**	—	—	ᵘ	—	—
Below average social class 4, 5	—	—	—	—	—	—	—	—	—	—
SAMPLE B (*Boys and Girls*)										
Above average social class 1, 2	†	—	—	—	†††	—	—	††		
Above average social class 3	—	—	—	—	††	—	—	††		
Above average social class 4, 5	—	—	—	—	†††	(††)	—	††		Only one version
Average social class 1, 2	†††	†	*ᵘ	—	—	—	—	*ᵘ†		of concept and
Average social class 3	(††)	††	—	**ᵒ	†††	—	(††)	††		verbal.
Average social class 4, 5	—	—	—	—	—	(††)	—	††		
Below average social class 1, 2	—	—	—	—	—	—	—	—		
Below average social class 3	—	—	—	—	—	—	—	—		
Below average social class 4, 5	—	—	—	—	—	—	—	—		

*ᵒ = gain favours non-streamed schools with Type 1 teachers.
*ᵘ = gain favours non-streamed schools with Type 2 teachers.
† = gain favours non-streamed schools (i.e. no difference between Type 1 and Type 2 teachers).
† = gain favours streamed schools.
one asterisk or dagger indicates gain significantly different at 5% level, two asterisks or daggers at 1% level, and three asterisks or daggers at 0·1% level.
— = no difference between streamed and non-streamed schools with Type 2 teachers.
† = non-significant.
(*), (†) = significant difference in means was accompanied by a significant difference in regression relationship (see Appendix 6).
For details of initial and final mean scores see Table 5.6, Appendix 6.

Factors other than teacher-type and type of school organization must account for the different results obtained from the two samples. This study confirms the work of American researchers in their conclusions that the method of grouping used is irrelevant to learning. It must be concluded from this study, too, that type of organization, even with the 'right type' of teacher (i.e. in terms of value-structure), makes no difference to academic progress as measured by objective tests.

These results may surprise many teachers who feel that they themselves have observed the effects of streaming or non-streaming on academic progress: they have seen in their own non-streamed class, for example, the slower pupils making tremendous gains and appearing to benefit from the presence of the more able pupils; or other teachers may have felt, in similar circumstances, that the brightest were not being 'stretched' to their limit. Two points can be made here. Firstly, attainment gains were measured in terms of objective tests, the content of which on the whole tended to be more concerned with understanding than with specific facts taught in class. Teachers making an assessment of progress would tend to use the latter specific criteria—which could account for their observations. Also, different teachers observe different effects in their classrooms: some teachers find that a certain type of pupil makes great gains, other teachers observe the same type of pupil making relatively poor progress. The findings of this study, however, refer to overall effects, and although variation obviously occurred among individual teachers, on the average there was no difference.

Another factor which is of interest here is the lack of relationship between the effectiveness of the teacher, as measured by pupil-progress, and his value-structure, as measured by attitudes and classroom practices. It would seem that a teacher may hold certain attitudes, and favour certain teaching methods, which are appropriate to the type of school in which he is teaching, but still be no more effective in terms of pupil-progress. In other words, no relationship was found between a teacher's attitudes, values, methods of teaching, and the types of lessons preferred, and his or her effectiveness as a teacher as measured by pupil achievement-gain. The failure to find such a relationship in the non-streamed school might be thought surprising. But two points should be borne in mind. Firstly, it was necessary on the grounds of sample-size to work with only two types of teacher (see Appendix 7B). This led to the combination of a number of specific differences between teachers which might well have been related to their effectiveness in this situation. Secondly, many children had teachers of different types in successive years; this could well have blurred the effects of any particular teacher-type.

Spread of scores

So far, the average achievement gains of pupils within each of the three ability groups have been examined and found unrelated to type of school organization. But another feature of test score distribution worth noting is the standard deviation or dispersion of test scores. Accordingly the spread of test scores (within sex and social class) in the compared groups was investigated. The standard deviation of test scores showed that there was a tendency for less homogeneity in performance in streamed schools (see Table 5.7, Appendix 6). Approximately 18 per cent of the comparisons indicated that the spread of scores was greater, reaching at least a 5 per cent level of statistical significance, in streamed schools, while the spread in non-streamed schools was never significantly larger (see Table 5.7, Appendix 6). This suggests that non-streaming tends to reduce the dispersion of test scores and streaming to increase it. That it does point to an organizational effect is supported by the fact that no consistent differences, in terms of spread of score, were found within non-streamed schools between the two teacher-types. It would seem that an outcome of separating children of different ability, which streaming implies, is a tendency to increase the difference between them. This supports the beliefs and findings of other workers (Yates and Pidgeon, 1959; Daniels, 1961).

Interpretation of these findings, however, should be treated cautiously, since one cannot state exactly what the greater score spread in streamed schools means. One might suppose that the greater spread implied that the brightest of the bright (i.e. top third) did better and the dullest of the dull (i.e. bottom third) did worse in a streamed school. But there was no evidence that this was so. It will be remembered that children in the two schools were matched for ability at 7+ (i.e. were allocated to one of three ability groups) and it was found that children of comparable ability made similar progress during their junior course in the two types of schools. If the bright or some of the brightest had made substantially greater academic progress in streamed schools and the number involved had been of any consequence, then this would have affected or 'pulled up' the average gain, but this did not occur.

67

Influence of social class on pupil-progress

The results already described (see Tables 5.1 and 5.2) have provided no evidence that children of different social classes did academically better or worse in one type of school organization than the other. However, a comparison of the progress made by the different social classes did provide some interesting results.

This was done by examining the relative change in performance in reading between the ages of seven and ten-plus. On the basis of their standardized score in reading at seven-plus, pupils were divided into five equal-sized groups: superior, above average, average, below average, and dull. The same process was repeated at 10+. The group to which each child had been allocated at seven-plus was then plotted against his group at ten-plus, and in this way it was possible to determine for each child whether he had gone up by one or more groups, moved down by one or more groups, or whether he had not changed his relative position.

All pupils who had obtained Reading test scores in the first and fourth year, and whose social class was known were included (N=4,673). The sample was divided into two groups on the basis of social class: a) pupils whose father's occupation was classified as professional, clerical or skilled (Classes 1, 2 and 3) and b) pupils whose father's occupation was classified as semi-skilled or un-skilled (Classes 4 and 5). Separate comparisons were carried out for boys and girls.

The results indicated that over the three years, the reading performance of children of the higher social class (1, 2, 3) 'improved', whereas that of the lower social class (4, 5) 'deteriorated'. In other words, the relative position of the two social class groups were further apart in terms of attainment score on a Reading test at 10+ than was the case at 7+. The findings were highly statistically significant and held for both boys and girls and all ability groups (see Table 5.3, Appendix 6).[1]

Why should the reading performance of children of lower social class origin fall off in relation to higher social class children? One of the more obvious reasons for this, shown by the Plowden Report, is the tendency for a poorer home background, in terms of 'cultural' stimulation and parental interest and encouragement, to be associated with lower class children. But in addition it is possible that teachers' attitudes have something to do with it—the tendency for them to

---

[1] Douglas (1964) also noted this tendency.

have lower 'expectancies' for children from lower social groups. A comparison was made of teachers' ratings of a child's ability and his actual performance on an English test, both these measures being obtained at the end of the third year. It was found that ability ratings given by teachers agreed with those obtained on the basis of the English test score for the majority of children, but of those not agreeing, lower social class children (groups 4, 5) were more likely than the upper social class children (groups 1, 2, 3) to be under-estimated, and the latter were more likely than the former to be over-estimated (see Table 5.4, Appendix 6).

In judging ability teachers in both streamed and non-streamed schools showed the same tendency to over-estimate the upper social group and under-estimate the lower social group. One outcome of this in streamed schools may well be allocation of lower working class children to too low an ability stream and middle class and upper working class children to too high a stream (see Chapter 7). In non-streamed schools, on the other hand, class teachers may develop an 'expectancy' towards the performance of their pupils which will tend to be lower in the case of lower social class children and higher for upper social class children than their actual potential.

If we take these two findings together—the teacher's tendency to under- or over-estimate ability according to social class and the children's tendency to drop off or improve in reading performance, correspondingly we might suggest a causal relationship here. One research worker, Rosenthal (1969), has in fact shown that what a teacher expects from a pupil is related to his rate of progress.

Conclusions

An examination was made of the progress of approximately 5,500 pupils in English, Reading, Mechanical and Problem Arithmetic, Number Concept, Verbal and Non-Verbal Reasoning during their junior school course. The results were analysed by three social class and three ability levels. Comparisons made between the achievement gains of pupils of comparable ability in 36 streamed and 36 non-streamed schools revealed no pattern favouring either type of school. Comparable pupils, whether bright or above average, average, or below average made similar progress in the two types of school. An additional analysis by teacher-type revealed no differ-ence in terms of the progress made by their pupils; but any effect may well have been blurred by pupils changing from one teacher-type to another in consecutive years.

There was no evidence that children of different social classes did academically better or worse in one type of organization than the other. But findings did indicate that the reading performance of children of lower social class origin (semi or unskilled workers' children) 'deteriorated' over the junior school course relative to higher social class children. Also it was found that there was a tendency for teachers to over-estimate the ability of higher social class children and under-estimate that of working class children. Taking these two findings together, it was suggested that there might be a causal relationship.

If one is to judge the streaming – non-streaming issue solely on the basis of academic performance, the findings of this chapter lend small support to either side. The decision to stream or non-stream must rest upon factors other than formal attainments.

This chapter has examined one aspect of the problem—the effects of school organization on cognitive development. Most people concerned with education, however, would consider that this is not the only or necessarily the most important educational goal. The rest of the book deals with the impact of organizational differences on other factors, such as the pupils' personal and social development.

References.

BARKER LUNN, J.C. (1967). 'The effects of streaming and non-streaming in junior schools', *New Research in Education*, 1, 46-75.

BLOOM, B. S. (1964). *Stability and Change in Human Characteristics*. New York: Wiley.

DANIELS, J. C. (1961). 'The effects of streaming in the primary school, II: a comparison of streamed and unstreamed schools', *Brit. J. Educ. Psychol.*, 31, 119-26.

DOUGLAS, J. W. B. (1964). *The Home and the School*. London: MacGibbon & Kee.

HEBB, D. O. (1949). *The Organization of Behaviour*. New York: Wiley.

PIAGET, J. (1952). *The Origins of Intelligence in Children*. New York: International University Press.

PIDGEON, D. A. (1969). 'Intelligence: a changed view', *Educational Research News*, no. 6.

ROSENTHAL, R. and JACOBSON, L. (1968). *Pygmalion in the Classroom: Teacher Expectation and Pupil Intellectual Development*. New York: Holt, Rinehart & Winston.

VERNON, P. E. (1960). *Intelligence and Attainment Tests*. London: University of London Press.

YATES, A. and PIDGEON, D. A. (1959). 'The effects of streaming', *Educ. Res.*, II, 1, 65-8.

CHAPTER 6

Divergent Thinking

DIVERGENT thinking or 'creativity' is a topic which has attracted a great deal of attention in recent years, and a considerable amount of work, particularly in the United States, has been devoted to the definition, measurement and encouragement of this type of ability[1]. The development of tests to seek out the 'divergent', non-conforming thinker, and the publication of guides to help teachers to make the most of their pupils' creative talents, reflect the opinions of many concerned with education that the present policies of many schools and teachers tend to stifle rather than develop this type of talent, which may result in a considerable loss to both the community and to individuals.

It has been suggested that a highly structured, authoritarian classroom atmosphere, where the emphasis is on the achievement of formal academic goals, is unlikely to foster the growth of divergent thinking.[2] The teacher who is unwilling to deviate from a rigid timetable to pursue the 'awkward' questions of the creative child will dismiss such questions as detracting from the 'real' purpose of the lesson. Under a more flexible and permissive approach, on the other hand, the deviations and 'red herrings' brought up by such a pupil will be welcomed and positively valued by the teacher, who will encourage the child to follow his own 'divergent' path of discovery.

It was felt that the introduction of a test of divergent thinking into the Streaming Project's battery would be of value in investigating

---

[1]Not everybody accepts that creative thinking must be divergent. Some assert that it can also be convergent. See Hudson (1966; 1968). Here, creativity is being used in relation only to the concept of divergent thinking.

[2]See Haddon, F. A. and Lytton, H. (1968). This study found that the performance of children from 'informal' primary schools on a test of divergent thinking was superior to that of children from 'formal' schools. An American study showed that nine-year-old children with 'lower-controlling' teachers obtained higher scores on a creativity test than children with 'higher-controlling' teachers. See Wodtke, K. H. and Wallen, N. E. (1965).

whether one type of school or teacher appeared to be more successful than another in encouraging the development of this particular type of ability. The findings of other researchers concerning the classroom atmosphere most and least conducive to the development of divergent thinking led to the prediction that the schools and teachers favouring a more informal, progressive approach to curriculum and methods would do more to foster divergent thinking than those preferring to adhere to the more formal methods associated with the achievement of accepted standards of academic attainment.

The tests

A test of divergent thinking was constructed especially for this investigation. The items it contained were of a very different nature from those characterizing the more conventional tests of ability and attainment. No single 'correct' answer was sought; on the contrary, the children were asked to think of as many, varied responses as they could to questions deliberately designed to present a new and unfamiliar frame of reference, e.g. by asking for as many unusual uses as possible for everyday objects such as a tin can (see Appendix 4).

The test was designed to measure three aspects of divergent thinking: fluency in ideas, flexibility of ideas and associations, and originality of response. *Statistical* originality was the criterion adopted here, with marks being awarded according to the rarity of the response among a representative sample (see Appendix 4). Two parallel versions of the test were constructed and administered to all Cohort 1 children, one version at the end of their third year, and the other at the end of their fourth year. The subsequent analysis was based on the scores in each year of a sample of approximately 1,800 children, consisting of the same children in both years (see Appendix 4).

A test of free writing in the form of essays was also administered in both years, and was specifically designed to encourage the expression of original and imaginative ideas. The children wrote two essays each year, choosing in each case from a list of topics which aimed at providing a stimulus for an interesting and imaginative story (see Appendix 4). The titles offered were deliberately unconventional in the ideas they presented, the aim being to lure the children away from producing a formal 'stereotyped' composition. Again it was hypothesized that in the more progressive type of school, teachers practising such methods would devote greater attention to the free expression of ideas, and would thus produce better results than teachers in schools where the more formal structured type of essay received greater emphasis.

It was further hoped to discover whether the contrasting types of school experience differed in their effect on the 'creative' performance of pupils of different ability levels; for instance, whether the effect of streaming was such that the curriculum considered appropriate for children in lower streams did not include the encouragement of free writing essays and expression. At the other end of the ability range the most able children might also be given less opportunity to develop their creative writing abilities in schools where formal academic attainment was given priority.

Since type of teacher seemed likely to be of importance in this, as in other areas of the streaming inquiry, it was decided to take this factor into account, as well as the organizational differences between schools. Again, children in streamed schools were not sub-divided by type of teacher, as the great majority of teachers in these schools were Type 2, holding similar attitudes and employing similar methods. Children in non-streamed schools, however, were divided into two groups:— (1) those whose fourth year teachers were Type 1, tending to be 'progressive' in their teaching methods and with typical non-streamer attitudes (see Chapter 4), and (2) children whose fourth year teachers were Type 2 and who were less in favour of 'progressive' lessons and, in terms of attitude and personality, more characteristic of the type of teacher found to predominate in streamed schools.

As the children had been classified according to the type of teacher they had had in their *fourth* year, it was at the end of this year that any differences due to this factor might be expected to make themselves evident. It was thus decided to look at the change of score between the third and fourth years, to see in which direction this lay and whether any differences emerged in the performance of children in streamed schools and those with Type 1 or Type 2 teachers in non-streamed schools. A further comparison was carried out to see whether there were any differences between the three groups at the end of the fourth year in the proportions of children obtaining high and low scores on the test.

The total distribution of scores on the tests each year was divided into five 'bands' or categories of score, each representing 20 per cent of the total sample, and these data were then used as a basis for comparison between the three groups. It must consequently be borne in mind that the results of this analysis represent a *relative* and not an absolute change in the performance of children in the three groups.

Results

(a) *Change of Score between* 9+ *and* 10+ *on Divergent Thinking Test*

When the change of score of children from higher and lower social class backgrounds was studied separately, a few significant differences emerged, indicating contrasting influences of different types of teacher and school. The 'flexibility' scores of lower social class (4, 5) boys in streamed schools showed a significant drop between 9+ and 10+ ($P < 0.01$), whereas comparable boys with Type 1 teachers in non-streamed schools showed an improvement in score which approached statistical significance. On the fluency aspect of the test, lower social class girls who had Type 2 teachers showed a significant drop in score ($P < 0.05$).

Since there was no consistent pattern of difference in score between higher and lower social class children, their scores were combined for further analysis.

The most striking fact to emerge from this analysis was that on each aspect of divergent thinking measured: fluency, flexibility and originality, the scores of boys in streamed schools showed a significant drop between 9+ and 10+ (fluency $P < 0.05$, flexibility $P < 0.01$, originality $P < 0.01$, using the Sign test).[1] The scores of girls in streamed schools also fell in each case, although the differences did not reach statistical significance.

The scores of girls in non-streamed schools who had Type 2 teachers in their fourth year also fell between 9+ and 10+, and in the case of 'originality' this drop was significant ($P < 0.01$). The scores of the corresponding group of boys also fell on the fluency and flexibility parts of the test but showed a very slight improvement on originality.

Both boys and girls in non-streamed schools who had had a Type 1 teacher, however, showed a slight improvement in score at 10+ in both fluency and flexibility, and in the case of girls' scores on 'flexibility', this change approached statistical significance. No consistent differences were found in the case of originality.

[1]See Table 6.4, Appendix 6.

These results indicate that the scores of children with Type 1 teachers tended to show a relative improvement, Type 2 teachers and those in streamed schools appeared to have had a negative effect on their pupils' performance in this field.

(b) *Change of Score between 9+ and 10+ on the Free Writing Essays*

In terms of change of score between 9+ and 10+, no significant differences emerged when the results on the Free Writing Test were analysed, nor were any consistent trends observed.

It should be pointed out that the Free Writing Test was very different in nature from the test of divergent thinking, and although the essay topics presented were made as stimulating and unstructured as possible, it is likely that this task was much more familiar than the more unconventional items presented in the divergent thinking test.

(c) *High and Low Scorers on the Divergent Thinking Test*

It was next decided to see if there were any differences between children in streamed schools and those with Type 1 or Type 2 teachers in non-streamed schools in the percentages obtaining high or low scores on the divergent thinking test at the end of the fourth year.

Firstly, taking the top 20 per cent of scores on the *total* distribution how many children from each of the three groups obtained scores falling within this top category? As Table 6.1 shows, in all cases but one, Type 1 teachers had the highest percentage of children in this category, while Type 2 teachers appeared to produce the smallest number of high scorers.

Turning to the children whose scores fell in the bottom 20 per cent of the total distribution it was seen that in every case except one Type 1 teachers had the smallest percentage of children in this group, while again in most cases the greatest percentage came from children with Type 2 teachers.

TABLE 6.1: *Percentage of children scoring in the top* 20 *per cent on the divergent thinking test*

Fluency

	Social Class	Non-Streamed Type 1	Non-Streamed Type 2	Streamed
Boys	1, 2, 3	23% (1)†	15% (3)	18% (2)
Boys	4, 5	14% (1)	8% (3)	12% (2)
Girls	1, 2, 3	31% (1)	21% (3)	26% (2)
Girls	4, 5	23% (1)	12% (3)	20% (2)

Flexibility

	Social Class	Non-Streamed Type 1	Non-Streamed Type 2	Streamed
Boys	1, 2, 3	23% (2)	19% (3)	24% (1)
Boys	4, 5	17% (1)	11% (2)	9% (3)
Girls	1, 2, 3	33% (1)	26% (2)	26% (2)
Girls	4, 5	23% (1)	7% (3)	15% (2)

Originality

	Social Class	Non-Streamed Type 1	Non-Streamed Type 2	Streamed
Boys	1, 2, 3	25% (1)	23% (2)	22% (3)
Boys	4, 5	25% (1)	13% (3)	14% (2)
Girls	1, 2, 3	26% (1)	18% (3)	22% (2)
Girls	4, 5	19% (1)	3% (3)	16% (2)

†Numbers in brackets refer to rank order.

TABLE 6.2: *Percentage of children scoring in the bottom 20 per cent on the divergent thinking test*

Fluency

	Social Class	Non-Streamed Type 1	Non-Streamed Type 2	Streamed
Boys	1, 2, 3	18% (2)†	25% (1)	18% (2)
Boys	4, 5	21% (3)	36% (1)	31% (2)
Girls	1, 2, 3	9% (3)	16% (1)	14% (2)
Girls	4, 5	34% (1)	29% (2)	26% (3)

Flexibility

	Social Class	Non-Streamed Type 1	Non-Streamed Type 2	Streamed
Boys	1, 2, 3	15% (3)	25% (1)	18% (2)
Boys	4, 5	20% (3)	38% (1)	36% (2)
Girls	1, 2, 3	14% (3)	19% (1)	17% (2)
Girls	4, 5	26% (3)	29% (2)	31% (1)

Originality

	Social Class	Non-Streamed Type 1	Non-Streamed Type 2	Streamed
Boys	1, 2, 3	18% (3)	22% (1)	20% (2)
Boys	4, 5	20% (3)	31% (2)	33% (1)
Girls	1, 2, 3	17% (3)	24% (1)	18% (2)
Girls	4, 5	28% (3)	29% (2)	32% (1)

†Numbers in brackets refer to rank order.

The results of the Free Writing Essays showed a similar tendency for Type 1 teachers to produce the greatest percentage of high scorers and the Type 2 teachers the smallest percentage (see Table 6.2). In the case of low scorers, however, no consistent pattern emerged (see Table 6.3b).

TABLE 6.3a: *Percentage scoring in the top* 20 *per cent on the Free Writing Essays*

	Social Class	Non-Streamed Type 1	Non-Streamed Type 2	Streamed
Boys	1, 2, 3	21% (1)†	18% (3)	21% (1)
Boys	4, 5	14% (1)	4% (3)	12% (2)
Girls	1, 2, 3	35% (1)	31% (2)	27% (3)
Girls	4, 5	20% (2)	16% (3)	21% (1)

†Numbers in brackets refer to rank order.

TABLE 6.3b: *Percentage scoring in the bottom* 20 *per cent on the Free Writing Essays*

	Social Class	Non-Streamed Type 1	Non-Streamed Type 2	Streamed
Boys	1, 2, 3	19% (3)†	21% (2)	28% (1)
Boys	4, 5	37% (2)	46% (1)	31% (3)
Girls	1, 2, 3	8% (2)	10% (1)	8% (2)
Girls	4, 5	18% (2)	15% (3)	25% (1)

†Numbers in brackets refer to rank order.

Type 1 teachers, therefore, were not only associated with the greatest number of high scorers, but also with the smallest proportion of children whose scores fell in the bottom 20 per cent on the test. Type 2 teachers, on the other hand, seem to be the least successful in developing the divergent thinking of their pupils. A possible explanation is that this type of teacher is something of a 'misfit' in non-streamed schools.[1] His allegiance to the aims of formal academic attainment often means that he practises, with a full ability range, methods suitable only in the context of a streamed class, no doubt increasing the difficulty of the perceived teaching task. This type of teacher is likely to have less time, if not inclination, than colleagues in streamed schools to create a classroom atmosphere in which learning can proceed in a self-initiated, unchannelled way.

'Highly creative' children

It was next decided to identify 'highly creative' children who, according to their scores on the test of divergent thinking were in the top 5 per cent. The aim of this was to determine which, if any, characteristics accompanied a high level of performance.

It is widely accepted that certain personality factors are strongly associated with a high level of divergent thinking, and it might be hypothesized that the really creative child will not be adversely affected by a detrimental school environment and may even, as Vernon (1964) has suggested 'thrive on rebelling against it'.

The 'highly creative' children were identified at the end of each year as those scoring in approximately the top 5 per cent according to the originality of ideas expressed in their responses. Although marked for *statistical* originality, the following examples show that their responses were original in the 'qualitative' sense also. When asked to think of unusual uses for tin cans, the majority of children were unable to break away from the conventional use as a container, whereas the 'highly creative' children saw the following possibilities:

> make collander, rotating sprinkler, crush to make armour, toy handcuffs, loudspeaker, morse-code transmitter, pipeline, conveyor belt, lampshade, adapt as scales, measure rainfall, water clock, measure distances, mirror, bullet-proof vest, pin-hole camera, pencil sharpener.

One hundred and ninety-five 'highly creative' children were identified in either the third or fourth year,[2] with boys and girls almost equally represented (95 and 100 respectively). There was little difference in the numbers from the two types of school, with 104 from streamed and 91 from non-streamed schools.

Looking at the ability level of the 'highly creative' children, it was found that, according to their scores on both the verbal reasoning

[1]For a discussion of this point, see Chapters 4 and 14.
[2]Children who were 'highly creative' in both years were included only once.

and English tests, approximately two-thirds were of above average ability while the rest were of average ability.[1] There was no difference between streamed and non-streamed schools in the proportions of children of average ability in the 'highly creative' group.

Other writers have suggested that level of ability may be a 'threshold' variable as far as creative thinking is concerned; that a certain minimum level of ability is needed, but beyond that there is little relationship between general ability and the ability to think 'creatively'. The fact that the 'highly creative' group with which we were concerned consisted almost exclusively of children of average and above average ability lends some slight measure of support to this claim.

Since many writers have suggested that level of creative thinking may be closely related to attitudes, it was decided to examine the scores of the 'highly creative' children on several attitude scales, and to compare these scores with those of other, less creative pupils. For the purpose of this comparison, the 'highly creative' children who were above average in ability[2] were compared with above average children who did not score in the top 5 per cent on the test of divergent thinking.

In terms of 'personality-related' rather than 'school-related' attitudes,[3] 'highly creative' children differed considerably from the less creative children.[4]

Both boys and girls who were 'highly creative' had higher scores on the 'social adjustment' scale than their above average counterparts, and also had much higher scores on the scale measuring 'academic self-image' (see Tables 6.6 and 6.7 in Appendix 6). On the 'anxiety' scale, too, it was found that 'highly creative' boys showed less anxiety than did the above average boys, more of the

[1]Above average were those scoring in the top third on the English or verbal reasoning tests and average were those scoring in the middle third.

[2]According to their scores on the English test.

[3]For details of children's attitude scales, see Chapter 9.

[4]There was a tendency for the highly creative boys to be more non-conforming (i.e. to score 0 or 1) than other boys of similar ability. This difference is interesting in the light of the finding reported in Chapter 9, that boys who had Type 1 teachers tended to be less conforming than boys taught by Type 2 teachers in non-streamed schools. The non-conforming behaviour of these boys may well be linked with a high level of divergent thinking and this may be permitted, or even encouraged to develop by the attitudes and methods of Type 1 teachers. There was little difference in the scores of girls on the conforming—non-conforming scale, although the scores of 'highly creative' girls tended to be more spread out (see Table 6.5, Appendix 6).

latter having low scores on this scale (see Table 6.8, Appendix 6). There was very little difference in anxiety level between the scores of 'highly creative' and other above average girls.

It would thus seem that 'highly creative' children are characterized by a greater degree of confidence in their abilities and a lack of inhibition in their behaviour, attributes which would seem to be conducive to a high level of performance in creative thinking.

Conclusions

It has been suggested (Haddon and Lytton, 1968) that the emphasis laid on self-initiated learning is the most important school factor in the development of creative talent, supported by a relaxed atmosphere in which children are free to pursue their own paths of learning and discovery. The results of this inquiry provide some slight evidence to support the claim that certain methods of teaching and certain types of teacher-pupil relationship do encourage this development more than others. Whether the optimum conditions for the encouragement of creative talent have yet been achieved, however, is much more doubtful.

References

HADDON, F. A. and LYTTON, H. (1968). 'Teaching approach and the development of divergent thinking abilities in primary schools', *Brit. J. Educ. Psychol.*, 38, 2, 171-80.

HUDSON, L. (1966). *Contrary Imaginations.* London: Methuen.

HUDSON, L. (1968). *Frames of Mind.* London: Methuen.

WODTKE, K. H. and WALLEN, N. E. (1965). 'The effects of teacher control in the classroom on pupil's creativity-test gains', *Amer. Educ. Res. J.*, 2, 2, 75-8.

VERNON, P. E. (1964). 'Creativity and Intelligence', *Educ. Res.*, VI, 3, 163-9.

CHAPTER 7

Biases in the Streaming System

QUITE a number of research studies in this country have revealed the presence of what Douglas (1964) calls 'unconscious biases' in the streaming system. These biases are associated with the over-representation of girls, middle class children, and those born between September and March in A-Streams (see Douglas, 1964; Jinks, 1964; Jackson, 1964; Sutton, 1967). One of the aims of this study was to examine and provide evidence on any biases in allocation of pupils to different streams.

For convenience and clarity, this chapter will be discussed in three parts: General biases; Wrongly allocated children; Transfers between streams.

GENERAL BIASES

Proportion of boys and girls in different streams

Information collected for the survey (Barker Lunn 1967a) indicated that the system of streaming appeared to favour girls: relatively more girls were found in A-streams and relatively fewer girls in B- and C-streams than would be expected by chance. The boys were more or less equally divided among the different streams.

To see if these differences disappeared as the children became older, the proportion of boys and girls (Cohort 1) in the different streams were compared when they were seven-plus and four years later when they were ten-plus. The differences were nearly as pronounced at 10+ and girls were still favoured (see Table 7.19, Appendix 6).

During the early junior school years it was found that girls were better than boys in reading and English. This was not true of arithmetic, particularly problem and number concept arithmetic, in which boys performed better. A possible reason for the higher proportion of girls than boys in A-streams is that schools give more weight to reading than arithmetic when allocating children from infant school to junior school streams.

Age of children in different streams

A number of researches (Jackson, 1964; Sutton, 1967) have shown that children in A-streams are significantly older than those in lower streams. The findings of the survey (Barker Lunn 1967a) confirmed this, showing that the average age tended to decrease from the A- to the D-stream. The table below is based on information obtained from 246 streamed schools as part of the survey. It can be seen that the top stream is always older than the bottom stream. The difference between the average age of the top and bottom stream is 0·9 of a month in the two-stream schools, 1 month in the three-stream, and 2·3 months in the four-stream schools.

TABLE 7.1: *Average ages of pupils in the first, second, third and fourth year 'streams'*

		FIRST YEAR PUPILS	SECOND YEAR PUPILS	THIRD YEAR PUPILS	FOURTH YEAR PUPILS
		Average Age	*Average Age*	*Average Age*	*Average Age*
2 streams	A	7yr 5·2m	8yr 6·5m	9yr 5·4m	10yr 6·1m
(159 schools)	B	7yr 4·4m	8yr 5·5m	9yr 5·2m	10yr 4·5m
3 streams	A	7yr 5·7m	8yr 6·4m	9yr 5·5m	10yr 6·2m
(66 schools)	B	7yr 5·3m	8yr 6·0m	9yr 5·7m	10yr 4·7m
	C	7yr 4·9m	8yr 5·0m	9yr 5·2m	10yr 4·5m
4 streams	A	7yr 8·4m	8yr 8·5m	9yr 6·0m	10yr 5·9m
(21 schools)	B	7yr 7·3m	8yr 7·3m	9yr 5·2m	10yr 4·6m
	C	7yr 5·0m	8yr 7·8m	9yr 5·0m	10yr 4·3m
	D	7yr 5·0m	8yr 6·7m	9yr 4·0m	10yr 4·1m

Under the present entry system, a child starts school either in or after the term which includes his fifth birthday and consequently autumn-born children have more schooling than younger children (spring and summer-born) in the same school year.

Of approximately 15,000 children involved in the cross-sectional sample (Barker Lunn, 1967b) only 26 per cent had completed a full nine terms in the infant school; 26 per cent had had *only six terms* in the infant school. In other words, they had missed a full year. Twenty-four per cent of the children had had seven terms and 24 per cent eight terms.

It can be seen in Table 7.2 below that there was a consistent trend for A-streams to have more children with nine terms infant schooling than would be expected by chance, and relatively fewer children who had spent a short time in the infant school. For the lower streams the trend was reversed. The differences between streams with regard to length of infant schooling were statistically highly significant ($P < 0.01$). It will be seen that the trend was more marked in three and four-stream schools and the composition of remedial classes (defined as the lowest stream combining two or more year groups or the E-stream of the largest schools) showed the same tendency to a startling degree. Nearly forty per cent of the children in remedial classes had missed a year in the infant school and had had only six terms. On the other hand, children who had completed the full nine terms in the infant school were unlikely to find themselves in a remedial class (only 12 per cent had this background).

TABLE 7.2: *Length of infant schooling of children in different streams*

	2-STREAM SCHOOLS (23 SCHOOLS)		3- TO 5-STREAM SCHOOLS (19 SCHOOLS)			
	A-stream	B-stream	A-stream	B-stream	C/D-stream	Remedial
6 terms in infants'	24%	31%	18%	26%	31%	39%
7 terms in infants'	21%	28%	22·5%	25%	26%	30%
8 terms in infants'	26%	22%	26%	23%	23%	19%
9 terms in infants'	29%	19%	33·5%	26%	20%	12%
No. of children (100%)	3,422	2,968	2,865	2,569	2,344	564

Data from this study were used to examine whether age differences between streams lessened as the children moved up through the school. Although they did decrease very slightly, pronounced age differences between streams persisted even in the final junior school year. In three-stream schools most children in A-streams were autumn-born and the oldest of the year group, most B-streams were winter-born, and most C-streams were summer-born, the youngest of the year group (see Table 7.3).

TABLE 7.3: *Time of year born and stream in the final junior school year* (*Cohort* 1)

NO. OF STREAMS	3-STREAM			2-STREAM	
	A	B	C	A	B
Autumn-born	41%	33%	23%	35%	24%
Winter-born	31%	35%	32%	37%	33%
Summer-born	28%	32%	45%	28%	43%
No. of children (100%)	578	614	401	643	568

Methods of allocating to streams and classes

A contributory factor to the differences in age between streams was that many headteachers did not use standardized tests or make age allowances in selecting children for different streams.

In the survey (Barker Lunn, 1967a) heads of schools were asked what criteria they used for assigning pupils to different streams. It was found that the most popular method at seven-plus, when pupils first entered junior school, was to allocate to streams on the basis of infant school records. These were probably based on the infant school teacher's assessment of a child's work or on school tests. A large number of schools used no objective tests (i.e. standardized tests): less than half used an intelligence test and even fewer used a standardized attainment test. Only about one quarter took age into account, see Table 7.4.

Evidence has already been given of a tendency for streaming to favour 'older' children in the year group and Table 7.4 shows that criteria such as age and standardized tests, which would diminish the 'younger' children's disadvantage, were employed by only a minority of schools.

TABLE 7.4: *Criteria used for assigning first year pupils to classes in schools using streaming*

	Streamed Schools
1. Infant school record	68%
2. Standardized intelligence tests	42%
3. Judgement	33%
4. Internal examinations	25%
5. Age of pupil	23%
6. Standardized attainment tests	16%
7. Others	7%
Number of schools giving information	258

Note: Schools may use more than one criterion.

Social class of children in different streams

The process of streaming brings about not only a separation of children on the basis of academic performance but also involves to some extent segregation of the social classes.

In 1964, teachers were asked to indicate the social class of children in their classes (see Appendix 4). It was found that there was a tendency for children from working-class home backgrounds to populate the lower streams; this was just as pronounced at 10+ as it was at 7+ (see Appendix 6, Table 7.20).

The table below shows the composition of each stream in terms of pupils' social class in the final junior school year.

TABLE 7.5: *Social class of parents of children in the different streams at 10+*

SOCIAL CLASS	2-STREAM SCHOOLS		3-STREAM SCHOOLS		
	A	B	A	B	C
Professional & Clerical (1, 2)	26%	11%	35%	14%	9%
Skilled (3)	46%	45%	44%	46%	34%
Semi- and Unskilled (4, 5)	28%	44%	21%	40%	57%
Number of children (100%)	643	568	578	614	401

The proportions of children from professional and clerical home backgrounds were highest in A-streams, and always a greater proportion from semi- and unskilled home backgrounds populated bottom or C-streams. These results partly stem from the fact that there is a relationship between academic performance and social class—middle class children on the whole tending to do better in school than working class children. Social class differences are greater for English than for arithmetic and therefore schools using English or reading as the major criterion for allocation to streams are likely to emphasize social class differences.

Another contributory factor was the tendency for teachers to over-estimate middle class children's ability and to under-estimate that of working class children. A comparison was made of teachers' ratings of a child's ability and his actual performance on an English test at the end of the third year of the junior school. Teachers' ratings agreed with test score ratings for most of the children, but in cases where they did not agree, working class children were more likely to be under-estimated and middle-class children over-estimated. (This tendency was also found in non-streamed schools—see Chapter 5.)

TABLE 7.6: *Teachers' ratings of pupils' ability (Cohort 1) of upper and lower social class origin in streamed schools compared with objective ratings based on an English test score*

SOCIAL CLASS	ABOVE AVERAGE† BASED ON ENGLISH TEST SCORE		AVERAGE BASED ON ENGLISH TEST SCORE		BELOW AVERAGE BASED ON ENGLISH TEST SCORE	
	Upper (1, 2, 3)	*Lower* (4, 5)	*Upper* (1, 2, 3)	*Lower* (4, 5)	*Upper* (1, 2, 3)	*Lower* (4, 5)
Teacher's rating of child's general ability						
Above average	69%	56%	15%	10%	—	—
Average	30%	44%	73%	69%	34%	28%
Below average	1%	—	12%	21%	66%	72%
Number of children (100%)	530	239	634	554	203	396

†Total sample divided into three groups of equal size on the basis of English test score.

The teacher's judgement was a criterion used for allocating to streams (see Table 7.4) but Table 7.6 indicates that the child's perceived ability was influenced to some extent by his type of home (see Douglas, 1964; Goodacre, 1968). It would seem that the over-allocation of upper social class and under-allocation of lower social class children to A-streams was not entirely warranted, and teachers' errors of judgement could have been a contributory factor in a number of instances.

Disabilities of children in different streams

It appeared that streaming had a tendency not only to separate children by age and social class but also by physical fitness. Teachers were asked to indicate whether each child suffered from a visual, hearing, speech or other physical disability (see Appendix 4). Similar results were obtained when the children (Cohort 1) were seven and ten-plus. Table 7.7 shows that more children in bottom streams suffered from physical disabilities.

TABLE 7.7: *Comparison of the number of physical disabilities of pupils aged* 10+ *in different streams*

	3/4-STREAM SCHOOLS			2-STREAM SCHOOLS	
	A	*B*	*C*	*A*	*B*
No disabilities	88%	86%	78%	88%	80%
One or more disabilities	12%	14%	22%	12%	20%
Number of children (100%)	578	614	401	643	568

Experience and age of teacher

The survey[1] indicated that teachers of A-streams tended to have more experience and consequently were older than teachers of other streams. This tendency is in line with the observations made by Jackson (1964) in the ten streamed schools that he studied.

[1]Barker Lunn (1967b), page 66.

WRONGLY ALLOCATED CHILDREN

Overlap in measured attainments between streams

It is generally believed that streaming is a system of separating bright from less bright children of the same age. Each school has its own method of accomplishing this, through the use of school tests, school records, standardized tests, teacher's assessments, or a summated total of some or all of these.

Whatever method is used, it cannot be perfectly reliable; some children will be wrongly allocated, no matter what the criterion of allocation may be. A number of studies have questioned methods of selection based on differences in ability or attainment (Yates and Pidgeon, 1957; Emmett, 1954; Daniels, 1959) and have shown that even the best available methods of allocation involve errors in prediction with regard to at least ten per cent of the children. Figures will be presented below which indicate that streaming produces a far from perfect separation of abilities or attainments.

The incidence of overlap in measured attainments between streams was investigated in 14 of the streamed schools.[1] At the end of each school year, the performance of pupils on both the English and Problem Arithmetic tests was examined separately in each of the 14 schools.

Table 7.8 shows the distribution of scores of second year pupils in one of the schools on the English test.

It can be seen from the table that there was some overlap between all the streams and considerable overlap between the B- and C-streams. Allowing for a margin of error[2] Table 7.9 shows the number of pupils in this school allocated to streams, using English score as a criterion, i.e. assuming that the top 31 pupils should be in the A-stream, the next 24 in the B-stream, the next 24 in the C-stream and the bottom 16 in the D-stream. The process was repeated for each of the 14 schools at the end of each school year[3] using the score obtained on the English test and again on the Problem

---

[1] The streamed schools in the 28 school sample. (See Appendix 5.)

[2] To allow for the unreliability of test scores a margin of ± 4 points was made for the English and ± 2 points for the Arithmetic test; these were based on the standard error of the test. Four points were added to the English scores of the bottom children in the A-stream and 4 points subtracted from the scores of the top children in the B-stream. Any overlap that still occurred was regarded as evidence of wrong allocation. A pupil's chance of scoring above or below this margin by error was 1 in 20.

[3] Except at the end of the fourth year when the children could not be transferred to another stream the following year because of the move to the secondary school.

TABLE 7.8: *English scores of second year pupils in a streamed school*

ENGLISH SCORE	A-STREAM	B-STREAM	C-STREAM	D-STREAM
0— 2				6
3— 5			2	1
6— 8			–	3
9—11			3	4
12—14		2	–	2
15—17		–	3	
18—20		3	4	
21—23		1	2	
24—26		7	4	
27—29		1	–	
30—32		2	1	
33—35		2	–	
36—38		1	2	
39—41	1	1	1	
42—44	2	3	1	
45—47	3	–	1	
48—50	5	1		
51—53	4			
54—56	7			
57—59	6			
60—62	3			
63—65	–			
Total	31	24	24	16

Arithmetic test. Here it must be pointed out that raw and not standardized test scores were used, and, had the latter been used, the overlap between streams would have been even greater owing to the age allowance necessary for lower streams. (See: Age of children in different streams; page 83.)

TABLE 7.9: *Number of pupils correctly allocated to streams in one streamed school using English scores as the criterion* (see *Table 7.8*)

NUMBER OF PUPILS	A-STREAM	B-STREAM	C-STREAM	D-STREAM
Placed too high	1	6	2	—
Correct stream	30	17	16	14
Placed too low	—	1	6	2

Children in the 'wrong' stream were identified. At the end of a school year one would expect a few children to be suitable candidates for transfer but, using the criteria described above, 13 per cent of the children were in the wrong stream at the end of the first and second year and as many as 18 per cent at the end of the third year, with their scores in English and arithmetic overlapping considerably with the scores of children in other streams. The percentage of children who were in too high or too low a stream was virtually the same. Also, the proportions of boys and girls identified as too high or too low were roughly equal.

Here it must be emphasized that the criterion used for identifying children as in the wrong stream was based on either the child's performance in arithmetic *or* English. Only one-eighth of the 'wrongly allocated' children were in the 'wrong' stream on the basis of both tests. Some may criticize the approach used here, arguing that if a child is not up to standard in both English and arithmetic the question of transfer would not arise and the claim that the child is in the wrong stream is unfair. This is accepted. But what is not unfair or misleading is to find out what happens to the academic progress of those children who were inappropriately placed for either English or arithmetic.

What happened to children in the 'wrong' stream?

Approximately 15 per cent of children were in the 'wrong' stream at the end of the school year. How many of these children were recognised by their school as being in the 'wrong' stream and corrected?

At the end of the first year a little over a third (36%) of the children identified as in the 'wrong' stream were corrected; three-fifths promoted, two-fifths demoted. At the end of the second year just under a quarter (22%) were corrected and put into a higher (15%) or lower stream (7%). Correction was not nearly so common at the end of the third year, and although the number identified as in the 'wrong' stream was highest at this time—probably because of failure to correct in earlier years—the number corrected was lowest of all years. Only 14 per cent, or a little less than three children out of twenty, were transferred; more were demoted (8%) than promoted (6%) to the correct stream.

Thus on average, over the three years, approximately three-quarters of the children in the 'wrong' stream remained in the same stream the following year. What happened to the academic performance of these children and what effect did remaining in the 'wrong' stream have on them? A comparison of the attainments of different streams at the end of the following year revealed that roughly half the children had 'conformed' and were now in the correct stream.[1] But half the children were still in the 'wrong' stream and had not conformed to the standard of their stream. This finding applied whether the children were in a stream which was too high or too low.

In order to make a comparison of the academic progress of children in the different years who were in too high or too low a stream, their raw scores in English and arithmetic were converted to standardized scores.[2] The table below shows the standardized scores of the children in Year A, the year they were identified as wrongly allocated, compared with their scores in Year B, the following year.

TABLE 7.10: *Academic progress over one year when in the 'wrong' stream (standardized scores)*

STREAM TOO LOW	ARITHMETIC	ENGLISH
Year A	108·09	107·84
Year B	103·06	104·93
No. of pupils	98	102

STREAM TOO HIGH	ARITHMETIC	ENGLISH
Year A	93·53	96·08
Year B	100·46	99·21
No. of pupils	120	104

[1] On the basis of the unreliability of a test, one would expect 5 per cent of the children who were identified as 'too high' to be really in the correct stream; therefore one would expect these children to regress towards the mean and obtain a higher score the following year but 50 per cent obtained a higher score. Similarly for those children identified as 'too low'.

[2] A standardized score of 100 is the average score; the conversion of a raw score to a standardized score takes age into account. A child of 8 years 2 months who obtains a raw score of 30 will have a higher standardized score than a child of 9 years 2 months who on the same test also has a raw score of 30.

When a child was kept in the wrong stream he tended to take on the characteristics of his stream, and his academic performance deteriorated if he were in too low a stream and improved if he were in too high a stream.

However, as was indicated earlier, some children were still in the wrong stream at the end of Year B and these had not deteriorated nor improved, as the case may be, although, as can be seen in Table 7.11, the tendency to conform can be seen among these children too.

TABLE 7.11: *Academic progress of children who conformed and of those who were still in the wrong stream at the end of a year (standardized scores)*

STREAM	ARITHMETIC		ENGLISH	
TOO LOW	*Conformed*	*Still Wrong*	*Conformed*	*Still Wrong*
Year A	108·54	107·59	105·94	109·48
Year B	99·79	107·37	100·43	108·78
No. of pupils	52	46	47	55
TOO HIGH	*Conformed*	*Still Wrong*	*Conformed*	*Still Wrong*
Year A	96·28	90·78	97·31	93·06
Year B	108·37	92·55	103·28	93·34
No. of pupils	60	60	52	52

These findings agree with those of Douglas (1964) who found that the less able children in upper streams improved whereas the relatively brighter children in the lower streams fell behind and conformed to the standard of the stream. The finding that is important is that children who should have been in a higher stream on the basis of one subject, English or Arithmetic performance, did not make the progress they should have made and deteriorated *relative* to other children of the same age over the year.

Characteristics of children who remained in the 'wrong' stream

(a) Sex

If streaming is based on the performance of children in both arithmetic and English there will always be some children who could justifiably be in a higher stream on the basis of one of these subjects—simply because there is not a perfect relationship between arithmetic and English. Also, difficulties are created by the fact that boys of junior school age tend to be better than girls at arithmetic and girls better than boys at English. Consequently, pronounced sex differences were found when children who were 'wrongly allocated' on the basis of English were compared with those identified on the basis of arithmetic. Boys who had been identified as in 'too high' a stream tended to be categorized as such on account of their poor English, whereas girls tended to be identified on account of their poor arithmetic performance. On the other hand, boys in too low a stream tended to do well in arithmetic and girls in similar circumstances to do well in English.

TABLE 7.12: *Comparison of the percentages of boys and girls identified as in too high or too low a stream, when using different criteria: test scores obtained on (a) Arithmetic, (b) English*

STREAM	ARITHMETIC		ENGLISH	
Too High	*Boys* 44%	*Girls* 65%	*Boys* 64%	*Girls* 36%
Too Low	56%	35%	36%	64%
No. of pupils (100%)	106	111	106	100

There is no clear cutting point, initially at any rate, between the bottom children of one stream and the top children of another, and these findings suggest that in the overlap areas there will be a tendency for boys to merit a higher stream on the basis of their arithmetic and girls on the basis of their English.

(b) Age and Length of Infant Schooling

As one would expect from the age differences found between streams, there were very significant differences in terms of age and length of infant schooling between those children who had experienced 'too high' and 'too low' a stream. As Table 7.13 shows, there was a pronounced tendency for children placed in 'too high' a stream to be in the oldest half of the year group and to have had the full or nearly the full number of terms in the infant school, whereas the children placed 'too low' tended to be younger and to have had less infant schooling. Sixty-three per cent of the 'too high' children had spent 8 or 9 terms in the infant school, whereas only 39 per cent of the 'too low' children had received that amount of infant schooling. Age is closely related to the length of time spent in the infant school and, as the table shows, children placed 'too low' tended to be in the youngest half of the year group and those placed 'too high' in the oldest half of the year group.

TABLE 7.13: *Length of infant schooling and age of children placed in too high and too low a stream*

LENGTH OF INFANT SCHOOLING	STREAM TOO HIGH	STREAM TOO LOW
6 or 7 terms	37%	61%
8 or 9 terms	63%	39%
Number of children (100%)	224	198

AGE	STREAM TOO HIGH	STREAM TOO LOW
Youngest half of year group	44%	57%
Oldest half of year group	56%	43%
Number of children (100%)	224	198

In order to find out whether there were any differences between those children who conformed and those who were still in the 'wrong' stream at the end of the year, comparisons were made between the ages and length of infant schooling of these two groups. It was found that children who were 'too low' and *still in the wrong stream* at the end of the year were more likely to be younger and to have had less infant schooling than those who conformed (68 per cent of children who were still wrong had had 6 or 7 terms infant schooling compared with 55 per cent of those who had conformed). Whereas the children placed 'too high' and 'still wrong' tended to be older and to have had more infant schooling than the conformers (68 per cent of 'still wrong' had had 8 or 9 terms infant schooling compared with 57 per cent of those who had conformed).[1]

[1] Note that raw and not standardized scores were used for identifying 'conformers' and 'wrongly allocated'.

Presumably these results were due to the fact that academic differences between 'older' and 'younger' pupils slowly disappear and the advantages of the 'older' and disadvantages of the 'younger' gradually become less as the children move up through the school.

(c) *Social Class*

The social class of children who remained in the wrong stream was next examined. The following table shows the social class distribution of boys and girls who were 'too high' and 'too low'.

TABLE 7.14: *Comparison of the social class of children in too high and too low a stream*

STREAM	BOYS		GIRLS	
	Too High	*Too Low*	*Too High*	*Too Low*
Upper social class (1, 2, 3)	63%	27%	50%	46%
Lower social class (4, 5)	37%	73%	50%	54%
Number of children† (100%)	115	97	104	103
Chi-square test	$\chi^2 = 11 \cdot 65, P < 0 \cdot 001$		Not significant	

†Number of children for whom information on social class was available.

While there was little difference in the social class distribution of girls who were 'too high' or 'too low', there were pronounced differences in the case of boys: those who were not corrected to the 'right' stream and were 'too high' tended to be from professional and skilled home backgrounds and those 'too low' from lower social class backgrounds. This tendency persisted using both the English and arithmetic tests as a criterion.

There were no social class differences between those children who conformed and were still in the wrong stream at the end of the school year.

TRANSFERS BETWEEN STREAMS

A characteristic of the streamed school is the occasional transfer of children from one stream to another during their school careers. After initial assignment to a class or stream in the first year of junior school, what were the pupil's chances of being transferred subsequently to another stream?

The survey carried out in 1963 indicated that the average number of children transferred in the school year 1961–62 was eight per cent. However, this information was not very satisfactory for only 69 per cent of streamed schools in the survey answered the question and recorded evidence of re-allocations. The eight per cent therefore was probably an over-estimate (Barker Lunn, 1967a).

Information obtained in the longitudinal study provided further evidence on transfers. In this analysis a study was made only of those children who were promoted or demoted by virtue of their academic performance and not those moving as a result of the school's internal re-organization. For example, if a school with two streams per year group in Year 1 introduced a third stream in Year 2, it is obvious that many of the children would be re-allocated to a 'new' stream. Such transfers would probably be on the basis of academic performance, but it is impossible to distinguish those children who would have been promoted or demoted had such a re-organization not taken place. Thus schools making a re-organization were excluded, leaving 30 streamed schools for study.

Considerable variation was found among schools in the number of children and the proportion of the year group moving up or down. At the end of the first junior year, on average, six per cent were transferred but this varied according to the number of streams in the school, and as would be expected more transfers (7%) were made in three and four-stream schools and fewer (5%) in two-stream schools. Overall, there were more promotions than demotions: at the end of the first year, five per cent in two-stream and six per cent in three and four-stream schools were promoted;[1] and five per cent in both two-stream and three or four-stream schools were demoted.

The average number of children moving at the end of the second year was the same as in the first year (6%), and at the end of the third year the number of transfers decreased to four per cent.

Overall, boys were more likely to be promoted and less likely to be demoted than girls ($\chi^2 = 5 \cdot 09$, $P < 0 \cdot 05$). There were no social class differences between children promoted and demoted. There were, however, age differences, and demoted children tended to be older than promoted ones (Boys: $\chi^2 = 7 \cdot 66$, $P < 0 \cdot 025$; Girls

---

[1] Percentages of promoted and demoted pupils are based on the number of possible promotions or demotions, i.e. those who are in top streams cannot be promoted and have been omitted in calculating the percentage promoted. Similarly, children in bottom streams cannot be demoted and have been omitted.

$\chi^2=8\cdot21$, P $<0\cdot02$). Demoted girls in contrast to promoted girls, also had more infant school experience ($\chi^2=7\cdot73$, P $<0\cdot025$). These results suggest that there was a tendency for the advantages that girls and 'older' children experience in the early years of the junior school to be corrected. But the numbers involved were too small to remove the initial biases. Movement between streams, however, was on the whole relatively small. Approximately 15 per cent of the year group were transferred to another stream during the four years of the junior school course. Once children had been assigned to their streams at seven-plus most of them remained in the same stream.

Academic performance of children promoted and demoted

To investigate what effects promotion and demotion had on academic performance, a study was made of pupils affected in this way in the 14 schools (28 school sample) involved in the analysis of pupils wrongly allocated. In these 14 schools 110 children were promoted and 66 demoted at the end of their first, second or third year.

The children who were promoted made very good progress and tended to make greater gains than others of the same age; but those demoted did not do so well and tended to 'deteriorate'[1] and become even worse (see Table 7.15).

TABLE 7.15: *Standardized scores obtained by children before and after transfer to a higher or lower stream**

	PROMOTED CHILDREN		DEMOTED CHILDREN	
	Arithmetic	*English*	*Arithmetic*	*English*
Year A (before transfer)	107·8	105·6	100·2	101·9
Year B (after transfer)	110·6	108·8	96·6	100·5
Number of children	102	106	59	59

*Children had to take the test in Year A and Year B to be included.

[1] i.e. deteriorate relative to the reference group

In an attempt to examine the relative success of the transfer, the child's scores on the English and Arithmetic tests were examined in relation to others to see whether he was in the top, middle or bottom third of his new class. Approximately 50 per cent of the promoted children were in the bottom third of their new class but 21 per cent were in the top third in Problem Arithmetic and 12 per cent in the top third in English.

TABLE 7.16: *Position in new class after transfer*

	PROMOTED		DEMOTED	
	Arithmetic	*English*	*Arithmetic*	*English*
Top third	21%	12%	(25) 41%	(38) 57%
Middle third	28%	35%	(20) 32%	(21) 32%
Bottom third	51%	53%	(17) 27%	(7) 11%
Number of children (100%)	108	110	62	66

After demotion, on the other hand, approximately 50 per cent were in the top third of their new class but over a quarter had sunk to the bottom third in terms of arithmetic and 11 per cent in terms of English performance.

However, some of the transfers were unexpected since, according to the children's scores on the Arithmetic and English tests, they were not in the overlap zone between streams and had not been identified on the basis of our tests as being in the 'wrong' stream. Thus one would expect these children to make less progress if promoted and to deteriorate less if demoted than children who had been in the 'wrong' stream (because relatively brighter or duller). This was found to be the case and children who were promoted and had been in the 'wrong' stream were less likely to remain in the bottom third of the class: 27 per cent were in the top third for arithmetic and 20 per cent in the top third for English. Also, what was remarkable was the success of children who had not been at the top of their class (i.e. not in the 'wrong' stream) but had been promoted: approximately a third of these children came in the middle or top third of their new class (see Table 7.17).

TABLE 7.17: *Class position after promotion of children who were and were not in the 'wrong' stream*

PRIOR TO MOVE IN	WRONG STREAM		NOT IN WRONG STREAM	
	Arithmetic	*English*	*Arithmetic*	*English*
Top third	(17) 27%	(13) 20%	(6) 13%	(—) —
Middle third	(20) 32%	(25) 39%	(10) 22%	(14) 30%
Bottom third	(26) 41%	(26) 41%	(29) 65%	(32) 70%
Number of children (100%)	63	64	45	46

Children who had been in the correct stream were more likely to remain in the top third of their new class, after demotion, than those who had been identified as in the wrong stream. But what was surprising was that similar percentages tended to drop to the bottom third of the new class, whether they had previously been in the wrong stream or not (see Table 7.18).

TABLE 7.18: *Class position after demotion of children who were and were not in the 'wrong' stream*

PRIOR TO MOVE IN	WRONG STREAM		NOT IN WRONG STREAM	
	Arithmetic	*English*	*Arithmetic*	*English*
Top third	(15) 35%	(22) 52%	(10) 53%	(16) 66%
Middle third	(16) 37%	(15) 36%	(4) 21%	(6) 25%
Bottom third	(12) 28%	(5) 12%	(5) 26%	(2) 9%
Number of children (100%)	43	42	19	24

Conclusions

This chapter has shown some of the biases in the streaming system. Such a process tends to be advantageous to autumn-born, middle and upper working class children, and to girls. Those who were slower or backward to start with—because of less infant schooling, or a home background which offered little parental encouragement and interest in education—were relegated to the lower streams. Here they encountered teachers who were younger and less experienced.

Many schools failed to give an age allowance in their allocation to streams: the study of children in the 'wrong' stream indicated that those who should have been in a higher stream tended to be the youngest in the year group.

At all times, whether in streamed or non-streamed schools, academic standards are related to age—autumn-born children tend to obtain higher marks than the winter-born who, in turn, tend to obtain higher marks than those born in the summer. This is probably partly a function of age and partly of length of schooling.[1] So at all times, age, within a year group, should be taken into account.

The problems involved in trying to separate children into different ability streams were numerous. Should school performance be the criterion for streaming without taking age into account? Where it is, the outcome is that children in any one stream are more homogeneous with respect to attainment level. But this process does not necessarily pick out the most able pupils, particularly at the borderline zones, and 'younger' able children are especially penalized. Another problem was the lack of perfect relationship between skills in different school subjects—children good at one subject are not necessarily equally good in another. In fact boys tend to be better at arithmetic than English, and girls better at English than arithmetic. The former is also true for working class children some of whom tend to be handicapped in English as a result of their home background. It is suggested that the preponderance of girls in A-streams could be due to schools placing more weight on reading and English in their allocation process—and as such boys, particularly working class boys, are often at a disadvantage. In the overlap zones between streams it was not uncommon to find boys who merited a higher stream on the basis of their arithmetic and girls a lower stream; and vice-versa for English.

Transfer from one stream to another is claimed to be an inherent and vital part of streaming. But it was found that approximately 6 per cent were transferred at the end of each year whereas on the basis of overlap between streams 15 per cent were known to be

---

[1] A further analysis is being carried out by the Foundation to determine the relative importance of length of infant schooling versus date of birth on scholastic performance.

incorrectly placed, on the basis of either arithmetic or English. The number of transfers decreased as the children moved up the school, and probably as a result of this, numbers in the wrong stream increased. Over the three years, approximately three-quarters known to be in the 'wrong' stream were not corrected. The effect of being left in the 'wrong' stream was a tendency for pupils to improve if they were in too high a stream, and to deteriorate if in too low a stream, although this was not the case for all children (see 'Robert', Chapter 15).

Children who were promoted tended to make very good progress, but children who were demoted tended to deteriorate and become even worse (see 'Julie', Chapter 15). In all cases, children tended to conform to the standard of their stream; promotion, or leaving a pupil in too high a stream, resulted in a higher academic performance; demotion, or leaving him in too low a stream, led to deterioration.

References

BARKER LUNN, J. C. (1967a). 'The effects of streaming and other forms of grouping in junior schools—Junior schools and their types of school organization', *New Research in Education*, 1, 4-45.

BARKER LUNN, J. C. (1967b). 'The effects of streaming and non-streaming in junior schools', *New Research in Education*, 1, 46-75.

DANIELS, J. C. (1959). 'Some effects of sex segregation and streaming on the intellectual and scholastic development of junior school children'. Unpublished Ph.D. thesis, Nottingham University.

DOUGLAS, J. W. B. (1964). *The Home and the School.* London: MacGibbon & Kee.

EMMETT, W. G. (1954). 'Secondary modern and grammar school performance predicted by tests given in primary school', *Brit. J. Educ. Psychol.*, XXIV, 2, 91-8.

GOODACRE, E. J. (1968). *Teachers and their Pupils' Home Background.* Slough: NFER.

JACKSON, B. (1964). *Streaming: An Education System in Miniature.* London: Routledge & Kegan Paul.

JINKS, P. C. (1964). 'An investigation into the effect of date of birth on subsequent school performance', *Educ. Res.*, VI, 3, 220-5.

SUTTON, P. (1967). 'Correlation between streaming and season of birth in secondary schools', *Brit. J. Educ. Psychol.*, 37, 300-4.

YATES, A. and PIDGEON, D. A. (1959). 'The effects of streaming', *Educ. Res.*, II, 1, 65-9.

CHAPTER 8

Children's Interests

OVER the years, a considerable amount of research has been devoted to the study of children's interests, seeking out the factors influencing their direction and development, the relationship between interest and success in any particular field, and developing techniques for measuring interests (Evans, 1965).

The experiences which a child has at school can clearly serve to stimulate and spark off interest in particular areas. It may be that the more informal type of school, in which creative work of all kinds is encouraged, fosters and stimulates creative interests and talent through the emphasis which is placed on developing the child's own interests, which, as far as possible, he is allowed to follow.[1] It was one of the aims of this study to see whether there were any differences in the pattern of interests of children who had attended streamed and non-streamed junior schools, and had experienced different types of teaching.

Some writers, notably Vernon (1964), have suggested that a person's interests and attitudes may be far more predictive of their 'creative talent' than the present existing tests of creative thinking. The investigation of children's interests was thus a supplement to the measurement of 'divergent thinking' provided by the tests described in Chapter 6.

Discussions were held with groups of 9- to 11-year-old children to find out which interests were popular at this age.[2] The information obtained was used in the construction of a 30-item questionnaire, which included a number of interests selected for their 'creative' content, and an equal number which were non-creative in character. (See Appendix 4.)

---

[1] Gardner, D. (1950) in a study of the interests of ten-year-old children, found that those in experimental schools, where the curriculum was 'interest-oriented', showed a higher level of activity in pursuing their interests than those from more 'traditional' schools. However, the method employed to measure interests was quite different from that used in this study.

[2] 'Interests' was one of the areas covered in the group discussions in which the main aim was the investigation of children's attitudes—see Appendix 3.

The children were asked to indicate their feelings about the interests listed by marking each activity in the following way:

> 2—like very much
>
> 1—quite like
>
> 0—never tried it or don't like it.

The questionnaire was completed by all the Cohort 1 children in the sample at the end of their third year in the junior school, and again at the end of the fourth year. Limitations on time and resources made it impossible to analyse all the scripts; a random sample of 2000 was drawn and these responses were subsequently scored.[1]

The questionnaires were initially scored on two factor scales,[2] both concerned with creative interests, but very different in content. The first of these consisted of a group of items which could be termed 'imaginative interests'; the second contained interests of a 'logical' nature. The two scales comprised the following activities:

Imaginative	*Logical*
writing stories	chess
making up plays	doing science experiments
making up poems	making models
painting pictures	reading encyclopaedias.
acting	
playing musical instruments	
reading poetry.	

Not unexpectedly in view of the items forming these two scales, there were marked differences in the scores of boys and girls. The 'imaginative' interests appealed much more to girls than to boys and the difference between their scores was highly significant ($P < 0.001$). It will be seen later in the chapter that several of the items in the 'imaginative' scale seemed to be actively disliked by boys, appearing in the list of the *least* popular activities. An examination of the scores on the 'logical interests' scale produced, predictably, the opposite result, with boys showing much greater preference for these activities ($P < 0.001$). Again, 'science experiments' and 'playing chess' were subsequently found to be two of the least liked activities among girls at all levels of ability. (See Table 8.4, Appendix 6.)

---

[1] The same sample was used in the assessment of divergent thinking—see Chapter 6 and Appendix 4.

[2] For details of the development of these scales, see Appendix 4.

The scores of both boys and girls on the 'imaginative' and 'logical' scales were related to level of ability. Both boys and girls of above average ability tended to score more highly on 'logical interests' than their less able peers (boys $P < 0.001$; girls $P < 0.01$). This result is not surprising in view of the activities making up this scale, all of which require a certain amount of ability or skill. On the 'imaginative' scale, on the other hand, the activities concerned were endorsed more by girls of below average ability ($P < 0.05$). A possible explanation for this lies in the tendency, noted elsewhere,[1,2] for children of low ability to be less discriminating and to register more unqualified approval of suggested activities than their more able peers. This tendency should perhaps serve as a caution against comparing the interests of different ability groups. However, it is still possible to compare within ability groups.

Comparison of scores of pupils in streamed and non-streamed schools on 'imaginative' and 'logical interests' scales

Since interest score varied by sex and ability level these factors had to be controlled before any comparison was made between streamed and non-streamed schools. Thus, in analysing the results obtained on the two interest scales at the end of the third year, the scores of boys and girls of similar ability[3] in the two types of school were compared.

As far as 'logical interests' were concerned, no differences emerged at any level of ability for either boys or girls. On the 'imaginative interests' scale the only significant difference revealed was in the scores of boys of average ability: those in streamed schools appeared to favour these activities more than their counterparts in non-streamed schools. However, examination of the scores of these children on the same scale the following year produced no such differences and the patterns of scores for the two types of school were practically identical.[4]

---

[1] For a discussion of similar results, see Stewart (1959).

[2] Evans (1965; p. 120) too, has pointed out that 'intelligence sometimes determines the level at which an interest may function rather than the choice of interest'.

[3] The children were divided into three ability groups on the basis of their Reading test score in the third year.

[4] Goldberg *et al.* (1966), using eight different 'areas' of interest, also found that in general, grouping pupils by ability seemed to have no consistent predictable effect on their interests.

The scores of the same sample of children were examined at the end of their fourth year to discover any changes in the interests of those who had experienced a Type 1 (non-streamer) or a Type 2 (streamer) teacher in the intervening year. [1]

On the 'logical' interests scale, the scores of boys and girls of all ability levels, and in the different school situations, were found to be very similar to those obtained a year earlier.

At all ability levels, boys in streamed schools showed a tendency to have lower scores on the 'imaginative interests' scale in the fourth year than they had in the previous year, and for boys of average ability, this difference was significant ($P<0.05$). (It may be recalled that this group of boys had appeared to score more highly than their non-streamed counterparts at 9+; this result at 10+ reflects the high degree of correspondence between the two groups at this age.) No such consistent trends were observable among boys in non-streamed schools with either type of teacher.

No significant changes were found in the scores of girls on 'imaginative' interests between 9+ and 10+; although at all levels of ability, and in all school situations, fewer girls had high scores at 10+ on this scale.

Very little change therefore took place in the pattern of children's interests between 9+ and 10+, at least as indicated by their scores on these two scales. The type of teacher also seemed to have little influence on their interests. The slight changes that were observed reflected a smaller number of high scorers on the 'imaginative' scale; this perhaps reflects an increasing selectivity of interests on the part of children as they mature, and a lesser tendency to register unqualified appreciation of the activities concerned.

Children's reading interests

Five of the items on the questionnaire were concerned with reading of some kind, i.e. comics, adventure stories, newspapers, poetry and encyclopaedias. These items were examined separately to see if there were any apparent differences in the reading habits of boys and girls of various ability levels attending different types of junior school. (See Table 8.6, Appendix 6.)

The results indicated that comics were the most popular reading matter among boys and girls of average and below average ability, while children of above average ability showed a preference for

[1] For discussion of teacher type, see Chapter 4.

adventure stories.[1] There were few differences in the reading interests of children in streamed and non-streamed schools. At all ability levels boys in non-streamed schools appeared to like reading newspapers more than boys in streamed schools, and at the average level of ability, this difference was statistically significant ($P < 0.01$). No corresponding pattern emerged, however, for girls. One might expect to find boys showing a greater interest in newspaper reading than girls (with a concentration on the sports pages), and in non-streamed schools this was so at all ability levels. In streamed schools, however, it was true only of children of above average ability.

The only other statistically significant difference in the reading interests of children in the two types of school lay in the tendency for the girls of above average ability in streamed schools to enjoy reading encyclopaedias more than girls in non-streamed schools ($P < 0.01$). Such activities may receive more emphasis or encouragement in the 'academic' atmosphere of the A-stream in which this group of girls would be concentrated.

Other noticeable differences in reading preferences concerned variations between boys and girls. In both types of school and at all ability levels a greater percentage of boys appeared to enjoy reading encyclopaedias, while more girls preferred reading poetry. Poetry was the least popular form of reading among all boys, except those of below average ability in streamed schools.

The finding that enjoyment of poetry reading appeared to increase as one moved down the ability scale may be a further reflection of the tendency, noted earlier, for less able children to endorse most activities. These children may also have scored it in terms of its popularity as a school activity rather than as a hobby or interest.

The most popular and least popular interests

It was next decided to find out which of the 30 interests included in the questionnaire were the most popular among boys and girls of different abilities and in different types of school, and also which interests appeared to be most rejected or disliked.[2]

---

[1] A study of leisure activities of 14- to 15-year-old boys and girls (Wragg, 1968) showed that comic reading remained popular with average and below average (secondary modern) children of this age (approximately 17 per cent reading comics more than once a week), but had been almost entirely abandoned by above average (grammar school) children.

[2] See Interests Questionnaire, Appendix 4.

The 30 interests were put into rank order (for boys and girls, different ability levels and streamed and non-streamed schools separately) according to the percentage of children who rated them '2—like very much' and for each group the six most popular interests were identified. As no differences were found in the preferences shown by children in streamed and non-streamed schools, the table below gives the results for the two types of school combined.

TABLE 8.1: *Most popular interests*

Boys

ABOVE AVERAGE ABILITY	AVERAGE ABILITY	BELOW AVERAGE ABILITY
1. Playing football	1. Going to the cinema	1. Watching T.V.
2. Climbing trees	2. Making models	2. Going to the cinema
3. {Playing cricket / Going to the cinema	3. {Playing football / Climbing trees / Watching T.V.	3. {Playing football / Climbing trees
5. Making models	6. Playing cricket	5. Making models
6. Reading comics		6. Reading comics

Girls

ABOVE AVERAGE ABILITY	AVERAGE ABILITY	BELOW AVERAGE ABILITY
1. Reading adventure stories	1. Going to the cinema	1. Watching T.V.
2. Going to the cinema	2. Sewing	2. Going to the cinema
3. Watching T.V.	3. Watching T.V.	3. Sewing
4. Sewing	4. Reading comics	4. Painting pictures
5. Reading comics	5. Drawing	5. Playing hide & seek
6. Doing crossword puzzles	6. Dancing	6. Playing hopscotch

The above table shows that 'going to the cinema' was the only interest which was universally popular regardless of sex or ability. 'Watching T.V.' was chosen by five of the six groups, missing only from the list of boys of above average ability. The range of activities chosen by boys appeared somewhat more restricted than that of girls (a total of 7 interests mentioned against 11 by girls). All boys chose 'football', 'climbing trees', 'making models' and 'going to the cinema', whereas the 'cinema' and 'sewing' were the only interests common to all three groups of girls.

Fewer differences appeared between the choices of boys of above and below average ability than between those of similar girls. In the former case, only one item on the list is different, in the latter there are three variations. Whereas the girls of above average ability chose 'reading adventure stories', 'doing crossword puzzles' and 'reading comics', all demanding a certain amount of concentrated mental activity, the girls of below average ability seemed to prefer the essentially 'play' activities of 'hide and seek' and 'hopscotch', and 'painting pictures'.

. It is interesting to note the very different nature of the most popular interests among boys and girls of above average ability, i.e. 'football' and 'reading' respectively. This may be one reason for the superior academic performance in English of girls at this age.

The items on the questionnaire were again put into rank order, this time according to the number of children who had rejected them (i.e. rated them '0'—'Never tried it or don't like it'). Again, the results for streamed and non-streamed schools were virtually identical and in the table below they have been combined.

TABLE 8.2: *Least popular interests*

Boys

Above Average Ability	Average Ability	Below Average Ability
1. Sewing	1. Sewing	1. Sewing
2. Dancing	2. Dancing	2. Dancing
3. Playing hopscotch	3. Playing hopscotch	3. Playing hopscotch
4. Writing daily diary	4. Making up poems	4. Writing daily diary
5. Making up plays	5. Writing daily diary	5. Reading poetry
6. Making up poems	6. {Making up plays / Reading poetry}	6. Making up poems

Girls

Above Average Ability	Average Ability	Below Average Ability
1. Playing chess	1. Playing football	1. Playing football
2. Playing football	2. Playing chess	2. Playing cricket
3. Playing cricket	3. Playing cricket	3. Reading encyclopaedias
4. Writing daily diary	4. Collecting stamps	4. Playing chess
5. {Collecting stamps / Doing science experiments}	5. Doing science experiments	5. Doing science experiments
	6. Writing daily diary	6. Collecting stamps

In this case no interest was universally disliked but 'writing a daily diary' was rejected by all groups except girls of below average ability. Diary writing is not an uncommon feature in junior schools and this may account for its lack of appeal to children as an 'interest' or hobby.

Among boys, all three ability groups rejected 'sewing', 'dancing' and 'hopscotch' in that order, no doubt regarding them as strictly girls' activities. Again only seven 'interests' were mentioned and the lists of all three groups were virtually identical.

Girls, too, were fairly unanimous in their rejection or lack of experience of certain activities; again, only seven items were contained in the lists. All girls disliked 'football', 'cricket' and 'doing science experiments' and perhaps more surprisingly 'chess' and 'stamp collecting'. The girls' rejection of science was matched by the boys apparent dislike of arts-oriented activites such as 'reading poetry', 'writing poems' and 'making up plays'.

Children's favourite hobbies

In addition to the thirty 'interests' constituting the questionnaire, an open-ended item was included which asked children to state their favourite out-of-school hobby.

A sub-sample was drawn of 844 children (436 boys and 408 girls) and their responses listed. A total of 89 hobbies or interests resulted, of which 66 had not been included in the questionnaire itself. These hobbies were then ranked according to their popularity and the six favourite hobbies of boys and girls of different abilities were listed. There were no differences between streamed and non-streamed schools and the table below gives the results for the two types of school combined.

In spite of the smallness of the numbers involved it can be seen that there was a large degree of correspondence between these lists and those of the 'most chosen interests' from the questionnaire itself. Only 'swimming' appeared as an almost universal favourite which was not included in the questionnaire proper. (It was, in fact, used as a practice example.)

The emergence of reading as *the* favourite hobby of girls of above average and average ability, and the second most popular among girls of below average ability, also confirms the earlier findings on the 'most popular interests' on the questionnaire. As suggested there, this may be of some educational significance. No group of boys showed enthusiasm for reading as a hobby; it appeared on the

TABLE 8.3: *Favourite hobbies*

Boys

Above Average (N=150)		Average (N=145)		Below Average (N=141)	
1.† Football	37%	1.† Football	34%	1.† Football	24%
2.† Making models	9%	2.† Making models	12%	2.‡ Swimming	11%
2. Collecting stamps	9%	3.‡ Swimming	9%	3.† Making models	7%
4.† Cricket	7%	4. Collecting stamps	6%	4. Cricket	6%
5.‡ ⌠Fishing	4%	5.‡ Fishing	3%	5. Collecting stamps	5%
⌡Swimming	4%	5.† Climbing trees	3%	6. Gardening	4%
		5. Reading	3%		

Girls

Above Average (N=145)		Average (N=145)		Below Average (N=118)	
1.† Reading	21%	1.† Reading	14%	1.‡ Swimming	18%
2.‡ Swimming	16%	1.‡ Swimming	14%	2.† Reading	8%
3. ⌠Collecting stamps	6%	3.† Dancing	8%	3.† Sewing	7%
⌡Dancing	6%	4.† Sewing	8%	4.† ⌠Hide and seek	5%
5.† Sewing	5%	5.‡ Riding	4%	⌡Hopscotch	5%
6.‡ ⌠Riding	4%	6.‡ Tennis	3%	6. Drawing	4%
⌡Skating	4%	6. Gardening	3%		
		6.† Hide and seek	3%		

†Also one of the 'most chosen' items on the questionnaire.
‡Item not included in the questionnaire.

list for the 'average' boys only, and even there was chosen by only 4 out of 145. Football was again the outstanding favourite among boys of all ability levels (though perhaps surprisingly, rather less so among below average boys). No activity appeared to enjoy a correspondingly high degree of popularity among girls.

It is interesting, and perhaps encouraging, to note that 'watching T.V.' did not emerge as a favourite pastime of any group in spite of being highly chosen on the questionnaire. In fact it was chosen by only 11 children out of the total sample of 844. Thus, while most children claimed to enjoy watching television, very few regarded it as their chief interest. This finding compares with that of Himmelweit, *et al.* (1958), who with a sample of 10- to 11-year-old children, found that over 50 per cent did not mention T.V. as one of their three favourite out-of-school activities.

Conclusions

The interests of children did not seem to be greatly affected by their attendance at a streamed or non-streamed school, or by their 'type' of teacher. This is perhaps not altogether surprising, for it is likely that individual personality traits and, especially at this age, factors associated with home background, exert a considerable influence on the choice of leisure activities. A father with a passion for fishing or electronics may well inspire a similar enthusiasm in his son.

The greatest single factor affecting the pattern of interests at the 9–11 age level was the sex of the child, with certain interests clearly identified as boys' or girls' hobbies, and a great deal of agreement as to which activities were unacceptable to one sex or the other. These sex differences were also noticeable in the reading preferences of children at this age level.

Children of below average ability showed a tendency to register undiscriminating approval of most activities, and this made comparisons between different ability groups of dubious validity. However, when the most popular interests and hobbies were examined, certain differences emerged which suggested that children of above average ability, and especially girls, showed a greater tendency to choose activities of a more demanding nature than the activities of the less able children.

References

EVANS, K. M. (1965). *Attitudes and Interests in Education.* London: Routledge & Kegan Paul.

GARDNER, D. (1950). *Long Term Results of Infant School Methods.* London: Methuen.

GOLDBERG, M. L., PASSOW, A. H. and JUSTMAN, J. (1966). *The Effects of Ability Grouping.* Columbia University, New York: Teachers College Press.

HIMMELWEIT, H. T., OPPENHEIM, A. N. and VINCE, P. (1958). *Television and the Child.* London: Oxford University Press.

STEWART, L. H. (1959). ' "Occupational level" scale of children's interests', *Educ. & Psychol. Meas.*, XIX, 3, 401-10.

VERNON, P. E. (1964). 'Creativity and intelligence', *Educ. Res.*, VI, 3, 163-9.

WRAGG, M. (1968). 'The leisure activities of boys and girls', *Educ. Res.*, 10, 2, 139-44.

CHAPTER 9

Attitudes of Pupils

THE effects of type of school organization on pupils' attitudes towards school has often been put forward as a crucial factor in the debate for or against streaming. The atmosphere in which the pupil finds himself seems to differ considerably between streamed and non-streamed schools, particularly for children of different ability levels. So one might expect to find that children in the two types of school display different attitudes to school and to teachers.

Very little research, however, has been carried out on this topic: the only British study is the one by Clegg (1964). His work was based on essays written by 160 children in C-, D- and E-streams of secondary modern schools on the topic: 'What I do and what I do not like about being in a C- or D-stream'. Reasons for liking the form included being with friends, easier work and personal attention. Reasons for dislike included feelings of personal neglect and blame, feelings of inferiority, insufficient responsibility in school and inability to get a job on leaving school. Unfortunately this was not a comparative study and so one does not know whether the same results would have been obtained with children of comparable ability in non-streamed schools.

Goldberg (1966) and Borg (1964) in the United States are among the few researchers to include pupil attitudes as a variable in the streaming/non-streaming controversy (see Introduction).

Exploratory research and construction of scales

Since only a small amount of research has been done in this country on pupils' attitudes, exploratory work in the form of discussions and interviews with children was carried out. The aim was to determine what attitudes children actually held and how these feelings were expressed. A full report of these discussions can be found in Appendix 3.

Briefly, the exploratory research indicated marked differences between streamed and non-streamed situations; it also confirmed the importance of the teacher, whose behaviour and attitudes appeared to determine the social and emotional climate of the classroom. The findings suggested that the type of teacher affected the pupil's behaviour and attitudes, particularly those concerning his relationship with the teacher, his motivation or desire to learn, his degree of anxiety in the classroom and his self-image (see Appendix 3).

Content analysis of the discussions provided a number of attitude areas crucial to the study. It was considered that scales to measure these would be the most profitable way of investigating further the trends indicated by the discussions. A review of the literature indicated that most of these areas had received little attention, although scales were available for four of them: *anxiety* (Himmelweit and Petrie, 1951; Sarason *et al.*, 1960; Casteneda *et al.*, 1956); *self-image* (Bills *et al.*, 1961); *attitude to school* (Fitt, 1956; Flanders, 1965; Jackson and Getzels, 1959); and *attitude to teacher* (Tcheschtelin *et al.*, 1940); unfortunately none of these scales seemed suitable for the present inquiry. Some of them had been developed for use with older children and most were constructed for a non-British population. It was considered necessary, therefore, to develop a total set of new scales for all areas. It was considered important that children's actual language should be used in constructing scales; consequently, a major principle was to obtain items from statements made by children in the group discussions. Each scale was made up of a number of items selected after factor analysis and scalogram analysis (see Appendix 3). Ten attitude scales were successfully constructed. These were: (a) academic self-image; (b) anxiety; (c) social adjustment; (d) relationship with teacher; (e) importance of doing well; (f) attitude to school; (g) interest in school work; (h) conforming versus non-conforming; (i) attitude to class; (j) other image of class. The scales were found to be positively intercorrelated, and thirty-six of the obtained correlations were significant at 0·05 or beyond, indicating a degree of overlap. The correlations fell rather neatly into two clusters, scales a-d dealing with personality and social relations, and scales e-j with attitudes towards aspects of school and school work. 'Relationship with teacher' correlated relatively highly with both clusters (see correlation matrix, Appendix 3.) (For a discussion of the relationship of the scales with other variables, see Barker Lunn, 1969.)

What do the scales mean?

The *'relationship with teacher'* scale emphasized the teacher's degree of concern for the child, as perceived by the child, rather than the child's liking for the teacher. Some of the items were: 'Teacher thinks I'm a trouble-maker', 'Teacher is interested in me', 'Teacher is nice to me' (see Appendix 3, items 4, 26, 39, 55, 58, 62). This scale's highest correlations were with 'interest in school work' and 'self-image'. Also it seemed that pupils having positive attitudes towards their teachers tended to be motivated to do well, to be conforming, and to like their class.[1]

The '*academic self-image*' scale reflected self-image in terms of school work (see Appendix 3, items 5, 7, 15, 18, 33, 47, 50, 56, 67). For example: 'I'm useless at school work', 'I'm very good at sums', 'My teacher thinks I'm clever'. Self-image seemed to depend somewhat on the child's relationship with the teacher, and if he had a good 'self-image' he also tended to be 'non-anxious'.[2]

The '*anxiety*' scale reflected anxieties, fears or worries in the classroom. For example: 'I would feel afraid if I got my work wrong', 'Children who can't do their school work feel ashamed', 'I'm scared to ask my teacher for help' (see Appendix 3, items 21, 29, 31, 35, 42, 70, 73). This scale correlated best with the 'self-image' scale; there was a complete lack of relationship with 'importance of doing well'.[3]

The '*social adjustment*' scale was concerned with the child's ability to get on well with his classmates. It included such items as: 'I have no one to play with at playtime', 'I think the other children in my class like me' (see Appendix 3, items 10, 22, 44, 51). This scale exhibited very low correlations (or no relationship) with 'attitude to school and school work'. It was, however, positively correlated with 'non-anxiety', 'relationship with teacher' and, highest of all, with 'academic self-image'.

The scale used to measure '*importance of doing well at school*' (see Appendix 3, items 11, 48, 49, 60, 78) stressed achievement orientation, for example: 'I work and try very hard in school', 'Doing well at school is most important to me'. The relationship of this with the other scales was interesting: the child who wanted to do well in school tended to have a favourable attitude to school and school-work, tended to be conforming and to have a good relationship with his teacher. There was no consistent tendency for this child to be either anxious or not.[4]

The '*attitude to school*' scale was concerned with general rather than specific aspects of school. It included statements such as: 'School is fun', 'I would leave school tomorrow if I could' (see Appendix 3, items 19, 27, 46, 53, 66, 72).

[1,2,3,4] See correlation matrix, Appendix 3.

The '*interest in school work*' scale was concerned both with school work in general and with particular lessons. An example of the former is: 'I enjoy most school work', and of the latter, 'We spend too much time doing arithmetic' (see Appendix 3, items 8, 13, 25, 34, 52, 79). Since the 'attitude to school' and 'interest in school work' scales were highly correlated (0·71) they are considered throughout as one area and discussed under the same heading.[1] Of particular interest were the significant intercorrelations of these two scales with all the others, with the exception of the social adjustment scale. The highest correlation for both was with the scale measuring 'importance of doing well': the child who liked school and school work not unexpectedly felt motivated to do well. Noteworthy here is the weak relationship between liking school and the personality of the pupil. It seems that a child can like school or be interested in his school work even if he is anxious in the classroom situation or does not get on well with his classmates.[2]

The '*conforming versus non-conforming*' scale covered the range of these two opposing types of behaviour. For example, the scale included items such as: 'I dislike children who are noisy in class', 'I like people who get me into mischief', 'When the teacher goes out of the room I play about' (see Appendix 3, items 3, 6, 24, 36, 38). The correlation matrix (see Appendix 3) indicates that conforming pupils tended to like school, school work and the teacher and believed that it was important to do well in school. There was no relationship between this scale and 'social adjustment'.

Items in the '*attitude to class*' scale referred to the favourableness or otherwise of being a member of a particular class. For example: 'I'd rather be in my class than the others for my age' and 'I hate being in the class I'm in now' (see Appendix 3, items 9, 14, 17, 20, 28, 37, 45, 71). This scale was more highly correlated with the 'interest in school work' scale than with any of the other scales. It also correlated well with the 'attitude to school', 'importance of doing well' and 'relationship with teacher' scales. It was unrelated to 'anxiety' and 'academic self-image' (see correlation matrix, Appendix 3).

[1] Factor analysis indicated only one factor in this area, but inspection of content revealed two areas, one dealing with general attitude to school and the other with school work; the two sets of items were used to form two separate Guttman scales. However, owing to the fact that they had a high intercorrelation and similar construct validity they are considered as one attitude area, rather than two. (See Barker Lunn, 1969.)

[2] See correlation matrix, Appendix 3.

The '*other image of class*' scale was concerned with the way a pupil felt other classes in the school viewed his class. For example: 'Other classes make fun of my class', 'Other children think we are nice in my class', 'Other classes think they are better than us' (see Appendix 3, items 16, 32, 40, 61, 65, 75). This scale is more meaningful to children in streamed schools and the fact that it was given to children in non-streamed as well as in streamed schools probably accounts for the lowish correlations in the matrix.

Sample and procedure

It was considered important that the attitude questionnaire should be administered by someone unconnected with the school. Since the cost and time involved in visiting schools were considerable, this part of the study was carried out in the 28 school sample only The sample consisted of fourteen matched pairs of streamed and non-streamed schools (see Appendix 5). Factors considered when matching the schools were the social background of the pupils, size of school, area, and whether or not it had an eleven-plus selection test. Again, partly due to the time required and to administrative problems, only a one in two randomly drawn sample of pupils in each class or stream was taken. The numbers in each testing session were restricted so that a careful watch could be kept on poor readers, making sure that they understood and knew what to do.

A one in two sample of the Cohort 1 children in the 28 schools completed the attitude questionnaire when they were in their third and fourth year, and a similar sample of the Cohort 2 children also participated when they were in their fourth year. So the the first administration involved both Cohort 1 and 2 children, aged nine and ten-plus respectively, and the second involved only the Cohort 1 children a year later. The Cohort 2 children were included to see whether any of the attitudes varied according to age, making it possible to know which attitudes would be expected to change over the year; the data were also used to confirm trends observed with the Cohort 1 pupils.

The main aim of the analysis was to determine whether there were any attitudinal differences between comparable pupils in streamed and non-streamed schools, taught by Type 1 teachers and Type 2 teachers.[1]

[1] The majority (86 per cent) of teachers teaching the third and fourth year (Cohort 1) in streamed schools (28 school sample) were Type 2—thus, results were not analysed by teacher-type in these schools.

117

The attitude results were examined in terms of actual scores, and in terms of change of score between the first and second testing. The former method, however, had serious limitations, since the non-streamed situation, in particular, was complicated by the effects of different teacher types. Nearly one-third of the pupils had experienced a change of teacher-type between the third and fourth year, and presumably an even larger number had experienced this at some time during their school career. Numerous other factors might also influence a pupil's score or his position on the attitude scale: these include infant school experience, pupil's personality, parents' values and their attitudes to school, the types of teacher in the past and in the present, as well as kind of school. Granted the complexity of the situation, particularly in non-streamed schools, it is difficult to assess when comparisons are based on actual scores how much of the difference is due to extraneous factors and how much is due to the effects of a *particular* teacher-type or type of school organization. A method of coping with this problem is to assess the pupil's development or change in attitude over time. This was, in fact, the method employed here. The attitudes expressed by the Cohort 1 pupils on the first and second occasion were therefore compared to detect whether any distinct pattern of change had occurred in pupils in streamed schools or under the direction of Type 1 or Type 2 teachers in non-streamed schools. The Sign test was used to assess the statistical significance of any change in attitude. [1]

An examination was made of both the actual scores obtained by children in the fourth year in the two types of school and with different types of teacher, and also the direction of attitude change in known circumstances; a number of precautions were taken with the former. Separate comparisons between the two types of school were made on the basis of data obtained from the Cohort 1 pupils when they were 10+ (i.e. streamed Cohort 1 versus non-streamed Cohort 1) and on the basis of data obtained from the Cohort 2 pupils when they also were 10+ (i.e. streamed Cohort 2 versus

[1] An objection that can be raised against this method of analysis is that the pupil's initial position on the scale may well influence the direction of change: those pupils whose starting position is either at the top or bottom end of the scale can move in one direction whereas those towards the middle of the scale can move in either direction. This is similar to the regression effect. This by no means accounts for all the changes observed in the data reported here, for, irrespective of starting point, it was found that some groups moved in one direction and comparable groups in another.

non-streamed Cohort 2). Also data obtained from the two cohorts were cross-checked (i.e. streamed Cohort 1 versus non-streamed Cohort 2, and streamed Cohort 2 versus non-streamed Cohort 1). Only when *results in the four comparisons were consistently in the one direction* have they been reported in the text. This was, in effect, a series of replication studies. Since the numbers when analysed by sex and ability were small, differences had to be large to reach a 5 per cent level of statistical significance—for this reason *trends* reaching a 20 per cent level of significance have been reported. The interpretation that follows is cautious; only where differences in attitude score have been confirmed by changes in attitude have they been regarded as conclusive.

For analysis purposes the children were divided into three ability groups:[1] (i) above average, (ii) average, (iii) below average. Separate analyses were carried out for boys and girls. The groups were further subdivided by type of school and, in non-streamed schools, by type of teacher.

The size of sample when attitude scores were examined, combining Cohorts 1 and 2, is given in Table 9.2.

TABLE 9.2†: *Number of Cohort 1 and Cohort 2 children whose attitudes were assessed at 10+ in streamed and non-streamed schools*

SCHOOL ORGANIZATION	NON-STREAMED		STREAMED
Teacher:	Type 1	Type 2	
Boys	306	215	505
Girls	295	185	502
Boys and Girls	601	400	1,007

†For Table 9.1 see Appendix 3, p. 304.

The three groups of pupils examined for attitude change were:
(i) Three hundred and twenty-seven Cohort 1 pupils in *non-streamed* schools who had been taught by 22 *Type 1* teachers

---

[1] The children were divided into three ability groups on the basis of their score on the English test: the Cohort 1 children on the basis of their score in the third year and the Cohort 2 on the basis of it in the fourth year.

(non-streamers) in the fourth year.[1]   One-third of these pupils had experienced Type 2 teachers (streamers) in the third year and the remaining two-thirds Type 1 teachers.

(ii) One hundred and sixty-three Cohort 1 pupils in *non-streamed* schools who had been taught by 13 *Type* 2 teachers in the fourth year.[2] Four-fifths of these pupils had experienced Type 2 teachers in the third year and the others Type 1 teachers.

(iii) Four hundred and ninety-two Cohort 1 pupils in *streamed* schools, taught by 35 fourth year teachers. (For details of the social class and ability of these three groups see Appendix 5.)[3]

It can be seen that there was a smaller number of pupils in (ii) and because this group was so small, the change in attitude had to be proportionally much greater to be statistically significant. For this reason information from this group is not as conclusive as it might have been had the numbers been larger.

ANALYSIS OF SCALES

This section covers the results for each scale in turn, providing first a summary and then a more detailed description. There are two sections. Part I deals with the scales concerned with the pupil's personality. Part II is concerned with the results obtained from the school-related attitude scales. At the end of Parts I and II there is a general discussion of the findings (see pages 130-5 and 146-50). **For the general reader, this discussion provides an adequate coverage of the findings.** For the more specialized reader the results obtained from each scale have been given in detail.

Part I—Personality scales

Since the emphasis in this study has been on the importance of teacher attitudes, values and classroom methods, it is proposed first to discuss the results obtained from using the 'relationship with teacher' scale.

[1, 2] Ideally, the attitude change of pupils experiencing one type of teacher and then the other should have been examined, but the numbers when analysed by sex and ability were too small for this type of analysis: therefore the data were analysed in terms of teacher-type in the fourth year.

[3] The social class of the three ability groups within the three sub-groups, i.e. Type 1, Type 2, streamed, were very similar, except that there were more boys in social classes 1 and 2, and fewer in 4 and 5 in the above average ability group in streamed than in non-streamed schools. (See Appendix 5, Tables A5.4 and A5.5.

'Relationship with Teacher'

The evidence indicated that, overall, children in non-streamed schools improved in their teacher-relationship when taught by Type 1 teachers; boys of average and below average ability, however, deteriorated in their teacher-relationship when taught by Type 2 teachers. In streamed schools this factor appeared to be influenced more by ability and by stream, perceived teacher-approval increasing among children of above average ability and decreasing among non-A-stream pupils and those of average and below average ability.

(*a*) *General findings.* Scores were related to the child's ability and sex. Girls, much more than boys, believed that their teacher liked them ($P < 0.001$); the greatest difference was in the proportion perceiving their teacher-relationship to be a poor one: 38 per cent of boys compared with 25 per cent of girls scored '0' or '1' (the maximum score on the scale was six). Brighter children were more likely than duller ones to see themselves as being liked ($P < 0.001$). There was no difference between the scores of third and fourth year children.

How did these findings fit in with the teachers' own feelings? Did they prefer brighter children to duller children and girls to boys? The class teacher rated each child on a four-point scale indicating how great a pleasure it was to have him in the class; these ratings were then tabulated against the pupils' perceived ability (as rated on a five-point scale).[1] The results confirmed the children's own beliefs (see Figure 1): teachers tended to find girls more of a pleasure than boys ($P < 0.001$) and brighter children more pleasurable than duller ones ($P < 0.001$).

It will be remembered that two basic types of teacher have been identified (see Chapter 4): Type 1 teachers were sympathetic towards the non-streamed school philosophy, and Type 2 teachers were antithetic to it. A comparison of the ratings given by the two types of teacher revealed that Type 2 teachers and teachers in streamed schools[2] found boys of average ability and boys and girls of below average ability less pleasurable to have in the class than did Type 1 teachers (see Figure 1, and Table 9.21 in Appendix 6).

There were no significant differences between the ratings given to girls of average ability by the two types of teacher in non-streamed schools, nor by teachers in streamed schools. Boys of above average

[1] For details of pleasurable and ability ratings, see Appendix 4.
[2] The analysis was not carried out in terms of 'type' of teacher in streamed schools (28 school sample) because the vast majority (86%) of teachers in the streamed schools were Type 2.

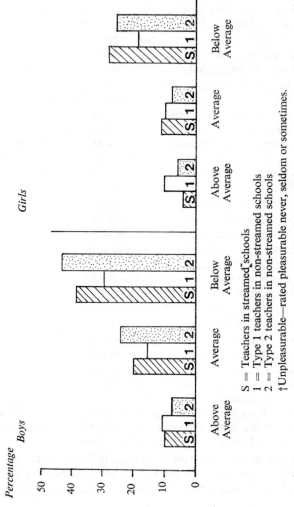

FIGURE 1: *Percentage of pupils rated unpleasurable† by teachers in streamed schools and by Type 1 and Type 2 teachers in non-streamed schools*

S = Teachers in streamed schools
1 = Type 1 teachers in non-streamed schools
2 = Type 2 teachers in non-streamed schools
†Unpleasurable—rated pleasurable never, seldom or sometimes.

(Figure 1 based on results obtained from total sample when pupils were aged 9+, N=5,452.)

ability received similar pleasurability ratings in both types of school and from both 'types' of teacher, but girls of above average ability received more unfavourable pleasurability ratings from Type 1 than from Type 2 teachers (see Table 9.21, Appendix 6). It is suggested that these results are due to different criteria used by the two types of teacher in judging a child's pleasurability. Type 2 teachers probably placed more emphasis on academic success and conformity (see Chapter 4) and these factors influenced their judgement, whereas, for Type 1 teachers, the personality of the child played a more important part.

(*b*) *Comparisons between school and teacher-types.* When the scores obtained in the fourth year were compared it was found that only one comparison was significantly different. Girls of average ability had a better relationship with their teacher in non-streamed schools: this applied whether the teacher was Type 1 or Type 2 ($P < 0.01$). (See Table 9.6, Appendix 6.)

Although none of the other comparisons was significantly different, boys of below average ability tended to perceive their teacher as liking them more if they were taught by Type 1 teachers than if they were taught by Type 2 or were in streamed schools ($P < 0.20$).[1]

The attitude change data indicated that in streamed schools children of above average ability tended to obtain a higher score (although only for girls did this reach the 5 per cent level of statistical significance), feeling that their teachers thought more of them in the fourth than the third year, but children of *average* and *below average* ability obtained a lower score ($P<0.05$). (See Figure 2.)

Moreover, there was a tendency for children other than those in 'A' or top streams to perceive their teacher as liking them less, but this change only reached statistical significance ($P < 0.05$) in bottom streams of three- or four-stream schools (see Table 9.20, Appendix 6).

In non-streamed schools where children had been taught by Type 2 teachers in the fourth year,[2] only one ability group made a significant attitude change: boys of average ability deteriorated ($P<0.05$) in their perceived teacher relationship. The trend was also in this direction, though not significantly so, for boys of below average ability (see Table 9.7, Appendix 6).

Figure 2 reveals that all ability levels in non-streamed schools who were taught by Type 1 teachers in the fourth year tended to improve

---

[1] See page 119.

[2] One-fifth of these children were taught by Type 1 teachers in the third year and the remainder were taught by Type 2.

FIGURE 2: *Percentage obtaining higher or lower scores on the 'relationship with teacher' scale*

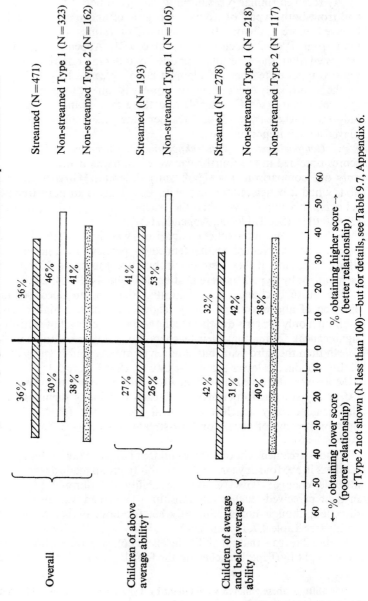

in their perceived teacher relationship[1] (overall—$P < 0.01$); an exception was girls of below average ability, but their change in attitude was not statistically significant. See Table 9.7, Appendix 6).

'Academic Self-Image'

There was little difference in the development of academic self-image of children of above average ability in the two types of school, although Type 1 teachers in non-streamed schools seemed to encourage the growth of a more favourable self-image in above average girls.

Children of average ability were affected by teacher-type: their self-image was best when they were taught by Type 1 teachers in non-streamed schools and poorest when taught by Type 2 teachers.

Boys of below average ability in streamed schools showed a more favourable development in self-image than their non-streamed counterparts. The findings were not conclusive for girls of this ability level.

(*a*) *General findings.* Boys tended to have a better academic self-image than girls ($P < 0.001$) and brighter children a better self-image than duller ones ($P < 0.001$). There was no difference in the scores obtained by third and fourth year children.

(*b*) *Comparisons between school and teacher types.* Examination of academic self-image scores in the fourth year indicated no differences between the two types of school or teacher at the above average ability level. This was not so at the other ability levels. More girls of average ability taught by Type 1 teachers had a good self-image and fewer had a poor self-image than comparable girls in streamed schools ($P < 0.05$), or than girls taught by Type 2 teachers in non-streamed schools ($P < 0.02$) (see Table 9.8, Appendix 6). Likewise, boys of average ability had a better self-image when taught by Type 1 than Type 2 teachers ($P < 0.02$) and tended, though not significantly, to have better scores when taught by Type 1 teachers than comparable boys in streamed schools (see Table 9.8, Appendix 6).

Boys of below average ability, on the other hand, tended to have a poorer 'academic self-image' in non-streamed schools, whatever the teacher-type ($P < 0.01$), and there were more high scorers among boys in streamed schools. There was no difference between

---

[1] One-third of these children had changed from a Type 2 to a Type 1 teacher between the third and fourth years.

125

girls of below average ability taught by Type 2 teachers and their counterparts in streamed schools; but fewer girls taught by Type 1 teachers in non-streamed schools had a good self-image (Type 1 versus streamed, $P<0.01$; Type 1 versus Type 2, $P<0.01$). Approximately half of the girls of this ability level in all three groups had a poor self-image. Since there was no evidence of girls with Type 1 teachers deteriorating and those with Type 2 teachers improving (see below) the lower scores of the girls taught by Type 1 teachers *vis-à-vis* the others should be interpreted with caution.

The data on attitude change showed that overall, the 'academic self-image' scores of children in streamed schools and those taught by Type 1 teachers in non-streamed schools tended to improve between the third and fourth years ($P < 0.01$) whereas there was a non-significant tendency for the self-image of those with Type 2 teachers in non-streamed schools to become poorer (see Figure 3 and Table 9.9 in Appendix 6).

The results became even more interesting, however, when the self-images of children of different abilities were examined. There was little difference for children of above average ability in the different schools (except that girls taught by Type 1 teachers improved their self-image in the fourth year—$P < 0.01$), and most of the difference occurred at the average and below average ability levels. An important factor appeared to be type of teacher. Figure 3 shows that there was little difference between the attitude changes made by pupils of average and below average ability in streamed schools and by pupils taught by Type 1 teachers; but it does clearly illustrate the different effect of Type 1 and Type 2 teachers on pupils of this ability level in non-streamed schools. More pupils of average and below average ability developed a poorer self-image when taught by Type 2 teachers. Table 9.9 in Appendix 6 gives separate details for each ability level and also for boys and girls. It can be seen from this table that most of the improvement in 'academic self-image' scores in non-streamed schools with Type 1 teachers was made by pupils of average ability ($P < 0.05$ for both boys and girls) and no significant move was made by those of below average ability. The only significant change in streamed schools was made by boys of below average ability, who improved their 'academic self-image' ($P < 0.01$, see Table 9.9 in Appendix 6).

Noteworthy here is the change in self-image of pupils in different streams: only children in lower streams changed significantly, and this was in a positive direction ($P<0.05$, see Table 9.20, Appendix 6).

FIGURE 3—*Percentage obtaining higher or lower scores on the 'academic self-image' scale*

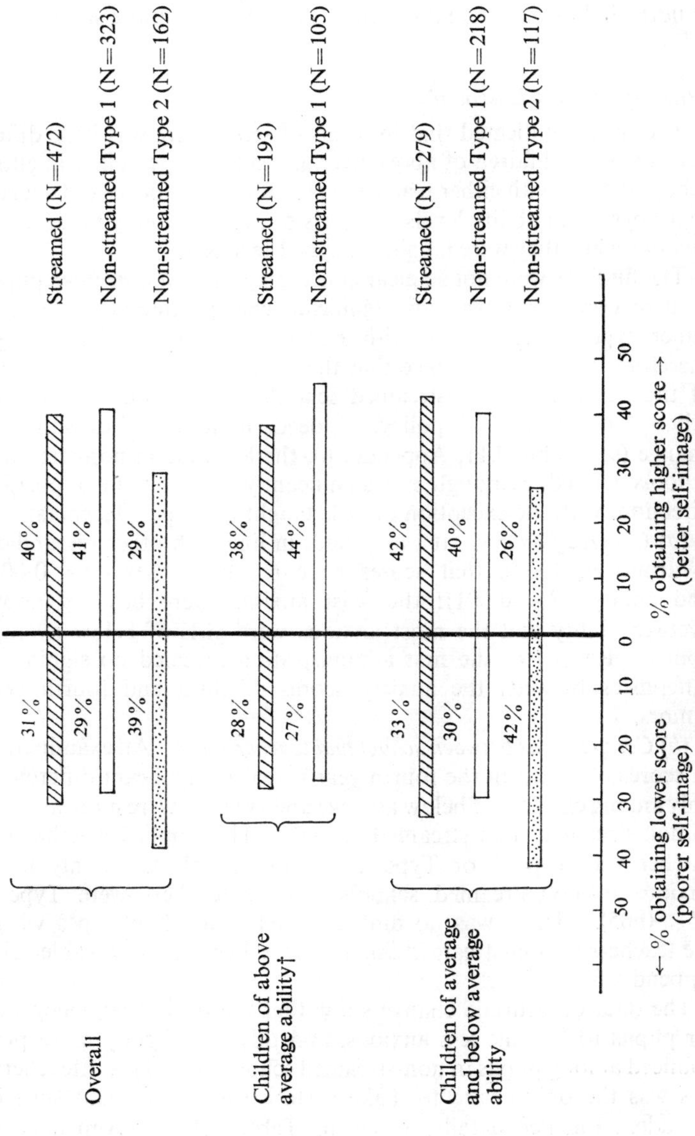
Overall
Streamed (N=472)
31%
40%
Non-streamed Type 1 (N=323)
29%
41%
Non-streamed Type 2 (N=162)
39%
29%
Children of above average ability†
Streamed (N=193)
28%
38%
Non-streamed Type 1 (N=105)
27%
44%
Children of average and below average ability
Streamed (N=279)
33%
42%
Non-streamed Type 1 (N=218)
30%
40%
Non-streamed Type 2 (N=117)
42%
26%
50 40 30 20 10 0 10 20 30 40 50
← % obtaining lower score (poorer self-image)
% obtaining higher score → (better self-image)

†Type 2 not shown (N less than 100)—but for details, see Table 9.9, Appendix 6.

It is interesting to observe, however, that most of the change came from B-streams in two-stream schools and little change was made by children in bottom streams of schools with three or more streams.

'Anxiety in the Classroom'

The results indicated that in terms of score there was little difference between children of above average and average ability in either school type or with either teacher-type. But the evidence did suggest that boys of all ability levels and girls of average ability became less anxious when they were taught by Type 1 teachers.

The findings were not so clear concerning the *below average* pupils —there were no statistically significant changes in anxiety level in either type of school or with either teacher-type. There was, therefore, no direct evidence that the lower scores (greater anxiety) of the less able in non-streamed schools were an outcome of the school's organizational policy. Indeed, in terms of direction of change (see Table 9.11, Appendix 6), the less able in non-streamed schools tended, although not significantly, to move in a positive direction, with the exception of girls taught by Type 1 teachers.

(*a*) *General findings.* It was found, in line with other researchers (Warburton, 1962), that scores were related to sex ($P < 0.001$) and ability ($P < 0.001$): the least anxious were boys of above average ability and the most anxious were girls of below average ability. Results of the first administration revealed no significant differences between the anxiety scores of third and fourth year juniors.

(*b*) *Comparisons between school and teacher types.* An examination of scores obtained in the fourth year revealed significant differences only among children of below average ability: boys were more anxious in non-streamed than streamed schools. This applied whether the teacher was Type 1 or Type 2 ($P<0.02$): girls were only more anxious in non-streamed schools if their teachers were Type 1 ($P < 0.05$). There was no difference between school types where the teachers in non-streamed schools were Type 2. (See Table 9.10, Appendix 6.)

The data on attitude change show that the overall tendency was for pupils to become less anxious, and this was slightly more pronounced among pupils in non-streamed schools with Type 1 teachers; this was the only group to make a statistically significant shift in attitude. Further details, given in Table 9.11 in Appendix 6, indicate that this same positive trend was found for boys of all

128

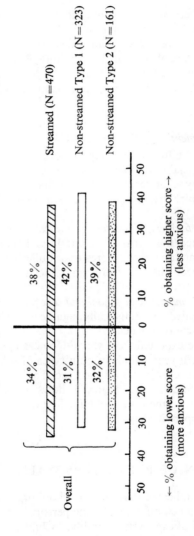

FIGURE 4: *Percentage obtaining higher or lower scores on the 'anxiety in the class-room' scale*

ability levels taught by Type 1 teachers, but among the girls, only those of average ability moved significantly ($P < 0.01$) in a positive direction.

Although there was no significant overall change in attitude in streamed schools, an examination of the anxiety scores of different streams did, however, reveal some movement: children in B-streams of two-stream schools became less anxious ($P < 0.05$); there was no significant shift in either direction in the top streams or in any of the other streams in three- or four-stream schools (see Table 9.20, Appendix 6).

'Social Adjustment'

The results obtained from using the social adjustment scale did not suggest that social development was superior in one type of school or with one type of teacher. (See Table 9.12, Appendix 6, and Chapter 10, which discusses social adjustment in terms of sociometric characteristics.)

(*a*) *General findings.* The results indicated that boys were more socially adjusted than girls ($P < 0.001$) and that brighter children obtained higher adjustment scores than duller children ($P < 0.001$). Also fourth year children were more socially adjusted than third year children: (Boys: $P < 0.05$; Girls: $P < 0.001$).

(*b*) *Comparisons between school and teacher types.* A comparison of scores revealed no statistically significant differences favouring either type of school or teacher.

As would be expected from the differences observed between the third and fourth year, pupils in both types of school and taught by both types of teacher increased their social adjustment score between the third and fourth year. Figure 5 shows that there was very little difference between the results obtained by the three groups (see also Table 9.12, Appendix 6).

DISCUSSION OF PUPILS' PERSONALITY ASSESSMENTS

The results indicated that neither school organization nor type of teacher made much difference to the personal and social adjustment of children of above average ability. Children of average ability, on the other hand, developed a better teacher-pupil relationship and academic self-image in non-streamed schools with a Type 1 teacher. Boys of below average ability had a more favourable teacher-pupil

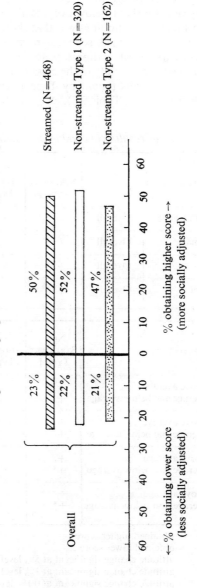

FIGURE 5: *Percentage obtaining higher or lower scores on the 'social adjustment' scale*

relationship in non-streamed schools with Type 1 teachers, but more of them had a good self-image in streamed schools. The findings were not conclusive for girls of below average ability.

One of the most interesting findings was that showing the influence of teacher-type in non-streamed schools—particularly in the development of the teacher-pupil relationship, academic self-image and, to a lesser extent, degree of anxiety in the classroom. In the attitude areas discussed so far, pupils taught by Type 1 teachers improved significantly in their score (see Table 9.3).

TABLE 9.3: *Summary of results concerning personality development*

ATTITUDE SCALE		NON-STREAMED TYPE 1	NON-STREAMED TYPE 2	STREAMED
Relationship with teacher	Overall	+**	+	—
Academic self-image	Overall	+**	—	+*
Anxiety	Overall	+**	+	+
Social adjustment	Overall	+***	+***	+***

ATTITUDE SCALE		NON-STREAMED TYPE 1	NON-STREAMED TYPE 2	STREAMED
Relationship with teacher	Above average	+**	+	+*
	Average and below average	+	—	—*
Academic self-image	Above average	+*	+	+
	Average and below average	+	—	+
Anxiety	Above average	+	+	+
	Average and below average	+*	+	+
Social adjustment	Above average	+***	+	+**
	Average and below average	+***	+***	+**

```
+   = obtained higher score
—   = obtained lower score
*   = attitude change significant at 5% level
**  = attitude change significant at 1% level
*** = attitude change significant at 0·1% level
```

132

These results are not surprising when one considers the different values held by the two teacher-types. Type 1 teachers were sympathetic towards the non-streamed philosophy and their approach tended to be more child-centred, their concern being for the all-round development of each pupil. Type 2 teachers, on the other hand, were opposed to non-streaming; they were more concerned with and interested in the bright child and emphasized academic success. These contrasting attitudes were reflected in the feelings of the two teacher-types about children of different abilities. Both expressed similar attitudes to pupils of above average ability and girls of average ability. But Type 2 teachers, in contrast to Type 1, had less sympathy for boys of average and boys and girls of below average ability, finding them less pleasurable to have in their class (see Figure 1, page 122).

Not surprisingly, there was a close agreement between the pupil's own opinion of what the teacher thought about him and the teacher's actual feelings, children of average and below average ability experiencing a more favourable teacher-pupil relationship when taught by Type 1 teachers. In the streamed situation, children of average and below average ability experienced a poorer teacher-pupil relationship. This was probably due to the fact that the majority were taught by Type 2 teachers. But since teacher relationship deteriorated between the third and fourth year, and type of teacher, on the whole, did not vary between the two years, it is suggested that the change was also due to the effect of school organization. The majority of children who deteriorated in teacher-relationship would have been in the lower ability streams since they were of average and below average ability; these changes could have been due to the child's growing awareness both of his own limited ability and of the high value placed upon academic success by the school and his teachers.

Type of teacher also affected the academic self-image of children of *average* ability, and the most favourable conditions for its growth seemed to be a combination of a Type 1 teacher and a non-streamed setting. Next best was a streamed school, and this was more favourable than a non-streamed situation where the teacher was a Type 2.

In non-streamed schools, teacher attitude and variation in classroom organization could together possibly account for the differences in 'academic self-image' of pupils of average ability. Type 2 teachers, on the one hand, tended to stream within the class, with the possible effect of accentuating ability differences and therefore creating greater consciousness of these. The child of average

133

ability was thus made aware that he was not as good as the 'top group'. Type 1 teachers, on the other hand, tended not to stream within the class and mixed ability groups were common; in such circumstances the child of average ability could probably contribute something to the group.

Another important factor influencing the child's 'academic self-image' was the teacher's attitude to the child: Type 1 teachers were more accepting of boys of average ability, although in relation to girls they were no different from Type 2 teachers. Different results obtained by the two types of teacher can thus be explained in terms of teacher attitudes and classroom practices.

For children of below average ability, the situation was different—a slightly more favourable pattern of growth was observed for boys in streamed schools. This was the only group of this ability level to improve significantly in self-image: all others showed a slight deterioration. An important factor, however, appeared to be the number of streams in the school: children in B-streams of two-stream schools improved their academic self-image in the final junior year, whereas little change was observed in the bottom stream of schools with three or more streams. The improvement of B-stream pupils in two-stream schools was probably partly due to their being one of the top classes and among the oldest children in the school. Since there was only one other class, they could regard themselves as 'superior' compared with the rest of the school. This was not as likely if they were in a C- or D-stream.

The image the child has of himself appears also to be based on his teacher's attitude, how well he can do his school work, and how he compares with classmates in terms of his work-standard, marks and even class position. *More* boys of below average ability in streamed schools had a 'good self-image' compared with a comparable group in non-streamed schools, presumably because, although they were likely to be in the lower ability stream, some of them could still be top or do the best work in their class: this being a much more unlikely feat for children in non-streamed classes. Girls of below average ability, however, had poorer self-image scores with Type 1 than Type 2 teachers or than similar girls in streamed schools. A possible reason for this is that girls are more sensitive than boys (according to their higher anxiety, and lower social adjustment scores) and regard their allocation to a low ability stream as incompatible with success.

It is interesting to note here that girls of below average ability taught by Type 1 teachers in non-streamed schools tended to have poorer scores on the self-image and anxiety scales than those taught by Type 2 teachers or than their counterparts in streamed schools. (There was little difference between the latter two.) A very tentative explanation for the higher scores of the less able girls with Type 2 teachers is that, in the non-streamed classroom organization, they are allocated to a 'bottom' group. In these circumstances, the child not only judges himself relative to other ability levels but also relative to those in his group. Boys tend to be inferior to girls in terms of work-standard, conscientiousness and conformity; the greater teacher-disapproval of boys which results (see Figure 1) may boost the self-confidence of the girls: there is someone in the bottom group worse than they are.

In contrast, Type 1 teachers frequently tended to form groups of children from all ability levels. The contribution to the group of children of below average ability will, for the most part, be minimal. In such circumstances they may feel inferior and, since they are in a minority, they may feel anxious about asking questions and asking for help. Type of classroom organization will probably make less difference to the academic self-image or anxiety level of boys, since in either situation they are more likely to be the poorer students.

Whether the less able child has these experiences in the mixed ability group depends, in part, on the other children, on past as well as present expectancies, on how the teacher sets the group up and what role she expects each child to play, and also on the general feeling in the school toward these children.

However, all this is speculative. It is obviously an area that needs further investigation. All one can say here is that since there was no evidence of the less able girl making a significant change on the self-image or anxiety scales when taught by Type 1 teachers, one cannot conclude that their lower scores were due to the effects of teacher-type.

Part II—School related attitudes

In Part II we discuss the results obtained from the school-related attitude scales: Importance of doing well, Attitude to school and interest in schoolwork, Conforming versus non-conforming, Attitude to class and 'Other image' of class. (For discussion, see page 146.)

Importance of Doing Well

Pupils taught by Type 1 teachers in non-streamed schools generally seemed to become more motivated to do well, particularly boys of average and below average ability. In streamed schools, on the other hand, only those in top or A-streams became more motivated, particularly boys of above average ability, whereas those in bottom streams became less motivated.

(*a*) *General findings.* Girls placed more importance on doing well at school than boys ($P < 0.001$). Motivation to do well increased with ability; these findings were highly statistically significant ($P < 0.001$). A comparison of the scores obtained by third and fourth year pupils suggested no difference in motivational level at the two ages.

(*b*) *Comparisons between school and teacher types.* There were no statistically significant differences between the scores obtained by children in streamed schools and those in non-streamed schools taught by Type 1 and Type 2 teachers.[1]

The data on attitude change revealed that the only children to make a significant overall shift in attitude were those in non-streamed schools taught by Type 1 teachers, and they increased their motivation to do well in school ($P<0.01$). (See Figure 6, and Table 9.13 in Appendix 6.)

It can be seen from Figure 6 that there was little difference between schools in the degree of attitude change of children of above average ability (for details of Type 2 see Table 9.13 in Appendix 6). There were differences, however, at the average and below average ability levels: more children in streamed schools showed a decrease in their motivation to do well, whereas more pupils in non-streamed schools taught by Type 1 teachers increased their motivation. Table 9.13 in Appendix 6 gives further attitude-change details, and it can be seen that at the average and below average ability levels, boys in particular made significant positive attitude changes when taught by Type 1 teachers. Only boys of above average ability in streamed schools made a significant shift in attitude, increasing their motivation to do well.

Streams were also examined for change in attitude: children in top streams increased their motivation to do well ($P < 0.05$) whereas children in lower streams tended to decrease in motivation, but this

---

[1] There was a trend indicating that boys of above average ability had higher scores (i.e. were more motivated to do well) in streamed schools than those taught by Type 1 teachers in non-streamed schools. ($P < 0.20$.) This trend was possibly due to the greater number of boys in social classes 1 and 2 and the smaller number in social classes 4 and 5 in streamed schools. (See footnote 3, page 120 and Table A5.4 and A5.5 in Appendix 5.

FIGURE 6: *Percentage obtaining higher or lower scores on the 'importance of doing well' scale*

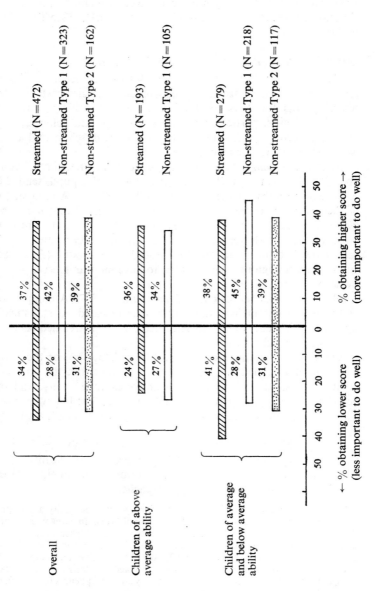

only reached a statistically significant level with children in bottom streams of three or four-stream schools ($P < 0.01$). (See Table 9.20 in Appendix 6.)

'Attitude to School' and 'Interest in School Work'

The findings indicated that there was little difference in relation to either school type or teacher-type; whatever the circumstances the tendency was for boys to develop more favourable attitudes to school, and girls, particularly those of average and below average ability, to become less favourably disposed towards school and school work in the final junior school year.

(*a*) *General findings.* Girls in both types of school had more favourable attitudes than boys ($P < 0.001$); also more able pupils tended to have higher scores on the two scales ($P < 0.001$). A comparison of the two year groups (Cohorts 1 and 2) indicated that *third year girls* had more favourable attitudes to school and school work than those in the fourth year ($P < 0.01$). On the other hand, *fourth year boys* had more favourable attitudes to school ($P < 0.05$) and tended, though not significantly, to have more interest in school work than third year boys.

(*b*) *Comparisons between school and teacher-types.* A comparison of the scores obtained in the fourth year revealed no statistically significant differences between streamed and non-streamed schools, whatever the teacher-type.[1]

It was found that the direction of attitude change was on the whole the same in streamed and non-streamed schools, but the improvement of boys, particularly those of above average ability, and the deterioration of girls, particularly the average, and below average, was more pronounced in streamed schools (see Table 9.14, Appendix 6).[2]

Among children in non-streamed schools taught by Type 1 teachers, only boys of average ability improved significantly (5%) in their attitude to school. There was no movement in either direction for any children taught by Type 2 teachers.

[1] There was a trend indicating that boys of above average ability had slightly more favourable attitudes to school and school work in streamed schools ($P < 0.10$). This trend could have been caused by the higher proportion of social classes 1 and 2 and lower proportion of social classes 4 and 5 in this sub-group in streamed schools. (See footnote 3, page 120 and Table A5.4, Appendix 5.)

[2] Analysis *by stream* in streamed schools revealed no statistically significant changes in attitude between the third and fourth year (see Appendix 6, Table 9.20) presumably because the improvement of the boys balanced out the deterioration of the girls.

'Conforming Versus Non-Conforming Pupils'

Children in general were less conforming in the fourth than in the third year: and more pronounced shifts in attitude were observed in streamed than non-streamed schools. The data, however, were not conclusive, for the actual scores suggested that boys of above average and average ability and girls of below average ability taught by Type 1 teachers in non-streamed schools tended to be the least conforming, those in streamed schools a little more conforming, and those taught by Type 2 teachers in non-streamed schools the most conforming.

(*a*) *General findings.* The following groups tended to be more conforming: girls compared with boys ($P < 0.001$); brighter compared with duller children ($P < 0.01$); and third year compared with fourth year children, particularly girls (Boys: $P < 0.05$; Girls: $P < 0.01$).

(*b*) *Comparisons between school and teacher types.* A comparison of scores obtained in the fourth year revealed a number of statistically significant differences. Girls of below average ability tended to be less conforming when taught by Type 1 teachers in non-streamed schools ($P < 0.01$); no difference was found between the scores of those taught by Type 2 teachers and their counterparts in streamed schools.

Boys of average ability were more conforming with Type 2 than with Type 1 teachers in non-streamed schools ($P<0.01$). (There were no consistent differences between these two groups of pupils of average ability and their counterparts in streamed schools). (See Table 9.15, Appendix 6.) Also there were non-significant trends indicating that boys of above average ability taught by Type 1 teachers were less conforming than their counterparts in streamed schools ($P<0.10$), but the latter were less comforming than those taught by Type 2 teachers in non-streamed schools ($P<0.20$).

The data on attitude change revealed that the tendency to become less conforming between the third and fourth year was more pronounced in streamed schools (i.e. overall, the change was significant at the 0·1 per cent level in streamed schools but was not significant in non-streamed schools—see Table 9.16, Appendix 6). In streamed schools the trend was in the same direction in all ability streams (see Table 9.20, Appendix 6).

Of those pupils taught by Type 1 teachers in non-streamed schools, only girls of below average ability made a statistically significant

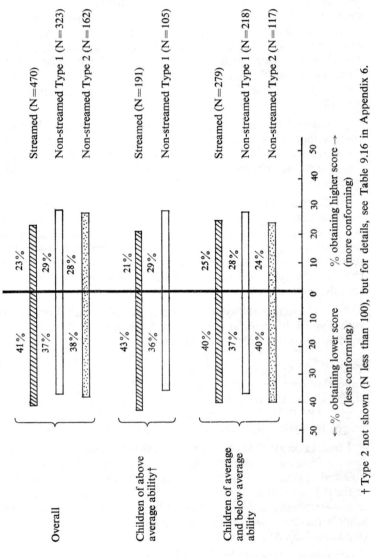

FIGURE 7: *Percentage obtaining higher or lower scores on the 'conforming' scale*

Overall

Streamed (N=470)

Non-streamed Type 1 (N=323)

Non-streamed Type 2 (N=162)

Children of above average ability†

Streamed (N=191)

Non-streamed Type 1 (N=105)

Children of average and below average ability

Streamed (N=279)

Non-streamed Type 1 (N=218)

Non-streamed Type 2 (N=117)

← % obtaining lower score
(less conforming)

% obtaining higher score →
(more conforming)

† Type 2 not shown (N less than 100), but for details, see Table 9.16 in Appendix 6.

attitude change ($P < 0.05$) and became less conforming. Note-worthy here is the non-significant tendency for boys of average ability taught by these teachers to become more conforming; their lower scores therefore can hardly be concluded as an effect of teacher-type. Of those pupils in non-streamed schools who had Type 2 teachers, only girls of average ability made a statistically significant shift ($P < 0.05$) becoming less conforming (for details, see Table 9.16, Appendix 6).

'Attitude to Class'

There was a strong tendency for children's attitudes towards their class to improve if they were in non-streamed schools and taught by Type 1 teachers. Children of average and below average ability in streamed schools were more likely to become disenchanted with their class, particularly if they were in the bottom streams of large schools.

(*a*) *General findings.* The results indicated that girls were more 'class involved' or satisfied than boys ($P < 0.001$); also the way in which a child felt about his class was related to his ability—brighter children feeling more satisfaction than duller ones ($P < 0.001$). No differences were found between third and fourth year children.

(*b*) *Comparisons between school and teacher types.* A comparison of scores obtained in the fourth year revealed two differences of statistical significance: boys of below average ability in non-streamed schools, taught by Type 1 teachers, had more favourable attitudes to their class than their counterparts in streamed schools ($P < 0.01$); this was also the case for girls of average ability in non-streamed schools whether taught by a Type 1 or Type 2 teacher ($P < 0.05$). (See Table 9.17, Appendix 6.)

Only pupils taught by Type 1 teachers made a significant improve-ment in attitude towards their class ($P < 0.001$), and, as Figure 8 and Table 9.18 in Appendix 6 indicate, the trend was the same for each ability level and for both boys and girls.

But it can be seen from Figure 8 that, in streamed schools, a greater deterioration in attitude was shown by children of average and below average ability relative to those of above average ability. This negative trend mainly concerned pupils in bottom streams of large schools: an analysis of attitude change by stream revealed that pupils in bottom streams of three- or four-stream schools deteriorated in attitude to their class, whereas pupils in middle streams improved (see Table 9.20, Appendix 6).

FIGURE 8: *Percentage obtaining higher or lower scores on the 'attitude to class' scale*

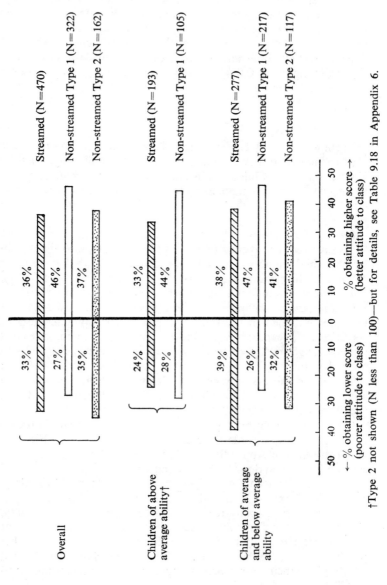

'Other Image' of Class

The results suggested that type of school organization was an important factor in determining 'other image' of a child's class. This varied very little for children of different abilities in non-streamed schools; in streamed schools, however, children of below average and average ability had a poorer 'other image' of their class than those of above average ability. The differences were more pronounced for girls. Children in lower ability streams also had a poorer 'other image' in the fourth year.

(*a*) *General findings.* Girls had a better 'other image' of their class than boys ($P < 0.001$) and brighter children held a more favourable 'other image' ($P < 0.001$). A comparison of third and fourth year children indicated that scores were more spread out along the scale in the fourth year and were therefore more discriminating at this age ($P < 0.01$).

(*b*) *Comparisons between school and teacher types.* Examining the scores obtained in the fourth year, it was found that children of above average ability in streamed schools had a better class 'other image' than those of average ability, who, in turn, were better off than pupils of below average ability. These trends were very pronounced for girls: 66 per cent of girls of above average ability in streamed schools had a high score on this scale, compared with 28 per cent of the below average girls (see Table 9.4). On the other hand, in non-streamed schools there was virtually no difference between the scores of different ability levels.

There was no statistically significant difference between the scores obtained by children taught by Type 1 or Type 2 teachers in non-streamed schools, which seems to suggest that streaming or non-streaming was a major factor in determining the class 'other image'. These results were confirmed by changes in attitude. Overall, the change in attitude in streamed schools was in a negative direction and it can be seen from Figure 9 and Table 9.19, Appendix 6 that this was particularly so for children of average and below average ability. When change in attitude was examined by stream, it was found that those in top streams made no significant shift in either direction whereas children in lower ability streams developed a poorer 'other image' between the third and fourth year ($P < 0.01$, see Table 9.20, Appendix 6).

No significant shift in attitude was made by children in non-streamed schools when taught by Type 2 teachers; of those taught by Type 1 teachers in the fourth year, only boys of average ability improved their class 'other image'.

TABLE 9.4: *Comparison of scores obtained on the 'other image of class' scale by children (Cohorts 1 and 2) in their fourth year in streamed and non-streamed schools*

Boys

'OTHER IMAGE' SCORE	ABOVE AVERAGE		AVERAGE		BELOW AVERAGE	
	Streamed	*Non-Streamed*	*Streamed*	*Non-Streamed*	*Streamed*	*Non-Streamed*
High	57%	44%	45%	44%	32%	41%
Medium	25%	34%	29%	29%	27%	30%
Poor	18%	22%	26%	27%	41%	29%
Number of children	170	131	164	192	171	198
Chi-square	$\chi^2 = 4\cdot87$ $P < 0\cdot10$		No significant difference		$\chi^2 = 6\cdot96$ $P < 0\cdot05$	
Inference	Better 'other image' in streamed schools				Better 'other image' in non-streamed schools	

Girls

'OTHER IMAGE' SCORE	ABOVE AVERAGE		AVERAGE		BELOW AVERAGE	
	Streamed	*Non-Streamed*	*Streamed*	*Non-Streamed*	*Streamed*	*Non-Streamed*
High	66%	52%	34%	54%	28%	45%
Medium	20%	27%	30%	30%	33%	33%
Poor	14%	21%	36%	16%	39%	22%
Number of children	224	173	158	183	120	123
Chi-square	$\chi^2 = 8\cdot17$ $P < 0\cdot02$		$\chi^2 = 21\cdot65$ $P < 0\cdot01$		$\chi^2 = 10\cdot36$ $P < 0\cdot01$	
Inference	Better 'other image' in streamed schools		Better 'other image' in non-streamed schools		Better 'other image' in non-streamed schools	

FIGURE 9: *Percentage obtaining higher and lower scores on 'other image' of class scale*

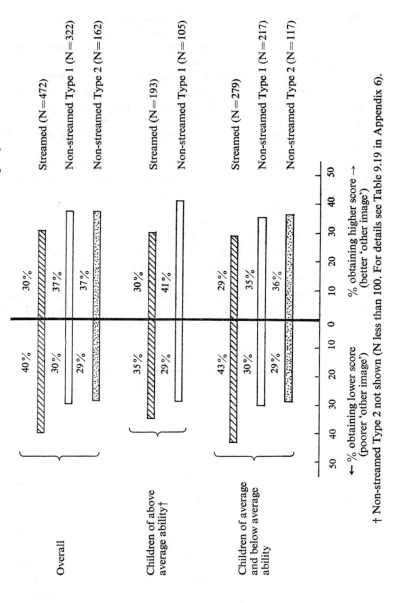

145

DISCUSSION OF SCHOOL ATTITUDES

Just as the personality scales had shown little difference between children of above average ability in the different circumstances, a similar pattern was found here; wherever they were, these pupils tended to have favourable attitudes.

Children of average and below average ability, on the other hand, became more motivated to do well in school and were more satisfied with their class and its 'other image' in non-streamed schools.

Children of all ability levels became more non-conforming in the fourth year; differences between school and teacher-type were not conclusive.

The school's organization seemed to play a more important part in the development of the children's attitudes to their class, their 'other image' of class and their motivation to do well in school, than in the development of their personal and social attitudes. In these three attitude areas, the non-streamed setting appeared a better environment for children of average and below average ability.

The table below, which summarizes the change in attitude results, shows that the tendency in streamed schools was for those of above average ability to improve and those of average and below average ability to deteriorate in their attitude scores. No such negative trends were observed among pupils of average and below average ability in non-streamed schools.

TABLE 9.5: *Summary of attitude change results*

ATTITUDE SCALE		NON-STREAMED *Type 1*	NON-STREAMED *Type 2*	STREAMED
Importance of doing well	Overall	+**	+	+
Attitude to school	Overall	+	+	+
Interest in school work	Overall	‡	—	—
Conforming versus non-conforming	Overall	—	—	—***
Attitude to class	Overall	+***	+	+
Other image of class	Overall	+	+	—

146

TABLE 9.5: *continued*

ATTITUDE SCALE		NON-STREAMED Type 1	NON-STREAMED Type 2	STREAMED
Importance of doing well	Above average	+	+	+
	Average and below average	+**	+	—
Attitude to school	Above average	+	+	+
	Average and below average	+	+	—
Interest in school work	Above average	+	+	+
	Average and below average	—	—	—
Conforming versus non-conforming	Above average	—	+	—***
	Average and below average	—*	—	—***
Attitude to class	Above average	+	—	+
	Average and below average	+***	+	—
Other image of class	Above average	+	+	—
	Average and below average	+	+	—*

```
+   = obtained higher score
—   = obtained lower score
*   = attitude change significant at 5% level
**  = attitude change significant at 1% level
*** = attitude change significant at 0·1% level
‡   = equal numbers obtaining a lower and higher score
```

The scales which discriminated most between pupils in the two types of school, were, not surprisingly, those concerned with school class—the pupil's degree of satisfaction and the way he felt others perceived it (i.e. 'other image'). Various educationists (Clegg, 1964) and teachers have suggested that children in lower ability streams suffer from the stigma attached to membership of these classes, since their status in the school *vis-à-vis* the higher ability streams is poor. Other teachers have denied that children think of differences or are even aware of streaming (see Chapter 14 and Appendix 2).

The results gave little support to the idea that children do not know that they are streamed. The evidence was that they did know and that they knew what it meant. Children of above average ability in streamed schools believed that others perceived their stream as superior; those of below average ability were more likely to believe that others did not think much of their stream. In streamed schools an inflated 'other image' of their class was held by those of above average ability and a deflated one held by children of below average ability.

The effect of being in a lower ability stream was reflected in the pupil's degree of class satisfaction—pupils of average and below average ability in streamed schools, unlike those in non-streamed schools, becoming less satisfied as they reached the final junior school year. All this confirms the exploratory research, and one can only assume that these growing negative feelings were due to a greater awareness at this age of the academic and status differences between streams (see Appendix 3).

What is the effect of dissatisfaction with one's school class? One study (Fox, *et al.*, 1964) found that pupils feeling this way tend to show a low level of utilization of their intelligence. The data available in this study do not allow us to confirm or refute this. What can be said, however, is that such dissatisfaction was associated with a declining interest or motivation in doing well at school.

It is worth noting here the apparent importance of the number of streams in the school: children in bottom streams of three- or four-stream schools appeared to be more negatively affected than those in B-streams of two-stream schools (see—teacher-relationship; academic self-image; importance of doing well; attitude to class; other image—Table 9.20, Appendix 6). This may be due to the fact that, the greater the number of streams, so the greater the differences in terms not only of academic performance but also of social class (see Chapter 7). Thus in a four-stream school, the A-stream would be very much 'higher' up the social scale than the D-stream. Given a social class difference, the pupils are able to perceive differences, other than academic, between various streams. Pupils in different streams are regarded as of different types, by both pupils and staff (see Chapter 14 and Appendix 3). They have a different way of speaking, dressing, different values, almost a different way of life. Perhaps it is these social class differences just as much as the academic ones which create the different aura surrounding different streams.

Although the results obtained on the conforming/non-conforming scale were not conclusive, they were interesting. A possible explanation for less conformity in the fourth year is as follows. On the basis of differences noted between third and fourth year children, it was expected that the follow-up (Cohort 1) children would express less conformity in their fourth year. This change can be regarded as a natural growing up process. There is ample evidence that children tend to become less conforming, even rebellious, as they approach and pass through adolescence. So the overall pattern of change was not unexpected. Differences between school and teacher-type were not conclusive. But a reasonable explanation for boys of above average and average ability and girls of below average ability having the lowest conformity scores with Type 1 teachers, would seem to be that these teachers create a freer atmosphere and are more 'permissive' in terms of discipline, rules and what they expect from their children. But why, on the other hand, should Type 2 teachers in non-streamed schools produce higher conformity in their pupils than similar teachers in streamed schools? It is suggested that the aims, attitudes and methods of Type 2 teachers are much more difficult to apply in a non-streamed setting. So, in order to carry them out, stricter discipline is enforced, a much more restrictive classroom atmosphere is created and the pupils are expected to be conforming. These findings tie in with the results obtained on the divergent thinking tests; pupils of Type 2 teachers tended to show the least divergencies of thought and to obtain the lowest scores, and pupils of Type 1 teachers tended to show the greatest divergencies (see Chapter 6).

There were no differences on the attitude to school and school work scales. Whatever the type of school or teacher, the tendency was for boys to become more favourably disposed and girls less favourably disposed towards school and school-work at the end of the fourth than at the end of the third junior year. But even though boys improved and girls deteriorated in their scores, the girls still had better attitudes to school and school work. Other research workers, noting that girls, at the junior level, like school better than boys, have generally attributed this to the belief that girls are more conforming and more amenable to discipline and order (Fitt, 1956). It could also be due to the fact that girls at the primary school level make faster progress and attain a higher level of achievement and therefore greater satisfaction than boys. But what is also observed among junior school children is a gradual narrowing of the gap in attainments between boys and girls—the large differences noted in the early years of the junior school, particularly in reading, are almost non-existent in the final year, and the differences between the sexes in their attitudes to school and school work also become smaller (see Morris, 1966).

Conclusions

The results indicated that organizational policy and teacher-type had little effect upon the attitudes of children of above average ability, but that they did affect those of average and below average ability.

Personal and social attitudes appeared to be influenced more by teacher-type than by kind of school, and on the whole, pupils taught by Type 1 teachers developed more positive attitudes. It is suggested that the different effects of the two teacher-types could probably be largely accounted for by their differences in attitude to the different ability levels.

Perhaps the most noteworthy trend was the preponderance of significant attitude changes indicating more positive attitudes in pupils taught by Type 1 teachers in non-streamed schools. Overall, these children improved in eight out of ten of the attitude areas, improvements reaching a one per cent level of significance on six of the scales (see Tables 9.3 and 9.5). Pupils in streamed schools, however, improved significantly on only two of the attitude scales. One reason for the fewer overall significant attitude changes in streamed schools was the tendency for children of different ability levels to move in different directions—the above average moving in a positive direction and those of average and below average ability in a negative direction—thus cancelling out or making what moves there were, statistically insignificant. This pattern was seen particularly on the school-related scales, and it is likely that in these areas the effect of streaming on different ability levels was most apparent.

A general finding was that attitudes varied by ability—pupils of average ability holding less favourable attitudes than bright children, and those of below average ability holding the poorest attitudes. In both types of school, children of below average ability had the poorest attitudes—they had the poorest teacher-relationship, academic self-image, and social adjustment and were the most anxious in the classroom situation—girls suffering more than boys in terms of lack of self-confidence. Also, children of this ability level had poor school-related attitudes—not surprisingly, since they had the least to offer academically. However, these negative

150

feelings, it is suggested, not only arose as a result of the child's own ineptitude but were exacerbated by the teachers' attitudes (see Figure 1; also Chapters 11 and 14).

The findings of this chapter suggest that type of school organization bears some relationship to the ways in which pupils' attitudes towards themselves and to school develop. In streamed schools, one of the most important factors appeared to be the child's stream, but in non-streamed schools it was the teacher. It is suggested that the more important and far-reaching effects of streaming or non-streaming lie much less in formal attainments than in personality and attitudinal factors.

References

BARKER, LUNN, J. C. (1969). 'The development of scales to measure junior school children's attitudes', *Brit. J. Educ. Psychol.*, 39, 64-71.

BILLS, R. E., VANCE, E. L. and MCLEAN, O. S. (1961). 'An index of adjustment and values', *J. Cons. Psychol.*, 15, 257-61.

BORG, W. R. (1964). *An Evaluation of Ability Grouping.* Co-op. Res. Proj. No. 577. Salt Lake City: Utah State University.

CASTENEDA, A., MCCANDLESS, B. R. and PALERMO, D. S. (1956). 'The children's form of manifest anxiety scale', *Child Developmt.*, 27, 317-26.

CLEGG, A. B. (1964). 'Children's attitudes to streaming', In: SIMON, B. ed. *Non-Streaming in the Junior School.* Leicester: PSW Educational Publications.

FITT, A. B. (1956). 'An experimental study of children's attitudes to school in Auckland, New Zealand', *Brit. J. Educ. Psychol.*, 26, 25-30.

FLANDERS, N. A. (1965). *Teacher Influence, Pupil Attitudes and Achievement.* Co-operative Research Monograph 12. Washington, DC: US Printing Office.

FOX, R. S., LIPPITT, R. O. and SCHMUCK, R. A. (1964). *Pupil-Teacher Adjustment and Mutual Adaptation in Creating Classroom Learning Environments.* Co-operative Research Monograph 1167. Washington, DC: US Department of Health, Education and Welfare.

GOLDBERG, M. L., PASSOW, A. H. and JUSTMAN, J. (1966). *The Effects of Ability Grouping:* Columbia University, New York: Teachers College Press.

HIMMELWEIT, H. T. and PETRIE, A. (1951). 'The measurement of personality in children', *Brit. J. Educ. Psychol.*, 21, 9-29.

JACKSON, P. W. and GETZELS, J. W. (1959). 'Psychological health and classroom functioning: A study of dissatisfaction with school among adolescents', *J. Educ. Psychol.*, 50, 295-300.

MORRIS, J. M. (1966). *Standards and Progress in Reading.* Slough: NFER.

SARASON, S. B., *et al.* (1960). *Anxiety in Elementary School Children.* New York: Wiley.

TCHESCHTELIN, M. A., HIPSKIND, M. J. and REMMERS, H. H. . (1940). 'Measuring the attitudes of elementary school children toward their teacher', *J. Educ. Psychol.*, 31, 195-203.

WARBURTON, F. W. (1962). 'The measurement of personality', *Educ. Res.*, IV, 193-205.

CHAPTER 10

Children's Friendship Patterns

A STUDY of children's friendship patterns was carried out in the summers of 1966 and 1967, when the main sample of children (Cohort 1) were in their third and fourth year of the junior school. The aim was to investigate the possible effects of streaming and non-streaming on friendship between children of different ability, social class levels and sex; and on sociometric status. The latter was to be examined in terms of academic performance, behaviour traits and social class.

This study was in part a repeat of an earlier one carried out in 1964 with a different sample of fourth-year junior school children, but from the same schools (Healey *et al.*, 1968).

A basic assumption of this study was that social relationships experienced at school are a crucial part of a child's education, possibly making just as important a contribution to long-term adjustment and fulfilment as the more formally attained skills. School usually gives the child his first experience as a member of a group outside his immediate family, and the way in which he copes may influence his personal interactions for the whole of his life (Northway 1968). Besides determining the ability to form friendships, social adjustment is related to scholastic performance and to the utilization of academic potential (see Buswell, 1953; Fox, Lippitt and Schmuck, 1964). Detjen and Detjen (1963) state that 'in order to concentrate on the business of learning a child needs to experience a mutual feeling of worth and friendliness with some of the children in his class; he must have at least one friend'.

In comparing streamed and non-streamed schools, two broad aspects of the development of children's friendships were held to be of particular importance. Firstly, the range of social contacts and experience which pupils were afforded in each type of organization; secondly, the degree of popularity or 'sociometric status' of pupils of differing ability, and the factors that influence it. Were certain types of children likely to be more or less fortunate in establishing friendships under one particular form of organization? It was thought that any differences of this kind between streamed and non-streamed schools would be important not only in terms of their effects on a child's social development but also because of their possible feedback effect on his academic progress. It was also hoped that the findings of this research would throw further light on the outcome of the different 'philosophies' of streaming and non-streaming.

In the earlier 1964 study (Healey *et al.*, 1968) a sociomatrix was filled in by the teacher after each child had indicated privately his first and second choice of best friend. The procedure in 1966 and 1967 varied slightly from this. Firstly, the administration was by questionnaire, which the pupils completed themselves so that their choices would be quite confidential and any bias from the teacher's influence eliminated. Secondly, two more criteria in addition to 'best friend' were added: the child was asked whom he would best like 'to work with', and whom 'to play with'. Thirdly, three choices were allowed on each of these criteria, and not two as in 1964; this was to bring the research into line with other studies reported in the literature.

Mutual pairs and their characteristics

The characteristics of mutual friends (i.e. child A chooses child B as well as being chosen by him) in terms of ability, social class and sex were of particular interest. Some important questions here were: did either form of organization promote or limit the formation of friendships in any determinable way? As ability and social class tended to be of a wider range in non-streamed classes, what happened to the pattern of mutual choices? Did pupils select friends from the whole range of ability and social class, or did they restrict them to those of similar ability to themselves?

Since the work involved in identifying mutual friends was considerable, the analysis was restricted to the 28 school sample[1] involving 2,036 pupils. Only information obtained in the fourth year was used and this analysis was further limited to the findings concerned with the best friend criterion.

Approximately three-quarters of the children were involved in at least one mutual pair: 73 per cent of the boys and 79 per cent of the girls in streamed schools, and 72 per cent of the boys and 79 per cent of the girls in non-streamed schools.

[1] For details, see Appendix 5.

153

(a) *Friendship between Children of Differing Ability Levels*

Mutual friends (i.e. those pairs of children who had chosen each other as best, second, or third best friend) were identified and categorized according to the degree of ability difference between them, based on the class teachers' (fourth year) ability ratings. Details of the five categories are given below:

Category 1 Mutual pairs where each friend had the same ability rating.

Category 2 Mutual pairs where the friends were one point apart on the scale, e.g. an 'above average' child in a pair with one rated 'average'; or one 'below average and possibly backward' with a 'dull and definitely backward' child.

Category 3 Mutual pairs where the friends were two points apart on the scale, e.g. a 'certain Grammar school' child in a pair with one rated 'average'.

Category 4 Mutual pairs where the friends were three points apart on the scale, e.g. a 'certain Grammar school' child in a pair with one rated 'below average and possibly backward'.

Category 5 Mutual pairs where the friends were four points apart on the scale, e.g. a 'certain Grammar school' child in a pair with one rated 'dull and definitely backward'.

The distribution of the mutual pairs on these five categories for streamed and non-streamed schools is shown in Table 10.1.

TABLE 10.1: *Comparison of mutual pairs in terms of similarity of ability ratings in streamed and non-streamed schools (best friend)*

TYPE OF MUTUAL PAIR	STREAMED	NON-STREAMED
Category 1	59%	42%
Category 2	34%	33%
Category 3	7%	23%
Category 4	—	2%
Category 5	—	—
Number of mutual pairs (100%)	559	590

The majority of children chose as friends pupils whose rated ability was the same, or only one point apart though this was more pronounced in streamed than non-streamed schools ($P < 0.001$). In non-streamed classes it was not unusual to find friendships between pupils of average ability and those rated 'certain of a Grammar school place', and friendships between average pupils and pupils rated 'dull and definitely backward' (i.e. category 3 friendships). Streamed classes, because of their greater homogeneity with respect to ability, did not permit such friendship patterns, and although children could have chosen outside their stream, only a very small percentage did so.[1]

In addition, a study was made of the influence of teacher-type in non-streamed schools on the degree of similarity of ability of mutual friends. An almost identical pattern of results was obtained: that is, type of teacher seemed to bear no relationship to the pattern of pupil friendships.

(b) Friendship between Children of Differing Social Class

Mutual pairs were also examined in terms of similarity of social class. A similar procedure to that described above was carried out and the pairs of friends were allocated to categories based this time on the children's social class.[2] A comparison of streamed and non-streamed schools revealed no difference between the distributions of categories. In both types of school, approximately 80 per cent of the mutual friends were of the same social class or one point apart, and this held for both sexes.

Again, there was no relationship between type of teacher and the pattern of their pupils' mutual friendship choices. (See Table 10.2, Appendix 6.)

(c) Friendship between Boys and Girls

Boys and girls appeared in the analysis as almost completely separate social groups and the children comprising a mutual pair were almost invariably of the same sex. In streamed and non-streamed

---

[1] The findings of this study indicated that the ability differences between mutual friends in non-streamed schools were more pronounced than those found in the 1964 study. This could be due to the change in administration of the instrument between the two testings—children might be less inhibited in recording a friendship with a child of differing ability on paper than in telling their teacher about it.

[2] For details of social class, see Appendix 4.

155

schools boys formed friendships with boys, and girls with girls. Only twelve of the 1,149 mutual pairs observed were between children of opposite sex, five in non-streamed schools, and seven in streamed schools. In all these cases the children were alike or only one point apart in rated ability.[1]

The findings on children's mutual friendships suggested a certain conservatism in the choice of friends by children of this age. In selecting which of their acquaintances should become friends, children tended to choose children of the same social class, ability and sex.

An important factor in the choice of friend was proximity; the vast majority of children selected friends from their own rather than other classes. Thus it was unlikely that children in streamed schools, which are in effect streamed by social class as well as ability, would compensate for this by choosing a friend outside their class. But even in non-streamed classes where there was an opportunity for the formation of mutual friendships between children of differing ability and social class, there was a strong tendency toward the 'bright' choosing 'bright' and the 'dull' choosing 'dull'. In terms of differences between the two types of school—all that can be said was that the tendency to choose children of similar ability as friends was less marked in non-streamed schools.

Sociometric status

Sociometric status can be thought of as a person's degree of popularity within a certain group. In this case the child's popularity in the social sense ('best friend', 'play with') was examined, as well as his academic popularity ('work with').

---

[1] A somewhat higher number of *unreciprocated* cross-sex choices was observed with a boy choosing a girl but not being chosen by her, or vice versa. Despite claims in the literature that girls are more likely to choose boys as friends than boys to choose girls, no difference was found in this study. Also, no differences were found between streamed and non-streamed schools, either in the overall amount of unreciprocated cross-sex choice, or in its distribution by sex or type of teacher. The one difference found was that children were more likely to choose the opposite sex as companions for work and play than as 'best friends'. The total number of such choices was three per cent on the 'best friend' criterion, five per cent on the 'work with' criterion and five per cent on the 'play with' criterion. This difference applied equally to boys and girls and to both kinds of organization, and suggests that the use of the term 'best friend' may mean a friend of the same sex to this age group. However, the strength of the tendency towards same sex association on all three criteria may be appreciated in that there were only 702 cross-sex choices out of a total of more than 15,000 made.

Based on the number of children choosing him as a 'best friend', workmate or playmate, the child was given a sociometric score for each. His *sociometric status* was then defined in terms of Bronfenbrenner's (1943) statistical framework for the analysis of sociometric choice patterns. This defines three levels of sociometric status: 'neglectee' (a child receiving no choices), 'star' (a child receiving seven or more choices), 'medium status' (a child receiving one to six choices).[1]

Since sociometric status is related to ability—brighter children have a higher sociometric status than below average or less able children (Bonney and Powell, 1953; Buswell, 1953; Bonney, 1955; Heber, 1956; Healey, Barker Lunn and Bouri, 1968)—it was expected that non-streaming, in which the full range of ability is in one class, would affect the pattern of sociometric choice. One might expect slow or less able children to be less 'popular' in non-streamed classes than comparable children in lower streams where all are of similar ability. Likewise, one might expect bright children to be more popular in non-streamed classes, where they are fewer in number, than in A-streams.

Another important factor was the effect of the teacher. Pearce (1958) in a study of two grammar school C-streams, found that the choices of the children increasingly clustered, over time, round a few highly chosen 'stars', but this happened less in an experimental form taught by co-operative and more 'progressive' methods. From this one might expect that the proportion of 'neglectees' and 'stars' would vary according to the type of teacher.

Separate analyses were carried out for each criterion, and the proportions of 'stars', 'neglectees' and 'medium status' children in streamed schools were compared with those in non-streamed schools having Type 1 (typical non-streamer) or Type 2 (typical streamer) teachers (see Chapter 4). Since the number of children having Type 1 teachers in streamed schools was so few, type of teacher was ignored.

---

[1] Expectations can be derived for any given number of choices allowed, and definitions for 'high' or 'low' sociometric status are thus given a meaningful statistical context. Although the precise level of expectancy associated with any given raw score varies with group size, Bronfenbrenner has given a list of initial raw status score values for diverse sociometric situations which hold with the values of $P < 0.05$ for groups between 15 and 35 persons, and does not exceed $P < 0.05$ for groups of size 10-50 persons. Since nearly 40 per cent of the classes fell within the narrower limits, and the remainder all contained less than 50 children, Bronfenbrenner's definitions were used to differentiate the statistically 'overchosen' children, or 'stars', and the statistically 'underchosen', or 'neglectees', from the normal choice range.

To control for differences arising from sex and ability, boys and girls of three different ability levels were examined separately.[1] The results which follow were obtained in the third junior year when the children (Cohort 1) were aged nine-plus.

The results indicated, as predicted, that there was a tendency for children of above average ability to be more 'popular' or to have higher sociometric status in non-streamed than in streamed schools, particularly in terms of someone to 'work with'. The trends for boys reached a level of statistical significance on the 'work with' ($P<0.001$) and the 'play with' criteria ($P<0.05$) but not on the 'best friend' criterion. Although the trends were in the same direction for girls of above average ability, none of the comparisons between streamed and non-streamed schools were statistically significantly different (see Appendix 6, Table 10.3).

The finding that boys of above average ability were more popular as workmates in non-streamed than streamed classes held whether they were taught by Type 1 ($P < 0.02$) or Type 2 teachers ($P < 0.001$) but the difference between the two types of school was greater when teachers in the non-streamed school were Type 2. Presumably this was because of their greater emphasis on the importance of academic success. The trends for girls of above average ability with a Type 1 or Type 2 teacher were similar to boys, but these did not reach a level of statistical significance.

Comparisons were made of the sociometric scores of boys and girls of average ability in the two types of school and with different types of teacher; no statistically significant differences were found. Also, no pattern or trend favouring one type of school or the other was apparent (see Appendix 6, Table 10.3).

As for the children of below average ability, there were tendencies in the case of boys for more 'stars' and fewer 'neglectees' in streamed schools—but these were not statistically significant on any of the criteria. No pattern or trend appeared for girls of below average ability: there were no statistically significant differences between the proportion of 'stars', 'medium status' and 'neglectees' in streamed and non-streamed schools or with different types of teacher.

To examine these trends further, the sociometric status of children of different ability levels within each type of organization was compared.

---

[1] The children were divided equally into three groups on the basis of their Reading test score at the end of the third year.

In streamed schools, the proportion of boys who were 'stars', 'neglectees' or 'medium status' did not vary by ability level. There was a tendency for more 'neglectees' and fewer 'stars' among the less able girls, and fewer 'neglectees' and more 'stars' among the more able girls—but only on the 'work with' criterion did this reach statistical significance ($P < 0.001$).

In non-streamed schools, the findings were similar to those for girls in streamed schools: on the 'work with' criterion children of below average ability were more likely to be 'neglectees' and less likely to be 'stars' than the more able (Type 1 Boys: $P < 0.001$; Type 2 Boys: $P < 0.001$; Type 1 Girls: $P < 0.05$; Type 2 Girls: $P < 0.001$). These tendencies were more pronounced when children were taught by Type 2 than Type 1 teachers. Even on the 'play with' criterion this trend was statistically significant for boys taught by Type 2 teachers ($P < 0.01$). None of the other comparisons on the 'play with' criterion were statistically significant, nor did any of the comparisons on the 'best friend' criterion reach statistical significance (see Table 10.4, Appendix 6).

Change of sociometric status between third and fourth year

The sociometric questionnaire was administered to Cohort 1 when they were in their third and fourth year, in order to investigate any changes that might have taken place. The results referred to above were based on third year data. The data obtained from the two years were compared and an analysis was made of the proportion of children who had increased or decreased in status in the fourth year; an investigation was then made of the patterns of change occurring in the sociometric status of children under the direction of Type 1 and Type 2 teachers, and in streamed and non-streamed schools.[1]

On the whole, the patterns that had been established in the third year remained. Of the changes that did take place, all were in the expected direction, confirming trends noted in the third year. (See Table 10.5, Appendix 6.)

On the 'work with' criterion, there was little change in sociometric status of children taught by Type 1 or Type 2 teachers in non-streamed schools, but in streamed schools girls of above average ability decreased in sociometric status (Sign test significant at

---

[1] This was based on the type of teacher the child had in the fourth year, irrespective of his third year teacher.

159

five per cent level). This resulted in an establishment of the tendency, already observed in the third year, for fewer girls of above average ability to be 'stars' and more to be 'neglectees' in streamed schools but, in comparing the two types of school, this only reached statistical significance when the girls in non-streamed schools were taught by Type 2 teachers ($P < 0.02$). There was no difference when they were taught by Type 1 teachers.[1]

There were some changes in non-streamed schools in the social status of boys taught by different teacher types. Boys of below average ability with Type 2 teachers became less popular on the 'best friend' criterion (Sign test significant at five per cent level) and boys of above average ability taught by Type 1 teachers became less popular on the 'best friend' and 'play with' criteria (Sign test significant at one per cent and five per cent levels respectively).

These changes were in the direction expected: Type 2 teachers emphasized academic success and found boys of below average ability less pleasurable to have in the class than did Type 1 teachers; the 'unacceptability' of boys of below average ability to Type 2 teachers was reflected in their lack of popularity among the other children. Type 1 teachers, on the other hand, placed less emphasis on academic success and this apparently resulted in success becoming a less important criterion to the children in their choice of friends: thus children of above average ability were less likely to become 'social stars' with Type 1 teachers.

What do these results mean?

Different factors seemed to influence the sociometric status of boys and girls. The sociometric status of boys was much more influenced by ability in non-streamed than in streamed schools. Boys of above average ability were more likely to be 'work' stars in non-streamed schools while there was also a non-significant trend for more boys of below average ability to be 'neglectees' in this type of school. These trends were much more pronounced on the 'work' than on the 'social' criteria and also with Type 2 teachers in non-streamed schools.

The sociometric status of girls was influenced by ability in both streamed and non-streamed schools: 'neglectees' tended to be the

---

[1] Another change observed in streamed schools was the decrease in 'work' status (Sign test 1% level) of boys of average ability. They also decreased significantly in social status (both criteria significant at 1% level) but there were still no statistically significant differences between streamed and non-streamed schools in the proportion of 'neglectees', 'medium status' and 'stars'.

below average, 'stars' above average. There was, however, one difference: the tendency for girls of above average ability to be 'work' stars was even more pronounced in non-streamed schools with Type 2 teachers, the trend being significantly greater than in streamed schools or in non-streamed schools with Type 1 teachers.

An important finding was that, over the total sample of boys and girls, the proportions of each who were 'neglectees', 'stars' and 'medium status' were approximately the same in streamed and non-streamed schools and with different 'types' of teacher (see Table 10.6, Appendix 6). Thus streaming or non-streaming made no apparent difference to the number of 'stars', 'neglectees' or 'medium status' children, although it did make a slight difference to the *type* of pupil, in terms of ability, who became a 'star' or a 'neglectee'.

Characteristics of 'stars' and 'neglectees'

What were the other characteristics of 'stars' and 'neglectees'? Were there any differences in streamed and non-streamed schools? An examination was made of the class position, social class, and pleasurability of the pupil, as perceived by the teacher, of 'stars' and 'neglectees' on all three sociometric criteria. In addition, their social characteristics, such as behaviour, social adjustment and degree of participation in school activities, were examined, but this time only on the social criterion of 'best friend'.

(a) Class Position

The tendency for 'stars' to be brighter and 'neglectees' to be duller than 'medium status' children was confirmed by their relative class positions (based on arithmetic). 'Stars' were more likely to be among the 'best' pupils and 'neglectees' among the 'poorest' pupils in the class in arithmetic. This trend was found on the 'work' and 'social' criteria ($P < 0.001$). (See Table 10.7, Appendix 6.)

In any comparison of streamed and non-streamed schools, it should be noted that 'position in class' has very different meanings in the two types of school: in non-streamed schools those at the 'bottom of the class' are below average and those at the 'top' are above average, in contrast to streamed schools where those at the 'top' or 'bottom' of the class can be of any ability level depending on which stream they are in.

Surprisingly, however, when children in non-streamed schools were taught by Type 1 teachers there was no difference between the two types of school in the proportion of 'neglectees' who were bottom, or 'stars' who were top of the class on any of the three criteria. On the other hand, there were differences when teachers in non-streamed schools were Type 2: proportionally more of the 'neglectees' in non-streamed than in streamed schools were among the poorest pupils in the class, not only on the 'work with' criterion but also on both social criteria ('work with': $P < 0.001$; 'play with': $P < 0.001$; 'best friend': $P < 0.05$); there was no difference in the class position of 'stars'.

(b) Social Class[1]

Neugarten (1946) has reported that children from homes with a higher socio-economic position tended to have higher sociometric status. She also found that when rejection choices were included these were given to children from homes with the lowest socio-economic status.

The findings of this study confirmed that 'neglectees' tended to be of a lower social class and 'stars' of a higher social class. Among 'neglectees', even on the social criteria, there were more children from social classes 4 and 5, and fewer from social classes 1, 2, 3, than among 'medium status' children ('best friend': $P < 0.01$). The 'stars', however, did not differ from the 'medium status' group.

Did this relationship hold in both streamed and non-streamed schools or were there any differences? The social class of 'neglectees' and 'stars' was examined in terms of the three sociometric criteria. It was found on all criteria that 'neglectees' followed a similar pattern to that indicated above in both streamed and non-streamed schools, and with different types of teacher—no differences were observed. Likewise there were no differences for 'stars' on the social criteria, but on the 'work with' criterion they were more likely to be from the highest social classes in non-streamed schools whatever the teacher type, in contrast to those in streamed schools (streamed versus non-streamed Type 1: $P < 0.05$; streamed versus non-streamed Type 2: $P < 0.05$; see Table 10.8b, Appendix 6).

Since ability is related to social class, the above results could be explained in terms of ability differences. Thus children may reach 'stardom' primarily as a result of their high ability, which happens to be associated with their high socio-economic background.

---

[1] For details of social class, see Appendix 4.

162

(*c*) *Pleasurability*

'Stars' and 'neglectees' were next examined in terms of their pleasurability as perceived by their class teacher (see Chapter 9, and Appendix 4). These confirmed the findings of an earlier study (Healey *et al.*, 1968): 'neglectees' tended to be perceived by their teachers as less pleasurable to have in the class than 'medium status' children ($P < 0.001$); there was no difference between pleasurability ratings given to 'medium status' children and 'stars'.

The pleasurability ratings of 'stars' and 'neglectees' were further examined for differences between streamed and non-streamed schools. There were no differences for 'stars' but the ratings given to 'neglectees' on the 'work with' criterion revealed some interesting differences when teachers in non-streamed schools were Type 2: 17 per cent, compared with 6 per cent in streamed schools, were rated as 'never or seldom a pleasure to have in the class' ($P < 0.01$). This rejection could partly be due to their low ability, for it has already been shown that Type 2 teachers found children of low ability unpleasurable.

The pleasurability ratings given to pupils who were 'neglectees' on the 'best friend' criterion differed in the two types of school: in non-streamed schools, whatever the teacher type, there was a tendency for more 'neglectees' to be given a low rating and fewer a high rating than in streamed schools ($P < 0.05$). (See Table 10.9, Appendix 5.)

(*d*) *Behaviour Ratings*

Since the child's behaviour, his social adjustment and his degree of participation in school activities could be described as social characteristics, the analysis here was restricted and carried out in terms of only one of the social criteria—that of 'best friend'.[1]

The class teacher rated each pupil on a four-point scale on four behaviour traits. These included the incidence of fighting or bullying, being picked-on or teased, social withdrawal, and disobedience or insolence. For the purposes of this analysis, an unfavourable rating meant that the behaviour had occurred at least once a week.

No different patterns emerged in the two types of school (see footnote 1) or with either teacher type. In both types of school 'neglectees' were perceived as significantly more likely to fight or

---

[1] 'Best friend' rather than the 'play with' criterion was selected because the former had been used in an earlier study—see Healey *et al.*, 1968.

bully other children; to be picked-on or teased; to be withdrawn in relationships with their classmates; and to be disobedient or insolent in class, compared with children in the medium range of sociometric status (see Table 10.10, Appendix 6). 'Stars' were distinguished from 'medium status' children in only one respect: they were less likely to be withdrawn.[1]

(e) Social Adjustment and Participation in School Activities

'Stars' and 'neglectees' on the 'best friend' criterion were also examined in terms of social adjustment[2] and their participation in school activities.[3] It was found that 'neglectees' tended to have poorer social adjustment ($P < 0.05$), and a lower level of participation in school activities ($P < 0.001$), and 'stars' a higher level of participation ($P < 0.001$) than 'medium status' children.

There was no difference between the social adjustment scores of 'neglectees' or 'stars' in different types of school or with different types of teacher. The level of participation of 'neglectees' in school activities did, however, vary with type of school and teacher: Type 1 teachers in non-streamed schools were more successful in encouraging their 'neglectees' to participate in school activities, having a higher level of participation than 'neglectees' in streamed schools or than those with Type 2 teachers in non-streamed schools (streamed versus Type 1: $P < 0.001$; Type 1 versus Type 2: $P < 0.01$). (See Tables 10.11 and 10.12, Appendix 6.)

Conclusions

Investigation of sociometric status revealed that the proportions of 'neglectees', 'medium status' and 'stars' on the three sociometric criteria: 'work with', 'play with' and 'best friend', in streamed and non-streamed schools, were almost identical. On the whole the type of child who became a 'neglectee' was similar in the two types of school. They tended to have low general ability, to be bottom or near the bottom of their class and to come from homes with low socio-economic status. On all behaviour ratings they tended to achieve poor scores; some responded to being friendless by belligerence and bossiness, and by being disobedient and insolent towards their teacher; some were picked-on and teased by their classmates;

---

[1] This tendency was noted in the earlier study, but did not reach statistical significance.

[2] For further details of Social Adjustment, see Chapter 9.

[3] For details of school activities, see Chapter 11.

others became shy and withdrawn. They tended to have poor social adjustment scores and to be infrequently chosen to participate in school activities. Besides being ignored or disliked by their classmates, their teachers, too, tended to find little pleasure in having them in the class.

However, there were some differences between the two types of school in terms of the type of child who acquired each sociometric status level. Brighter and middle class children were more likely to be sought after as work-mates in non-streamed than in streamed schools. The wide range of ability in non-streamed classes ensured that children of above average ability were the most able in their class and as work-mates these children were frequently chosen by their less able classmates. This was in contrast to the streamed situation where children of above average ability were together in one class and therefore were not so likely to attain the same degree of popularity as their counterparts in non-streamed schools. However, what is of interest here is that when they were taught by Type 2 teachers in non-streamed schools, children of above average ability were even more popular as work-mates, while children who were bottom of the class were more likely to be 'neglectees'. Type 2 teachers placed greater emphasis on academic success and their pupils, it appeared, responded to this value in their choice of work-mates.

The influence of the teacher was even more interesting in using the social criteria. Type 1 teachers in non-streamed schools found 'neglectees' on the 'best friend' criterion slightly less pleasurable than did teachers in streamed schools, although they did not rate 'neglectees' on the 'work with' criterion similarly. This suggests that these teachers judged their pupils' degree of pleasurability in the same way as the pupils themselves. Although they found 'neglectees' ('best friend') less pleasurable than other children, Type 1 teachers were more successful than Type 2 teachers, or those in streamed schools in bringing the social 'neglectees' into the life of the school.[1]

The number of differences, however, between the two types of school was greater when teachers in non-streamed schools were Type 2. It appeared that Type 2 teachers' emphasis on academic success and also their 'dislike' of below average children was transmitted to

---

[1] Another difference in the third year was that boys of above average ability with Type 1 teachers were more popular as playmates than similar boys in streamed schools, but this was not the case by the end of the fourth year.

their pupils, who tended to select friends in accordance with their teachers' own feelings. With Type 2 teachers, there was a greater tendency for social 'neglectees' to be at the bottom of the class in contrast to those in streamed schools and those taught by Type 1 teachers in non-streamed schools, and probably as a result of their being at the bottom of the class they were less pleasurable to their Type 2 teacher than similar children in streamed schools.

Differences between boys and girls were noted. The sociometric status of girls in either type of school in contrast to boys was influenced more by ability and there was less difference between the two types of school. Boys, on the other hand, were more affected than girls by the type of school organization, and only in non-streamed schools did ability appear to have a major influence on sociometric status. Both sexes were sensitive, but boys slightly more so, to the type of teacher.

There was some evidence that children tended to identify with the values of their teachers in choosing friends and work-mates. For example, in the non-streamed situation, there was a strong tendency for duller members of the class to be 'neglectees': this association was much weaker where there were Type 1 teachers, part of whose value structure involved greater sympathy for the duller child. Under the same circumstances, there was a much smaller tendency for brighter children to be 'stars'.

The difference in ability range between streamed and non-streamed classes had some effect on the pattern of mutual choices. Opportunity to choose friends of different ability level and social class was greater in non-streamed classes and children in these classes did have a wider range of friends in terms of ability, though not in terms of social class. On the whole, however, children seemed to choose each other as friends when they were of similar ability and social class. Thus, although children in streamed classes were inevitably restricted in their range of choice, the presence of a mixed ability group of children, as in the non-streamed situation, did not necessarily ensure that friendship choices were wider.

References

BONNEY, M. E. (1956). 'A study of constancy of sociometric ranks among college students over a two year period', *Sociometry*, 18, 531-42.
BONNEY, M. E. and POWELL, J. (1953). 'Differences in social behaviour between sociometrically high and sociometrically low children', *Amer. J. Educ. Res.*, 46, 481-95.

BRONFENBRENNER, U. (1943). 'A constant frame of reference for sociometric research: Part I, Theory and technique', *Sociometry*, 6, 363-97.

BUSWELL, M. M. (1953). 'The relationship between the social structure of the classroom and the academic success of the pupils', *J. Exp. Educ.*, 22, 37-52.

DETJEN, E. W. and DETJEN, M. F. (1963) *Elementary School Guidance*. London: McGraw-Hill.

FOX, R. S., LIPPITT, R. O. and SCHMUCK, R. A. (1964). *Pupil-Teacher Adjustment and Mutual Adaptation in Creating Classroom Learning Environments*. Co-operative Research Monograph 1167. Washington, DC: US Department of Health, Education and Welfare.

HEALEY, P. B., BARKER LUNN, J. C. and BOURI, J. (1968). 'Some sociometric characteristics of children in streamed and non-streamed junior schools'. Unpublished paper.

HEBER, R. F. (1956). 'The relation of intelligence and physical maturity to social status of children', *J. Educ. Psychol.*, 47, 158-62.

NEUGARTEN, B. L. (1946). 'Social class and friendship among school children', *Amer. J. Sociol.*, 51, 305-13.

NORTHWAY, M. L. (1968). 'The stability of young children's social relations', *Educ. Res.*, 11, 54-7.

PEARCE, R. A. (1958). 'Streaming and a sociometric study', *Educ. Rev.*, 10, 248-51.

CHAPTER 11

Participation in School Activities

PARTICIPATION in activities outside the classroom context and not directly related to the learning programme would be regarded by most people concerned with education as an important part of a child's school experience. Not only can such participation stimulate and develop a child's interest in various fields; it also provides the opportunity to take part in co-operative group activities and can serve to satisfy what Fleming (1958) has called 'a human need to participate in the affairs of some intimate and friendly group.'

There has been little or no previous research devoted to the study of such activities in schools. It seems likely, however, that this is an area in which schools will vary considerably, both in provision and in the participation which they encourage among their pupils. One of the questions which this inquiry hoped to answer was whether streamed and non-streamed schools differed in the encouragement shown to pupils of different types to take part in school activities. As reported elsewhere,[1] a number of teachers who favoured streaming held the view that 'it's a fallacy to believe that because a child is *not* good at reading and arithmetic he will be good at something else'. Did this attitude result in a tendency in streamed schools for children in lower streams to be left out of activities as a result of their perceived inability to succeed at anything? And how did the less able children fare in the non-streamed situation? It might be hypothesized that the emphasis on child-centred methods and social development associated more with non-streamed schools would lead to teachers in these schools attaching a greater degree of importance to *all* pupils taking part in such activities than their colleagues in streamed schools.

One of the questionnaires completed by the schools was concerned with the provision of different types of school activity. Table 11.1 shows the percentage of schools undertaking each of the activities mentioned in the questionnaire in 1964, when the Cohort 1 children

---

[1] See Appendix 2 and Chapter 13.

were aged 7+, and again in 1967, when they were in their fourth and final junior school year.

TABLE 11.1: *Types of school activity*

	1964 (BASED ON 84 SCHOOLS)	1967 (BASED ON 72 SCHOOLS)
1. School sports team	99%	99%
2. School choir, orchestra or recorder group	91%	82%
3. Individual children taking a special part in morning prayers, such as reading the Lesson	90%	90%
4. School clubs, such as chess, stamps	63%	67%
5. School prefects	61%	58%
6. School play	44%	51%
7. School dancing display	49%	43%
8. School holiday	33%	26%
9. School magazine	11%	10%
10. School visits, such as a visit to the fire station or zoo	Not asked	86%

Only in one instance was a difference found between streamed and non-streamed schools: this was in the existence of a prefect system, which was found in 75 per cent of streamed schools but only 40 per cent of non-streamed schools. It was likely that prefects' duties varied considerably from school to school, but no further information was available.

It can be seen from the list of activities above that, with the possible exception of numbers 4, 8 and 10, participation probably depended on being chosen by the teacher to take part. Thus, any variations found in the level of participation of different children in different types of school can be said to reflect the degree of encouragement shown by the teachers in each case.

In order to obtain information on each child's level of participation at 7+ and again at 10+, teachers were asked to indicate which activities the pupil had taken part in during the school year in question. A participation ratio score was subsequently calculated for each child, *relating the number of activities in which he had taken part to the total number available in the school.* In this way variations between schools in the number of activities was controlled.

As might be predicted, the level of participation in school activities was very low in the first junior school year, particularly among children of below average ability. Ability level was closely related to participation, with children of above average ability taking a much greater part.

An examination of the participation ratio scores of children of comparable ability levels in streamed and non-streamed schools revealed statistically significant differences even at this early stage in the junior school career. At each level of ability boys and girls in streamed schools were found to take less part in school activities than their counterparts in non-streamed schools (all χ^2 tests highly significant). At the below average level of ability more than 80 per cent of children in streamed schools had very low scores compared with about two-thirds in non-streamed schools (see Table 11.2, Appendix 6).

Little difference was found in the level of participation of boys and girls at this age, except that girls of above average ability in non-streamed schools tended to have higher scores than boys ($P < 0.05$). No other comparisons produced any differences.

A much higher level of participation in school activities was reported when the children were in their fourth (10+) year. Also, differences had appeared in the degree of participation of boys and girls, especially at the above average and average levels of ability, with more girls than boys obtaining high scores. The type of activities offered by the school may have held more appeal for girls than for boys.[1]

Both the level of ability and social class background were related to participation, with, predictably, children of higher ability and social class taking a greater part in school activities. Consequently these factors were controlled when streamed and non-streamed schools were compared, with each ability group and social class being examined separately.[2]

Participation in streamed and non-streamed schools

Firstly, boys of above average ability from each of the three social class groups were compared, and, although there was a trend favouring boys from non-streamed schools, the differences were not statistically significant.

[1] Four of the items: school orchestra, school play, school magazine, school dancing display, involve activities which were more favoured by girls than boys according to their scores on the interests questionnaire. See Chapter 8.

[2] Children were divided into three ability groups according to their score on the Reading test, and three social classes: professional and clerical; skilled; and semi and unskilled (see Appendix 4).

Boys of average ability from semi- and unskilled homes had a significantly higher participation ratio in non-streamed schools ($P < 0.001$), as did those from skilled home backgrounds ($P < 0.05$). A similar, though non-significant, trend was observed among boys from professional and clerical backgrounds.

Among boys of below average ability only those from semi- and unskilled backgrounds showed a significantly higher level of participation in non-streamed schools ($P < 0.001$), although the trend was in the same direction for the other two social class groups (see Tables 11.3 and 11.4, Appendix 6).

A comparison of the participation scores of girls in the two types of school revealed similar results to those reported for boys, although slight differences emerged. Girls of above average ability from skilled home backgrounds and in non-streamed schools showed a significantly higher level of participation ($P < 0.05$). A similar, though non-significant, trend was found in the scores of those from semi-skilled and unskilled home backgrounds, but there was no difference in the participation of girls of above average ability from professional and clerical homes in the two types of school.

Only one significant result was found among girls of average ability: the scores of those from semi-skilled and unskilled homes showed a significant difference in favour of non-streamed schools ($P < 0.05$).

In the case of girls of below average ability, highly significant differences in favour of non-streamed schools were found among those from skilled, semi-skilled and unskilled homes ($P < 0.01$) and $P < 0.001$ respectively); and although there was no significant difference in the participation of those from professional and clerical home backgrounds, the trend favoured those in non-streamed schools (see Tables 11.3 and 11.4, Appendix 6).

The provision of activities was very similar in streamed and non-streamed schools but the number and type of pupils taking part varied greatly. Furthermore, the results suggested that these differences were most striking at the average and below average levels of ability and, within these groups, among children from lower social class backgrounds. The effect of social class seemed to increase as one moved down the ability scale: among children of above average ability it was relatively unimportant; at the average level, however, the greatest difference between streamed and non-streamed schools was in children from semi-skilled and unskilled homes; while at the below average level of ability, children in streamed schools who came

171

from either unskilled, semi-skilled or skilled homes showed a considerably lower level of participation than their counterparts in non-streamed schools. In the final year of junior school 39 per cent of boys of below average ability[1] in streamed schools had low participation scores compared with only 19 per cent in non-streamed schools, and the corresponding figures for girls were 43 per cent and 24 per cent respectively (see Table 11.5, Appendix 6). Since participation was probably dependent upon teacher choice, a certain amount of 'rejection' of the less able child seemed to take place in streamed schools in particular, and the child who was not academically bright did not seem to be expected to shine at anything else.

Children's participation ratio scores in terms of their position in class[2] revealed similar differences in favour of non-streamed schools. This result is perhaps surprising for children at the bottom of a class, since those at the bottom of a non-streamed class will usually be of below average ability, while in a streamed school, this group will include children at the bottom of A-streams. Bearing in mind the relationship between ability level and participation, one might hypothesize that the difference between streamed and non-streamed schools in the number of low participants would be to some extent evened out here, since A-stream children would be likely to take more part in school activities. However, this was not the case: there was still a significant tendency for children at the bottom of their class in streamed schools to take less part in school activities ($P < 0.01$ in case of both boys and girls). Therefore, being in an A class may be no guarantee of encouragement to take part in activities for a child who is at the bottom of that class (see Table 11.6, Appendix 6).

Participation and teacher behaviour ratings

Since children's participation in school activities depended to a large extent upon teacher choice, the teachers' view of the child was considered important. We therefore examined the level of participation of boys and girls in streamed and non-streamed schools in terms of the ratings given to them by their teachers on certain aspects of behaviour.

In both types of school the children regarded as unpleasurable in class were more likely to have a low participation ratio than their

---

[1] As defined by teachers' ratings.
[2] As rated by their teachers in arithmetic. See Appendix 4.

more approved peers (all χ^2 tests highly significant). It seemed that children who were not particularly liked by their teacher were less likely to be encouraged to take part in school activities. (see Table 11.7, Appendix 6).

Boys in streamed schools who were regarded by their teachers as prone to fighting were more likely to have a low participation ratio than those who were not rated in this way ($P < 0.01$). No significant difference was found in non-streamed boys, however. Fighting is probably more common among boys of low ability and low social class, and this association may explain the low level of participation in streamed schools, while teachers in non-streamed schools, as was found in Chapter 10, may nevertheless encourage participation of children whom they perceive as having unfavourable characteristics. Few girls in either type of school were prone to fighting and no differences emerged in their participation ratio scores. In both types of school both boys and girls who were perceived as 'withdrawn' were more likely to have a low participation score than those who were not. It would seem probable that the relationship between a low level of participation and a tendency to be withdrawn or prone to fighting is a circular one. To be left out of school activities is likely to increase the tendency to be withdrawn in a child who already exhibits such behaviour; while exclusion from activities of a boy who is seen as a nuisance will no doubt strengthen the tendency for his energies to be released in antisocial ways (see Tables 11·8 and 11.9, Appendix 6).

Conclusions

In both types of school, level of participation was found to be related to ability and social class background.

Comparing participation in streamed and non-streamed schools, however, it was found that, with the exception of higher social class girls of above average ability, children in streamed schools took less part in school activities than those in non-streamed schools. These differences were particularly striking among children of average and below average ability and from lower social class backgrounds. These results indicate that greater importance is attached in non-streamed schools to the encouragement of *all* children to take part in such activities. In streamed schools, a combination of low ability, low stream and low social class background makes it likely that a child will be left out of school activities, and that those who could perhaps benefit most from this enrichment of their school experience are being deprived of the opportunity to do so.

173

Children in both types of school who were thought by their teachers to have unfavourable behaviour traits were less likely to take part in school activities than other children. Yet these are the children for whom participation in various activities would be most advantageous and therapeutic in helping them to overcome their difficulties, and exclusion will probably only intensify their unfavourable characteristics.

References

FLEMING, C. M. (1958). *Teaching: A Psychological Analysis.* London: Methuen.

CHAPTER 12

Attitudes of Parents

THE importance for children's educational progress of factors associated with their home background is nowadays virtually unquestioned. In recent years however (cf. the Plowden Report), increasing attention has been drawn to the influence of *parents' attitudes*, in addition to the more tangible factors associated with material standards in the home and parental occupation.

It is likely that the relationship between parents' attitudes and their children's attainment operates in both directions; as the Primary School Report (Department of Education and Science, 1967) says: 'The children's very success or failure in school work may increase or weaken parental aspirations'. Factors such as a child's stream, his position in class and his performance in relation to other children may well affect the way in which his parents assess his potential and, in turn, their aspirations for his future.

The purpose of this part of the research was to discover whether a child's being in a streamed or non-streamed class made any difference to his parents' opinion of his performance in school and to their hopes for his future education and training. A brief questionnaire was constructed with the aim of obtaining information on parents' aspirations for their children's secondary schooling and further training. This was sent to a sample of about 3,900 parents which included children of Cohorts 1 and 2 when in their third and fourth year respectively, in the 28 schools (for details, see Appendix 5). Brevity and simplicity were considered essential features of the questionnaire and the final version consisted of a few straightforward, pre-coded questions in a form which, it was hoped, would produce a high response rate.

The questionnaires were sent to the schools in sealed envelopes and distributed to the children by their teachers. The envelopes also contained a covering letter to parents, explaining the purpose of the inquiry and stressing the confidential nature of their replies. No names or addresses appeared on the questionnaire—only the research code number of the child concerned. The questionnaires were returned to the schools, and thence, unseen by teachers, to the NFER.

The questionnaire included four questions which were of importance to the study. The first asked parents to indicate the age at which they wanted their child to leave school—15, 16 or 17+. The second question asked which type of secondary school parents would prefer their children to attend (irrespective of any allocation already made)—grammar, comprehensive, secondary modern or technical. The third dealt with subsequent training, asking parents to choose among university, technical college (for one or two years), apprenticeship of some kind or no further training of any sort. Finally, they were asked to rate their child's ability at school work as either very good, good, average or not so good. A fifth question, included primarily as a 'buffer' item, asked whether children could recite nursery rhymes, count up to ten and read simple books before starting infant school. As expected, this item received a very high proportion of affirmative responses and was not analysed further.

Approximately 87 per cent of parents completed and returned their questionnaires. The subsequent analysis was carried out on responses of parents of all children for whom social class information and teachers' ability ratings were available. As it was considered possible that the effects of the 11+ selection test might alter parental aspirations of the fourth-year children, the two cohorts were initially analysed separately. The 11+ factor, however, appeared to make little difference, and in the following report, results for the two cohorts have been combined.

How parents rated their children's ability

Parents were asked: 'In your opinion how good is your child now at school work?' and rated their children on a four-point scale ranging from 'very good' to 'not so good'.

There was no overall difference between streamed and non-streamed schools in the ability ratings given by parents. Furthermore, no differences emerged when children were divided into three ability levels according to their *teachers'* estimates, and comparisons were made between parents' ratings of children of above average, average and below average ability in streamed and non-streamed schools.

There was, however, a noticeable sex difference in the ratings parents gave their children, with both social classes tending to rate girls more highly than boys (see Table 12.1). This finding was consistent with both teachers' ratings of pupils' abilities and with the results of attainment tests at this age level.

TABLE 12.1: *Parents' ratings of children's ability*

ABILITY RATING	HIGHER SOCIAL CLASS†		LOWER SOCIAL CLASS	
	Boys	*Girls*	*Boys*	*Girls*
Very good	13%	18%	6%	12%
Good	36%	38%	25%	29%
Average	44%	40%	61%	52%
Not so good	7%	4%	8%	7%
Number of parents giving information (100%)	961	948	801	811

† Social class categories are based on teachers' ratings of father's occupation. The higher social class group includes professional/managerial, clerical and skilled workers, whilst the lower social class group consists of semi-skilled and unskilled workers. For details, see Appendix 4.

As Table 12.1 shows there were also significant differences in the ratings given by parents of different social classes. Higher social class parents were more likely to rate their children as 'very good' or 'good'. Comparatively few parents of either social class, however, were willing to regard their children as being below average in ability. A considerable discrepancy was found to exist between parents' and teachers' ratings of children perceived as below average by teachers: only 23 per cent were rated 'not so good' by their parents; 68 per cent were seen as 'average' and the remaining 9 per cent as 'good' or 'very good'. The higher the ability rating given by teachers the greater the correspondence between that and the rating given by parents. Among children rated 'average' by teachers almost two-thirds were rated similarly by their parents, whilst over 80 per cent of the parents of 'above average' children considered them as 'good' or 'very good'.

Choice of secondary school

First it was decided to compare parents' choice of secondary school for their children with the actual pattern of allocation. Table 12.2 shows the percentage of parents choosing the four different types of school and the percentage of children concerned who were subsequently allocated to each type of school at the end of their fourth year.[1]

TABLE 12.2: *Preferred type and actual allocation to secondary schools*

TYPE OF SCHOOL	% OF PARENTS CHOOSING	% OF PUPILS ALLOCATED
Secondary Modern	22%	58%
Comprehensive	20%	19%
Technical	13%	1%
Grammar	45%	20%
Other	—	2%
Number of parents giving information (100%)	3,479	

Clearly the grammar school continues to maintain primacy of esteem over other types of secondary school—everywhere the choice of grammar school far outweighed the provision of places. The same was true for technical schools, but the percentage of children allocated to comprehensive schools was almost equal to that of parents choosing this type of school. Only in the case of secondary modern schools was the supply of places considerably in excess of demand (see Table 12.2).

Further evidence that parental choice of secondary school was unrelated to provision of places and actual allocation lay in the fact that in 13 of the junior schools in the study for which no comprehensive or technical schools were yet available, parental choice of such schools ranged from 6 per cent to 25 per cent.

Comparing the choice of secondary school made by parents of children in streamed and non-streamed schools, it was found that the grammar school was the first choice of all higher social class parents, but among lower social class parents the grammar school was the first choice of parents of non-streamed children only; lower social class parents with children in streamed schools showed a clear

[1] Information on secondary school allocation was available only for the Cohort 1 children. It is unlikely, however, that the pattern of allocation of Cohort 2 children (who left junior school a year earlier) would have differed more than slightly.

preference for the secondary modern (see Table 12.3). At first sight then, it would appear, in the case of the lower social class, that attendance at a non-streamed junior school heightened parents' aspirations for an academic secondary education for their children while attendance at a streamed junior school depressed them. This was perhaps further reflected in the greater percentage of lower social class parents of non-streamed children who expressed a preference for the comprehensive school, perhaps regarding this as an alternative route to an academic secondary education.

TABLE 12.3: *Parents' choice of secondary school by type of junior school, social class and sex of child*

	HIGHER SOCIAL CLASS*				LOWER SOCIAL CLASS			
	Boys		Girls		Boys		Girls	
	Strea-med	Non-Strea-med	Strea-med	Non-Strea-med	Strea-med	Non-Strea-med	Strea-med	Non-Strea-med
Secondary Modern	13%	10%	16%	11%	34%†	25%	41%†	33%
Comprehensive	18%	18%	21%	24%	19%	24%	14%	24%
Technical	16%	16%	8%	5%	19%	17%	13%	9%
Grammar	53%†	56%†	55%†	60%†	28%	34%†	32%	34%†
Number of parents giving information (100%)	513	432	490	447	392	411	417	377

*For definition, see Table 12.1, page 171.
†Most popular choice

Comparing the rank order of choices made by parents of children of similar ability in the two types of school, it was found that at the above average level[1] grammar school was clearly the most popular choice among all groups (see Table 12.6, Appendix 6).

Among higher social class parents, almost the same percentage in both types of school chose grammar school, although a significantly higher percentage ($P < 0.05$) of lower social class parents of above average boys in streamed schools chose the grammar school (see Table 12.6b, Appendix 6).

[1] Ability levels based on teachers' ratings.

It is interesting to note, however, that a higher percentage of lower social class parents of bright boys in non-streamed schools preferred the comprehensive to the grammar school and more or less equal proportions in the two types of school chose the secondary modern. There were no statistically significant differences in the type of school chosen by parents of lower social class girls of above average ability.

At the average level of ability,[1] grammar school remained first choice of all higher social class groups, but among lower social class parents the secondary modern was the most popular, except for parents of non-streamed boys, for whom grammar school was still the most popular choice.

At the below average level of ability there was a tendency for parents of children in non-streamed schools to have slightly higher aspirations for their secondary education (see Table 12.6, Appendix 6): grammar school remained the first choice of higher social class parents with sons in non-streamed schools, but was the *least* chosen type of school among parents with boys in streamed schools; these parents showing a preference for the secondary modern. Higher social class parents of below average girls in non-streamed schools chose the comprehensive school first, with grammar school a close second; those with girls of similar ability in streamed schools, however, showed a clear preference for the secondary modern school with grammar school only third choice. While the secondary modern school was first choice of all lower social class parents of below average children, it was much more popular among those with children in streamed schools. Parents with below average children in non-streamed schools were more likely to hope for grammar, or comprehensive places, rather than confine their aspirations to the secondary modern school (see Table 12.6, Appendix 6).

Streaming therefore seemed to have had the effect of depressing the aspirations of parents with children of limited academic ability. Bearing in mind that no differences were found in the ability ratings given by parents of streamed and non-streamed children, it seems that the mere fact of a child being in anything but the top stream has the effect of lowering parental expectations and aspirations for a grammar school place. While a parent of a non-streamed child may be aware that the child is 'not so good' or only 'average', he may feel that his chances of success have not been prematurely limited by his being placed in a low stream.

[1] Ability levels based on teachers' ratings.

Age of leaving

Parents were also asked to state at what age they would like their children to leave secondary school.

TABLE 12.4: *Age of leaving desired by parents*

AGE OF LEAVING	HIGHER SOCIAL CLASS†		LOWER SOCIAL CLASS	
	Boys	*Girls*	*Boys*	*Girls*
15	9%	12%	34%	35%
16	25%	32%	37%	38%
17+	66%	56%	29%	27%
Number of parents giving information (100%)	941	936	802	815

†For definition, see Table 12.1, page 177.

Comparing the choices of parents of children of perceived equivalent ability levels[1] in the two types of school, it was found that at the above average level, a higher percentage of parents of children in streamed schools chose a later leaving age (17+). In the case of higher social class girls and lower social class boys, these differences were statistically significant ($P < 0.05$ and $P < 0.01$ respectively, see Table 12.7 in Appendix 6).

Little difference was found in the age of leaving chosen by parents of children of average ability in the two types of school, but at the below average ability level, there was a tendency for parents with children in streamed schools to choose an earlier leaving age than their counterparts with children in non-streamed schools, and in the case of parents of higher social class girls this difference was significant ($P < 0.05$, see Table 12.7 in Appendix 6). This finding is consistent with that which indicated that parents of children of below average ability in non-streamed schools had somewhat higher aspirations for their secondary education.

Not unexpectedly, a close relationship existed between the type of secondary school chosen and the school leaving age expected. Parents who wished their children to go to grammar school were also prepared for them to stay at school longer: 18 was the most popular age of leaving for boys and girls of both social classes whose parents

[1] See footnote, page 179.

181

had chosen grammar school. Those who chose technical or comprehensive education also tended to want their children to remain at school beyond the statutory leaving age, with 16 being the most popular choice in almost all cases. The secondary modern school appeared to have the least 'holding power' of all types of secondary school with 47 per cent of higher social class parents and 62 per cent of lower social class parents wishing their children to leave at the age of 15.

As Table 12.4 shows there were marked social class differences in the expected age of leaving, with higher social class parents showing greater willingness for their children to remain at school longer. As with choice of secondary school these differences remained even when each category of ability (as indicated by parents) was examined separately.

Whatever the type of secondary school chosen, the same social class differences in desired leaving age were found to persist. These were particularly marked among the parents who had chosen grammar schools and among those boys whose parents preferred comprehensives. For example, 44 per cent of lower social class parents who wished their sons to go to grammar school also wanted them to leave at or before 16, compared with only 16 per cent of higher social class parents. In the. case of comprehensive schools, 41 per cent of higher social class parents were willing for their sons to remain at school until 18, as against only 15 per cent of lower social class parents.

More boys' than girls' parents were prepared to let them remain at school until 18, especially among higher social class parents (see Table 12.4). Bearing in mind the tendency for parents to rate their girls as more capable in terms of ability, this finding perhaps reflects the greater importance attached by parents to the education of their sons.

The choice of further education

Information on parents' aspirations for further education or training for their children was obtained by asking them if they wanted their children to enter university or training college, go to a technical college for one or two years, take up an apprenticeship of some kind, or to have no further training of any sort.

As Table 12.5 shows, university was easily the most popular choice of higher social class parents of boys and girls. Lower social class parents on the other hand, clearly favoured apprenticeship for

Attitudes of Parents

their sons, and a one-year technical college course for their daughters although the preferences for girls were less concentrated. Only in the case of lower social class girls did a substantial number of parents express a wish for no further training.

TABLE 12.5: *Type of further training preferred*

| | HIGHER SOCIAL CLASS† | | LOWER SOCIAL CLASS | |
	Boys	Girls	Boys	Girls
None	1%	4%	4%	12%
Apprenticeship	26%	13%	60%	26%
Technical College—1 year	7%	29%	5%	34%
Technical College—2 years	20%	9%	15%	9%
University/College—3+ yrs.	46%	45%	16%	19%
Number of parents giving information (100%)	928	911	785	763

*For definition, see Table 12.1, page 177.

It was found that the overall pattern of choice of further training made by parents of children in streamed and non-streamed schools was very similar.

Comparing the aspirations of parents of children of equivalent ability[1] in the two types of school it was again found that, at the above average level, there was a tendency for more parents of children in streamed schools to hope for university or college places than their counterparts with children in non-streamed schools, although this difference was significant only in the case of higher social class girls ($P<0.05$, see Table 12.8 in Appendix 6). Little difference emerged in the percentage choosing university among parents of children of average ability in the two types of school.

At the below average level, however, higher social class parents of boys in non-streamed schools were more likely to choose university or three year college than were those with sons in streamed schools ($P<0.01$).

As in all previous cases there were marked social class differences in the choice of further training. Higher social class parents were

[1] See footnote page 179.

183

more likely to opt for further training, especially in terms of university education. It is interesting to note that hope for a three year college or university education appeared, unlike the other alternatives, to be influenced at this age almost solely by social class, and hardly at all by the child's sex.

Again, it was found that parents of different social classes had different aspirations for their children even when their estimates of their child's ability were the same. Of parents who thought of their children as 'very good' or 'good' at school work, roughly twice as many higher social class as lower social class hoped for a subsequent university education. Higher social class parents who regarded their children as above average in ability tended to restrict their choice of further training to a three year college course or to university; the lower the perceived ability level, the more their choices became dispersed among the alternatives. With lower social class parents the opposite occurred. The higher the rated ability, the more scattered were the choices; those who rated their children as average or below confined their aspirations to apprenticeship.

Not unexpectedly in view of the other associations established, a strong link existed between secondary school preferred and choice of further training. Grammar school was regarded as the main route to a university education, with the comprehensive as a possible alternative. Apprenticeship was seen as the most likely follow-up to a secondary modern education.

Conclusions

This study has provided some evidence that parents' aspirations for their children's educational and vocational future are influenced by the type of junior school attended by their children, and that the direction of this influence (i.e. either raising or depressing aspirations) is related to the child's ability level.

Attendance at a streamed school of children of above average ability appeared to raise parents' aspirations, and particularly the aspirations of lower social class parents.

Attendance at a streamed school appeared to have the opposite effect on the hopes of parents of children of below average ability. Compared with their non-streamed counterparts, these parents had lower aspirations for their children's secondary education in that fewer hoped for a grammar school place and more opted for the secondary modern school; also they were more likely to choose an earlier leaving age and to be less ambitious in their choice of further training. Aspirations and expectations are closely linked, and the early classification of pupils which streaming implies seems to be interpreted by parents as an indication of what the educational future of their children is likely to be. Placement in a top stream seems to make parents more ambitious for their children, but allocation to a low stream is regarded by parents as a sign that their children's academic future is strictly limited.

Greater differences in aspirations were found among parents of children of different ability levels in streamed schools than in non-streamed schools. The difference in the parental aspirations for average and below average children, in particular, was much greater in streamed than in non-streamed schools (see Tables 12.6, 12.7, 12.8 in Appendix 6).

The results of this survey produced some evidence to support the claim that parents have higher educational aspirations for their sons than for their daughters. They were more willing for boys to remain at school until 17 or 18, and showed a tendency to choose selective secondary schools (grammar and technical) for their sons rather than for their daughters.

As each point in the analysis, lower social class parents appeared to demand less of the education system than higher social class parents. Fewer desired grammar school places for their children, fewer were willing for them to stay at school beyond the statutory leaving age, and their hopes for further education or training were considerably more limited. Even within each level of rated ability, lower social class parents expressed lower aspirations in each area studied. There thus appears to be a pattern of progressive self-elimination of lower social class children by their parents at each stage of the educational system, which clearly contributes to the 'wastage of ability' so consistently reported in investigations in this field.

It should be emphasized here that this survey was based on parents' intentions; the follow-up study through secondary school will reveal what actually happens in terms of leaving age and type of further training.

References

DEPARTMENT OF EDUCATION AND SCIENCE: CENTRAL ADVISORY COUNCIL FOR EDUCATION (ENGLAND). (1967). *Children and their Primary Schools* (Plowden Report). London: H.M. Stationery Office.

CHAPTER 13

Occupational Aspirations of Children

MUCH has been written of the self-fulfilling prophecy—the tendency for children to conform to what is expected of them. Streaming is claimed by some to depress the aspirations of children in lower ability streams and increase those of children in higher ability streams. Non-streaming, on the other hand, is often thought to increase the aspirations of lower ability children. It might, of course, be argued that streaming makes children's aspirations more realistic in relation to their ability. In order to test these hypotheses the children in streamed and non-streamed schools were questioned about their occupational aspirations.

All the children, at the end of their fourth year in the junior school, were asked: 'What would you like to do when you grow up?'[1] Since the work involved in coding this open-ended question was considerable, only a random sample was taken. The responses of just over 2,000 children were recorded (see Appendix 4)[2].

Status of occupational aspiration

Since his ability and his parents' social class were found to be related to the child's occupational aspiration, it was decided to hold constant these two factors while examining the responses of boys and girls in the two types of school. Whether a child chose to be an architect or a doctor was of no particular interest at this stage of the inquiry. What was of interest was whether children of similar ability and background had career aspirations of a higher or lower occupational status in the two types of school. For example, would children of average ability from similar types of home background have higher or lower aspirations in terms of occupational choice in the streamed or the non-streamed school? The occupations desired

---

[1] This question was also asked at the end of the third year; the information obtained then was used to provide a coding frame for the fourth year data.

[2] The same sample was used in the assessment of divergent thinking and interests—see Chapters 6 and 8.

by the children were categorized and allocated to one of three occupational status groups: (*a*) professional, (*b*) skilled, (*c*) semi-skilled or unskilled. The occupations were graded on the basis of the *Registrar-General's Classification of Occupations* and Reiss' (1961) *Scales of Occupational Prestige*.

For the purposes of analysis the children were allocated to one of three groups according to their father's social class or occupational status and to a further one of three groups on the basis of ability.[1] Nine groups resulted from this and in each, comparisons were made between streamed and non-streamed schools.

No significant differences were found between the occupational status of career aspirations of children in streamed and non-streamed schools. When the responses of boys and girls were examined separately in terms of the above still no differences were found. From this it can be concluded that in general, streaming or non-streaming *per se* makes no difference to the status or aspirational level of occupational choice of children of comparable ability and similar home background.

Occupation aspired to in streamed and non-streamed schools

Next, the actual occupations desired by boys and girls were examined. First an overall comparison was made, and, as can be seen from the following table, the percentages choosing each occupation ran almost parallel in streamed and non-streamed schools.

For boys, the most desired occupation was to be a professional footballer or other type of sportsman; this was the only career aspiration which was significantly more popular in non-streamed than streamed schools. It is difficult to say why this should be so. One possible reason is that streamed schools concentrate more on a select few (see Chapter 11) and as a consequence dampen the enthusiasm of some of their boys. Another possible explanation is that more of the non-streamed schools were in areas with a First Division team which may have increased the popularity of football.

The second most popular choice for boys was the Forces, which included Merchant Navy, and if air-pilot and navigator are also included in this category, the percentage increases to 15 per cent.

Engineers/Mechanics accounted for nine per cent and seven per cent of the choices in streamed and non-streamed schools respectively. This usually consisted of stating a desire to be an 'engineer', but

---

[1] Children were assigned to ability groups on the basis of Reading test scores.

some boys were more specific and expressed their wish to be an electrical engineer, motor mechanic and so on. Transport drivers of various kinds, especially bus, lorry and train, were the choice of seven per cent and four per cent of boys in streamed and non-streamed school respectively.

These were the major categories. The specific occupations given in the table accounted for 82 per cent. The other choices, although interesting in themselves, were too infrequent to form a category (less than one per cent), and were therefore allocated to an 'others' category according to occupational status.

Turning now to the choice of the girls in Table 13.1, the first point to note is that there were no significant differences between streamed and non-streamed schools.

TABLE 13.1: *Occupational aspirations of fourth year junior school boys and girls (10-11 years) in streamed and non-streamed schools*

Boys

DESIRED OCCUPATION	NON-STREAMED	STREAMED	TOTAL
Footballer/Sportsman	28%	19%	23%
Forces and Merchant Navy	11%	9%	10%
Air-pilot/Navigator	5%	6%	5%
Engineer/Mechanic	7%	9%	8%
Driver (bus/train/lorry)	4%	7%	5%
Policeman	3%	5%	4%
Scientist	4%	3%	3%
Naturalist/Zoologist/Zoo-keeper	3%	3%	3%
Teacher	3%	2%	2%
Architect	2%	3%	3%
Veterinary Surgeon	2%	2%	2%
Farmer	2%	†	2%
Carpenter	2%	3%	3%
Electrician	1%	3%	2%
Fireman	1%	2%	2%
Builder/Decorator	1%	1%	1%
Artist/Art teacher	1%	2%	2%
Doctor	1%	1%	1%
Shop assistant	1%	1%	1%
Other professions	4%	4%	4%
Other skilled	7%	7%	7%
Other semi- and unskilled	7%	8%	7%
Number of boys giving information (100%)	430	472	902

Note: † = less than 0·5%

Girls

DESIRED OCCUPATION	NON-STREAMED	STREAMED	TOTAL
Hairdresser	15%	16%	16%
Nurse	15%	14%	14%
Teacher	14%	13%	13%
Secretary/Office worker	11%	15%	13%
Shop assistant	6%	5%	6%
Air-hostess	5%	6%	5%
Work with animals	4%	4%	4%
Horse rider or instructor	3%	1%	2%
Veterinary Surgeon	2%	3%	2%
Dancer/Dancing teacher	1%	3%	2%
Fashion designer	3%	1%	2%
Actress/Film star	1%	2%	2%
Dressmaker	2%	1%	1%
Swimmer/Swimming instructor	2%	1%	2%
Artist	1%	1%	1%
Librarian	1%	1%	1%
Doctor	†	1%	1%
Telephonist	1%	†	1%
Model	†	†	1%
Other professions	5%	2%	3%
Other skilled	5%	4%	4%
Other semi- and unskilled	3%	6%	4%
Number of girls giving information (100%)	416	483	899

Note: † =less than 0·5%.

The second point is that in contrast to the boys, the girls were less diffuse in their choice: half chose to be either a hairdresser, a nurse, a teacher or a secretary/office worker. Surprisingly, only a few chose the more glamorous jobs. The number giving their choice as 'pop-star', for example, was too small to include as a separate category; other glamorous jobs such as a horse-rider or a dancer, both of which included teachers of these skills, or a model, were chosen by two per cent or less.

Occupational aspiration and ability

The occupational aspiration of boys was less influenced by ability than that of girls. Above average boys in both types of school chose in order of preference, footballer or other sportsman,

189

air-pilot, and the Forces. For average boys, the most popular choice was again footballer, followed by the Forces. Footballer, too, was the most popular occupation among below average boys, with engineer/mechanic (13 per cent) as second choice in streamed schools (eight per cent chose this in non-streamed schools), and the Forces (11 per cent) coming second in non-streamed schools (eight per cent chose the Forces in streamed schools). (See Table 13.2, Appendix 6.)

Choice of occupation for the girls was clearly associated with ability. The pattern for girls of above average ability in both types of school was the same: teacher was the most popular choice, followed by nurse and then secretarial or office work.

There was, however, a difference between the schools for girls of average ability: secretarial or office work was more often chosen by average girls in streamed schools (21 per cent) than in non-streamed schools (10 per cent), this being the first choice in streamed schools. Hairdresser was the most popular choice in non-streamed schools (16 per cent) even though more girls chose this occupation in streamed schools (19 per cent). Teacher was the second choice for average girls in non-streamed schools (12 per cent) closely followed by nurse (11 per cent). Nurse (13 per cent) occupied third place and teacher came fourth (7 per cent) for average girls in streamed schools.

More or less the same choices were given by girls of below average ability in the two types of school. Hairdresser was the most desired occupation, followed by nurse, secretarial or office work and shop-assistant. (See Table 13.2, Appendix 6.)

Conclusions

Whether the desired occupation was based upon fantasy or otherwise, there was little difference between the choices of children in streamed and non-streamed schools.

The aspirations of boys seemed to be much more unrealistic than those of girls and ability had less effect on their choice. The majority of boys did not seem able to dissociate their major interest, football, from their occupational choice (see Chapter 8) and the vast number of those desiring to be professional footballers or sportsmen bore no resemblance to the actual or possible number and indicated the fantasy level or idealized nature of their choice. The numbers of boys desiring occupations other than that of professional footballer or sportsman were similar to those reported in the literature concerning secondary school boys (Veness, 1962).

190

Girls' career aspirations seemed to be influenced considerably by ability but the effect of being in a streamed or non-streamed school appeared to have little influence. Comparing the results obtained with secondary school girls (Veness, 1962) it seemed that some of the jobs, such as hairdresser, teacher, air-hostess, or work with animals, were over-chosen, and that secretarial or office work was under-chosen. The proportions choosing nursing, including children's nurse, were remarkably similar at the two ages.

Although parents' educational aspirations for their children appeared to be influenced by the type of school attended (see Chapter 12), this was not true of the children's own occupational aspirations. This may have been because the children were un-realistic in their choice and their chosen occupations were simply fantasies or daydreams, but in any case the fact remains that stream-ing or non-streaming had little effect.[1]

References

Registrar-General's Classification of Occupations. (1960). London: H.M. Stationery Office.

REISS, A. J., *et al.* (1961). *Occupations and Social Status.* New York: Free Press of Glencoe.

VENESS, T. (1962). *School Leavers—Their Aspirations and Expectations.* London: Methuen.

---

[1] An analysis of the non-streamed schools by type of teacher indicated very little difference between the occupational choice of children having a Type 1 or Type 2 teacher. One interesting point did emerge, however: more boys wanted to be a policeman if they were taught by a Type 2 teacher than a Type 1 teacher.

CHAPTER 14

An Intensive Study of Six Schools[1]

DURING the final year of the Streaming Project's longitudinal study, six of the schools in the main sample were selected for further, more intensive study. These comprised three streamed and three non-streamed schools.

Earlier results had suggested that teachers' attitudes and methods might exert a greater influence on pupils' performance than the actual organization of the school. Matters demanding close investigation were the variations in attitudes towards children of different ability levels and social backgrounds, the extent to which teachers support the aims associated with the type of organization under which they work and how far they succeed in fulfilling or modifying these aims in the classroom. One of the chief aims of the intensive study was to throw some light on these questions.

Since it had been found that teachers in non-streamed schools in particular did not necessarily favour their school's organizational policy it was decided to select three non-streamed schools on the basis of the proportion of their staff in apparent support of the prevailing system of organization.[2] The *non-streamed* schools selected were as follows:

Beech Grove. The majority of staff were in favour of non-streaming and only one member of staff favoured streaming.

Oak Lane. Only the head favoured non-streaming; all the staff were in favour of streaming.

---

[1] Elsa Ferri was primarily responsible for writing this chapter and the next and for carrying out the fieldwork on which it is based.

[2] The attitudes of *all* staff in the school were measured in the first year of the study (1964) but in later years only the attitudes of teachers of the follow-up children were assessed. These latter teachers were also classified into Type 1 and Type 2 teachers according to their attitudes and teaching methods. The proportions given above refer to the figures obtained in 1964. The picture remained much the same when teachers of the longitudinal study only were examined in terms of teacher-type: Beech Grove: 9 Type 1, 3 Type 2; Oak Lane: 2 Type 1, 8 Type 2; Ash Valley: 4 Type 1, 11 Type 2. In the streamed schools the teachers (longitudinal study) were as follows: Red Hill: 6 Type 2, 2 Type 1; Grey Ridge: 10 Type 2, 1 Type 1; Green Mount: 13 Type 2, 3 Type 1.

Ash Valley. Half the staff favoured streaming and the other half were uncertain or favoured non-streaming.

The three *streamed* schools were selected so as to roughly match the non-streamed schools in terms of socio-economic background. Since it had been suggested by the exploratory work that the number of streams per year group was an important factor in streamed schools, a two-stream (Red Hill), a three-stream (Grey Ridge) and a four-stream school (Green Mount) were selected. The majority of staff in all three streamed schools favoured streaming and could be described as Type 2 or 'typical streamers'. In each school, however, there were at least one or two Type 1 teachers ('typical non-streamers').

Thus the two kinds of school differed in their type of organization, and within the schools there was a varying range of opinion and practices among teachers. In the sections of this report which deal primarily with teachers' attitudes the schools are not described individually, but the views of teachers from the various schools have been combined to present the different extremes of opinion expressed. For obvious reasons the school names and the names given to teachers in this chapter are fictitious.

One week was spent by members of the research team in each of the schools involved in the intensive study. Information was obtained chiefly by tape-recorded semi-structured interviews with the head and individual members of staff, backed up by as much classroom observation as was possible in the time available.

The three streamed schools

Red Hill was a two-stream junior school, built in the 1950s, and serving a stable, middle-class suburban area. Material standards in the area were very high, and, according to the head, who had been at the school since it opened, the majority of parents were co-operative, interested and 'education conscious'. The children in the school reflected their materially secure backgrounds; without exception they looked healthy and well-fed and almost all wore school uniform.

Grey Ridge was a three-stream junior school serving a large corporation housing estate. The head, who had been at the school for about fifteen years, felt that, on the whole, the children in the school were materially well cared for, but home backgrounds were not particularly 'cultured'.

Green Mount was a large four-stream junior school situated on a council estate in an industrial area; most of its pupils were children of semi- or unskilled workers employed in local factories. The majority of the children looked clean and well cared for and a number wore school uniform. The present head had been at the school for only two years.

The three non-streamed schools

Oak Lane had three classes in each year group and was built in the early 1950s. It served a council estate on the outskirts of a large industrial town. The head, who had been at Oak Lane since it opened and who unstreamed the school some years ago, felt that economically the homes of the children in his school were 'fairly comfortable', but culturally, parental interest was confined mainly to 'the TV, the pub and the club'.

Beech Grove was also a three-class entry junior school and was built in the late 1950s. It was situated in a solidly middle-class suburban area and parental interest in education and all matters affecting the school was intensely keen. The school had been unstreamed since it opened; the present head had held his post for several years.

Ash Valley was a large junior school with four classes in each year group. It was built in the 1950s and was situated on a large council estate. The material standards of the children's homes were probably slightly higher than those of Oak Lane. The present head had been responsible for unstreaming the school.

How the children were allocated

(a) The Streamed Schools

The survey of organizational practices in junior schools had revealed that the most popular criterion for assigning first year pupils to classes in streamed schools was infant school records. Sixty-eight per cent of schools used this method either alone or in conjunction with some other criterion, such as a standardized intelligence test or internal examinations.

Two of the three streamed schools under study did in fact carry out their initial streaming on the basis of infant school records alone, although in Green Mount school, the children were already in streamed classes in the infant school and they simply remained in these classes when they moved up to the adjoining junior department. When the present head came to Green Mount he found that the practice in the infant school had been to stream the children on the basis of number attainment, and he had suggested that if they insisted on streaming at that stage, reading performance might be a better criterion.

At Grey Ridge School initial allocation to classes was made on the basis of infant school records. These children, however, had not been streamed at any stage in the nearby infants school: classes there were formed on the basis of a 'family group' system, so that the age range in any one class was from five to seven years. At the end of the children's final year in the infant school, the headmistress sent the junior school a record card covering each child's progress while in the school. On the basis of this information the headmaster carried out a 'tentative streaming' during the holidays. In October of their first term in the junior school the children were given standardized non-verbal and reading tests, and if any 'obvious mistakes' in initial allocation were subsequently revealed, children were transferred appropriately at half-term.

The children who came to Red Hill Junior School, like those at Green Mount, had been in streamed classes during their time in the adjoining infant department. Originally the junior school accepted the class placings allocated by the infant department, but had changed the procedure as a result of 'pressure from parents'. The children were subsequently split into two groups alphabetically when they came into the junior school, and then given the school's 'own particular test'. This test included reading, spelling and writing, and, according to the head, 'a test to see if they are quick on the uptake or have to be told what to do a few times before they get the message'. At the end of a fortnight during which all these assessments took place, the children were divided into two streams, or, as the head preferred to call them, 'faster and slower workers'. A fortnight was the maximum time it took to 'sort the children out'. The head felt that this procedure worked very satisfactorily and had been accepted by parents as a fair method of allocation.

Since at neither Green Mount nor Grey Ridge had standardized tests been used at any stage in the infants school, it can be seen that in all three schools initial allocation to streams was based on assessments which were to a greater or lesser degree subjective, i.e. teachers' estimates of children's progress or internally devised tests whose validity or reliability were unknown.

As with the initial allocation to classes, the decision to transfer a child from one stream to another seemed to be based, in each of the three schools, on similarly subjective criteria, such as teachers' recommendations and/or the results of internal school examinations.

The table below shows the number of transfers in each direction which took place within one year group of children during their time in the schools concerned.

TABLE 14.1: *Number of transfers in the three streamed schools*

	GREEN MOUNT				GREY RIDGE				RED HILL			
	†Prom.	*Dem.*	*No. in Group*	*% transferred*	*Prom.*	*Dem.*	*No. in Group*	*% transferred*	*Prom.*	*Dem.*	*No. in Group*	*% transferred*
1964	7	5	159	7·5	2	3	93	5·4	1	1	63	3·3
1965	9	5	143	9·8	2	0	85	2·4	0	0	52	0
1966	5	0	138	3·6	1	1	81	2·5	3‡	0	49	6·1

†Prom.=Promoted   Dem.=Demoted

‡1 child a recent arrival in the school

In spite of size differences in the schools, it can be seen from the table that considerably more transfers took place at Green Mount than at the two other schools. (The difference in the pattern of transfer at Green Mount in 1966 may or may not reflect the policy of the new head.) The practice at Green Mount was for the teacher to make a recommendation to the head, who then studied the child's work and progress. It was claimed, also, that parents were 'consulted', although this seemed to consist merely of informing the parents that the school felt that transfer would be in the child's interest. Teachers at Green Mount varied in their readiness to recommend children for transfer. One teacher claimed she had had 'several' moved from the A- to the B-stream. Another member of staff was much more wary about moving children: 'If the teacher is absolutely *positive*—I don't think I've ever done it—I feel it is better for a child to be top of the D than lagging in the C'.

Very little re-grading appeared to take place at Red Hill, where the head seemed to think of transfer in terms of movement between one group and another *within* the class. One member of staff was disturbed that there was 'practically no transfer' in the school, and felt that 'if one is going to have a streamed school I think there *should* be'. This teacher felt that there was a considerable overlap between streams in terms of ability in all year groups, and this opinion was echoed by several other members of staff (see Table 14.2).

The official policy regarding transfer at Grey Ridge was that the top one or two and the bottom one or two pupils in each class (on the results of internal examinations) were nominated for transfer at the end of each school year. The head emphasized, however, that the decision to move a child or not was influenced less by his or her class position than by the views of himself and the teachers concerned on the probable effect of any change on the child's confidence and subsequent progress. In this school too, a number of teachers felt that not enough transfer between classes took place and that they would like to see a more flexible system, especially in year groups, in which they felt that the overlap of ability between classes was considerable.

The following tables (pages 198-200) show the overlap between streams in all three streamed schools in terms of the standardized scores obtained on a reading test at 7+ and at 10+.

From these tables (pages 198-200) it can be seen that there is a considerable overlap between adjacent streams in all three schools, and in Grey Ridge and Green Mount there is also a clear overlap between the A- and C-streams at both 7+ and 10+.

(b) The Non-Streamed Schools

The survey of types of organization in junior schools had disclosed that age of pupil was the most commonly used single criterion for assigning pupils to classes at 7+ in non-streamed schools. This method was, in fact, employed by all three of the non-streamed schools under study; the children had been placed in classes according to age in the infant schools and remained in these classes when they moved up to the juniors. In each year group, therefore, classes represented either the oldest, middle or youngest children in the age group, with an age range in each class of three or four months, according to the number of classes in the year group.

Only at Beech Grove was any doubt expressed as to the efficacy of this method of allocation and an attempt made to modify the system introduced. It had been noticed over a period of years at Beech Grove that the older children in the year group tended to be more advanced and mature than their younger counterparts. Several teachers felt that a random allocation of children to classes would give more truly parallel groups.

TABLE 14.2: *Standardized reading test scores obtained by the same children at 7+ and 10+ at Red Hill School*

Red Hill

Standardized score	7+		10+	
	A-stream	*B-stream*	*A-stream*	*B-stream*
140+			2	
135–9			–	
130–4	1		3	
125–9	3		–	
120–4	3	2	2	
115–9	1	–	6	3
110–4	2	–	1	2
105–9	3	4	2	2
100–4	3	4	1	3
95–9	1	4	–	2
90–4		1	–	–
85–9		3	1	2
80–4		1		2
75–9				–
70–4				2
70—				
N†	17	19	18	18
Mean score	114·35	100·16	118·72	98·39
Number in class at 7+:	32	29	Number in class at 10+: 35	31

† To be included a child had to have a reading test score at 7+ and at 10+.

TABLE 14.3: *Standardized reading test scores obtained by the same children at 7+ and 10+ at Grey Ridge School*

Grey Ridge

Standard- ized score	7+			10+		
	A-stream	B-stream	C-stream	A-stream	B-stream	C-stream
140+				2		
135–9	1			–		
130–4	–			–		
125–9	–			3		
120–4	1			3		
115–9	7			5		
110–4	3			7	1	
105–9	4	3		3	3	
100–4	4	3		3	3	1
95–9	5	4		1	5	–
90–4	2	5	1	5	9	2
85–9	1	6	3		2	3
80–4	3	2	3		1	6
75–9	–	1	2		1	3
70–4	1		3			
70—			4			
N†	32	24	16	32	25	15
Mean score	103·88	93·25	78·06	111·88	95·40	84·67
Number in class at 7+:	39	31	22	Number in class at 10+: 37	34	19

† To be included a child had to have a reading test score at 7+ and at 10+.

TABLE 14.4: *Standardized reading test scores obtained by the same children at 7+ and 10+ at Green Mount School*

Green Mount

Stand-ardized score	7+				10+			
	A-stream	B-stream	C-stream	D-stream	A-stream	B-stream	C-stream	D-stream
140+	1							
135–9	1							
130–4	–	1						
125–9	1	–			1	1		
120–4	2	1			3	–		
115–9	9	1			4	1		
110–4	9	3			6	4		
105–9	3	7			5	7	4	
100–4	1	13	3		7	5	2	
95–9	1	5	6		1	8	4	1
90–4	1		15	4		3	8	2
85–9			2	5		2	6	–
80–4			3	5		1	4	1
75–9				4			1	5
70–4				4				2
70—								12
N†	29	31	29	22	27	32	29	23
Mean score	114·59	105·39	92·69	82·23	110·33	101·84	92·52	75·30
Number in class at 7+:	42	45	41	31	Number in class at 10+: 36	42	38	30

† To be included a child had to have a reading test score at 7+ and at 10+.

How the teachers were allocated

The head of a junior school enjoys virtual autonomy in the use he makes of his staff. His policy in the allocation of teachers to classes may vary from a deliberate regular interchange of staff between different age and ability levels to a more static situation where teachers remain for an indefinite period with a particular class.

(a) The Streamed Schools

One of the arguments advanced for non-streaming is that it has a beneficial effect on staff relations and morale, since no teacher can be favoured or discriminated against by being compelled to spend a disproportionate time with a particular ability level. Certainly none of the staff in the streamed schools in the intensive study expressed unanimous satisfaction at the system of staff allocation in operation.

The head of Green Mount was fairly new to the school, and had so far made only tentative alterations to a system of teacher allocation which he found profoundly disturbing. His own view was that while a preference for teaching younger or older children was perfectly acceptable, a teacher should be able and prepared to teach any ability level. The situation at Green Mount until his arrival had been very static: the A-stream teachers, and to a lesser extent the 'B' teachers, had kept the same streams for as long as 15 years, while there were regular vacancies for 'C' and 'D' teachers. It was obvious, the head felt, that some teachers thought of themselves as 'A teachers' and were highly satisfied with the prevailing situation: 'I've had 4A since 1954—some of the happiest years of my teaching life'— A-stream teacher.

Teachers of lower streams, however, were less content. One D-stream teacher complained of the tendency to get the same class year after year. 'I think all heads let teachers stick with the D's if they're mug enough not to complain.' Another 'D' teacher felt that those taking C and D classes would like to move, but 'the others seem to have been there so long you don't like to ask'. Even those teachers who felt specially committed to helping the more backward children considered that to be allocated a C or D class every year was an unfair burden.

A similar situation existed at Grey Ridge where, although the head maintained that there was 'no rigidity' in the system of staff allocation, a number of teachers had stayed with the same class for a considerable time. One A-stream teacher had been firmly ensconced in this position for the last fifteen years. He admitted that he preferred to stay where he was and, while agreeing that teachers should be able to adapt to any age or ability range, he felt that 'if you're doing well somewhere, I don't really see any point in moving'.

Another teacher, who had had a C-stream for 'most of the time' that he had spent at Grey Ridge, felt that some teachers in the school had 'a label round their necks', and that it was 'very frustrating to be kept with the same stream year after year, as goes on here'. He believed that teachers should be moved around regularly whether they welcomed the change or not, since 'you get stale at teaching more easily than in anything else I can think of'. This teacher felt that the A-stream teachers at Grey Ridge were 'very happy in their jobs'; the B- and C-stream teachers on the other hand would welcome more movement of staff. 'The A's have more marking but we have stresses that they don't have!'

Unlike the head of Green Mount, the head of Red Hill considered efficiency with different *ability* levels rather than with different age groups to be the deciding factor in teacher allocation. He felt that some teachers were best suited to taking the 'fast, quick-witted streams' and 'it would irk them to have the slower ones'. On the other hand there were teachers who were more sympathetic to the slower child and 'it suits their personalities to work at that pace'.

Another feature of the system of staff allocation at Red Hill was that the teacher who took the third year 'A' class moved with them into the fourth year. Although the head claimed that this practice was attempted with both classes in the year group, there was no evidence that it had been the case with the 'B' classes, and one teacher referred to the practice as having been introduced 'especially with the top class as it was helpful for the 11+'.

It emerged that the two most experienced members of staff at Red Hill had for several years taken the third and fourth year 'A' classes consecutively in the manner described above. Both, however, felt that it was undesirable for the same teacher to have the same class year after year. Although one admitted that while he disapproved in theory, in practice he was highly satisfied with the situation as it affected him personally: 'I don't *approve* of the scheme whereby the same teachers take the top "A" class all the time—it's not fair on the other teachers. But I've had "A" classes all the way and—being purely selfish—it's very nice! I've been spoiled—and I love it.'

From the comments of the teachers in the three schools it was clear that where the system of staff allocation was relatively static, it had led to feelings of resentment on the part of teachers of lower streams. Dissatisfaction and frustration invariably focussed on the fact that certain teachers became entrenched as 'A teachers' and had a monopoly of bright children. While many teachers were willing to take the more backward children, few wanted to take them all the time. That A-stream teachers enjoyed higher status was perceived by teachers of all streams—'It was a question of the disciplinarians being *relegated* to the C-streams' (C-stream teacher). In all three schools, teachers of lower streams agreed that 'movement would encourage teachers—they wouldn't be able to say "you couldn't get an A class at that school—that's why I left".'

(b) The Non-Streamed Schools

In a non-streamed school where age is the only factor which differentiates classes, the question of staff allocation is less likely to lead to comparisons and friction. In all three non-streamed schools head and staff agreed that teacher allocation was much simpler when the streaming factor was absent. 'In a streamed school you always got someone coming along saying: "Can I have the A class again?" The poor young people are given the E-stream and told it's the opportunity class!'

To the teachers in the non-streamed schools, especially those who had had no experience of streamed schools, the question of staff allocation was of little importance. At Beech Grove it was summed up as 'very democratic—the head asks for your preferences and gives you what you want if he can'. Only at Oak Lane did the head adhere closely to a policy of moving staff around regularly. He felt that teachers were basically very conservative and would, if allowed, opt to remain in the same situation where the pattern was familiar. This, however, led quickly to staleness and should be avoided at all costs for the good of both teachers and children.

How the teachers saw the children[1]

Teachers' attitudes towards, and evaluation of, different types of children tend to be expressed in terms of social background and ability level.

The way teachers feel about children of different backgrounds and abilities is related to their views of the aims of education and of their

---

[1] For an investigation of infant teachers' assessments of and attitudes towards their pupils' home backgrounds, attributes and other characteristics, see Goodacre (1968).

role as educators. For the 'knowledge-centred' teacher, the goal of education is the acquisition of information and the attainment of set academic standards; the function of the teacher is to impart this information and his efficiency is measured in terms of his pupils' academic success.

At the other extreme is the 'child-centred' teacher who believes that the aim of education is to develop to the full the interests and potentials of each individual child. This view was summed up by the head of Ash Valley: 'The aim of education is to draw people out, not cram things in'.

The 'Knowledge-Centred' Teachers

Teachers falling into the first category tended to favour children of high ability who came from a home background where academic success was highly valued, and a positive attitude to school was instilled by the parents.[1] The rapid visible progress made by bright children gave satisfaction to the teacher, who saw them as keen, eager to learn and responsive—'children—I'm speaking mainly about *bright* children—*want* to learn'. Academic results were the crucial factor for these teachers—one A-stream teacher went as far as to say that, since many of his current A class were not really 'A' standard, 'only about 10 children in the class were really worth teaching!'

A number of teachers also expressed the belief that a high level of general ability was associated with superiority in all fields. One Red Hill teacher expressed surprise that most of the school's current football team were boys from the B class—'It's normally the other way round—if you've got it "up there" you've got it elsewhere'.

Dull children were regarded as not only less able but also less interested in non-academic school activities. Several teachers at Grey Ridge drew attention to the greater interest and participation of A-stream children in school activities such as the recorder group, which was composed predominantly of 'A' children, with a few B's. On one occasion a C-stream child had put in an appearance, but had never returned. C-stream children, it was felt, were 'just not interested' in this sort of activity, or in the more common pursuits of the brighter children, such as reading, music or stamp collecting.

The inability of less able children to approach the standards by which such teachers measure progress and success led in many cases

[1] Goodacre (1968) found that pupils from middle class areas were more likely to be perceived by their teachers as 'quiet', 'serious' and 'hardworking'. Children in lower working class areas, however, were more often described as 'talkative', 'generous', 'humorous', 'enterprising' and 'lazy'.

to a dislike of teaching these children. Several teachers intimated that they would find teaching the slow child irksome—'I wouldn't like the lack of production of a finished article when I had done my stint of teaching'—and would be irritated by the need to give individual attention to the more backward ones 'who can't even find the right page—I think it's dreadful!'

There was also a tendency among teachers who favoured the bright child to equate low ability or backwardness with laziness. One teacher felt that a large number of the less able children were simply 'apathetic types who just don't want to know'. The same opinion was held by one of the heads who claimed that 'you always get a minority who have a built-in resistance to learning. I don't think they would benefit from *any* sort of education'.

The unfavourable attitudes of many 'knowledge-centred' teachers towards dull children were expressed not only in terms of their inability to achieve certain academic standards, but focused also on behaviour and attitudes which, these teachers felt, characterized children who were of limited ability and who came from lower social backgrounds (see Appendix 2).

The association between ability and social class was clearly apparent in the larger streamed schools. At Green Mount, the four-stream school, the majority of 'A' children wore school uniform, but the proportion decreased as one proceeded 'down-stream'. In the D-streams were concentrated the rather 'scruffy' minority who were noticeable in the school. At Grey Ridge, too, the A-stream children looked neat and well cared for, while a number of 'C' children appeared poorly dressed and less well-nourished. A number of teachers expressed open hostility towards children, and parents, whose way of life and values were often quite alien to those which the teacher upheld. Strong disapproval was directed at parental standards by a number of teachers in each of the schools in which a large proportion of children came from lower social class backgrounds—'They can't handle money properly—they spend it in the wrong way—on drink and cigarettes'.[1] One teacher felt that these 'pure council house types' displayed complete indifference towards school and teachers—'I think they not only resent but *despise* the learning you have yourself—they don't want their children to know'. It was felt that such attitudes had been adopted by the children, resulting in an 'inbred suspicion' of teachers and antagonism towards school.

[1] Goodacre (1968), pages 24–5.

Many teachers commented on the poorer standards of behaviour which they perceived in children from such home backgrounds. 'You have to teach good manners in an area like this—they're not taught at home. They think nothing of coming into the Staff Room without knocking'. Any friendliness or permissiveness on the part of the teacher towards such children was considered impossible:

'You can't allow too much latitude with this type of child—they think it's weakness. It's because of their background—manual workers, benchworkers—they're not ready for it. It's like the black natives who want home rule and don't know what to do with it—they just fight among themselves.'

While some teachers were clearly disturbed at their inability to evoke a co-operative response from these children, others tended to dismiss it as an endemic problem which had to be coped with— 'That type simply *is* that type—however much we try to help them'.

At Red Hill, a two-stream school in a middle class area, no visible differences between A- and B-stream children were apparent. However, a number of teachers perceived substantial differences between children in upper and lower streams in terms of attitudes and behaviour which they felt reflected basic differences between children of high and low ability. One teacher remarked that while watching children going home he had noticed that 'the boys who were climbing fences, pulling down trees and destroying gardens' invariably came from the lower stream of a year group. For a number of teachers the only way to deal with these children was to 'clamp down and shock them now and then', and the most essential quality for a C- or D-stream teacher was to be a 'tough disciplinarian'; 'you give them an inch and they take the odd three miles'.

To sum up, the teacher whose approach to education was 'knowledge-centred' tended to favour the bright child, whom he regarded as more worthy of attention, more industrious and well-behaved, and whose attitudes to school and work closely resembled his own. There was a tendency to regard the perceived deficiencies of the low ability child as due to factors beyond the sphere of school and teacher—poor attitudes to school and unsatisfactory behaviour standards were products of a poor home background; backwardness or lack of progress was frequently attributed to inherent laziness, and an apparent lack of interest or participation in non-academic school activities merely reflected the child's inability to do anything well.

The great majority of teachers in the schools under study who fell into this category were found in the streamed schools.[1] Quite a number, however, in non-streamed schools[2] (nearly all at Oak Lane) also subscribed to these views and expressed dissatisfaction at having to teach all ability levels—'I've been very upset some years to find nice, promising children held back because they have to be in a class with behaviour problems'.

The 'Child-Centred' Teachers

A number of teachers in non-streamed schools, especially those at Beech Grove, fell into the 'child-centred' category. Convinced that education should aim to develop the potentialities of *all* types of children, many felt that the dull ones needed more help and attention if this aim was to be fulfilled. Several teachers of C- and D-streams at Green Mount also held these views and felt that the greatest problem facing dull or backward children was lack of self-confidence. Aware that other children were much more capable, they became 'despondent and miserable'. It was this lack of confidence, it was felt, which led to the unfavourable attitudes to school and the undesirable behaviour traits of which the other teachers complained —'They try to assert themselves in different ways to prove that they have certain qualities which the others haven't got!' These teachers emphasized the need to 'make the backward children feel important —that they have something to contribute'.

Unlike their more 'knowledge-centred' colleagues, these teachers emphasized the duty of school and staff to stimulate and awaken the interests of each individual child. One teacher at Green Mount felt that the approach adopted by the school to average and below average children was basically wrong; that if the work was made sufficiently interesting 'any child could be made keen'. It was felt that too many teachers measured the success of their efforts in terms of academic results and all that they offered was a watered-down version of the syllabus for the brighter children.

Whereas many of the 'knowledge-centred' teachers had displayed hostility towards the attitudes and behaviour of children from lower social class backgrounds, the 'child-centred' group, while expressing awareness of the negative factors associated with home background, felt that these could and should be mitigated by the efforts of school and teacher. The head and several members of staff at Ash Valley emphasized the extra obligations of a teacher in meeting the needs of

[1,2] See footnote 2 page 192.

children from poorer homes—'It's very easy to be soft on the good-looking, pleasant-mannered ones—but the others often need it far more'.

Thus, the 'child-centred' teachers, while also recognizing differences in attitudes and behaviour between children of high and low ability, tended to explain these differences in terms of the disadvantaged position in which dull children found themselves, and to stress that maximum help and attention should be devoted to these children to counteract these disadvantages.

Most of the teachers interviewed fell somewhere between the two extremes of opinion outlined above, although more 'child-centred' teachers were found in non-streamed schools, and more 'knowledge-centred' teachers in streamed schools. Where extreme views were represented within the same school, staff relations had noticeably suffered.

Several teachers at Green Mount made little secret of the fact that they disapproved of and resented each other's attitudes. One very pro A-stream teacher found the tendency of a couple of members of staff to give most attention to the less able 'criminal in this day and age'. Conversely, a D-stream teacher resented the fact that 'some people think that because children are in the D-stream they're no good at sports, art or anything—and they're quite stunned when you bring something into the staff room—"Gosh" they say—"Did one of *yours* make that?"' This particular teacher had campaigned successfully the previous year to have a D-stream child appointed as a prefect, and admitted that since the advent of the new head, there had been a 'healthier attitude' towards the less able child, although in a number of cases teachers had merely adopted a superficial attitude to please the head—'underneath they just don't want to know'.

These basic differences of opinion and attitude between various members of staff at Green Mount had produced a deleterious effect on staff relations. Endorsement of one view was interpreted by teachers holding the other as an undermining of their own work and status. A strained atmosphere or even open friction was not infrequently observable in the staff room, particularly when trivial incidents became inflated and interpreted by those involved as a challenge to their conflicting principles.

Clearly the way in which teachers regard the children will affect the way in which the children regard themselves and each other. The importance of teacher attitudes in modifying or accentuating the effects of streaming or non-streaming on a child's self-image and awareness has been stressed elsewhere. As one head pointed out: 'If a teacher *likes* the children, some of them wouldn't know if they were streamed or not'. The teachers' attitudes and expectations can also, of course, aggravate a situation and reduce children's self-confidence: 'I took 1C for handwork and said to them—"why can't you do such and such?" One boy said "we can't—we were told we can't. We were told we're the dunces of the school".' An A-stream teacher at Green Mount claimed that his children did not regard themselves as 'superior beings' and said that if they did he 'would soon knock it out of them'. When a visitor left his classroom to go to a 'D' class, however, he called out, 'Good luck—you'll need it there!' and joined in the gale of laughter which this evoked from the class.

Attitudes to streaming

Just as teachers' attitudes to children of different ability levels are related to their views on the aims of primary education, so both of these factors appear to be associated with their feelings about streaming.

The 'knowledge-centred' teacher tended to support streaming, and its perceived academic advantage to children of high ability. The more 'child-centred' teacher tended to favour non-streaming as giving a fairer opportunity to all ability levels, and as socially more desirable in that it avoids the segregation and 'labelling' of children which streaming implies.

Teachers representing these different viewpoints were found in each of the schools under study.[1] While nearly all staff in the streamed schools tended to support the prevailing type of organization, this was not so in the non-streamed schools, particularly in Oak Lane where a *majority* would have preferred a different system.

In each of the streamed schools a number of teachers who preferred teaching bright children were strong supporters of streaming in the interest of these pupils. In a non-streamed class they felt, the bright child would be held back, would be irritated by the slowness of the other children and would consequently become 'bored and frustrated'. Many were very strongly opposed to mixed ability classes and regarded the effects of non-streaming as pernicious:

'Non-streaming will do a lot of harm to some kids before they find out it's bad. Most harm will be done to the brightest kids—they won't get on as fast as they want to.'

[1] See footnote 2 page 192.

Teachers holding such views were not only found in streamed schools, however. One teacher at Oak Lane compared her present school unfavourably with a streamed school in which she had previously taught—'It was very encouraging there—you really could see marvellous results at the top and we improved our results every year'. For this teacher satisfaction in her work came from seeing bright children reach a high standard of academic achievement. She felt that a non-streamed class deprived both herself and the children of the needed incentive of established academic goals—'A teacher can never have the satisfaction of obtaining really first-rate results. I would rather take my turn at teaching the C- or D-stream once every few years for the pleasure of having an 'A' or 'B' class in the other years'.

The competitive spirit which many advocates of non-streaming criticized as an undesirable concomitant of streaming was regarded by these teachers as 'good for the soul' and conducive to a high level of achievement—'Children like to struggle against each other and do better'. The use made by different teachers of class places, team points and stars reflects the extent to which they endorsed the idea of competition in class and their criteria for allocating praise and reward. At Green Mount the children in 3A were given a team point 'if they got 20 out of 20 and Miss N. thought the work was good' (3A pupil). Mrs. S. in 4D, however, believed in giving a lot of points—'I tell my class—when I look at your work I'm not comparing you with anyone—if you've tried hard, you'll get a star'.

This illustrates the different attitudes of the 'knowledge-centred' and the more 'child-centred' teacher—in the first case a team point was given for attainment of a required standard; in the second it was given to a child who had done his best. The first viewpoint was shared by the head of Red Hill: 'I never give full marks—no one's work is absolutely perfect and full marks implies perfection'.

In the non-streamed schools considerably less emphasis (and in Beech Grove, active discouragement) was given to individual rivalry, especially in the academic sphere. Class placings were never given as this was considered 'very disheartening to those of lower ability'. While many teachers in the non-streamed schools disliked the principle of awarding team points for work, others merely felt that it was impractical with non-streamed classes. 'The same ones would get points all the time—you'd be looking round for something to give the slow ones points for so it would become completely false'. These teachers clearly believed that merit lay in the achievement of a fixed standard rather than in improvement and progress in terms of each individual child's capacity.

Almost without exception, the arguments in favour of streaming were stated solely in terms of its effect on attainment and academic progress. Differences in ability were regarded as 'a fact of life which has to be faced sooner or later', and the question whether streaming had social or psychological effects was either ignored or discounted— 'I've never believed in this theory that if you tell the less able child it is less able, it affects it. In some cases it affects it in the right way— makes it decide to try harder!' Many pro-streaming teachers believed that the social effects of streaming were greatly exaggerated: children were regarded as either not really conscious of being streamed or they accepted it as a normal part of school life. One teacher felt that any feelings of inferiority were more likely to be found in the lower part of the *A-stream*—'in the lower streams', he said, 'they don't notice it so much if they can't read or write'.

Just as academic attainment was the factor of primary importance in the views of the pro-streaming teachers, the social aspect of education was that which received most emphasis in the arguments of those who preferred non-streaming. While the pro-streamers regarded segregation by ability as simply acknowledging a fact of life, the anti-streamers condemned it as 'artificial—it does not reflect real life' and considered it 'criminal to label a child A, B or C'.

The perceived social effects of streaming had led the heads of the non-streamed schools to abolish segregation by ability. All three felt that streaming aggravated the distinctions between children and led to the formation of an ' "A" class aristocracy—all uniformed, clean and smart' and a concentration of problem children in the bottom streams. One head felt that streaming 'directed these children into delinquency by stigmatizing them at the age of seven'. Different streams did not mix in the playground, except in the form of skirmishes caused by resentment on the part of lower stream children of the superior attitude adopted by the 'A's. According to one head the effects of streaming were also noticeable outside the schools— 'Families wouldn't speak to each other because their children were in different streams'. Before Ash Valley was de-streamed, a graph of participation in school visits and activities had shown a gradual dropping off from the A-stream downwards. Since de-streaming, the head claimed, all children took part in these activities (see Chapter 11).

All three non-streamed heads agreed that since de-streaming a great deal of the anti-social behaviour which had characterized the lower stream children had disappeared and that a 'much happier atmosphere' existed in the school.

A number of teachers in the non-streamed schools who had also taught in streamed schools claimed that they would 'never do it again'. Apart from their conviction that segregation was socially wrong, they criticized the tendency in many streamed schools to give preferential treatment to the top streams in terms of material facilities and better teachers—'The A's got everything and the C's got nothing. We had a rotten room and desks with splinters in them. The children kept saying "Why don't we get anything?" ' The execution of administrative details served to emphasize the 'status hierarchy' of streams and the inferiority of lower stream children— 'When classes are read out—you start at A and go through to D. They're even lined up in assembly that way—little things like that count'.

Although the social aspect was that which most concerned the teachers who advocated non-streaming, they also tended to feel that academically non-streaming was more desirable, especially for the child of lesser ability. These teachers laid stress on the fostering of a co-operative rather than a competitive atmosphere in the classroom and felt that the bright children could help the less able, to the benefit of each. 'I have seen so often how the less able gain from the bright. Jeremy would have been in a "C" class but he has gone up and up each time—he has gained enormously from his friends.' This teacher did not feel that the bright children had been held back in any way—'It helps the bright ones to explain to someone else'.

Both the heads of Ash Valley and Oak Lane felt that the level of attainment in a school was determined less by the type of organization than by the quality of individual teachers. 'If the teacher is poor it won't make any difference if they're streamed or not. Some teachers would be just as much at sea in a streamed class but it wouldn't be so apparent.' It was generally felt that non-streaming made considerably greater demands on teachers in terms of planning and organization, but some of them regarded this as more stimulating and enjoyable and harsh criticism was levelled at those who 'prefer streaming because it's easier—they give no thought to how the children will benefit'.

As mentioned earlier, there were in each of the six schools a number of teachers who would have preferred a different type of organization from that under which they were working. While a few teachers in the streamed schools expressed themselves in favour of non-streaming, it would be misleading to suggest that they felt constrained by or in basic conflict with the organization under which they worked. Most of those who criticized the effects of streaming were teachers of lower streams and their greatest concern was that the less able child should have the maximum possible attention from understanding and skilful teachers. A non-streamed class with an unsympathetic teacher, it was felt, would not overcome the lack of confidence and negative attitudes which characterized the backward child.

In the non-streamed schools, however, were a number of teachers who would have preferred a streamed system. In each case non-streaming was criticized in terms of attainment; the social factor was regarded as irrelevant or of less importance. However, there was little consensus among these teachers, even in the same school, as to the effect of non-streaming on the attainments of children of different ability levels. Whereas one teacher asserted that 'non-streaming helps the average but neglects the bright and the dull', another felt that 'non-streaming is against the interests of the middle group—there's a tendency to work to the top or the bottom'. These conflicting views perhaps reflect the personal difficulties experienced by individual teachers in coping with mixed ability classes and their concern for the interests of a particular ability group.

It is reasonable to assume that teachers will, consciously or unconsciously, as far as they are permitted, adopt classroom methods and practices which are in accordance with their own views on the aims of primary education (see Chapter 4). How far individual teachers in the schools under study succeeded in fulfilling or, in the case of some, in modifying, the aims associated with the organization under which they worked, is discussed in the following section.

Teaching methods

The methods of teaching and classroom practices favoured by individual teachers are likely to be those considered most efficient in fulfilling what they regard as the aims of primary education. The 'knowledge-centred' type of teacher tends to prefer formal and abstract methods and separate subject lessons, with an emphasis on class teaching and individual work as opposed to group work. A competitive spirit is encouraged in the classroom, but co-operation between children is not favoured. The classroom atmosphere tends to be non-permissive: children are expected to remain in their seats and work in comparative silence. The 'child-centred' teacher, on the other hand, makes use of more informal practical methods, concentrating on stimulating the children's interest. Group work and co-operation are encouraged and children have greater freedom to talk among themselves and move freely about the room.

In practice, of course, a considerable number of teachers do not fit exactly into either category. Some may employ formal methods in a highly permissive atmosphere, and vice versa. Also within each school, there was considerable variation among teachers in the methods used. In the two larger streamed schools, for example, class teaching was the most popular method, but a number of teachers also used similar or mixed ability groups for different lessons, while at Red Hill almost every teacher employed ability grouping at least for basic subjects (perhaps reflecting the wider ability range in a two-stream school). In the non-streamed schools the picture was even more varied. At Beech Grove, where the majority of teachers were 'typical non-streamers', emphasis was placed on individual work or co-operative, mixed group work. At Ash Valley, almost all teachers grouped by ability for basic subjects and many used mixed groups for other lessons. As noted earlier, very few teachers at Oak Lane supported the system of non-streaming and this was reflected in the teaching methods, which consisted mainly of class teaching with some ability grouping. Many teachers would no doubt consider class-teaching practicable only with a streamed class which had a narrow range of ability.

The degree to which any teacher is free to develop his own methods and ideas is determined in part by the policy of the head in such matters as timetable and curriculum organization, and the extent to which he attempts to establish a uniformity of approach among his staff. In fact, in all six schools under study, teachers claimed that considerable freedom was given them to develop their own methods, and this had to some degree permitted the wide variations found within the schools. At Green Mount the head had presented each member of staff with a blank timetable in the hope of encouraging a more flexible approach, but had found that 'some teachers immediately wanted to write in exactly what they were going to do and when. They've got very little improvisation—it's easier to do page 22 this week and page 23 next'.

Only at Beech Grove was a consistent attempt made to analyse and discuss teaching methods and relate them to the professed aims of the school. While almost all members of staff employed methods in keeping with the informal child-centred approach, one or two still preferred more formal methods. One teacher felt that he needed a 'canon of judgement' and that by 'putting sums on the board you can then compare children with each other'. This teacher also believed in the value of occasional class lessons—'The good ones need refreshing, the middle are just reaching that point and the bottom might pick up a crumb of knowledge'. The head of Beech Grove, while personally not supporting such methods, held the view, in common with the other five heads, that it was better to allow a teacher to develop the methods which he or she preferred and considered most successful than to attempt to impose an approach which the teacher regarded as unsuitable or felt personally unable to carry out.

What follows is a description of the classroom practices of individual teachers. The first two typify the 'knowledge-centred' teacher in a streamed school and the 'child-centred' teacher in a non-streamed school as encountered in the present study. The second two descriptions show the extent to which teachers, holding different values from those associated with their particular type of school, succeeded in modifying the school's professed aims in the classroom by adopting methods more in accordance with their own views. The names given to the teachers are fictitious.

1. Knowledge-Centred Teacher: Streamed School

Mr. Kay had taken a 3rd year A-stream class for a number of years and considered himself one of the most formal teachers in the school. He admitted that he preferred to teach the top stream and regarded the backward as 'not my cup of tea'. He employed class teaching most of the time—'You get more home that way. I like children to be sitting listening when I'm talking'. He occasionally divided the class into ability groups for arithmetic but felt this method was often unsatisfactory—'Certain groups produce good work, others do nothing—they need chasing up the whole time'.

Mr. Kay saw education as the acquisition of a body of knowledge and held that at any given age, all children should have reached a certain stage in this process. He had little sympathy for the idea of a curriculum based on the development of a child's interests—'I don't believe in the idea that a child will work when he wants to. When he comes into my class he works when I say so, otherwise I don't want to know him!'

By the end of the third year, Mr. Kay expected his class to be able to apply the 'four rules' to number, weight, capacity, money, and cope with long division, fractions and decimals. He had little time for the 'colour factor' method which had been introduced in the school in recent years—'I haven't used it. In my opinion it's silly. They've got to know plus and minus before you can do anything.'

In English Mr. Kay made considerable use of formal textbooks—'One was a sort of Bible years ago for the 11+ and is still very good, lots of work on adjectives and pronouns and comprehension exercises'. The children also wrote stories once a fortnight but Mr. Kay stressed that he did not 'fall in with the school of thought that says, "bags of writing and no corrections". 'I like the child by my side to see what's *wrong*. So many these days just read through and say "very good". To my mind that's not *marking*.'

The class did occasional project work, but Mr. Kay had reservations about its value unless it was 'really organized'. This view was clearly opposed to the child-centred teacher's view of project work as being child-initiated research and discovery. Mr. Kay felt that children of this age had to be told exactly what to do and supervised —'You can't just say "go and find out"—you get screeds of stuff that means nothing!' He referred to a recent 'project' on the voyage of Sir Francis Chichester, undertaken by a student teacher. Some of the work, he said, was 'very good—*factual*, but others had drawn pictures of fish and seaweed—nothing to *do* with Chichester!'

He concentrated on subject lessons and enjoyed teaching the 'old favourites'—English, Arithmetic and History. He said: 'I think I'm good at these things—and Music—and I know I'm not much good with Nature Study and Science—I haven't got the interest. And it rubs off on the children—if I say to my children—we'll do Nature Study—they groan—it's true!'

The children in the class sat in long rows in an atmosphere of quiet concentration.

2. Child-Centred Teacher: Non-Streamed School

Miss Field had a 4th year non-streamed class. The children sat where they liked at tables arranged in small groups. The emphasis in Miss Field's class was on individual work, especially in basic subjects, while in other subjects children worked in friendship groups of two, three or four.

The work in mathematics was geared to a workbook which each child went through individually and which guided him into a considerable amount of practical work. Numerous practical aids were available in the classroom for this purpose. New processes were explained to each child individually, since Miss Field felt that this was ultimately less time-consuming—'Once they've grasped something you *know* they have. If you teach from the board half the class possibly hasn't understood and then they get it wrong'.

In English Miss Field devoted a great deal of time to oral discussion and story writing. She emphasized the need to follow or arouse the children's interest and also encouraged a lot of creative writing using various concrete stimuli. Apart from the more conventional sources such as music and pictures, she had also employed more vivid stimuli, such as burning a newspaper in front of the class and asking children to record their impressions. She stressed the need to encourage children to express their feelings and emotions and suggested that school work should be 'related to their own lives, not alien to them'. Her approach to various subjects was to integrate rather than compartmentalize—a description or experience written about in English would be depicted visually in an art lesson. Project or 'discovery' work involved the choice of a topic by the children themselves and their own research into various aspects which might cover a number of 'subject' areas.

Miss Field was experimenting with an 'Integrated Day' approach, in which the classroom was divided into different areas of interest, such as Maths, Craft, or 'discovery' corners, where each child found materials, books and work cards suitable for his or her particular ability level. Each child was given a certain amount of work to cover but was free to choose what he did and when, and to organize his own day—'Often a child gets carried away with something and sticks at it all day—that's fine as far as I'm concerned'. This system inevitably entailed a considerable amount of movement around the room and a steady buzz of conversation from children working together. Miss Field felt that a normal level of conversation was to be expected in a classroom—'They can talk, move about—do what they like as long as they're working. It works extremely well'.

3. Knowledge-Centred Teacher: Non-Streamed School

Miss Lee taught a 3rd year non-streamed class. She was strongly critical of the system of non-streaming which she felt had an adverse effect on the attainment of both bright and dull children. She herself preferred teaching the bright children who made swift progress and adopted the values which she herself held—'Bright children love to see a book full of ticks—they like to show their work off'.

Like many of the more formal, knowledge-centred teachers, Miss Lee found the methods associated with non-streaming quite foreign to what she regarded as the function of a teacher, and had reverted to practices more in accordance with a streamed system. 'Grouping for each subject *sounds* ideal but the day isn't long enough to have three groups in Maths and English—we're working to a very tight timetable'. She liked to follow a 'scheme of work' so that 'nothing gets left out'. Having tried grouping the class for basic subjects, she found that 'the top groups made good progress but the bottom ones got left behind', and while admitting that the same result occurred under class teaching, she preferred the latter method, which involved less strain on the teacher—'I don't believe in using more energy than you need'.

Having reverted to class teaching for most of the time, Miss Lee explained that she 'tended to aim at the middle'. She had a 'guilty conscience about the slower ones' who, she felt, made very little progress, but 'If I spend half-an-hour on one, I achieve very little, so I might as well concentrate on others who gain more'.

As far as lessons were concerned, Miss Lee concentrated on the formal teaching of basic subjects. Although the school was experimenting with Nuffield Maths, she preferred to stick to traditional maths—'There are so many things they *must* know: like the four rules and tables. I don't see the point of teaching a lot of fancy number systems if children can't reckon money'. She had introduced the 'new maths' for one lesson a week and found that 'the children like it better than I do'. She herself was still convinced that the old system was best—'I reject a lot of the new Maths. I'd have to learn it myself! I've got by without it all these years, so I don't see the point of bothering children with it'.

In English, too, the emphasis was on the formal. Graded spelling tests were held each day; when the child had 80 per cent correct, he moved on to the next group of words—'Then they are *aiming* at something—and they *work*!' Stress was also laid on basic principles of grammar and comprehension, and handwriting was checked once a month. In previous years Miss Lee had allowed the brighter children to 'do a topic' but felt that the present top group was not large enough to make this worthwhile.

The children in Miss Lee's class were seated according to their ability in arithmetic and remained in these places for all lessons. Thus, as far as seating was concerned, the children were clearly streamed within the class, although they were taught less frequently in these ability groups and more often as a class.

Miss Lee made no attempt to mask differences between groups or her attitude towards them—she indicated in a loud voice that 'these are my bright children, these are the middle group, and those are the dull ones'. One of her chief dislikes about teaching a non-streamed class was that 'you always have the slow ones with you'. Miss Lee felt that she was not trained to teach backward children and was clearly frustrated and irritated by their presence in the class. The classroom atmosphere was non-permissive: talking was discouraged and children were frequently admonished for clattering feet or rulers. Co-operation between children was also discouraged—'I don't believe in the bright ones helping the others—they are interested in their *own* attainments and are in school to *learn*, not to teach'.

4. *Child-Centred Teacher: Streamed School*

Miss Carr taught a fourth year D-stream class and was firmly convinced that the formal methods of the knowledge-centred teacher were unsuitable, especially for less able children. In her classroom there was a lot of movement and a steady buzz of conversation. Several different activities were going on at once, some children reading quietly, some doing arithmetic, and another group was involved in building a kiln with alternative layers of sawdust and green pottery. Miss Carr was usually lost from sight, dividing her time between the craft group and the individual problems of the other children.

Since many of the children had reading difficulties, Miss Carr felt that it was important that they should learn to express themselves orally and concentrated a great deal on free talking and oral composition. She used books to try and pick out good descriptions—'to get them to appreciate good English and express themselves'. The children wrote stories 'about things they *know*—family, pets— things they feel and think about'. On the classroom walls, among the large, colourful display of children's paintings and models, were cards of spellings that the children needed to use frequently. Miss Carr said that she reluctantly had to give some time to more formal work—'I talk about nouns because the secondary school will want them to know, but I can't really see much point in it'.

She refused to keep a set timetable—'If what some people call a red herring crops up and the children are interested, it's worth pursuing'. She criticized teachers who had not so much a method as a routine—'now is the time to put up picture No. 4!'

The children were seated in small groups of three and four and chose their own places. The relations between them and their teacher were relaxed and informal. Miss Carr was very conscious of the effect on the children of the teacher's attitudes and approach. 'You can tell a teacher by her class. If the teacher talks loudly, it's a noisy class. If she has a cool approach, the children aren't friendly at all. If the children are pushing and rude, I think the teacher must be.'

Discussion

It is clear that the two types of teacher have very different expectations of what their role in the classroom should be, and what children should be doing. The knowledge-centred teacher emphasized correctness and accepted academic standards—'I like copperplate work and good English'; whereas the child-centred teacher encouraged self-expression and stimulated the child's interests—'I don't correct creative writing—it stops them producing ideas'. Knowledge-centred teachers also tended to lay stress on behaviour training and self-discipline—'Sitting properly in class and control of one's body are most important things'. The other type of teacher believed, however, 'that if a boy writes better kneeling on the seat, that's okay with me'.

The teachers succeeded to a considerable degree in practising the methods which they preferred, even in a school in which such methods would seem inappropriate.

The great amount of experimentation in method in non-streamed schools showed considerable variation in ideas and approach, but certain common factors were regarded as crucial by all who supported non-streaming. The fostering of a co-operative atmosphere in the classroom was stressed as one of the most important features of non-streaming. It was felt that the competitive spirit associated with streaming was out of place and served no useful purpose in a non-streamed class. An emphasis on self-improvement and progress rather than a comparison with others, and encouragement of children working together and helping each other exemplified the approach which sought to establish a feeling of co-operation.

The abandonment of a set timetable which divided the day rigidly into sections, each devoted to a separate subject, was also seen as a prerequisite of a learning programme which aimed primarily at developing children's interests. Flexibility in grouping too, was considered essential: the emergence of rigid, static groups suggested a streamed system in the classroom context. Most teachers employed at some time a form of ability grouping for basic subjects but emphasized that movement between groups should be expected and facilitated. In some schools a system of 'setting' was employed for basic subjects; children were taken from their own class and grouped with children of a similar ability level from the other classes in the year group, returning to their own class for all other lessons.

A variation on the idea of combining classes for different purposes was that of 'team teaching' where two or more classes were combined into a 'unit'. 'Areas of work' were spread over the classrooms involved, and teachers shared responsibility for the different activities which went on simultaneously. One advantage of this system, it was claimed, was that teachers had freedom to develop their own particular interests or talents. The system, by its very nature, entailed considerable co-operation, discussion and interchange of ideas between various members of staff which was considered of great value, especially for younger, less experienced teachers. Children in many non-streamed schools were also responsible for organising their own work and timetable for the day, or even the week, under the guidance and supervision of the teacher. Many teachers encouraged children to keep their own records of the work they had covered, the teacher herself becoming more concerned with the child's personal development, and his approach and reaction to various situations and problems.

In spite of the great variations between school and school, and between teacher and teacher, the approach of those favouring nonstreaming was guided by the conviction that learning should be child-centred, geared to the children's interests and undertaken in an atmosphere of co-operative activity.

Relations of heads and staff

The relations between a head and his staff are clearly of crucial importance in the smooth running of a school and for the morale of all who work in it. Schools vary greatly in the extent to which head and individual teachers share the same views on the aims of primary education and the means whereby they, as educators, should strive to achieve these aims. It has already been seen that very different ways of thinking were represented among the staff in the schools under study and that these were manifested in the varying attitudes, expectations and methods.

(a) The Streamed Schools

The head of Green Mount, while adhering personally to the more progressive, child-centred view of education, had reduced friction and discontent among his staff by allowing them the maximum

221

freedom to organize their own classes and work. He had done little more than *suggest* that more flexible and progressive approaches should be adopted, and he was aware that among the older teachers little change had, in fact, taken place. As most of them were nearing retirement, however, he felt it more advisable to leave them to carry on as before than to try to convert them to new ways of thinking. Regular staff meetings were held at Green Mount and the head's relations with his staff were friendly and informal. He clearly commanded the respect of all members of staff, including those whose views differed radically from his own.

At Grey Ridge official staff meetings were infrequent. Several teachers deplored this fact, especially the lack of meetings to find out what others were doing in their classes. There had been little discussion about the introduction of a new system of mathematics and no attempt to evolve an integrated approach—'I don't know what other people are doing. I seem to be sailing away on my own little track, and I'm sure other people feel much the same'. Not only were the number of staff meetings at Grey Ridge considered inadequate; one or two teachers also expressed dissatisfaction at the form which they took—'They are meetings for imparting information. The framework of school administration is decided elsewhere'.

The staff as a whole seemed to feel that constructive discussion of any matter affecting the school was largely a waste of time, as 'we don't feel there's much chance of a change!' The head was regarded as rather traditional and conservative, and most teachers felt it was not worthwhile suggesting innovations. The reaction to someone's suggestion that a parent-teacher association should be established was: 'Oh—the head would never consider *that*!'

The head of Red Hill considered the school small enough to enable head-staff relations to be kept on an informal level, and to remove the need for official staff meetings. Occasionally he might hold a form of staff meeting 'making it short and sharp .... I just go through the points I want to, then everyone knows'; or he would adopt the more informal method of 'popping in at lunchtime to tell them what I want or to give information'. Although preferring the informal approach, the head felt that 'certain things *have* to be done formally', such as the need to criticize a pupil or teacher. In such cases he would deal with children and staff in the same way—'I rarely reprimand as such any member of staff—just call them to order and indicate that I would like something altered'.

The staff at Red Hill were unanimous in their feelings of disapproval and frustration at the lack of two-way communication in the form of regular staff meetings and discussions. The general feeling was that if any changes were to take place in the school, the head would decide and tell them. A meeting had been held to discuss the adoption of a particular method of teaching mathematics, but, as one teacher put it: 'We were on a sticky wicket as we hadn't seen it!' A similar case quoted concerned the abolition of progress reports several years previously—'He just came in one day and said, "No more reports!" And that was that.'

The poor relations and lack of communication between head and staff at Red Hill seemed to have had an adverse effect on staff morale. An atmosphere of lethargy pervaded the staff room and very little discussion on matters relating to the school or education generally took place, even among the younger teachers who might have been expected to show enthusiasm in the suggestion of new methods or ideas.

(b) The Non-Streamed Schools.

In the three non-streamed schools patterns of communications and relations between heads and their staff presented as varied a picture as in the streamed schools.

At Oak Lane the staff without exception regarded the level of discussion and communication in the school as inadequate. Official staff meetings were 'infrequent' and held 'to discuss such matters as the Christmas party and Sports Day'. Informal discussion with the head was rare, and between teachers was considered pointless, as 'the head decides and tells us'. Concern was expressed at the lack of co-ordination in policy and teaching methods—'We're all apt to remain in our own little cocoon'. Newer members of staff were particularly aware of a lack of guidance and directive—'Information just filters down. The head only comes to see you if there is something wrong'.

The poor relations existing between head and staff at Oak Lane were perhaps partly explained by the fact that the head was virtually alone in his support of non-streaming. Almost every member of staff was highly critical of the system and practised in the classroom methods which were more in accordance with their own ideas.

Quite a different situation prevailed at Beech Grove where a great deal of discussion took place on matters affecting school policy. Frequent meetings were held to discuss particular topics such as the Plowden Report, and to discuss 'what to teach and when'. The head found these meetings useful and successful—'My staff are very articulate and always have plenty to say'. Relations between head and staff appeared to be excellent, and there was a high degree of consensus as to the aims and methods which the school should adopt.

At Ash Valley, too, regular staff meetings were held to discuss routine school matters and to co-ordinate teaching methods in such areas as Reading, Maths and French, which the head felt required a standardization of approach. No lack of communication or consultation was felt by members of staff; on the contrary, approval was expressed of the head's democratic approach—'He always talks things over—he never just says we *will* do so-and-so'.

Conclusions

In three of the six schools involved in this study the relations between head and staff were, in the views of the teachers concerned, far from satisfactory. Lack of consultation and discussion on the school's policy and aims, and the absence of any attempt to co-ordinate approaches and methods throughout the school had in each case led to a lowering of staff morale, and, in Oak Lane, to a situation where teachers were practising methods clearly inappropriate to the aims of the school as envisaged by the head.

An adequate level of communication and interchange of ideas between head and staff seems to be essential if any school, whether streamed or non-streamed, is to achieve the aims associated with its particular type of organization.

In spite of the limitations on time and resources in carrying out a thorough intensive study, the picture obtained of the six schools which were visited confirmed the powerful influence of teachers' attitudes and behaviour in determining whether a school does, in fact, manifest the features associated with its type of organization. Both the streamed and non-streamed schools had teachers who differed radically in their views on the aims of primary education, the type of school best suited to achieve these aims, and their own contribution as teachers.

A non-streamed organization appeared particularly susceptible to modification at the hands of teachers who did not support its principles. Especially in the absence of constructive guidance, encouragement and an integrative approach on the part of the head, many teachers withdrew into the isolated domain of their own classroom and continued to practise methods and approaches at total variance with the supposed aims of the school. A positive, co-ordinating approach on the part of the head is, however, likely to be a necessary but not sufficient pre-requisite of a school's success in fulfilling its aims. Unless teachers' attitudes are considered when appointing them to a non-streamed school in particular, the school is likely to be non-streamed in name only.

Reference

GOODACRE, E. J. (1968). *Teachers and their Pupils' Home Background.* Slough: NFER.

CHAPTER 15

Case Studies of Individual Children

THE effect which a school has on its pupils' progress and development is by no means related simply to its type of organization, i.e. whether it is streamed or non-streamed. Variations in teaching methods and in the attitudes and personalities of teachers and pupils are important aspects of the environment in which learning takes place.

The streaming study has been chiefly concerned with the overall effects of different types of junior school experience, not only on attainment, but also on the social and personal development of the children under study. How have these different types of experience affected individual children? Overall comparison must inevitably obscure such information under cover of general trends and differences. It was therefore the aim of this part of the study to focus attention on the junior school careers of a number of individual boys and girls, and in so doing, to spotlight the factors which seemed to have had a crucial influence on the child's academic progress.

It was decided to select for this purpose a number of children whose progress during the junior school course had been highly successful and a corresponding number whose junior school careers appeared to be characterized by failure.

A child's progress and development is likely to be affected by his school, home and personality. Some factors will assume greater importance than others, but each child's development is nevertheless the product of the cumulative interaction of all the relevant influences. Thus a poor performance, due primarily to learning difficulties in the classroom, may be exacerbated by a lack of incentive and encouragement at home.

The case history perhaps most closely related to the streaming question is that of ROBERT, a boy who was allocated to the 'wrong stream'[1] throughout his junior school career. Although his test scores each year showed him to be superior in performance to many

[1] See Chapter 7.

A-stream children, he remained in a 'B' class for all four years of the junior course. The slight drop in some of his scores in the fourth year suggested that he was finally conforming to the standards of the B-stream, but in most cases they remained as good as those of some A-stream children who, unlike Robert, were subsequently allocated to grammar school.

While a warm personal relationship with the teacher may be of greater importance to some children than to others, it is unlikely that a poor relationship between teacher and pupil will have anything but an adverse effect on the child's progess. Wall *et al.* (1962) have pointed out that 'if *rapport* between teacher and pupil is poor, then one of the first essentials in the learning situation has been neglected.'

An illustration of this is provided by SANDRA, an A-stream child of average ability who had the misfortune to spend two consecutive years in the class of a teacher with whom she had a very unsatisfactory relationship. Sandra believed, quite correctly, that she was disliked by her teacher, and feeling herself incapable of pleasing, became tense and nervous in class and lost all interest in school work. A child less sensitive than Sandra and less in need of constant praise and encouragement might have survived the situation, but it is highly probable that this poor teacher-pupil relationship was a causal factor of Sandra's general deterioration in performance in her second and third years of junior school.

Sympathetic understanding and positive encouragement from the teacher may be needed to overcome handicaps to progress which stem from other sources. JIMMY's erratic test scores suggested that he was not performing as well as he might; he was also regarded by the school as a behaviour problem. Investigation of Jimmy's case indicated that his behaviour in school was associated with emotional problems stemming from his home environment. A complete lack of *rapport* between home and school had led to each attributing to the other the blame for Jimmy's poor performance, resulting in little being done to help the boy.

Although themselves influenced by previous experiences at home and school, the child's own emotions, drives and motivations are of crucial importance in determining his adaptation to each learning situation and his subsequent progress. ALEX, at seven, was below average in attainment, but displayed great personal drive and determination to succeed in his school work. He showed considerable improvement each year and finally obtained a grammar school place. This success may have been achieved in spite of, rather than with the help of, tremendous pressure from a highly ambitious father, which, in another child, might have produced only self-defeating tension and anxiety.

In the case of DAVID also, pressure from home might well have exercised an adverse effect on his progress. A boy of very high ability, David was a natural left-hander, who, at his father's insistence, had been made to write with his right hand. The outcome of this was a dislike of writing which almost assumed the proportions of a phobia and an antipathy towards any activity involving handwork. In spite of his excellent progress, David had been unhappy at school, except when in the class of a sympathetic teacher, who felt that he would make better progress with less pressure and more encouragement.

In contrast to those children who had been submitted to considerable pressure to succeed were a number whose poor performance seemed due primarily to a lack of sufficient motivation and encouragement, either from home or school, or both.

JULIE made very little progress during her four years in junior school and her performance in arithmetic especially had been very poor. While her parents showed no lack of concern for her welfare and happiness, no interest was expressed in her educational progress. No attempt was made to hide the fact that they considered the progress of her brother of much greater importance. Little had been expected of Julie—and little had been achieved.

NORA, too, had made little or no progress during her period in the junior school. Her score on the Problem Arithmetic test in her second junior year had been 13; two years later she scored only 8 on the same test! All Nora's teachers remarked on her helpfulness, and had encouraged her to do chores round the school rather than concentrate on her obvious learning difficulties. Her home background provided no mitigating influences; her parents had had little education themselves, and their occasional attempts to help her with her difficulties had produced only greater confusion and anxiety on Nora's part.

It is, of course, impossible to specify the environmental and personality factors which will combine to produce maximum progress in school. As has been indicated here, some children made good progress in circumstances which might have been thought to exert a detrimental effect. It is a somewhat simpler task to identify the factors which appeared to have contributed to failure in particular cases. In most instances this seemed to be the result of a combination of adverse circumstances; even where the immediate cause seemed fairly clearly discernible, it was found to be reinforced by other factors. Limitations of time and resources precluded an exhaustive examination of all the factors which might have influenced the progress of the children concerned. The aim of this study has been to highlight those factors which seemed to have played an important role in the success or failure of these children in the junior school.

Sample and method of investigation

Children for case study were restricted to those attending the six schools described in the previous chapter. The studies were carried out in the fourth year and children were selected on the basis of their academic performance in the previous three years. Only 'improvers' or 'deteriorators' were chosen for study. For the purposes of selection both raw and standardized scores were used. The performance of children whose standardized scores showed an increase or decrease from one year to the next could be said to have improved or deteriorated relative to other children of that age. Since the same test (or a parallel version) was administered each year, it would be expected that all children would show at least some increase in *raw* score each year. However, a number of children selected for their poor performance were found to show a *drop* in raw score between one year and the next; that is to say, they achieved less on the same test than they had a year earlier.

Recorded interviews with each child were carried out by members of the research team.[1] The aim was to obtain the children's views on their own work and progress, attitudes towardssc hool and factors associated with school, and to discover any problems or anxieties which they might have encountered either in or out of school.

Each home was visited and a recorded interview was also held with the child's mother to find out the parents' opinions of their child's physical, mental and social development and progress, their level of interest and participation in the child's education, and their aspirations for his or her educational and vocational future.

Discussions were also held with the head of the school and, where possible, with all teachers who had taught the child, to obtain their views on his progress, development and personality.

In all, 30 children were studied. It would have been impractical to include all of these in this report; the seven case histories which

[1] Interviewers were Elsa Ferri and Peter Healey.

follow represent those in which the factors associated with good or poor progress seem most clearly discernible. Details of the other 23 case-studies are available.

ROBERT—*who was in the wrong stream*

Robert was a tall, well-built anxious looking boy who rarely smiled. He had spent all four junior school years in a 'B' class, although, on the basis of his annual test performance he had been identified as a 'wrongly allocated'[1] pupil who should have been in the A-stream. He was, in fact, one of a small group of children who were found to have remained in the 'wrong' stream thoughout their junior school careers.

TABLE 15.1: *Robert's test scores*

AGE	READING		ENGLISH		PROBLEM		MECHAN-ICAL		CONCEPT		VERBAL		STREAM
	Stan.	*Raw*	*Stan.*	*Raw*	*Stan.*	*Raw*	*Stan.*	*Raw*	*Stan.*	*Raw*	*Stan.*	*Raw*	
7+	105	17	109	15	106	7	88	4	–	–	–	–	B
8+	125	34	112	31	112	14	94	9	122	32	111	56†	B
9+	113	33	117	50	115	21	118	30	131	48	116	26	B
10+	110	36	114	56	116	26	107	26	130	53	110	29	B

†A different test used at 8+

Note: Stan.=standardized score; Raw=raw score

Like many children who had been placed in too low a stream, Robert was one of the youngest in his year group. This fact also made him characteristic of those wrongly allocated children who did not 'conform' to the standards of the stream in which they had been incorrectly placed (see Chapter 7).

In spite of the fact that Robert's scores in English and Problem Arithmetic at 9+ and 10+ placed him about half-way up the A-stream, he was rated only 'average' by his teacher each year.

[1] For definition of 'wrongly allocated' see Chapter 7.

230

His mother was bitterly disappointed that he had not been promoted to the A-stream, and felt that his chances of success were being seriously lessened by his remaining in a 'B' class—'You've got to be able to go from B to A or you don't stand a chance at 11+'. She had gone to see the headmaster about this, and had been told that it was felt, in Robert's case, that if he was 'pushed too soon he might drop back'. Robert's mother could not accept this—'I should have thought that the prestige of going up to the A was better than staying at the top of the B, with nothing to aim for.' According to his mother, Robert, too, was acutely disappointed when he was not promoted—'It knocked all the enthusiasm out of him'.

Robert himself obviously felt that he would be more stimulated by the work in 4A—'They learn a lot more, and the questions are harder—not like in our class. And they do a bit of homework in 4A'. While in the third year he had actually asked his teacher if he could have some homework, but had met with little encouragement. His desire to be in the 'A' class was matched by feelings of frustration and dissatisfaction with the work and pace of his present class—'I like the teacher but she always does things too *slow*.' Robert read a great deal at home and especially enjoyed working through historical topics in his encyclopedia—'Then you come to school and the teacher takes three lessons to read three pages, when you can read it in half-an-hour! It gets a bit boring'. His favourite teacher was the one who had made him work hardest—'He always gave you hard things and you just got on happily. I think I worked best for him'. Robert made no secret of the fact that he would be glad to leave his present school, and expressed a wish to go to Grammar school, because 'you pass most exams there and I'd like to get through quite a lot of exams'. He had a longstanding desire to become a veterinary surgeon, and had 'studied' biology on his own.

Robert was an only child who had been brought up in an authoritarian atmosphere, due chiefly to a very strict father. Like many children in this position he had spent a great amount of time in adult company. Both his parents were keen climbers and he had been obliged to become keen too, as most weekends and holidays were spent climbing and hostelling with his parents. His father, according to his mother, was a strict disciplinarian—'Robert knows authority. Most friends' children can talk to us "on a level", but Robert always treats an older person as such—he doesn't say what he likes'. His mother, however, was convinced that her husband was *too* strict. She also felt that he was less interested in Robert's education and progress than she—'He doesn't take an

231

outstanding interest in schooling. He says: "If he's clever enough he'll come on; if not, he won't." But I think with an only child you're a bit more ambitious'.

Here were two possible areas of conflict and tension between Robert's parents with regard to their son's upbringing and progress. Although his mother emphasized that she would never challenge her husband in front of the boy, Robert could hardly fail to be aware of this potential, if not overt, conflict in his home. He felt that his parents would 'like him to get through', although there was little talk of school at home. 'It's just: Have you done your piano lesson, have you done this, have you done that?' His attitude towards his father seemed to be one of docile but sullen submission, unaccompanied by any sense of respect or admiration—'I'd like a nice exciting life—not like some people—like my dad—he just goes round climbing—he doesn't really *do* much'.

Robert's mother felt that her son's 'rather different upbringing' had led to his feeling a gulf between himself and the other children at school. The headmaster had remarked that Robert was timid and reserved with other children and his teacher said that while the others 'didn't object to him', he had no close friends and liked to be by himself.

Robert however, saw himself as being almost totally *rejected* by the other children—'They don't often let me play. They let me play some games, yet they never seem to like me'. Why should Robert be rejected by his classmates? Firstly, he was considerably superior to almost all of them in terms of ability and attainment. Secondly, as an only child who had spent overmuch time in adult company, he was more serious and sober, and probably more mature in outlook than most of his companions. This rejection, however, was by no means one-sided. Robert was highly critical of, and apparently unable to comprehend behaviour which many would regard as typical of high-spirited 11-year-olds. 'Alan, he's always going round as if there's a *war* on—kicks the classroom door open, imagines he's got a tommygun.'

The behaviour of other boys seemed at times to puzzle and disturb him to an almost obsessive degree and his disapproval was expressed in language which one might expect to hear from an adult who finds children's behaviour irksome. Quite probably he had borrowed this language from the adult world with which he had so much contact. Robert *was* different from the other children—he was quiet and gentle and, according to his teachers, 'placid as they come'. Yet there was some evidence to suggest that beneath the surface was a latent desire to 'break out', and 'yell and throw things' as the others did. In three out of four essays, administered in years 3 and 4, violence, war and fighting were his predominant themes.

'There was a cry and a loud clatter of feet. The time had come. We ran forward and they ran forward. We started fighting, finding our swords cutting them in half, going through their swords. After two hours of fighting we walked through them knowing they were not there.'

It seemed that the discipline and restraint imposed on him at home had been, at most, superficially effective, but as a result Robert was unable to form satisfactory relationships with other children.

He seemed to have experienced similar difficulties in his relations with teachers. All agreed that he had considerable ability but said that he was making little progress and, in fact, underachieving. But Table 15.1 shows that in the first three years this was not so and he made considerable progress. His teachers, however, were unanimous in attributing this so-called 'lack of progress' to sheer laziness on the boy's part—'He's bone idle—will work to get by, but won't do anything else'. Not only was he lazy, but one teacher felt that 'he showed no enthusiasm for anything—gave the impression of being thoroughly bored'. While all were ready to dismiss him as 'bone idle', however, they all likewise confessed to having failed to 'get through' to him, and his mother was disturbed when, on Open Days, teachers had told her that they 'just couldn't understand Robert'.

It could be that his laziness and boredom, as perceived by his teachers, stemmed from his being in a class with children of considerably lower ability than himself, where the work was too easy for him; he longed for the more stimulating atmosphere of the A-stream. The only therapy his present teacher could suggest, however, was 'a kick up the backside'.

His scores at 10+ were all within the range of those accepted for grammar school, with the exception of mechanical arithmetic which showed a drop in raw score from the previous year. Yet although he was as good as some A-stream children who were selected for grammar school, Robert was allocated to a secondary modern; selection being based largely on the recommendations of the head, taking account of the class teachers' assessments—assessments which, as we have seen, were unlikely to increase Robert's chances of success. Having been in the 'wrong 'stream for four years, it seems that his teachers' limited expectations have possibly led to his being 'wrongly allocated' once again.

SANDRA—*a poor teacher-pupil relationship*

Sandra was a rather plump, very talkative girl who had been in an A-stream all through her junior school career. Her scores on the attainment tests at 7+ were somewhat above average, but deteriorated steadily after that in practically all subjects; at times even in terms of raw score.

TABLE 15.2: *Sandra's Test Scores*

AGE	READING		ENGLISH		PROBLEM		MECHAN-ICAL		CONCEPT		VERBAL		STREAM
	Stan.	*Raw*	*Stan.*	*Raw*	*Stan.*	*Raw*	*Stan.*	*Raw*	*Stan.*	*Raw*	*Stan.*	*Raw*	
7+	112	26	116	35	108	12	111	17	–	–	–	–	A
8+	107	29	117	49	98	13	110	22	98	17	106	60†	A
9+	98	29	108	50	91	13	98	18	105	32	99	19	A
10+	100	34	109	54	94	18	104	30	93	28	101	26	A

†A different test used at 8+

Note: Stan.=standardized score; Raw=raw score

The change in Sandra's class position on these tests emphasizes the deterioration in her performance compared with that of other children in the class; at 7+ Sandra was in the top third of her class but at 9+ and 10+ in the bottom third. Also she had been rated 'above average' in ability by her first year teacher, but in later years only 'average'.

TABLE 15.3: *Sandra's class position*

	READING	ENGLISH	PROBLEM	MECHAN-ICAL	NO. IN CLASS
7+ class position	13th	9th	12th	13th	42
9+ class position	36th	33rd	37th	37th	37

One of the main reasons for her poor progress in school seemed to be a very poor relationship with her teacher in her second and third year. She did well in her first year at junior school and had a good report from her teacher with whom she got on very well—'She was strict but kind and always had a friendly smile'. In her second year, she moved into the class of a middle-aged teacher who was perceived by Sandra as very strict and who she felt did not like her. Encouragement was not forthcoming and however hard she tried, the teacher had not praised or rewarded her efforts—'If I got 19 out of 20 this wasn't good enough for Miss M.' Unfortunately for Sandra, the same teacher remained with the class for the subsequent third year. According to her mother, 'Sandra went completely haywire', while in this teacher's class. 'She didn't like Miss M. and I don't think Miss M. particularly liked her. . . .She lost all interest in school, she didn't want to go, she wouldn't do her homework—she just couldn't care less.'

Not only did Miss M. fail to encourage and motivate Sandra, but her 'bad temper' and 'shouting' had also frightened and intimidated her. 'When people shout at me I got very scared and nervous. I don't like nerves. Mum and Dad try to calm me down but it is no use—I start nodding my head and twitching—I can't help it. And Miss M. had such a catty look—it upset me and I get terrible nerves.'

As soon as Sandra's name was mentioned to Miss M., the teacher's immediate comment was: 'Oh—that lump!' Sandra's claim that Miss M. disliked her appeared correct; Miss M. made no attempt to hide or excuse her rejection of the girl—'She could be helpful if you wanted, but I never wanted!' The nervous symptoms which Sandra described had not gone unnoticed by Miss M. She remembered that Sandra had gone through a bout of sleeplessness and had been very 'nervy and jumpy'; but she clearly considered this of little significance, and far from regarding Sandra as a highly nervous and sensitive child, summed her up as 'a non-functioning *lump*—a suet pudding'. Although she placed Sandra in the bottom third of the class in terms of ability, she felt that the girl should have made considerably more progress than she had, but had 'made no effort at all' and was 'as lazy as they come'. According to Miss M. too, 'grumbling at Sandra just didn't register', but the teacher was apparently unable to offer any other approach to a child whose work was not up to standard.

Sandra's unhappy two years in Miss M.'s class were probably made worse by the fact that she was not popular with her classmates. In her third year at school she was a 'neglectee', not being chosen as a friend by any other child in her class. This may partly be explained by the fact that she had a friend in another class and spent more time with her than with her own classmates. Also, her timidity of teachers who shouted at her was carried over into her relationship with her peers—'Some of the children in my class are big bullies and they shout at you. I don't like that'. In her fourth year, however, Sandra was chosen as a friend by a girl whom she herself had selected. Her teacher felt that she got on well with the others and joined in everything, whereas Miss M. was of the opinion that the other children merely tolerated her and 'she was never the centre of attraction'.

In her final year at the school, Sandra had had a male teacher whom she liked very much. He had given plenty of praise and encouragement and she had gained self-confidence. Throughout the two years she was in Miss M.'s class she had only twice received a star for her work, whereas in the term and a half she had spent in the fourth year class she had already collected 35. Praise seemed particularly important to Sandra and, as her mother said: 'If her father says she's good there's no limit to what she'll do'. Both Sandra and her parents were aware of the difference in her work and attitude to school since changing classes. 'She spends all her time with her books—does *pages* of homework. She wants to please him.' Sandra had made a conscious effort to do well at school this year and, in her own words, had been 'trying very hard'. Her scores at 10+ did show a slight improvement and her teacher considered that she was progressing 'at a normal rate'.

Although Sandra's parents felt that she had improved greatly in her fourth year, they were also of the opinion that 'it's a bit too late for this school to bring out any good', and accepted that Sandra would go the following year to a secondary modern school. The 11+ examination had been abandoned in the area, and selection for secondary school was carried out on the basis of teachers' reports over the four years in the junior school. Sandra's mother felt that as Miss M. would thus be involved in the assessment, Sandra's chances of getting to a 'better' school were virtually non-existent. She clearly felt that Sandra's lack of success at her present school had been solely due to her unfortunate experiences with Miss M., and was relieved to think that at the secondary school she would have different teachers for separate subjects and so would not be 'dependent on one for all results'.

Although 'education conscious', Sandra's parents were probably more concerned for her happiness and peace of mind than her academic progress and may therefore have 'played down' the importance of school work during her time in Miss M.'s class when she had been performing so badly, and was so miserable at school.

Sandra felt that school work was important and wanted to do well. Although she talked of going to secondary modern school, she had not quite relinquished all hopes of a grammar school place, even though she had heard it was 'strict', 'Because I'd like to get somewhere in the world. I want to have a good background. So I'm just hoping . . .'

Sandra was a sensitive girl who needed plenty of praise, incentive and encouragement if she was to produce her best. Had it not been for her unhappy experiences in Miss M.'s class, unfortunately, extended to two years, she may have made better progress. Perhaps the following excerpt from her story[1] about a horse expresses her own feelings and sense of injustice when in Miss M.'s class:

'I was sold to this fellow Smith. He used to crack the whip three times a day and hurt us. So I kicked him and he whipped me. I was so sad—he used to treat all the other horses beautifully, but never me. I never will go back to him. He will always treat me nastily. But I can tell I will be happy with you for ever.' 'I hope so', said the farmer. 'I hope so too.'

JIMMY—*an underachiever*

Jimmy was a behaviour and work problem to his school. The school was non-streamed, and the children were allocated to classes by age. Jimmy was one of the youngest children in the youngest class. His progress had been mixed, showing sudden spurts in some subjects—for example, concept arithmetic between 9+ and 10+—and relative standstills in others.

It can be seen that Jimmy made almost no progress in reading in his second year, his raw score on the *same* test increasing by only one point, and his standardized score declining considerably. There is a discrepancy between much of Jimmy's attainment and his standardized score of 115 points at 8+ on a primary verbal test—the eighth highest score in a class of 32. The gaps in the table of standardized scores suggests a pattern of absence from school. In his second year Jimmy lost 16-20 days schooling through absence, in his third year 21-25 days, and 16-20 days in the fourth year. Over these three years his rate of absence was the highest in his year group.

---

[1] See Chapter 6 for details of essays.

TABLE 15.4: *Jimmy's test scores*

AGE	READING		ENGLISH		PROBLEM		MECHAN-ICAL		CONCEPT		VERBAL		STREAM
	Stan.	*Raw*	*Stan.*	*Raw*	*Stan.*	*Raw*	*Stan.*	*Raw*	*Stan.*	*Raw*	*Stan.*	*Raw*	
7+	118	23	110	13	93	3	102	8	–	–	–	–	Non-streamed school
8+	108	24	absent		absent		absent		absent		115	61†	
9+	110	32	113	46	104	16	98	14	107	26	110	22	
10+	absent		absent		absent		absent		121	48	absent		

†A different test used at 8+

Note: Stan.=standardized score; Raw=raw score

Jimmy also stood out from his fellow pupils in not being accepted by them and by his teachers. He received no choices from his classmates in a sociometric test in his first and fourth years, and in his third year he was chosen only to play with (not as a friend) by a boy and a girl. Both of these children, like Jimmy himself, were rated as 'quite often withdrawn' by their teacher, and one of them received very few choices from the other children. Jimmy had also received a succession of unfavourable ratings from his teachers on both his attainment and his behaviour. In the third year he was rated as one of the poorest in his class in reading. In fact, his standardized reading score was 110 at this time—well above the class average. Each year he had been rated 'a poor or lazy worker', and the headmaster summarized the staff's feeling that 'Jimmy is not by any means achieving up to capacity'. None of his teachers had rated Jimmy as a 'pleasure to have in the class', and he had also been consistently regarded as disobedient and liable to fight or bully other children.

His fourth year teacher was the most sympathetic towards his work and behaviour problems. He regarded Jimmy as a particular responsibility, and felt that the boy had not been handled patiently enough lower down the school. He was willing to absorb a certain amount of aggression from Jimmy in the hope that their relationship would improve to a point where he might have some influence. He agreed that Jimmy did misbehave in class, but had noted that he was also capable of good work if he felt involved. Jimmy had responded to this in terms of sentiment—'I like Mr. C. best of all the teachers I've had', but his behaviour in the class was largely unmodified: 'When I feel I've done enough, or I want to talk to the person sitting next to me, I talk to them.'

His feelings about work were more mixed than this statement would suggest. When asked what age he would most like to be he said: 'I should like to be back as a baby . . . because I'd get a second chance at my work at school'. He didn't like work particularly, but thought this was because 'I don't really catch on with it'. He wanted to please Mr. C., however, and added that if he had a chance to be a teacher, he would be a strict one—'I don't think that children ought to talk in class, but I like to'.

Most of the other teachers' patience did not last as long as Mr. C.'s, and during his first year Jimmy's behaviour was referred to the headmaster. The head represented Jimmy's disobedience and underachievement as simply the behaviour of a truculent and somewhat lazy child. But he drew attention to the fact that Jimmy had a younger brother who was educationally sub-normal and who naturally had received a great deal of attention from the parents, and suggested that this was probably an important factor in Jimmy's problem: since he had gone to a residential school in Jimmy's second year, he said, Jimmy's work and behaviour had improved.

His problem seemed to be located by the school exclusively within himself and his home background. There was an awareness that he was 'not among the normal run of boys in this school'. His home background was, in fact, different. His father worked in the retail trade, but the parents of most of his classmates were in professional and business occupations. Although most of the parents were claimed to be very keen on non-streaming and the school's associated developments in individual teaching and the child's planning of his own work, Jimmy's parents suspected it—being something entirely divorced from their own experience. They located the cause of their son's underachievement in the school, just as firmly as the school had located it in the home—'In the reports we get, every time it says: "Jimmy could do better, but he won't". But that's *their* problem, to make the child work; that's what he's there for.' They were not unambitious for Jimmy, and wanted him to go to university, but had found it difficult to help him with his work, since the school's methods were unfamiliar to them. When methods did seem similar

239

they often varied in detail only, a variation which to them seemed merely perverse. Their lack of understanding of the school's methods added to their conviction that modern education methods were 'a soft option for the teacher', and 'shirking the problem of discipline'.

Their bewilderment was increased when the head abolished homework entirely because he said it wasn't necessary for boys of that age. 'All I know is that it's necessary for Jimmy.' His mother also had some hard things to say about 'choice-time' where the children chose their own work-programme—'It's absolutely fantastic. If there's any time over, the child should be coached at the subject he's worst in'. If Jimmy misbehaved in class, this was likewise considered the school's problem—'They should punish him—I shan't complain'. Much of his behaviour at school was explained by his parents as related to the school's teaching methods —'The devil finds mischief for idle hands'. In support of this they claimed that he was well behaved at home—'If we *do* have any trouble—my saying is: "You're not at ———school now, my boy!" '

Both parents felt inhibited when they visited the school. Although they endorsed the greater discipline and formality of their own school experience, it had left them reluctant to challenge the authority of the teacher. As a result they felt their views went partly unrepresented, partly ignored. Opportunities for contact with the teachers were few. Finding themselves in a queue with other parents, and with a very short time available, they came away frustrated, feeling that a lot had been unsaid. They had formed a deep dislike of the school, and admitted to letting Jimmy stay away on occasions when it would have been better to insist on his going.

Jimmy's home background had also complicated his difficulties at school. Firstly, his misbehaviours had stood out amongst the tractable middle class children of which the school was chiefly composed. Secondly, it had been all too easy for the school to label Jimmy's problem as 'home background' rather than to look for ways in which the school could help. The boy was clearly in need of psychological help, but the school records revealed that he had had only one interview with someone from the Mental Welfare Department, which had yielded one brief and quite unclinical report. If his school and parents had effectively communicated to each other their aims and intentions for the boy, and had tried together to reach a solution, Jimmy's behaviour and attainments might have been much improved.

ALEX—*who was determined to succeed*

Alex was the eldest of four children of Central European parents of different nationalities. He was born in this country and went to an infant school situated in a largely immigrant area of an industrial city. Just before he was of junior age, however, the family moved out to a suburb of the city and Alex began his junior school career in that area. His scores at 7+ showed him to be somewhat below average, but since then he had made excellent progress, obtaining a grammar school place at the end of his fourth year.

TABLE 15.5: *Alex's test scores*

Age	Reading		English		Problem		Mechan- ical		Concept		Verbal		Stream
	Stan.	*Raw*	*Stan.*	*Raw*	*Stan.*	*Raw*	*Stan.*	*Raw*	*Stan.*	*Raw*	*Stan.*	*Raw*	
7+	89	9	92	5	93	5	104	12	–	–	–	–	Non- streamed school
8+	96	20	99	24	97	11	97	12	105	21	94	37†	
9+	101	30	102	42	107	21	110	26	109	34	91	12	
10+	111	39	102	46	111	25	121	39	115	48	95	20	

†A different test used at 8+

Note: Stan. = standardized score; Raw = raw score

For the first three years at the school Alex was rated by his teachers as 'below average' in ability. In the fourth year, however, his ability rating moved up three places and he was considered 'certain of a grammar school place'.

Alex's teachers had not only considered him of limited ability, but had also regarded him as less than an unqualified pleasure to have in their class. His first year teacher remembered him as 'reticent— odd—he would never come and confide. You could never "get hold" of him'. He also felt that, although not handicapped by language difficulty, Alex was unable to express himself fluently, and was generally 'not very capable'. His fourth year teacher described him in similar terms, as 'an introvert who never contributes anything to class, and who shows little interest in anything'. Far from being of limited ability, however, she felt that he was 'much brighter than he appears' and at times produced surprisingly excellent work, especially in maths. Both teachers agreed that Alex's unforthcoming attitude in class was due chiefly to basic laziness and indifference. From his teacher's unfavourable opinion of Alex, it would seem unlikely that he had sensed much encouragement or motivation from them to do well.

Alex's unresponsive attitude as perceived by his teachers was perhaps understandable, in view of the fact that his home background was very different from that of most of his classmates who came in the main from professional homes. These children were used to hearing and being included in adult conversations at home; they were themselves highly articulate and were encouraged in school to express their opinions and ideas freely. Alex, on the other hand, came from a lower social class background (his father was occupied on shift work in a city factory) and English was not the mother tongue of either of his parents. It was not surprising, therefore, that Alex seemed, and probably felt, different from his classmates. To interpret his unforthcoming attitude as laziness and lack of interest, however, would seem far from accurate, and was perhaps a rationalization on the part of his teachers to explain their inability to understand him.

Like many immigrant parents, Alex's father was very concerned that his children should do well at school, obtain good academic qualifications and 'better themselves'. His high aspirations were already suggested by the family's moving from a depressed immigrant area to a solidly middle class suburb and were further reflected in the desire that Alex should stay at a grammar school until he was eighteen and then go on to university. According to Alex's mother, her husband was very strict and authoritarian—he was determined that Alex should go to grammar school and his attempts to motivate his son to work towards this goal took the form of threats rather than encouragement. 'He says Alex has *got* to pass the 11+ or he'll not get to grammar school—and he *must* get to grammar school'. When he had visited the school on an Open Evening it was to stress to the teacher in broken English that Alex must be made to work— 'If he does not work—you smack!' The constant pressure to succeed had not, however, been accompanied by any attempt by Alex's father to take an active interest in the boy's education or to help him with his work. According to Alex, his mother would occasionally help him with homework, but 'Dad's always in the garden doing jobs'.

242

Alex's mother was somewhat less forceful in her ambitions for her son. She did not expect him to obtain a grammar school place— 'I know he's improved but I don't think he will go to grammar school. But I think it's better to be top in a secondary modern than bottom in a grammar'. Although she herself was willing to accept whatever situation came about, she was clearly worried as to what her husband's reactions would be if Alex did not fulfil his hopes.

According to his mother, Alex's reaction to the constant pressure from his father to get to grammar school was to assume a 'don't care' attitude. This would seem to be merely a superficial defensiveness, however, as he took his school work very seriously and had high aspirations for his future education and career.

He had found the work at his infant school in a depressed immigrant area comparatively easy, and was disturbed to find that much higher standards were expected at the 'new' junior school in the middle class area. He had not got on well with his first year junior teacher, who, he said, 'kept pulling my ears if I did anything wrong'. He began to worry that he was falling behind with his work and, although the children were not given homework to do, he began to take his books home 'to catch up'. According to his mother this was his own idea—'He would come home and sit and work and never play. He would say: "Oh, I've got to do this to catch up".' She felt that his excellent progress in the junior school was due solely to his own determined efforts and hard work. Alex himself was very conscious of the improvement in his work, and was hoping very much to get a grammar school place 'because you learn a lot and get a good job'. The importance of 'getting a good job' had been impressed on him by his father, and his mother, too, was keen for Alex to 'be something'. He expected to stay at school until he had passed his A-level exams, and would like to go on to college. He also had high aspirations for his subsequent career—'I am thinking of being a computerist (!)—feeding it with programs—or perhaps be an engineer and make one.'

His determination to work and do well at school extended even to subjects which he admitted he did not like very much—'I don't like some lessons, but I say to myself, if I didn't have them I wouldn't be clever, and wouldn't know as much as I do now'. How far this attitude was merely an echoing of his father's strictures is open to question; however, the effect it had had on Alex's performance is undoubtable. The motivation towards academic achievement which he had received at home had no doubt been reinforced by his school surroundings. Most of his classmates came from professional homes where academic success was highly valued and school achievement was at a premium, and they, too, were keen to do well at school.

At playtimes, Alex liked to 'walk around with my friends—and discuss things—how we're getting on'. His work and progress seemed never to be very far from his thoughts; unlike most boys of his age, when given three wishes, the only thing he wished for was 'to be a wise man'.

His own drive and determination seemed to be the chief factors contributing to his good progress and success, stimulated by pressure from a highly ambitious father. He had met little encouragement from his teachers—in fact, their attitude might well have had a *discouraging* effect on him. However, he had clearly adopted his father's high aspirations for him, and this had spurred him on to make tremendous progress and even to obtain the grammar school place which was out of the question in his early junior school years.

It is worth noting that had Alex attended a streamed school, he would certainly have been in a B-stream, and possibly even a 'C' class on the strength of his scores at 7+. This leads one to speculate what effect being in a lower stream might have had on his drive to succeed and also on his subsequent progress.

DAVID—*a left-handed 'problem'*

David was a rather small, serious boy, with exceptional vocabulary and powers of self-expression for his age. He came to his junior school late in the summer term of his first year, his parents having moved from another part of the country. He was placed provisionally in the B-stream of a three-stream school, but moved to the A-stream at the beginning of his second year. In this second year particularly he made outstanding progress, and became one of the highest achieving children in his year group. His rate of progress in maths, however, had begun to show a marked decline in the fourth year.

David did not enjoy life in his second year class. He described his relationship with Mr. J., the teacher of 2A—'We didn't get along together, and I never got along in that class.'

Mr. J., who regarded David as 'a boy of immense potentialities', pressed him very hard in his second year, particularly on improving his handwriting, which was at times nearly illegible. The difficulty about David's handwriting seemed to have arisen from his father's refusal to acknowledge the boy as a natural left-hander, and his insistence that he should use his right hand. He found right-handed writing extremely difficult, and a number of arguments resulted between him and his father, and between his father and his mother, who was convinced that the problem had been over-emphasized. 'I didn't agree at the time. My husband has realized since that he was wrong, and he shouldn't have forced David to do it.' The infant school, when it found out about this, had tried to encourage David to write with his left hand, but encountered no greater success. David relished the thought of owning a typewriter, so that he might avoid the physical act of writing. Even so, one of his main spare time activities was writing imaginative stories, for which he had taken his own pseudonym.

TABLE 15.6: *David's test scores*

AGE	READING		ENGLISH		PROBLEM		MECHAN-ICAL		CONCEPT		VERBAL		STREAM
	Stan.	*Raw*	*Stan.*	*Raw*	*Stan.*	*Raw*	*Stan.*	*Raw*	*Stan.*	*Raw*	*Stan.*	*Raw*	
7+	93	10	94	3	73	0	123	18	–	–	–	–	B
8+	126	35	122	45	125	21	115	20	114	25	121	68†	A
9+	131	42	116	50	137	28	127	36	124	43	134	35	A
10+	141	46	115	57	116	25	119	36	117	46	119	34	A

†A different test used at 8+

Note: Stan.=standardized score; Raw=raw score

David's dislike of handwork may also have been associated with his early difficulties in writing. His mother described him as having little patience in learning skills requiring manual co-ordination—'Whereas Michael (his younger brother) will keep at it until he gets it right, David will just give up'. There seemed to be nothing wrong with his general physical co-ordination and he played in the school football team. Instead, his learning of manual skills, especially if associated with school work, seemed to have become the subject of a large emotional block. The pressure exerted by Mr. J.

in this field may have provoked David's negative reaction to the teacher. He certainly found Mr. J.'s. general approach unacceptable —'Even in a school football match, when I fell over injured, he called out "Get up, you fool".'

Mr. J. complained that David used to interrupt his lessons with questions and this broke the flow of class teaching. If corrected on this, David's reaction was not to pursue the point, but to withdraw completely—'A wall came down between us, and I couldn't get through to him'. Sometimes, he felt, David's questioning interruptions were of genuine interest, 'but unfortunately I couldn't pursue them or the whole lesson would be lost'. David's mother added another explanation for the bad relationship with Mr. J.—'David has always talked to adults more as equals, as if he was an adult too. I think Mr. J. may never have got used to this, and may have thought David was being rude'.

The relationship became so bad that the head saw David's mother half-way through the second year, and warned her that David might have to be transferred back to the B-stream. She was told at that time that his work in a number of subjects was deteriorating. Both his parents were upset about this, since they had believed that his unhappiness at school was associated simply with his difficulty at making new friends, and were unaware that there were also difficulties in his relationship with his teachers and in his school work.

David did survive his second year in the A-stream, and went on to 3A, and a woman teacher. Here, according to David, his parents, and the headmaster and staff, he made spectacular progress which he felt would have been made in the second year had he not been inhibited by his poor relationship with Mr. J. As his mother put it: 'David came on wonderfully in the third year teacher's class. She seemed to know David and to understand him'.

The third year teacher was very sympathetic towards David. She thought that his ability had not been allowed to develop under Mr. J.'s demanding approach, and adopted a compensating protective attitude towards the boy, trying to coax his best work out of him. When David expressed a strong dislike for handwork and craft lessons, she arranged for him to read during the period instead; generally, the pressure on David declined. It was only kept high in one area, and David, at the request of his parents, was given handwriting exercises to do at home. But his parents demanded perfection in this exercise, and he became anxious and tense and the practice was dropped. The teacher explained: 'I felt that this approach would probably lead to more tension and less progress in

David than if we left him to progress at his own rate'. David felt that this third year teacher was the best he had had—'She was just likeable, and she always gave individual attention; I think that's important as well'.

Although he did make progress in the third year in most subjects, this was far less spectacular than the progress he actually made in his second year, under the disliked Mr. J. (see Table 15.6). According to his attainment test results his progress during the second year in Reading, English and Problem Arithmetic was exceptionally good, and it is difficult to understand how the school could have come to believe that this year was one of standstill or decline. Possibly both the headmaster and Mr. J., in their anxiety about David as a behavioural problem, failed to reach an objective assessment of his attainment level. In terms of academic performance, Mr. J.'s pressure on David was clearly successful, although it exacted its price in David's poor behaviour and unhappy relationship with his teacher.

Pressure was also consistently high from David's parents. His father, particularly, had high aspirations which, according to his mother, were to some extent a compensation for his own failure to get on in the world. David described how 'they interrogate me nightly' on the work he had done during the school day. Although more realistic, and more immediately demanding of their son, his parents' aspirations for him were unlikely to be as high as David's for himself. He spoke of himself as an M.P., and a possible Minister of Education. He also wanted to be a computer programmer, a professional footballer, and a jockey.

David's scores on the children's attitude questionnaire suggested a fairly confident boy, considering school work important, but who was not satisfied with his present class and teacher. He had very definite ideas on what an ideal teacher should be like—'He shouldn't be dull, but should be doing new things all the time'. Boredom as a result of too much revision was one of his major problems in the fourth year, and it may be that the failure of his fourth year experience to extend him sufficiently had been the cause of the wide ranging decline in his scores at 10+.

JULIE—*who had uninterested parents*

Julie was a friendly, likeable girl who, in her fourth year, was the most popular girl in her class. She began her junior school career in an A-stream but was demoted to a 'B' class at the end of her first

247

year. Her test results over the four years in the school indicated very poor progress and while her reading and English were average at seven-plus, her arithmetic was very poor.

TABLE 15.7: *Julie's test scores*

AGE	READING		ENGLISH		PROBLEM		MECHAN-ICAL		CONCEPT		VERBAL		STREAM
	Stan.	*Raw*	*Stan.*	*Raw*	*Stan.*	*Raw*	*Stan.*	*Raw*	*Stan.*	*Raw*	*Stan.*	*Raw*	
7+	106	22	100	12	68	0	82	4	–	–	–	–	A
8+	100	24	95	17	81	4	76	4	78	5	97	43†	B
9+	92	23	99	35	73	4	80	8	83	11	87	10	B
10+	91	28	95	43	89	15	76	8	83	16	94	19	B

†A different test used at 8+
Note: Stan.=standardized score; Raw=raw score

Julie's first year teacher had been surprised when the girl went down to the B-stream; she felt that she had held her own in the 'A' class during the year and it was 'a mystery' to her when Julie 'got nowhere in the exam'. Subsequent teachers, however, had considered Julie 'definitely a B-stream child'. This view was echoed by the head, who had no recollection of Julie ever having been in an 'A' class.

Julie's teachers agreed that although her English and reading were fairly satisfactory, as far as arithmetic was concerned there was an 'absolute blank'. Her fourth year teacher felt that she was very slow to grasp new ideas and methods and would become panic-stricken if she did not understand. Rather than ask for help, however, she would sit and 'muddle along' and if not carefully watched would simply 'down tools and sit there'. Her previous teacher had also noticed this tendency and felt that, although Julie worried about her inability to cope, she hated to be singled out for individual attention as she felt that the other children were laughing at her. Julie herself admitted her difficulty with arithmetic and her consequent dislike of the subject—'I hate sums; I can't do them. I don't like the working out—I like to write the answer straight down'. According to her teachers Julie's way of overcoming her difficulty in arithmetic was to ignore it—'She thinks things are easy because she only does what she can'.

Going down to the B-stream did not appear to have worried Julie a great deal. She greatly preferred her present class to the A-stream where 'they do harder work'. Her demotion did not appear to have caused any concern at home either—her mother, in fact, like the head, had completely forgotten that Julie had ever been in an 'A' class, and could only remember that her younger brother, Paul, had gone down to a 'B' class at the end of his first year! Paul, according to the children's mother, was definitely the 'brighter spark of the two'. 'Julie's work just doesn't compare with Paul's—and you do compare the two.' Paul was also much more lively and inquisitive than Julie, who tended to be quiet, take life very seriously and would 'never be brilliant'.

Julie's father was an ex-regular serviceman who was employed in a factory in the area, and according to her headmaster, who had visited the home, discipline was strict and based on army lines. Her father's apparent sole concern regarding Julie's school performance was that she should cause no trouble and do as she was told. Both parents were aware that her academic progress at school had not been good and that she found maths especially difficult. On the whole they felt she was 'just average'—'Sometimes she's bright and amazes us—other times you could shake her!' They had made little attempt to help her at home with work which she found difficult, feeling it better to leave such things to her teachers 'who know best'. Her father also held the view that 'they are at school all day—they need freedom of an evening'. Julie's home pastimes were not of an academic nature—her favourite hobby was baby-sitting, or taking babies for walks. She also spent a considerable amount of free time watching television and writing 'scary stories' based on episodes she had seen on the screen (her favourite subject at school was composition). Julie claimed that she enjoyed reading, especially fairytales, comics and similar books. She had only a few books at home, all of which she had read several times. At home she made very little mention of school or school work. As her mother put it: 'Julie likes to come home and forget she's ever been to school'.

Neither of Julie's parents held very high aspirations for her educational or vocational future. They would be content for her to attend the local secondary modern school until she was 16, which they assumed would be the minimum age for leaving by that time (otherwise she would definitely leave school at 15)—'I don't want her to stay on unless she makes some remarkable improvement and I can see some future'. Her parents had not given any thought to her eventual career or employment; her mother did not feel it was a question of great importance as 'only one girl in a thousand makes a good career woman'. Julie, she had noticed, was already displaying strong maternal instincts—'Her aim in life is to get married and have children—even at 11!' Julie's only idea of a future career was to work in a home for unwanted babies—'she's very concerned about people not wanting their children'. Her mother felt that ultimately Julie would 'probably just be an ordinary housewife', and expressed the hope that she would make a happy marriage—'That will suit us'.

Both parents clearly showed more interest and concern in their son's future. His mother expressed the hope that he would manage to work back into the A-stream, which, she felt, was an advantage which was 'more important for a boy'. She and her husband had already discussed nine-year old Paul's future, and were hoping that he would obtain a place at grammar school. The boy's subsequent career had also been discussed and his father was keen for him to take up an apprenticeship of some kind. Both parents clearly believed that education and training were of far greater importance for a boy than for a girl—'After all, he is the breadwinner in the end'.

Julie's aspirations for her own future were, like those of her parents, extremely limited. She was hoping to go to the local secondary modern school which her closest friend attended, and had no conception of, or interest in, what it would be like, other than the fact that 'you swap round (classes) every 40 minutes'. Her ideas on the age at which she would leave school seemed to have been conditioned by the fact that 'Mum said it would be 16'. She personally felt that she would rather be at work than at school, although: 'My Dad said you'll regret the day you start work'. Her current aspirations were completely unrelated to any educational or scholastic goals; she wished she were 16 so that she would 'be able to go to dances', and when given three wishes her only ambition was 'to be one of those millionaires'.

It would appear that home background had contributed at least in part to Julie's lack of progress during her four years in junior school. Her parents had very low aspirations and gave no encouragement, if at all it was to 'forget all about school' when she came home; they had made little attempt to help her with her obvious difficulties or to motivate her towards greater success in school work. Little was expected of her in the academic field, and Julie could hardly have failed to become aware of this.

NORA—*a 'helpful' girl*

Nora was a friendly, talkative, 'motherly' sort of girl whose voice and manner of speech suggested a middle-aged woman rather than a child of eleven. Her progress during her four years at a large, non-streamed junior school, had been poor, especially in arithmetic, in which she began somewhat above average and deteriorated drastically in terms of both standardized and raw scores.

TABLE 15.8: *Nora's test scores*

AGE	READING		ENGLISH		PROBLEM		MECHAN-ICAL		CONCEPT		VERBAL		STREAM
	Stan.	*Raw*	*Stan.*	*Raw*	*Stan.*	*Raw*	*Stan.*	*Raw*	*Stan.*	*Raw*	*Stan.*	*Raw*	
7+	86	8	88	4	109	12	109	15	–	–	–	–	Non-streamed school
8+	82	11	85	8	100	13	80	6	95	14	82	19†	
9+	80	16	87	20	73	4	81	9	95	21	90	12	
10+	81	20	88	28	76	8	76	9	83	17	90	17	

†A different test used at 8+

Note: Stan.=standardized score; Raw=raw score

Nora's first year teacher rated her as 'average' in ability; since then she had been considered 'below average and possibly backward' each year. Her fourth year teacher felt that her progress had been very slow, that she suffered from all-round reading difficulty and seemed unable to grasp new processes in arithmetic.

According to Nora's school reports, her most outstanding quality as perceived by her teachers had been her 'helpfulness'. As her fourth year teacher put it: 'She has a flair for tidying up—she does jobs thoroughly'. As a result of this Nora had been entrusted in her fourth year with certain staffroom duties, which, in her own words, involved 'cleaning the staffroom, washing the cups, seeing to the kettles, tidying chairs, and cleaning out the ashtrays'. Nora spent a considerable amount of time each day thus occupied, while the rest of her class were having lessons. From time to time she could also be seen approaching members of staff to ask if they had any jobs for her to do.

Nora had been popular with her teachers, all of whom had remarked in reports how 'helpful and reliable' she was. Her mother had found these comments satisfying but did not altogether approve of the amount of time Nora spent tidying up the staffroom 'because while she's doing that, the others are doing lessons, so she gets behind'.

Nora's enthusiasm for domestic chores was also exercised at home. Much of her free time was spent 'helping Mummy with work— washing up, making beds, lighting fires, helping with dinner on Sundays'. She seemed to have little inclination for hobbies and pursuits more normally associated with children of her age—'I feel a bit lost on Sundays, there's not much to do after helping Mummy'. On the 'interests' questionnaire Nora listed her favourite hobby as 'baby-sitting'—frequently during her spare time she and a friend 'take babies out so their mothers can get on with their work'.

Nora's home background was described by her teacher as 'not very strong—there's not too much care'. Both parents went out to work—her father at a local factory, and her mother at a factory some distance from home. This necessitated her leaving home early in the morning and returning late in the evening, so that a neighbour 'saw to' the three children in the morning and they returned to her until their mother arrived home in the evening. The general appearance of the home and the family was one of carefree untidiness.

Nora's mother was aware of the poor progress which the girl was making at school and particularly of her backwardness in arithmetic. This, her mother felt, was because 'she don't know her tables and it's pulling her back'. She had in fact, tried to help Nora to learn tables but had made no headway and abandoned the attempt in impatience, 'I tried to learn her but it just doesn't sink in. If you shout at her she just sits down and cries—just doesn't want to know. I just give up—she's not going to *attempt* it.'

A similar attempt to help Nora's elder sister with her homework had likewise ended in friction, due to the fact that the mother could not comprehend the method of subtraction taught in the school—'I said the teacher was definitely *wrong!*'

Arithmetic presented the biggest worry to Nora—she knew she was 'a bit left behind'. Her mother felt that this was due to the fact that she became very nervous if she didn't understand something, and instead of asking for help would struggle to do it by herself and consequently get hopelessly left behind. Nora herself seemed more concerned about her slowness than her lack of understanding—her teacher pointed out that she was more worried about finishing her work than about getting it right. As far as understanding the work was concerned, Nora seemed to be repressing any doubts as to her ability to cope—'I'm not very good at the moment, but I'm hoping I soon will be.'

Her poor reading was also a source of anxiety for Nora, and she seemed to try to compensate for this by helping her young sister (aged 9) and her friends with their reading difficulties. She helped them to 'split the words up' in the same way that her teacher helped her, and clearly found pleasure and self-confidence in this.

Although her parents showed some concern over her lack of progress and had made a token attempt to help her with her work, it was clear that they had little idea of what the school was doing and were not well-informed about educational matters generally. Her mother expressed indignation that she had been told at a meeting about secondary education that Nora would not 'go up' to grammar school. This meeting had been held in November and, as the children did not take the 11+ exam till January, Nora's mother felt that this was prejudging the issue unfairly—'I thought—well! it just might be one of them things that she could sit down and *do*! That don't give the child confidence.' Apart from this however, Nora's parents were not greatly concerned about the 11+; at the time of the exam, her elder sister had been in hospital and her mother 'didn't have much time or interest for it'. She felt that the local secondary modern school seemed quite suitable, and like Nora, laid more emphasis on domestic rather than academic subjects—'They learn to cook—there's two domestic science rooms and needlework rooms—I'm not sorry she's not going to an "upper" school'. She expressed willingness for Nora to stay on at school until 16 'if she wants to', and while having no clear aspirations for her vocational future, would like her to 'be something', although this seemed restricted to a disapproval of factory work which she herself had taken up and 'thought it was silly afterwards'.

Nora's own ambitions were also limited. She was apprehensive about going to another school and was 'wondering what the work is going to be like'. Her only interest in her next school lay in the introduction of cookery and other domestic lessons. As far as a future career was concerned, hairdressing or 'working in a shop' were the most popular alternatives, plus the somewhat unrealistic one of 'working in a stable with horses'.

In spite of her difficulties with work, she was happy at school; she liked her teacher and got on well with her own particular friends. Having failed to distinguish herself academically, she seemed to have concentrated all her efforts in obtaining approval at home and in school in the field in which she excelled—domestic chores. She clearly found great pleasure in being commended by the head for her work in the staffroom—'Sometimes he says I'm very helpful'.

Nora had lost a great deal of ground in basic subjects since she first came to school. The little help she had received at home was inadequate to overcome her difficulties, and although recognized as 'below average' by the school and clearly in need of help, she had been allowed to spend time in the staffroom while she would clearly have been better employed in her class.

An attempt has been made in these case studies to examine reasons for success or failure in school. It was found that although one factor in a number of the studies stood out as an obvious cause, usually success or failure was a result of a whole pattern of interacting influences.

References

WALL, W. D., SCHONELL, F. J. and OLSEN, W. C. (1962). *Failure in School.* Hamburg: Unesco Institute of Education.

CHAPTER 16

Dynamics of Change[1]

A Study of Three Schools Making an Organizational Change

IT was suggested that schools undergoing a change of organization from streaming to non-streaming or vice versa might be worthy of particular attention because: (i) a school in the transitional stage may highlight the essential differences between these forms of organization, and, in particular, the extent to which each form of organization delineates particular curricula and/or methods of teaching; (ii) because it was expected that the initial attitudes of the staff, plus the manner in which the change was introduced, would be important factors in determining the extent to which the change was 'successful'.

The seventy-two schools in the longitudinal study had all, with one exception, kept the same form of organization during the years of the research programme. A number of them had, however, introduced organizational changes with children younger than those being studied. By 1967, the last year of the study, three schools which had gradually introduced change had experienced the new form of organization for three years. In all cases the change had been introduced with children entering the school a year later than the longitudinal study children. The other schools referred to above were in much earlier stages of organizational change. These three schools were therefore the ones selected for detailed study.

School A, which changed from streaming to non-streaming, was situated on a large council estate. It was designed as a three form entry junior school but the number of forms per year group varied between three and four. There were approximately 30–35 children in each class. By 1967, only the fourth-year children were still streamed.

School B, which also changed from streaming to non-streaming, served a mixed urban area. Its pupils came from a broad cross-section of home backgrounds, although a higher proportion came from professional and clerical homes than in Schools A and C.

---

[1] This chapter was written with the assistance of Peter B. Healey, who was responsible for the fieldwork.

255

This was a two form entry junior school and there were approximately 30–32 children in each class. The school completed the change in three years instead of four and had non-streamed the longitudinal study children at the beginning of their fourth year.[1]

School C, which changed from non-streaming to streaming, fell between the other two in terms of social class background, serving an older, more established council estate. This was a three form entry junior school and had about 100–110 children in each year group, the number of children in the class varying according to stream. In 1967 only its fourth year was non-streamed, the other years having been streamed from entry. This school was the only one in the study known to be changing from a non-streamed to a fully streamed form of organization.

Financial and staffing considerations limited the scope of this inquiry to firstly, classroom observations and discussions with teachers as to their teaching methods: and secondly, a longer intensive interview with the head, his deputy and three other members of staff. In both types of school, where sufficient variation in the staff's opinion allowed, at least one teacher holding each of the following views was interviewed:

(a)   initially pro-streaming.[2]
(b)   initially undecided or neutral.
(c)   initially anti-streaming.

The aim of the interviews was to make a detailed study of the teacher's attitudes and approaches to his job, and of his reaction to the introduction and workings of the new type of organization.

In addition to the direct fieldwork, a short programme of testing—Problem Arithmetic and English—was carried out with the 1966-67 second and third year children, so that some comparison could be made between the attainments of these children (who had experienced only the new form of organization) and the children in the longitudinal study at the same age. A direct, but limited, comparison between the levels of attainment associated with both streaming and non-streaming within the same school was therefore possible.

Initial attitudes of staff to streaming

All three schools introduced their organizational change in 1964-65. In order to estimate the sort of reception it would receive

---

[1]As the follow-up children in school B experienced an organizational change they had to be omitted from the longitudinal study analysis.

[2] On the basis of score on the attitude to streaming scale (see Chapter 3).

staff attitudes and the numbers of Type 1 (typical non-streamer) and Type 2 (typical streamer) teachers were examined.[1]

In Schools A and B, which changed to non-streaming, the majority of staff, just before the change, believed in streaming and were typical 'streamers' or Type 2 teachers. In School A, only one teacher believed in non-streaming but four (including this teacher) used teaching methods and held views typical of the non-streamer, while the remaining fourteen were classified as typical streamers. It might be added here that the head of School A did not initially favour non-streaming but was willing to experiment. In School B, only the head and the deputy head supported non-streaming. Only School C, which changed to streaming, had a majority of teachers with views supporting the change: eight were typical 'streamers' and the remaining four were typical 'non-streamers'. Three of the non-streamers were to leave at the end of the term, giving the head an opportunity to select new staff favouring streaming.

This, then was the picture of staff opinions in the three schools at the end of the summer term just before the new form of organization was introduced.

School A's change to non-streaming started with the headmaster's experiment of non-streaming a first year group, which was then streamed in the normal way in the second, third and fourth years. When this group had reached the fourth year, its attainments were compared with previous fourth years and the headmaster found ('to my surprise') that the experimental group had done better. Despite all the imponderables in sampling, control and evaluation of this experiment, the headmaster, normally a convinced streamer, thought that non-streaming in the first year had been responsible for the higher attainment; and although he and most of his staff still favoured streaming the comparison had prepared the ground for a tempering of attitudes. The start of the complete changeover to non-streaming came at the beginning of the 1964-65 school year. The head said: 'Although I was very much for streaming, I thought there might be something in non-streaming' and 'was willing to give it a try'. He gave various reasons as to why the change took place, one being that the classes were of a reasonably small size, but the clearest picture came from combining his views with the consistent observations made by his staff.

The local education authority was, it seemed, in favour of non-streaming and if the school wished to introduce non-streaming, it

[1] See Chapter 4.

would ensure that sufficient staff and finance were forthcoming to overcome initial difficulties. The change was agreed to and one additional assistant teacher was added to the school's quota. This teacher arrived in the 1963-64 school year and enabled the head to organize his first year children into four smaller, instead of three streamed classes. In addition, the head created a new position—a head of department for the lower juniors (first two years) who was to be responsible for the development of the curriculum and teaching methods for these years, with special reference to the new non-streamed classes.

In School B which also changed to non-streaming the head was the major influence behind the change. On arrival at the school as a new head, he found it rigidly streamed and timetabled, and, having previously only experienced schools too small to stream and having always wanted to stream, he thought at first he had discovered his ideal school. Shortly, however, he began to have doubts. He found that 'at any time it would be possible to interchange the top 20 per cent of the B-stream and the bottom 20 per cent of the A-stream without any effect on the relative attainment of the two classes'. This overlap implied some flexibility to the head, at least in the teachers' perceptions of the children's ability. But he found none —'A' children were 'A' children, and as such, better than 'B' children. The head then began to doubt how far his original belief in the equivalence of the top 'B' and the bottom 'A' children was justified, since it seemed likely that the 'B' children were being held back by the limited expectations of their teachers. Thus, the first seeds of doubt were laid. It was only when he came to see other disadvantages during the next few years that he finally decided to change to non-streaming.

In School C, six years after the introduction of non-streaming, streaming began to be re-introduced. Non-streaming, as an organization affecting the *whole* school, had lasted only three years. Unlike the other schools, the staff in School C appeared to play an important role in determining the change.

Although the head paid lip-service to non-streaming, one might ask how deep his commitment was and why he favoured it. He believed in the 'social advantages' of non-streaming but felt that there was no difference in the academic standard reached in the two forms of organization. It seemed that the need to preserve order and discipline was stronger than the desire to introduce an increasingly child-centred educational atmosphere. The social doubts about streaming which he had during his first headship, centred on the problems generated by the anti-social elements in the lowest ability streams, rather than on the disadvantages of individual children. When he became head of School C, he had introduced non-streaming because of problem children who 'were dispersed—and it was just as though the school had had a tranquillizer'.

He believed, however, in the need for experienced teachers to take non-streamed classes because 'it's more demanding'. When he first introduced non-streaming he considered that, even if there were 'weak links' among the staff, the balance of experience at that time was favourable. To upset the balance however, it only required a few experienced teachers to leave. The younger replacements, in most cases taking up their first teaching post, found the demands of a non-streamed class somewhat beyond them, their problems being mainly of a disciplinary nature. It was at this time that the head re-introduced streaming. The rest of his staff favoured streaming— most were identified as typical streamers—but it is doubtful whether this was a determinant in the change. Anxiety was felt by many of the staff at this time about the performance of their children in the eleven-plus and this may have reinforced the head's decision to re-introduce streaming, but probably more important was the loss of experienced teachers.

Methods of introducing the change

One reason for slowing the pace of a major educational change, such as the introduction of streaming or non-streaming is that it allows the school a period of adjustment. It also enables the head-master to postpone the evil day for 'oppositionists' on his staff by offering them jobs in the old organization at the upper end of the school for two or three years ahead. This is certainly a long enough period for such a teacher to look for another post in a school whose policy more closely reflects his own approaches. If a school loses its staff before the change is completed, the headmaster may be able to turn the situation to his advantage by recruiting replacements sympathetic to the new form of organization.

In School A, the staff were given a half-term's warning that a change to non-streaming would take place in the new school year. This was communicated through the staff-room noticeboard in the list allocating staff to classes for the 1964-65 session. Since it was a gradual change, only teachers of the first year children were immedi-ately concerned and, for the new four-form intake, three teachers were recruited from outside and only one member of the existing staff was involved. New staff taking up their posts in September 1964 had their first intimation of the change at that time. There was no official staff meeting prior to September 1964, either about the fact that change was taking place, or to discuss the teaching methods thought to be appropriate to the new scheme. The head, had however, discussed the change 'with the more responsible members of staff'.

As the head of School B became doubtful about streaming, he began to challenge the opinions of his staff and 'somewhat ruthlessly exploited these differences', as a result of which most of the staff resigned within the following two years. For two years, the head made no changes. The time-lag was considered necessary, partly because he was a new head and felt that 'it's a very exceptional head who can make the school his own without appointing his own staff' and also 'simply because it was not the kind of staff you could do it with: they were "too traditional".' Therefore, he was grateful when the 'old' staff departed.

Then followed the period of 'educative discussion', usually quite informally with one or two staff members, and his deputy, who also favoured non-streaming. Both the head and his deputy claimed that they preferred these small groups to formal staff meetings. The head felt that his arguments would be better received on an individual basis than by a group 'whose individual reservations add up'. The deputy head, on the other hand, felt that a series of individual meetings of this sort ensured a better representation of staff opinions. The head's view of the discussion process was probably more nearly correct, and certainly this gradual approach, extending over two years, was relatively successful in terms of staff stability: only one member of staff had left since the change was introduced. (Four teachers, however, had left in the term preceding the change). Despite having the say on overall policy, the head did not specify what teaching methods the staff should employ, but he did emphasize his dislike of streaming within the class.

As in School A, the staff in School C were uninvolved in the decision-making on the organizational change. Indeed, there was no meeting between head and staff to inform them of the introduction of streaming. The head in School C saw himself as a 'benevolent autocrat' acting in relation to his staff 'in the same way', he believed, 'that they should act towards their pupils'. Decisions about school policy came from the top and the staff were there to put them into effect. The head had allocated the new first year to streams on the basis of infant school records and only by noticing differences between the three classes had the staff become aware of streaming. But at no time was there an indication from the head that streaming was replacing non-streaming. The head, of course, may have had reasons for doing this; he believed that there were social disadvantages with streaming, and he may have hoped for a while at least to avoid these by not labelling the classes and not announcing the fact to the school or staff. The staff did not agree on the reasons for introducing non-streaming and then streaming: one teacher thought that streaming had been re-introduced because the 'A' children were not being fully extended, another because the 'C' children were falling behind, and the third suggested that the head should be asked. The lack of communication was on the whole accepted: 'When streaming was introduced it was without consultation, which the head, of course, has a perfect right to do' (this was from a teacher who demanded 'respect rather than liking' from her children).

Attitudes of staff to the change

In all three schools, the staff played a chiefly passive role in the change. The role of the head was authoritarian: he could run his school in the way he liked whatever the preferences or wishes of his staff. If they did not like it, they could resign. Only the head in School B communicated with his staff, although they, too, were quite powerless. The staff in School C were relieved when the changeover to streaming was re-introduced and, as far as they were concerned, the sooner it applied throughout the whole of the school the better. In School A, most of the staff were not in favour of non-streaming, and in School B, they were apathetic about the change and 'almost all the staff had no strong opinions about it either way'.

By introducing non-streaming in the first year initially with new or 'sympathetic' teachers, the heads of Schools A and B had avoided opposition or trouble. As one head put it: 'It was my policy to keep the older, more traditional teachers away from the non-streamed classes at first'. But in both schools, the staff had not realized that the change would gradually extend right through the school, and this misunderstanding had affected their initial reaction: 'I felt it would not affect me personally', and 'When I heard it was being introduced lower down the school, I didn't think too much about it, because it didn't affect me at the time'. However, when it was continued into the second year, both staffs became not only aware of the implications of the change but also more involved. In School A, a number of staff meetings, both formal and informal, were held before non-streaming was extended to the second year and most of the staff were against the change, although as one member put it: 'Everyone could see the advantage of never being landed with a C-stream class'.

In neither school, A or B, were meetings held during the first year or before the second year to discuss or perhaps evolve possible teaching techniques. So that some teachers felt 'apprehensive' about taking a non-streamed class, others 'felt incompetent', and one teacher 'wondered what the others were doing'. As one teacher said: 'When I first started taking a non-streamed class, I knew I would have to change my teaching method, but I was very ill-informed of what had been happening in the non-streamed classes'. Teachers kept their problems and what went on in their classroom to themselves. This lack of communication about teaching methods probably stems from the perceived role of the teacher whose classroom is his kingdom and who is free to do whatever he likes in his own room. This is supported by the comment of one of the heads, who said: 'They are competent professionals, and on principle I would not visit a classroom without special need'.

Although there was very little formal discussion of the new teaching methods required, both Schools A and B had introduced the 'new maths' a number of years before changing to non-streaming. One teacher in particular, in School B, thought that the timing of the introduction of the Nuffield Maths was intended to 'soften-up' some of the more reluctant teachers to the introduction of new teaching methods involved in non-streaming.

After experiencing non-streaming, satisfaction with it seemed to depend on the teacher's ability to cope with group teaching and also on his attitudes to the different ability levels. For example, those who were sympathetic to the average and less able child mentioned the social and academic advantages of non-streaming: 'It's a good leveller and children accept each other more readily', or 'There's no antagonism or "looking down" that existed under streaming'. 'Non-streaming seems to help those who would be in a 'B' or 'C' class because they get a better example and a better atmosphere'. However, some teachers—both for and against non-streaming—believed that the academic progress of the bright child suffered under non-streaming and 'that brighter children do better in an A-stream'.

A few did not accept the new system and attacked the difficulties associated with teaching a non-streamed class—'I think it's a stupid system because the teacher of a non-streamed class is teaching at many different levels (in her case, nine) whereas in an A-stream, if you split them into A's, B's and C's you can cope with *three* levels in a class', and 'I find it very difficult to work with five different groups'. These teachers also tended to be more interested in teaching the bright child—'I resent the time I have to spend teaching a child to read when the time could be spent in extending the brighter children. I prefer not to have this child in my class—I'm more interested in the brighter child'.

Why did these teachers stay at the school if they were opposed to the school's organizational change? They could have left and found another post elsewhere.[1] It seemed, that rather than do this, they accepted the organization, externally at least, and adjusted to it. The heads did not seem to concern themselves too much with classroom practice, so that a teacher could choose his own methods—those which gave him most satisfaction, and fulfilled the aims which he considered important. These may or may not have been the aims of the head.

In School C, the staff welcomed the change back to streaming. The four teachers interviewed held similar views on education (in favour of eleven-plus selection, against secondary re-organization, in favour of streaming all children, with the possible exception of the middle ability group) which could be described as more typical of the views held by teachers in streamed schools. For them, the aim of education was to obtain high marks on attainment tests:

'During non-streaming, the better ones were passing for grammar school but not at a really high mark—they found when they got there, having scraped in, they suddenly shot ahead—so they had obviously been held back—if they had been pushed, they might have done a lot better . . . The percentage of grammar school places didn't change'.

But these teachers, too, like those opposed to the system in Schools A and B, saw no inconsistency in remaining in the school under the non-streamed organization and externally, at least, accommodated themselves to its demands.

---

[1] In School A, only four members of staff out of a possible sixteen remained from September 1964 to early 1967, when the fieldwork took place. After the first year of non-streaming seven members of staff left; all had legitimate personal reasons for the move, and it is impossible to know what part, if any, the change in school policy played in their decisions.

Although School B also had a large change in staff after the arrival of the new head, most of these took place before any organizational change came about.

After the change

The successful introduction of a new system would seem to depend on tact and patience on the part of the head and also on the changing consensus of staff opinions. But, in addition to this, it requires different attitudes, and new methods and approaches. This section will attempt to illustrate how new teaching methods in the classroom may be essential accompaniments of a new organization if the aims associated with it are to be fulfilled.

In School A, the methods were a mixture, reflecting an intention by some staff to ensure that the non-streaming principle was carried into the detail of classroom practice, and the wish of others to continue to group by ability. During the first year, the staff in School A were left to themselves, and it was not until the fourth term, when non-streaming had reached the second year, that difficulties and the head's dissatisfactions with the system were brought to light. The head had discovered that a number of the staff were streaming within their classes and 'they had a group of A children and a group of C children sitting in different places and doing different work'. As the head said: 'I didn't want to impose my will on the staff but—'. So he called his staff together, criticizing their present approach—'which defeated the purpose of reorganization'—and suggested that they should use the method adopted by one of the more 'successful' members of staff. He had devised a system based on the division of the class into five or six mixed ability groups. Normally there would be one bright, one dull and four children of middle range ability in each group. In addition to the ability criterion, the groups were also made up on the basis of children's friendships. He had five activities—English, Maths, 'Topic' (a social studies project), Painting and Reading, and the idea was that each group did each activity in rotation, but that at any given time not more than one or two groups were involved in any given activity. The teacher who devised the scheme said that if all the members of the class were working individually or in groups on the same material, he found he would get many simultaneous requests for help from children who had reached the same problem-stage. Under his scheme the pressure was lessened. Subjects such as Painting and 'Topic' were claimed to need less attention, and this enabled the teacher to concentrate on the groups doing English, Maths and Reading.

After this, some variant of the approach was adopted in nearly all the non-streamed classes of School A, but with the difference that ability tended to remain as the criterion for grouping the children. Teachers allocated to groups chiefly on the basis of reading, one group having the best readers, another the next best, and so on down to a group of the poorest readers. The children remained in the same group for the teaching of all five activities.

The physical organization of the classrooms also reflected differences in approach: in the fourth year classes (still streamed) the desks were in traditional rows, focusing on the teacher who dispensed knowledge from the front of the class. In all except two of the non-streamed classes (staffed by two of the older teachers) this pattern was broken into small groups of desks, the room having lost its overall 'polarization'.

For most of the staff at School A, then, the formal introduction of non-streaming meant a gradual transfer from streaming between the classes to streaming within the class. Nevertheless, in most cases, aspects of the children's educational experience had changed. They were now being taught primarily in small groups, using less directive methods, and new equipment, particularly in Maths. Only in the case of the teacher who devised the above system and two of the younger teachers with experience of non-streamed schools were these methods integrated into a fully non-streamed approach. In these three classrooms a deliberate attempt had been made to ensure that each group contained both brighter and slower children, and, within these groups, co-operation took the place of the competition which characterized much of the work of the single ability groups in other classes.

Although individual teachers at School A were unhappy about small group methods, most of them were satisfied with the particular streaming/non-streaming compromise which they had reached with their class. Despite the original moves against streaming within the class, it had continued to take place, and the head seemed to have reached a tacit understanding with his staff and allowed them to do what they wished as long as the results were good. Of these he was very conscious and he kept records of the children's progress. But he had found that different teachers were obtaining different progress rates; with some teachers the brighter children were making faster progress than the average or lower ability children, and with others the progress made by different ability levels was much more consistent. The former teachers seemed as perplexed as he was, and he was forced to conclude that it was something to do with the teacher's personality and 'a question of their attitude towards different children'. Interviews with the former teachers, in fact, indicated their preference for streaming and their emphasis on 'stretching' the bright child.

The head of School B realized, too, that non-streaming required major changes in teaching methods, and set out to reduce the resistance which he felt sure that these would arouse by introducing them in the form of the Nuffield Maths project before the organizational change. In most cases this worked, and teachers accepted not only the pre-prepared Nuffield work-cards, but started to make their own work-cards for other subjects. The extent to which work-cards were integrated into the routine of class life (as distinct from serving simply as a 'fill-in' between more formal endeavours) varied from class to class. So did the amount of 'project' or 'assignment' learning, although in two or three classes this was highly developed. Class teaching had given way almost completely to individual or group teaching, for, as one teacher said: 'I've gone off class teaching altogether—I don't think anybody listens'. He divided his class into mixed ability groups, and these functioned for Reading and sometimes for Maths and other subjects. He tried to teach Maths individually, and English and project work was often done in pairs, with a child of good reading ability with one less proficient, and they were encouraged to work together.

As in School A, one or two teachers in School B streamed within the class, despite the head's formal insistence that streaming within the class was not allowed. Both he and the head of School A may not have been aware of its existence, but more likely they felt that the individual teachers had the final say on what went on in the classroom.

Groups seemed to be regarded in School B largely as a transitional phase on the way towards truly individual teaching and the head was trying to reach a generally agreed approach on this and other details of classroom practice. He also planned further changes, some of which 'underlined' the non-streamed nature of the school: he was, for example, at the time of fieldwork, trying to encourage the first year teachers to look upon the *whole* year group rather than the individual class, as their responsibility. This involved such arrangements as exchange of classes for occasional lessons—this did not arise out of specialist teaching—and one teacher took a large group for a television lesson while the other gave intensive work to a small group of backward pupils; or both teachers took the whole year group in a form of 'team teaching'.

School C's methods were remarkably stable from the original period of streaming, through non-streaming, and the change back to streaming again. At the time of the field work the fourth year (non-streamed) classes were taught as a class for all subjects, except English, where 'setting' had been introduced. The staff criticized non-streaming on the grounds of the 'impossibility' of class-teaching the non-streamed class—'the lesson cannot be pitched at a level which will guarantee that neither the slower pupils are "left behind" nor the faster pupils "held back".' This is not to say that no change in methods was associated with the non-streamed period. In particular, a form of individual project work called 'assignments' in English and Maths had been introduced and the vestigial remains of this work-cards system persisted under streaming in some of the classes. But none of the new methods involved a complete breakdown of the class unit; even during 'assignments' it was usual for a teacher to answer individual points of difficulty by stopping the children in what they were doing and explaining the point to the whole class.

One can conclude that class, group or individual teaching can be used with streaming, but for a non-streamed organization to be successful, it requires the abandonment of the class as the basic teaching unit. Where this does not occur, the staff may express dissatisfaction, either directly with the teaching process itself, or with the results in terms of assimilated learning. Which of these two forms of disillusion occurs will depend on the allowed amount of 'feedback' from the class: a teacher who is constantly interrupted by children who are 'either bored or bewildered' by the pace of exposition is likely to say that teaching mixed ability classes is impossible, while a colleague who allows only a one-way traffic of information during a lesson, and later 'tests' for the amount of information absorbed, will simply claim it is ineffective with certain ability groups.

Statistical findings

In all three schools English and Problem Arithmetic tests were administered to the 1966-67 second and third year children. This enabled a direct, though limited, comparison to be made between the 8+ and 9+ children under the new organization, and the longitudinal study children, at these ages, under the old organization. The results for each school can be seen in Tables 16.1—16.6 in Appendix 6.

Only 10 of 36 comparisons showed significant differences and these did not consistently favour one form of organization or the other. None of the significant differences could be attributed to

267

differences in social class distribution. In one of the newly non-streamed schools (School B) the non-streamed organization did better with one year group and the streamed organization better with the other. Also, a significant difference was found between two of the parallel classes in this school and the performance of pupils of a teacher who had developed a work cards system and other individual teaching approaches was superior, although it should be added that the member of staff of School A who was in a similar position did not obtain better results than his colleagues who employed more conventional methods. (See Chapter 5.)

Conclusions

A study was made of three schools which had introduced an organizational change in the form of streaming or non-streaming. Two of the schools had changed from streaming to non-streaming and had non-streamed their children from entry to the school; the other had re-introduced streaming with each new intake. In all three cases the change was a gradual process intended to extend eventually right through the school. All had experienced the new form of organization for three years, and in one more year the changeover would be completed.

The study was based on interviews with the heads and members of staff and also on classroom observation. The aims were to examine the reasons for the change, the manner in which the change was introduced, initial attitudes and the reactions of the staff to the change.

The role of the staff in the organizational change was chiefly passive. The heads did not consider the attitudes or views of their staff before changing to non-streaming, although they may have been taken into account in the school changing back to streaming. For, in this school, most of the staff had a streaming orientation, but probably the major factor in determining the re-introduction of streaming was the loss of experienced teachers whom the head considered essential in a non-streamed organization.

In both schools introducing non-streaming most of the staff were not in favour of the change. In one school the head believed in non-streaming and so introduced it. But in the other school the head, like his staff, was not in favour and his decision to non-stream seemed to be influenced by the attractive incentives, in the form of staff and materials offered by the LEA, and also by his desire to test the organization out.

Discussions in two of the schools between the head and staff concerning the change were minimal. The head changing back to streaming did not communicate this fact to his staff; they had to discover it for themselves. One of the two heads changing to non-streaming informed his staff of the change in a list on the staff-room notice board. The other head, who believed in non-streaming, had had discussions on an individual basis with each member of his staff prior to the change.

All three heads used a different method, but in each case the head was the policy maker and it was his decision to bring about the change. Those changing to non-streaming found that, by itself, non-streaming was not a panacea and, unaccompanied by a change in attitude and different teaching techniques, the only change was from streaming between classes to streaming within classes.

The new teaching methods required by non-streaming were probably more easily introduced than changes in teachers' attitudes. But, as the heads discovered, neither were so easy to bring about as the organizational change itself. Both heads changing to non-streaming involved their staff in the 'new maths' in the hope that these methods would be transferred to more general teaching. In some cases this plan worked and teachers accepted group teaching, individual assignments, co-operative work, and mixed ability groups. But a few teachers could not accept the methods, since they clashed with their aims and their beliefs in the function of primary education. The heads accepting the competent professional view of their staff made no attempt to force methods upon their teachers, and their only action was to lay down, but without enforcement, that there should be no streaming within the class. In practice some teachers did stream within the class, this being their way of coping with the new organization, and continued as they had always done.

In the school which changed back to streaming, 'new teaching methods' resulting from non-streaming had not been fully developed and the major method during non-streaming had been class teaching. The attitudes and teaching methods of the staff in this school were typical of those in a streamed school and it is probable that the era of non-streaming had been one in name only. There were no problems in the change back to streaming, simply because the staff wanted the change and were equipped to cope. The same would probably apply in a school changing to non-streaming if the staff, as well as the head, were prepared and wanted the change.

Why was there a lack of communication between the head and staff concerning the organizational change and its consequences? Initially, they may not have been aware that there would be any consequences. But, more probably, it stemmed from the traditional idea that the head is the policy maker and his staff are there to put his ideas into practice. Similarly, the head's reticence to discuss changes in teaching methods with his staff probably arose from the traditional idea of the role of the teacher—the convention that a teacher is free to teach in the way he chooses. But unless new approaches and techniques were discussed with the staff they were not automatically implemented.

For some teachers—even if they had adopted new teaching methods—a change of attitude, particularly to different ability levels, did not necessarily follow. Some teachers whose values were firmly rooted would probably never change; nor would they ever accept the philosophy and aims associated with non-streaming. They would always stream within the class and have 'the "dim" boys who shouldn't be there'. In one non-streamed school it was found that teachers placing more importance on the 'stretching' of the bright children, obtained better academic progress from them and poorer progress from the other children than other teachers who were less partial in their favours. This particular head was very aware of the need for an attitude change, but felt that he could have little influence.

One may ask what alternative strategies the heads of these schools might have adopted to bring in the new system. Several attempts have been made to distinguish the methods by which small-scale social changes might be introduced, most of which concentrate on the use of the social group and group decisions to increase the commitment of the individual involved. Lewin (1958) found that new ideas were more likely to be accepted when the introduction to them was through a group discussion and decision rather than through a lecture followed by individual decisions. The direct application of this to educational change might be thought limited but new ideas, organizational change, and even attitude change are more likely to be effected through group discussion and decision than through the relatively dictatorial methods used by the heads in this study.

The findings of this study indicated that a number of questions should be considered by a head before making an organizational change. Most of these concern his staff. How do they feel about the changeover? How flexible are they, and can they cope with new classroom methods? What are their attitudes to the different ability levels and what does each member of his staff consider his role to be as a teacher? And also what does each consider the aims of primary education to be?

The findings of this study and the work of people like Lewin seem to indicate that where changes are to be introduced there needs to be full consultation with the teachers. And new approaches and different techniques of instruction will only arise out of discussion and possibly in-service training, and not from a simple organizational *fait accompli.*

In fact, the whole of the research on streaming indicated that the streaming/non-streaming controversy is more complex than propagandists on either side would have one to believe. There is a crucial difference between the demands of the two types of situation. The streamed school can tolerate a greater diversity, both of teaching methods and teacher attitudes without its objectives being disrupted. The success of non-streaming, however, depends upon the acceptance by teachers of the objectives of the system, and unless accompanied by this, any change to non-streaming will be in name only.

In conclusion, three main points can be made. Firstly, the issue of streaming or non-streaming is complex. In examining non-streamed schools it is essential to take into account both the methods adopted, and the attitudes held by teachers.

Secondly, academic performance, in the main, is unaffected by the kind of school organization adopted or by teacher-type. Progress seems to be more a matter of the effectiveness of the individual teacher. Minority groups in streamed schools are, however, affected. These include children in the overlap zone between streams and those promoted and demoted. Whether these children gain or lose from the system, academically, depends upon whether they are in—or move to—a higher or lower ability stream.

Thirdly, the main effects of school and teacher-type are on the child's social and emotional development. These influences have a marginal effect on bright children but operate strikingly on children of average and below average ability. This is, in the final assessment, one of the most important findings to emerge from the streaming study.

Reference

LEWIN, K. (1958). 'Group decision and social change'. In: MACCOBY, E. E., NEWCOMBE, T. M. and HARTLEY, E. L. *Readings in Social Psychology.* New York: Holt, Rinehart & Winston.

Very useful

CHAPTER 17

Summary[1]

THE aim of this study was to examine the effects of streaming and non-streaming on the personality and social and intellectual development of junior school pupils.

The major part of the research was concerned with the follow-up of approximately 5,500 children through their junior school course. This involved seventy-two junior schools: thirty-six streamed and thirty-six non-streamed. The pupils were initially tested at seven years old, in 1964, and then annually until 1967 when they were in their final junior school year.

The instruments of measurement were tests and questionnaires designed to assess pupils' performance and attitudes in nine different areas: (i) attainment in reading, English, number concept, problem and mechanical arithmetic (ii) verbal and non-verbal reasoning (iii) 'creativity' or 'divergent thinking' (iv) interests (v) school-related attitudes (vi) personality (vii) sociometric status (viii) participation in school activities and (ix) occupational aspirations.

Information was also obtained on teachers' attitudes to streaming and other educational topics and on their classroom practices and teaching methods. In addition a limited study was made of parents' attitudes. Two additional studies were carried out: one was an intensive study of six schools and the other concerned problems and methods of organizational change.

1. One of the most important findings concerned the role of the teacher. Teachers within streamed schools were more united in both their views on educational matters and their teaching methods, in contrast to non-streamed schools where there was a wide divergence of opinion. Only about half the staff in non-streamed schools could be called 'non-streamers'. The others held attitudes more typical of teachers in streamed schools. This finding was important, for this group of teachers appeared to create a 'streamed atmosphere' within

---

[1] At the end of each chapter there is a concluding section which covers the main findings. Only the most significant results are given here.

their non-streamed classes. Their teaching methods, their lessons and their attitudes tended to reflect the pattern found in streamed schools. They even streamed their children so that different ability groups were seated in different parts of the classroom. They seemed to be counteracting, consciously or unconsciously, the aims of a non-streamed school. As this could well result in modifying and thus masking the true effects of an organizational policy of non-streaming, all analyses were carried out in terms of two teacher-types: Type 1 held attitudes and used teaching methods typical of non-streamed schools and Type 2 was typical of streamed schools.

The typical 'streamer' can probably be described as 'knowledge-centred'. For these teachers the emphasis was on the acquisition of knowledge and the attainment of set academic standards; they were particularly interested in and concerned for the bright child. They concentrated on 'traditional' lessons and gave more emphasis to the '3 Rs'. Competition was encouraged, and the eleven-plus selection test and streaming were approved of as a means of adapting to individual differences. These teachers believed in firmer discipline and their classroom atmosphere was more formal.

By contrast the approach of the typical 'non-streamer' was more 'child-centred', with a greater concern for the all-round development of each pupil. Their teaching tended to place more emphasis on self-expression, learning by discovery and practical experience. They were likely to encourage a co-operative environment in which pupils worked together in groups and helped each other over difficulties. A more 'permissive' classroom atmosphere, in terms of less discipline and a greater tolerance of noise, was preferred. These teachers disapproved of streaming and the eleven-plus test because of the differentiation implicit in such procedures. (See Chapters 3 and 4.)

2. Comparisons between streamed and non-streamed schools revealed that there was no difference in the average academic performance of boys and girls of comparable ability and social class. The effect of being taught by a particular teacher-type also appeared to bear little relationship to academic progress, but any effect may well have been blurred by pupils changing from one teacher-type to another in consecutive years (see Chapter 5).

3. 'Divergent thinking' tests indicated that a higher level of this type of thinking was associated with non-streamed schools when pupils were taught by 'typical non-streamer teachers'. It is suggested that the higher scores were not so much a direct outcome of the form

of school organization but were rather due to the teaching techniques used and the more 'permissive' atmosphere created by these teachers. (See Chapter 6.)

4. There was no evidence that children of different social classes did academically better or worse in either type of organization. But the findings did indicate that children of lower social class origin 'deteriorated' in reading performance over the junior school course relative to children of higher social class. Also there was a tendency for teachers to over-estimate the ability of higher social class children and under-estimate the ability of lower working-class children. One outcome of this in streamed schools could well be an unwarranted allocation of some lower working-class children to too low an ability stream, particularly where the teacher's judgement is the criterion for allocation. In non-streamed classes, on the other hand, teachers may develop an 'expectancy' towards the performance of their pupils which will tend to be lower than the actual potential of the lower social class children and higher than the potential of the upper class children. Teachers' under-estimations of the abilities of lower working-class children may well be a determinant of the children's decline in performance. (See Chapters 5 and 7.)

5. A study was made of the characteristics of pupils allocated to different ability streams in streamed schools. There was a tendency for A-streams to comprise an undue proportion of girls and of autumn-born and of middle-class and upper working-class children; and for lower streams to comprise an undue proportion of boys, summer-born children, and those coming from lower socio-economic home backgrounds.

6. An assessment of the extent to which children can be accurately allocated to school classes on the basis of attainment showed that, at the end of the school year, approximately 15 per cent were in the 'wrong' stream on the basis of either their arithmetic or English performance, this percentage being lower in the early years and higher in the later years. At the beginning of the next school year, on average a quarter of these children were moved into their 'correct' stream, but the other three-quarters remained in the 'wrong' stream. Children remaining in too high a stream tended to improve and those in too low a stream to deteriorate in academic performance, but this was by no means universal (see Chapter 7).

7. Many schools failed to give an age allowance in their allocation to streams: an examination of children in the 'wrong' stream indicated that those who merited a higher stream tended to be the

youngest in the year group and to have least infant schooling; and vice versa for children who should have been in a lower ability stream (see Chapter 7).

8. Transfer from one stream to another is claimed to be an inherent and vital part of streaming. But it was found that only about 6 per cent were transferred at the end of each year whereas on the basis of overlap between streams 15 per cent were known to be incorrectly placed on the basis of either arithmetic or English performance. The number of transfers decreased as the children moved up the school and probably as a result of this, numbers in the 'wrong' stream increased (see Chapter 7).

9. Children who were promoted to a higher ability stream tended to make very good academic progress, but children who were demoted tended to deteriorate and become even worse (see Chapter 7).

10. The results, in general, indicated that neither school organization nor teacher-type had much effect on the social, emotional or attitudinal development of children of above average ability, but that they did affect those of average and below average ability (see Chapter 9).

11. Children of *average* ability were particularly influenced by teacher-type in the development of their teacher-pupil relationship and academic self-image, and, in these two areas, pupils who were taught by 'typical non-streamers' in non-streamed schools were better off than their counterparts in streamed schools. The poorest attitudes were held by pupils taught by 'typical streamers' in non-streamed schools (see Chapter 9).

12. Boys of *below average* ability also had the most favourable teacher-pupil relationship with typical non-streamer teachers in non-streamed schools (see Chapter 9).

13. More boys of below average ability had a 'good academic self-image' in streamed than non-streamed schools (see Chapter 9).

14. The school's streaming or non-streaming policy influenced the development of certain school-related attitudes—attitude to class, 'other image' of class and motivation to do well in school—in children of average and below average ability. In these three areas, children in non-streamed schools held more favourable attitudes than children in streamed schools. (See Chapter 9.)

15. The number of streams in streamed schools appeared to be important, and although pupils in A-streams tended to improve and those in lower streams to deteriorate in their attitudes, this effect was more pronounced in the bottom streams of three or four stream

schools. It is suggested that the greater the number of streams, the greater the possibility of pupils in lower streams regarding themselves as socially segregated, with the concomitant humiliation which such segration may imply (see Chapter 9).

16. A study of mutual friendships has revealed that children in both streamed and non-streamed schools taught by either teacher-type tended to choose those of similar ability and social class as friends, although a greater number of mixed ability friendships were observed in non-streamed classes (see Chapter 10).

17. A study of the social popularity of children of different ability levels revealed that there was little difference between those in streamed schools and those taught by 'typical non-streamers' in non-streamed schools. However, of those taught by 'typical streamers' in non-streamed schools, more children of below average ability were friendless or neglected by others. It seems reasonable to suggest that the emphasis of these teachers on academic success and their dislike of the below average is communicated to other pupils who in turn reject the below average children (see Chapter 10).

18. A comparison was made of the type of pupil chosen to take part in school activities, such as the school play, school teams, etc. More children in non-streamed schools participated in school activities, but in both schools the bright children and children from higher social classes tended to be more active. This tendency was very much more pronounced in streamed schools (see Chapter 11).

19. A survey of parents' attitudes revealed that the classification of pupils which streaming implies is interpreted by parents as an indication of their children's future. The educational aspirations and hopes of parents of children attending non-streamed schools were less linked with the child's ability than the hopes of parents of 'streamed' children.

20. The whole of the research indicated a greater union in the objectives of teachers in streamed schools and a tendency for many teachers in non-streamed schools to hold attitudes or implement policies at variance with the avowed policy of their school. The children's academic performance, in the main, was unaffected by their school's organizational policy or their teacher's attitude to streaming, although the attainments of children who were promoted or demoted were certainly affected. The most striking finding was that the emotional and social development of children of average and below average ability was strongly affected by streaming or non-streaming and by teachers' attitudes.

Appendices

Major Hypotheses of Research

1. There will be no difference between the achievement gains of children of similar ability and social class in streamed and non-streamed schools.

2. Teachers' attitudes and opinions will not be related to the achievement gains of children in streamed and non-streamed schools.

3. There will be no difference in the number of pupils changing from one ability group to another in streamed and non-streamed schools.

4. There will be no difference in the gain in divergent thinking score of children of similar ability and social class in different types of school and taught by different teacher-types.

5. There will be no difference in the proportions of boys and girls in different streams.

6. There will be no difference in the proportions of children born at different times of the year in different streams.

7. There will be no difference in the proportions of children with physical disabilities in different streams.

8. There will be no difference in the experience and age of teachers of different streams.

9. There will be no difference in the academic progress of border-line children in different ability streams.

10. There will be no difference in the type of child (e.g. sex, age, social class) who is transferred to a higher or lower ability stream.

11. Promotion to a higher and demotion to a lower ability stream will make no difference to academic performance.

12. There will be no difference between the interest scores of boys and girls of similar ability in streamed and non-streamed schools.

13. There will be no difference in change in interest scores for boys and girls of similar ability in different types of school and taught by different types of teacher.

14. There will be no difference between the occupational aspirations of boys and girls of similar ability and social class in streamed and non-streamed schools.

15. There will be no difference between the 'prestige' level of the occupations aspired to by boys and girls of similar ability and social class in streamed and non-streamed schools.

16. There will be no difference between the degree of participation in school activities of boys and girls of similar ability and social class in streamed and non-streamed schools.

17. There will be no difference between the sociometric score of children of similar ability and social class in streamed and non-streamed schools.

18. There will be no relationship between the sociometric status of pupils of different ability level and their teacher-type.

19. There will be no difference in the ability levels and social background of mutual friends in streamed and non-streamed schools.

20. There will be no difference between the change in sociometric score of children of different ability levels taught by different types of teacher and in different types of school.

21. The characteristics of 'stars' and 'neglectees' will not vary between streamed and non-streamed schools.

22. There will be no difference in the change of attitude score between the third and fourth year of boys and girls of similar ability taught by different types of teacher and in different types of school.

23. There will be no difference between the attitude scores of boys and girls of similar ability in streamed and non-streamed schools.

24. Teachers' attitudes and opinions will not be related to children's attitude scores.

25. There will be no difference in the aspirational level, i.e. age of leaving school, type of secondary school, or further training, chosen by parents of children of similar ability and social class in streamed and non-streamed schools.

Exploratory Research Stage 1: Interviews with Teachers

The aim of the exploratory research

Since little was known about the nature of streamed or non-streamed schools, it was decided to carry out exploratory research in the form of semi-structured interviews with teachers.

These interviews made available data about prevailing teaching techniques, and the values and aims of teachers in streamed and non-streamed schools. They also provided a general picture of teacher attitudes and made available statements for use in developing attitude scales.

This appendix contains a report of the main findings of the interviews. It is intended to paint a picture of the streamed and non-streamed school as reported by the teachers. It also provided the basis for many of the hypotheses and attitude scales (see Chapter 3 and Appendix 1) in this study.

Method and sample

A total of 31 interviews were carried out during October 1963 in twelve schools situated in Essex, Buckinghamshire, Berkshire and London.

Teachers interviewed were selected on the basis of stream, age of children taught, their sex, and their number of years' experience, so that all types of teacher were included.

Each teacher was interviewed in private for about one hour and was encouraged to talk about many aspects of the junior school. The interviewer adopted a permissive and non-critical role but at the same time developed opportunely each theme which was related to any area he had been briefed to investigate. An interview schedule had been prepared beforehand and was used as a rough guide. Each interview was taped and later transcribed.

Report on the exploratory interviews

The 31 interviews were divided among three interviewers.[1] Based on a verbatim record of the interviews, an individual report was written by each interviewer. The results which follow are a condensation of the three individual reports. For convenience they are discussed in three sections:

I. Attitudes to streaming.
II. Methods of teaching.
III. Discipline.

I. ATTITUDES TO STREAMING

Attitudes towards streaming

Most of the teachers in streamed schools interviewed supported streaming; most in non-streamed schools were against streaming. A number of teachers in both types of school were critical of the organization used by the head. In some schools the head had imposed an organization apparently without explaining his reasons to the staff; as one teacher said: 'The head had some reason for introducing non-streaming but I don't know what it was'.

The teachers who supported streaming evaluated it in quite different terms from those who did not support it. The attitudes of these two groups will be discussed separately.

Attitudes of teachers in favour of streaming

(*a*) *Streaming Ensures that Brighter Children Make Maximum Progress.*

Many teachers emphasized the advantage which they felt streaming gave to the bright child. The evaluation of streaming with respect to the bright child, giving less emphasis to the needs of the average and slow, was partly related to the eleven-plus selection test. 'Each child must be given the best chance in the eleven-plus and therefore streaming is essential to push the "A" child'.

Although the bright child was commonly the major consideration when evaluating streaming, quite often it appeared that 'bright' also meant that he came from the 'right' home background for success. Children from home backgrounds where success at school was praised were especially valued. Some teachers believed in

[1] Interviewers were J. C. Barker Lunn, C. J. Tuppen and J. H. Hewlett, members of the research team.

separating these children from those who came from 'less good homes' who were perceived as being less interested in school work and less well-behaved. One teacher said: 'Children from better home backgrounds are more likely to succeed academically, therefore they should be streamed off, with only the very best from the poorer home backgrounds.' Another said: 'If I have two children and one must go into a "B" class, I would choose the one from the poorer home background because I know the child from the good home has a much greater chance of succeeding in an "A" class'.

The advantage of having the bright children in one class where the ability range is smaller was seen as 'stretching the bright children' and 'time is not lost on the dull ones'.

(b) Streaming 'Removes' the Dull Child

Acquisition of knowledge and proven learning appeared to be very important factors for these teachers, and for this reason many found dull children difficult to accept and indeed were openly hostile towards them. They would have deeply resented being given a lower stream to teach. One teacher said: 'Most teachers don't really like teaching backward classes. They prefer to teach bright ones where they can see rapid progress and results for all their efforts.' Other comments were: 'If you've got all the dregs, life becomes a bit of a grind'; 'There is too much work of no avail spent on backward children. They should know what's in the teacher's mind without too much explaining'.

Another reason for the dislike of dull children and lower streams, quite apart from lack of academic progress, seemed to be their association with lower working class backgrounds. Some teachers looked down on the way of life of the parents: 'They are more like animals than human beings'. Consequently: 'Children in C-streams are much more difficult to like—they don't treat you as a person, they don't talk to you the same way as bright children'. Moreover, 'backwardness and naughtiness go together'. These children were thought to have other failings too: 'Dull children can't concentrate'. 'They don't have a sense of humour'. The extremists believed that it was impossible for a dull child to 'shine' at anything: 'It's a fallacy to believe that because a child is *not* good at reading and arithmetic, he will be good at something else.'

(c) Streaming Ensures Backward Children Receive Special Education

By no means all teachers were unfavourable to backward children. Some teachers who were pro-streaming evaluated it in terms of the slow child. These teachers believed that it was important that dull children, for the sake of their social, personal and academic development, should be segregated from bright and average children. It was felt that their low attainments and apparent lack of ability relative to other children in a non-streamed class resulted in emotional problems and even lower attainments and greater backwardness. These teachers believed that slow children should be taught in small classes, given as much individual attention as possible and a curriculum to suit their needs.

(d) Teaching is more Efficient and Easier for the Teacher when Classes are Streamed

It was felt that streaming reduced the range of ability within each class so that a syllabus and teaching method appropriate for the intellectual level of the class could be used, thus making the task of teaching easier: 'It's definitely to the teacher's advantage to have a smaller ability range'.

A number of teachers appeared to evaluate streaming and non-streaming in terms of teaching the class as a whole and had rejected or had given no thought to the idea of a different approach or method: 'In a non-streamed class, the work is too simple for some, while others are just sitting there unable to do it'. 'It isn't fair to hold the bright ones back and it isn't fair to neglect the dull ones to give the bright ones more attention'. Those using class teaching methods and who had considered group teaching claimed that 'group teaching is acceptable in theory but does not work in practice'. Using class teaching in a streamed class, 'you could get a good standard of work', and 'the whole "A" class can move as a unit'.

Attitudes of teachers in favour of non-streaming

(a) Non-streaming Gives Each Child a Fair Chance

Non-streamers disapproved of labelling a child as 'A', 'B', or 'C' and felt that when labels were given, they became permanent. They also mentioned the difficulty of making accurate assessments of a child's capabilities when he first entered the junior school. They stressed the ways in which a child may be incorrectly allocated to a stream: 'Streaming is very bad for the late-developers'. With non-streaming, 'Children who have spent less time in the infant school are not permanently handicapped nor are those who have been ill'.

(b) Non-streaming Leads to Better Social Adjustment

The idealist and firm believer in streaming would claim that each child receives an education suited to his own particular abilities, that society needs all kinds and levels of abilities and that every child is equally esteemed, whatever his abilities may be.

Many teachers, both in streamed and non-streamed schools denied that this was a realistic picture. They felt that differences of status existed for everyone involved, children, parents and teachers. It was believed that feelings of inferiority and unworthiness were produced in a child who was not in the A-stream, and that labelling a child A, B or C or in any other way, could only have harmful effects on the child's development:

'Children know they are C, B or A even if given other names.'

'Children in lower streams have less confidence, they feel inferior.'

'I'm sure that if you say "they are B" they become B.'

'The child who is in the B-stream feels he is there for life.'

Many of the teachers who believed in non-streaming felt that these problems would be overcome in non-streamed schools, where slow children, they claimed, did not have the same fear of failure, lack of self-confidence or feelings of defeat: 'In a non-streamed class, the bright children set a responsible tone which helps the teacher to integrate difficult children into classroom activities.'

(c) Non-streaming Results in a Happier Staff

Some teachers said: 'With streaming, all the problem children would be in one class, and it's unfair on the first year teacher who may have thirty non-readers in the class'. Other teachers reported their own feelings of apathy when told they were to teach a 'C' class; others believed that many 'C' class teachers were discouraged right from the start of the school year and, expecting poor results and deviant patterns of behaviour, this was what they got. On the other hand, some of the A-stream teachers felt that having an A-stream reflected their high status as a teacher, being entrusted with the potential grammar school children.

Some teachers felt that staff generally were happier with non-streaming: 'It's more taxing, but more rewarding'. It was felt that teachers were often disappointed if they were given a 'B' or 'C' class and non-streaming was a way of avoiding this: 'Each teacher has the advantage of having some bright children. We all like to see progress.'

Criticisms of non-streaming

A number of teachers in non-streamed schools had criticisms of non-streaming.

(a) Bright Children are Neglected or Mis-used

'I sometimes feel I'm wasting the time of the bright ones.'

'If any child is neglected in a non-streamed class, it is the bright child. There is always the risk that a bright child will be used as an uncertified teacher in a non-streamed class.' It was pointed out several times, that often a child can explain something to another child more clearly than the teacher can, and while some teachers seemed to favour the use of bright pupils in this way, others appeared much more concerned that the bright children should forge ahead.

(b) With Non-streaming, Backward Children Continue to Feel Inferior

'They realize quite soon who is bright and who isn't. Children are very cruel, I think. They turn round and say: "that's simple—is that all you're doing?" It's not very good for the backward to be reminded that the others are better. One boy didn't want to come to school because he realized he was dim.'

'Within a non-streamed class the less bright will feel at a great disadvantage.'

This pattern of events, however, appeared to be modifiable. Others felt that non-streaming must be based on a spirit of co-operation rather than competition and from the outset had tried to encourage this. 'The bright have to consider the slow child and can help him, which helps to develop their character.'

(c) Non-streaming is only Possible with Small Classes

Many teachers felt that large classes were preventing the introduction of 'progressive' methods such as non-streaming. In the interviews, several statements were made such as: 'The question of streaming versus non-streaming is bound up with class size' and, 'you can't teach a large class other than by formal method'.

II. METHODS OF TEACHING

Formal versus informal approach to teaching

Two extreme views concerning the function of the primary school could be distinguished. One emphasized learning and the acquisition of knowledge; the other emphasized the child, interesting him and developing his potentials.

Broadly speaking, the more 'knowledge-centred' teachers favoured the use of streaming, the eleven-plus examination and special academic education for the bright child. They used abstract rather than practical methods of teaching, class teaching and individual work rather than group work, and they tended to prefer teaching bright rather than slow children.

The more 'child-centred' teacher, on the other hand, tended to feel that non-streaming was desirable and that practical experience was the ideal way in which a child should learn; they tended to have children working together in groups, often on 'projects'; they were more interested in a broad curriculum with special emphasis upon self-expression in drama, music and art. They were less concerned that children should be clean and tidy and relatively quiet and placed less emphasis upon discipline.

Many teachers, of course, belonged to neither one extreme or the other, their methods and attitudes being a mixture of formal and informal.

The attitudes of the two types of teacher to various aspects of teaching are examined below.

(a) Teachers Using Formal Methods

Teachers using formal methods tended to be in streamed schools. They believed that formal methods were more efficient: 'The old fashioned method of blackboard and chalk is still the best'. They had little enthusiasm for more practical methods; for example, the use of concrete methods in arithmetic was considered by some not only a waste of time, but a possible hindrance to the child's development to think abstractly. 'When I teach area, I teach length times breadth equals area, and then the children have to apply the formula —none of this nonsense of racing round measuring up the school yard!' Another teacher said: 'I don't think there's any point in messing around with toys and glue when the important thing is to know tables and be able to manipulate figures'.

On the other hand, many felt that formal teaching methods were the most effective for preparing children for the eleven-plus selection test: 'I believe in formal methods, especially if the eleven-plus test is going to continue'.

(b) Teachers Using Informal Methods

Teachers using informal teaching methods tended to be in non-streamed schools. These teachers stressed the importance of children discovering things for themselves. 'When a child says,

"Cor, look 'ere!", then I feel that somebody has learnt something there.' Formal abstract methods were considered unsuitable: 'Children may be able to learn abstract ideas, but they cannot apply them when they come up against a difficult problem'. 'Getting sums right is not as important as knowing what they are doing and why.' They felt that making children interested in school was a major aim, particularly with children from poorer homes where there was little interest in education. 'The formal approach has killed interest in mathematics, though basically juniors are very interested.'

Use of informal methods required first of all a non-traditional classroom. While the 'knowledge-centred' teacher would say: 'I like my desks in rows and not in groups', 'child-centred' teachers might be in favour of 'octagonal classrooms with bays and work-spaces with many activities going on at the same time'.

The fact that a teacher used projects was not necessarily an indication of the use of informal methods. The teacher who said: 'I give them a topic and then tell them how to read about it, to draw a picture and to write sentences about it, and I even give them the page numbers' could hardly be described as child-centred. This is quite different from the approach of a teacher, whose class when engaged on project-work may be either working in groups or individually, with many activities taking place at once so that some may be reading or writing, and others measuring, painting, or making models.

Many 'knowledge-centred' teachers rejected projects of the child-centred type, believing that it was impossible to interest all children by any method. 'There's an awful lot of waffling about method and how we interest the children—it doesn't matter how you put it to them, eighty per cent of them won't be interested. We're not going to tread the paths of our forefathers and beat it into them, but they must appreciate that there's a lot to be learned, whether interested or not.'

Thus, two distinct approaches can be seen—a formal and an informal. The use by 'knowledge-centred' teachers of abstract rather than concrete or practical experience meant that skills in arithmetic were acquired through rote learning and the use of symbols. Formal teaching methods in English involved learning lists of spellings, understanding parts of speech, writing class-prepared compositions, and so on.

Informal teaching methods emphasized individual discovery, practical experience, and gradual comprehension of the principles involved. In arithmetic this involved measuring, shopping, sharing and the use of apparatus (Colour Factor, Dienes, etc.). In English the emphasis was on creativity and keeping the child's interest rather than on correct spelling, punctuation and class-prepared compositions.

The curriculum and the timetable

'Knowledge-centred' teachers tended to favour a narrow curriculum, with great stress laid on the basic subjects and with time carefully allocated to them: 'I have to do arithmetic at the same time every morning, for my own peace of mind'. They tended to feel that 'if we covered fewer subjects and did them more thoroughly it would be better in the long-run'. 'We are trying to cram more and more in and we are failing to give them the basis in arithmetic and reading necessary for the secondary school to build on.'

On the other hand, the philosophy of the more 'child-centred' teacher was that the curriculum should be broader and based on the children's interests: 'I try to make a lesson around anything they bring to school to show me'. This approach meant far less adherence to a fixed timetable: 'If you follow a timetable rigidly, then when a child brings something in, you cannot discuss it', or 'There's so much overlap in lessons, and when you have aroused enthusiasm, it would be fatuous to stop it and start another lesson'. Some teachers felt apprehensive about their departure from the timetable. 'I follow the timetable; the headmaster here expects us to follow it.' Another teacher said, 'Is the head going to listen to this interview?' Interviewer: 'No.' Teacher: 'Well, I never stick to my timetable!'

Attitude to noise

Teachers' attitudes towards noise in the classroom appeared to vary along a scale of tolerance. The more 'knowledge-centred' teachers used methods which did not permit or encourage much talking. Even in art and craft one teacher felt that 'the best results in craft, needlework, painting come from a quiet atmosphere'. Another said: 'I have yet to hear anything worthwhile in a class that talks while it works'.

Some teachers appeared to perceive noise as a threat to their authority: 'I cannot stand talking—it's a wonder some teachers are not in a mental hospital with the amount of noise they put up with'. Or noise for some appeared as a major discipline problem: 'I speak in a quiet voice and they have to listen to hear me, but the noise gradually builds up and we have silence again'. 'I can never under-stand why they don't have discipline refresher courses—it seems to me that discipline is the major thing.'

The 'child-centred' teachers used methods which by their very nature allowed more freedom and noise. They were, however, more tolerant of noise and felt that 'it's not natural for children to be quiet', and 'I don't mind children talking to one another and seeking advice, it can be very helpful'. 'Children can work very well in an atmosphere which can hardly be described as quiet.'

III. DISCIPLINE

There appeared to be two main aspects of the subject of discipline. The first, emphasized by 'authoritarian' teachers,[1] was an insistence that children should show a respect for adults and authority and that rules and regulations were to be obeyed. Quiet classroom atmos-phere, good deportment, clean and tidy appearance and good manners were important to these teachers. The second aspect was much more emphasized by the 'democratic' teachers[2] and con-cerned the effect of one child's behaviour upon another or society in general.

Teachers of the first type would make remarks such as: 'I do demand clean hands and faces' or 'I would like to see in the junior school much more emphasis on self-control—sitting properly in class, not biting nails, sucking fingers, fidgeting.' 'Control of one's body is a most important thing; once you have personal control, you can listen.' The ideal child was perceived as 'responsive, very polite, gets on with his work and does exactly as you ask him'.

Fewer rules were laid down in the 'democratic' approach and the basis of these was that they were made for the protection of society, and by keeping to the rules, the child showed consideration for those about him and protected himself from harm.

Teachers of the second type might agree with one head who said: 'Don't expect good manners from my children because you won't get them'. She believed her children were spontaneous, individualistic and natural and would keep these qualities if not subjected to rules about things which, as far as she was concerned, were relatively unimportant.

[1] Teachers holding 'authoritarian' views also tended to be 'knowledge-centred'.
[2] Teachers holding 'democratic' views also tended to be 'child-centred' (see Appendix 7 and Chapter 3).

Punishment

The more 'authoritarian' teachers were prepared to use physical punishment in order to make children conform to school rules. They felt that smacking children was an effective and justifiable punishment:

'I'm quite prepared to smack bottoms and legs for disobeying rules.'

'A good slap in the right place at the right time does an awful lot of good.'

'If the child goes over the line it's punished—all this soppy talk about hurting its ego with a good smacked bottom is a lot of nonsense.'

'I've been in this business long enough to know that a slap on a child's leg is far more effective than talking to him like a Dutch uncle.'

Other teachers completely ruled out physical punishment: 'It is completely unnecessary'. 'If I can't deal with a child by talking to him about what he's done, then I feel there is something wrong.'

Several teachers stated that discipline problems were very rare in the junior school and that most classroom problems could be dealt with by a stern look.

The majority, however, fell between the two extremes of opinion. Most considered that the use of the cane was more limited nowadays, but while deploring the idea of a return to the days when every teacher had one, they were also of the opinion that there was 'nothing wrong with a quick slap'.

Exploratory Research Stage II: Discussions with Children

SINCE only a minimal amount of research has been done in this
country on the attitudes of pupils in streamed and non-streamed
schools, it was decided to begin the study with some exploratory
research to find out what attitudes actually existed.

The purpose of this research was twofold. One objective was to
provide a representative picture of the way in which children viewed
school and to use the information in the formulation of hypotheses
relevant to a study of streaming. The second objective was to provide a source of statements for the construction of attitude scales
needed to test these hypotheses.

The exploratory research consisted of two stages. In the first
stage the aim was to find a method which allowed a child to express
his views freely. The second stage was to adopt the most fruitful
method found in stage one and use it on a larger group of children.

The search for a suitable technique for eliciting children's attitudes

As the children in the longitudinal study of the Streaming research
would be in their third or fourth year of the junior school by the time
any instrument developed would be used, it was decided to restrict
the exploratory research to the nine- and ten-plus age groups.

Various methods were tried out. A composition entitled, 'What
I like and what I dislike about being in Class —' was written by all
third- and fourth-year children in two schools—a streamed and a
non-streamed school.

A number of other methods were also tried out in a further two
schools. These were: relatively unstructured individual interviews;
group discussions (again semi-structured) with various numbers of
children, some mixed and some single sex groups; projective
pictures; incomplete sentences. The discussions and interviews
lasted from half an hour to sixty minutes. The projective pictures
and incomplete sentences were tried out in a group situation.

Only a minority of compositions showed a convincing degree of
spontaneity, and almost all consisted largely of material such as: 'I

like making up stories and going to games on Fridays', and 'I hate having to wright out pomes and storyes and I don't like sumes'.

The less able children, in particular, were handicapped here by their lack of verbal skills. This was also the case when they came to deal with the incomplete sentences—many of the children were unable to express their feelings in writing, even though they had been told that spelling did not matter.

The group discussions were by far the most successful. Of the different sized groups, it was found that *four* children of the same sex was the optimum number. Too much time was spent in the 'warming up' stages when interviewing individuals or two children. This tended to result in a 'question and answer' situation. The groups of three children were reasonably successful, but there was a tendency again for the same result as a two or one child situation. Groups of eight and six children were too large; in every group there would be one child or a couple of children who would sit back, withdrawn and would not contribute anything to the discussion.

Mixed sex groups were not so successful and as discussion of the opposite sex in their class was a usual topic brought up by the children, it was considered that this could be discussed more freely if the groups were restricted to one sex.

Thus, for this particular age group of nine- and ten-year-old children, it appeared that for the purpose of studying attitudes, groups of four children of one sex would be the most productive. It was possible with this size of group to establish 'rapport' in a relatively short time, and also for the children to have a discussion without feeling inhibited by the size of the group.

The decision was therefore made to carry out a further set of group discussions of this size in a number of streamed and non-streamed schools.

Group discussions

Heads who had previously expressed their willingness to take part in the research were approached and their co-operation secured. These were *not* participants in the Streaming research.

Seventeen group discussions were held in five schools, of which three were streamed and two non-streamed. In the streamed schools, children were selected at random from the class registers. In the non-streamed schools, groups were picked at random in one case and selected in the other by class teachers to give contrasting groups of 'bright' and 'dull' children.

The group discussions were carried out in a room where no disturbance by other children or members of staff was likely. In most cases the room was a spare classroom. The role of the leader of the group discussion[1] was to steer the conversation to relevant topics and to encourage development of certain ideas, but at the same time to appear permissive and unobtrusive.

A schedule had been prepared beforehand and this was used as a rough guide by the leader. The group discussions were taped and later transcribed.

The children were told that the team were 'writing a book' about school children. Several schools called their project-lessons 'research', and where children were familiar with this word, a parallel could be drawn with their own work. They were shown the tape recorder and assured that none of their teachers would hear what they had said, and if things they did say were put into a 'book', nobody would know *who* had said them.

For the most part, attitudes were coherently formed and the children had no difficulty in expressing them in the group situation.

The records of the group discussions yielded a mass of material, much of which was relevant to the study of streaming. These records were thoroughly examined and the different viewpoints sorted, enabling broad hunches and hypotheses to be formulated.

What follows is a report of the group discussions. This consists mostly of quotations, these being chosen to be representative of all viewpoints expressed. A number of attitude dimensions emerged in the discussions and the results are examined under these headings. The aim is to give some idea of the richness and quality of the attitudes, and at the same time to illustrate the complex of variables affecting them.

A. ATTITUDES TO STREAMING/NON-STREAMING

Attitudes of children in streamed schools

(a) *Awareness of Streaming*

Most children in streamed schools were aware that they were streamed and knew what this meant.

Heads who numbered or lettered their classes did not succeed in concealing from their pupils the true nature of the stream, i.e. 'A', 'B', 'C'.

---

[1] The leaders were Joan Barker Lunn, Janet Bouri, and Christopher Tuppen, all members of the Streaming research team.

A group of A-stream girls referred to 'the boys slightly lower down than us, you know, in Class 4 . . . they're very rough boys compared with ours'. When asked if Class 4 was a class of younger children, they all began to talk at once. 'It's a lower grade'. 'We have June tests . . .' 'We have A, B, C, D, E, etc. . . .' (N.B. The classes were numbered throughout the school.) 'They can take us up or take us down at the end of the term.' 'They're lower because, you see, they can't work as well as us and they just can't take things in as we can or work things out; they have different kinds of maths from us.'

The D-stream children from the same school did not all talk at once about streaming—they showed distinct restraint when asked how Class 1 (A-stream) was different from their own. 'We don't have to do so much hard work as they do.' 'They're in a higher class, the top class, so they'll have to do harder work, won't they?'

Some A-stream girls from another school told how 'they (B-stream girls) say they are in an A-class and that we are in a B-class. We test them out and we know they don't know the answers'.

One school (out of two streamed schools) which contributed compositions seemed particularly aware of streaming and its implications. Remarks included:

'I like being in the highest class of the year. I have been there ever since I started school.'

'Class A is the highest class of the year.'

'Mr. P. gives us hard things. I like being in Class A because I have a good chance of going to grammar school.'

(b) Attitude to their Own Class and to Other Streams

All the A-stream children interviewed preferred their own class, partly because of the better opportunities, but the main reason being that 'it is a better class'. 'It's the top class in the school.' 'I like being in the highest class.' 'I've got some good friends in there (the B-stream) in the football team, but I would not like to be in that class—it's the dunces' class.' 'B-stream are dunces, well not actually dunces, but they're not as clever as us.' 'Children in 4C are very rough—they are not very clever, the girls are rough and are bullies.' 'They can't add up—they're dumb.' 'I'd feel terrible; I wouldn't like to be in the B-class.' 'Even the teachers say they can't add up—if you can't say your tables, teacher says, you'll go down into the B-stream.'

Apart from intellectual differences, the children in lower streams were regarded as different in other ways too—'They're untidy, rough children, they're always fighting'. 'They're always laughing and don't take any notice of the teachers. But since they've been changing over teachers, they're getting naughtier.' 'They're noisy, as well.' 'They stand up and talk and walk around when someone's talking to them.' 'When they sing with us, they ruin it, because they've got growling voices.'

Equally B- and C-stream children regarded the A-stream children as different. 'A-stream speak right posh.' '4A are silly, they play baby games.' 'They're snobs.' 'They are goody goodies.' 'They are boastful.' 'The A-stream has the best workers in it.' '3J (A-stream) is the hardest class.' 'They have to work harder.'

Unlike the A-stream children, who preferred their own class, B- and C-stream children were divided on this.

Some preferred their own class 'because the work is easy', whereas in the A-stream, 'they have to work too hard'; also, 'they have homework.' 'Because I am not in the top class, who do a lot of hard work . . . the work is not a worry to me.' 'I am the best in my class, I went up into their class, but I couldn't do the work, so I asked to come back to my old class.'

Children may try to minimize their feelings of being in a lower stream by pretending that differences do not exist:

'I'd rather be in 3B, there's more time to think. There's not much difference in standard.'

Those children who would have preferred to be in a higher stream usually gave reasons relating to academic or perceived status differences:

'In the other class, almost everyone passes the 11+. I would like to be there. Mr. K. brings you on.'

'If you're in that class, you go to grammar schools—I'd like to be there.'

'I'd like to go into 4A, if the other children weren't there, because they're the top.'

Another reason given for preferring a higher stream was the preferential treatment given to the A-stream.

'I wish I were in Class 1 (i.e. 4A) and then I could go swimming.' (D-stream)

'I don't like our class, it's used as a canteen, too.' (D-stream)

'Nobody thinks about us in 4C or any of the C-stream classes.' (C-stream)

'The A-classes do all the jobs.' (C-stream)

'When it's a nice day, 4A and 4B go down to the park and we have to stay in school doing lessons.' (C-stream)

'4A and 4B were going to the ballet in L. and I asked the teacher if we could go too, and she said, all surprised, "Do you want to go?"—we went, though.'

(c) *'Other' Class Image*

The children, on the whole, had a realistic picture of what other streams thought of them.

Pupils in lower streams echoed back what the A-stream had said of them. 'People in A-streams say C's are dunces.' '4A are awful: they think we're right dunces.' 'They call us slobs, not snobs, slobs.' 'They don't like us; they think we're awful.'

A-stream children, too, had good social perception. 'They say we're goody goodies.' 'They think we're show-offs, just because we're clever.' 'They think we're boastful.'

A-stream children appeared to be contented with their role and status, but the above must not be interpreted to mean that all lower stream children were discontented. Their state of contentment seemed to depend on a number of factors. One was the school— the status of the lower stream appeared to vary from school to school. In one northern school, the children from the D-stream perceived their status as very low and this had certainly coloured their attitudes to school, work, teachers, even society—they were antagonistic and rebellious. In another school, however, the status of their class—a B-stream (lowest)—had never been questioned and these children had accepted that 'the only difference is that they (the A-stream) do slightly harder work than us.' No apparent resentment was shown by these children.

Attitudes of children in non-streamed schools to their own class and other ability levels

So far the streamed school and the attitudes of children to other pupils of different ability levels have been examined. Streaming seems to bring problems, but these are not automatically eliminated by a non-streamed organization.

The attitude of children to each other in the non-streamed class seemed to vary. It would seem that at least two factors appeared important. Firstly, the composition of the class in terms of ability and social class appeared influential, and the more homogeneous the class, the less reference made, antagonistic or otherwise, to the other ability levels. But perhaps the most important factor of all was the teacher and her attitude towards pupils of different ability levels.

It seemed quite common for teachers not to like teaching lower ability children.[1] One teacher had said to the writer in front of her class: 'I don't like teaching dull children; I wasn't trained to teach them. Those are my clever children over there (pointing to a row by the window), the average are in the middle and the dull children are over there' (pointing to a row at the other side of the room). It was quite obvious to the children in this class who was wanted and who wasn't.

If the teacher accepted all ability levels and attempted to integrate her class, then much of the antipathy between different pupils, one suspects, would disappear. It appeared from the discussions that there were some teachers who tried to do this but they were not too common.

'We have group work—everybody does something, there's a clever person in charge, but we all help. Everybody does something. The class is split up into four or five groups and we all have a project.'

It appeared that differences in ability had been accepted by this class of children, and they were able to regard everybody as useful in some way.

More commonly though, it appeared, from what the children said, that they were streamed within the class. In such cases the children were very aware of their differences, so that they constantly referred to the 'top group' or the 'bottom group' or the 'clever children' or 'not clever children'. In such cases it was felt that the teacher preferred the brighter ones—'She hopes for clever pupils in her class'—and that they, the duller pupils, took second place.

Social, as well as academic differences, were reported between 'clever' and 'not clever' children.

'I think the bottom group are a bit jealous of the top group. They think we're snobs.' (See A-stream remarks)

'Most spend their time walking round the classroom having fun.'

'Most of the children (dull) don't like school; they hate it because they can't do their school work.'

'Some of them smoke (not so clever children); they think themselves big.'

'They go out with girls.'

Whereas the lower ability children claimed that the brighter children were 'boastful' and 'show off' and say, 'I've passed my prelims.'

It is interesting to note that some of the differences between A- and C-streams and bright and dull children can be laid down to

[1] See Appendix 2 and Chapter 11.

social class factors. For instance, in both types of school different ways of speaking and dressing were noticed. Also, different patterns of behaviour were observed—A-stream children were still playing 'baby' games when the lower ability children were smoking and 'going out' with the opposite sex. Other work has also shown that working class children take on adult modes of behaviour earlier than middle class children.[1]

B. OTHER ATTITUDES

Relationship with the teacher

The children had experienced relationships with a variety of teachers and had, for the most part, firmly rooted attitudes toward 'teachers' in the abstract. In particular, they had formed ideas of what sort of teachers they liked and what sort they disliked.

Two dimensions could be distinguished. The children seemed to evaluate their teachers in terms of 'nice' versus 'not so nice', that is, desirable versus undesirable personality attributes, and also in terms of 'good' and 'poor' as a teacher.

(a) 'Nice' Teachers

'Nice' teachers were those who were perceived as kind, fair, having a sense of humour, and who did not shout or use physical punishment.

'He came to see me in hospital.'

'She lets you lie down if you have a headache.'

'My teacher is a nice teacher—she's lovely. I call her me Mummy, she likes to be fair with everyone'.

'I didn't like our teacher in 2A because she had lots of pets and she hardly ever put our paintings up on the wall—only her pets.'

'There's a poor person in our class whose got awful clothes—when the other children call her names, the teacher takes no notice. She should smack them.'

'I don't like our teacher because she won't let us have library. We have only had it three times this term.'

'We have only had football once this term so far—because we're naughty.'

'I like Mr. B.; he cracks jokes and is usually cheerful.'

'I like Mr. E.; he can take a joke, most of them can't.'

[1] McKennell, A. C. and Thomas, R. K. (1967). *Adults' and Adolescents' Smoking Habits and Attitudes.* (Ministry of Health: Government Social Survey). London: H.M. Stationery Office.

'Our teacher is very nice because he hasn't shouted and hasn't smacked once.'

'He keeps shaking you and knocking you over if you have done anything wrong.'

'She scolds you even if you can't sing properly.'

'I'm worried about going up into the next class. Mrs. H. says, "Don't you dare talk or get out of your seat or move or anything— or the first one, I'll slap you".'

(b) *'Good' versus 'Poor' Teacher*

The children also evaluated their teacher in terms of how good a teacher he or she was. A 'good' teacher was one who was able to give the pupil many satisfying and very few frustrating experiences.

Some of the lower ability pupils in non-streamed schools mentioned the difficulty of the work and their consequent dislike of it. 'It's all boring', and 'It's so dull'. Their lack of interest was often associated with failure or perceived to be due to inadequate explanation.

Teachers who gave the child successful experiences came in for much praise.

'I used to worry about my arithmetic, but I don't now. I've improved—he's a good teacher and shows you how to do it when you don't understand.'

'I've improved a lot with Mrs. M. 'cos when I had the other teacher, I don't want to be horrible, but well, they just told you the sum and you had to get on with it, but now I've got Mrs. M., I've improved such a lot.'

The teacher, it would seem, influences the pupil's interests in *school work*, his *degree of confidence* and his *self image*.

Interest in school work

Not surprisingly, there was a tendency for the child to like the subjects he could do and dislike the others. Some of the remarks from successful children were as follows:

'I like arithmetic because I don't do too bad.'

'I like tests because I feel I'm going to come top.'

'I like arithmetic because I'm quick and always finish first.'

Whereas less successful children claimed:

'I don't like having a spelling test because I can't spell very good.'

'I don't like doing sums because she gives us hard ones.'

'I really hate science because it's so hard to understand.'

300

'I don't like reading, the books are too hard to read.'

It became apparent from the discussions that many of the children wanted to do well, less for the reward or satisfaction of success than through fear of failure. They showed considerable anxiety about failure in school—A-stream children in particular.

Confidence versus anxiety in the classroom

More often than not, children expected punishment or ridicule rather than sympathy when they did not understand or got their work wrong. Some feared what their teacher might say if they 'owned up' to their confusion or ignorance, and therefore did not bother to ask for help when it was needed.

'She shouts at you if you don't know your work and you feel so awful.'

'We're scared to say we don't understand because she shouts.'

'When I get stuck, I ask the teacher but I feel guilty (embarrassed?) —he asks you simple questions like "What's three nines?" ' '

Fear of asking seemed to be exacerbated in those classes where a competitive atmosphere had been encouraged, particularly in A-streams. The child appeared to be afraid to ask because of the embarrassment resulting from the jibes of others in the class.

'A lot of children don't like asking because others would say, "Ha! Ha! Look at her, she can't do it".'

'We're scared to tell the teacher, we're frightened of her in a way, but the boys turn round and make fun of us.'

'The boys tease us if we don't understand, they say, "Look at little baby, she didn't understand the first time".'

It seemed that those children who were afraid to ask had teachers who punished or blamed them in some way when they got their work wrong.

'If you don't get your sums right, teacher shouts at you.'

'He shouts at you for the slightest mistake.'

'I dislike arithmetic, because if we get them wrong we have to stay in.'

'If you get over a certain mark, you go out to games, but if you don't, you stay in.'

Threats of: 'If you get your sums wrong, you'll move to a new group', or 'If you can't say your tables, you'll go into the B-stream' were claimed to have been used.

The main source of anxiety seemed to be the shame associated with failure.

'Teachers ask: "How many have you got right—put up your hands, 50, 49, 48" and so on, if you have many wrong, you feel ashamed. You feel yourself go red. Everyone laughs and you feel stupid!' (A-stream)

'You feel so awful when teacher shouts at you when you don't know your work.' (Dull non-streamed)

'If I get my sums wrong, I don't tell my parents, they wouldn't shout at me, they'd say, "You can only do your best", but I'd feel awful and ashamed.'

'If we don't pass the eleven-plus, we will be so ashamed and disappointed.' (Non-streamed bright)

'I hope I go to grammar school because otherwise I'd feel so low— a dunce.' (A-stream)

The child's image of the 'ideal pupil'

The teacher-pupil relationship was also investigated by examining the pupil's perception of the ideal pupil. Projective pictures were used for this. Most of the children believed that the teacher desired clever and well-behaved pupils only. 'Teacher wonders if the new girl is a good speller—if she's a good girl and clever'. 'She's hoping the new girl will be good at work and might come and be top of the class.' 'She hopes for good pupils who work hard.'

A group of 'rebellious boys' from a low stream, when asked what teacher would be thinking of a new girl, declared unanimously: 'She's hoping she's a nice girl and would be a good worker—be top of the class.'

A group of low stream girls, who gave the basis of their friendship as solidarity in the pursuit of fun and 'trouble', thought that the teacher would hope to have 'good pupils who work hard.' 'A good pupil works hard and does not play about.'

Self-image in terms of school work

Most children had a clear self image of their ability. Their assessment of themselves was, of course, coloured by the other children they had met, with whom they or their teacher had made a comparison. Also, if they were in a streamed school, the 'stream' they were in had influenced their self-concept. Knowing his stream made a child fully aware of his ability relative to the rest of his age group—'We are very clever in this class', or 'I'd prefer to be in 4B because they're cleverer'.

302

Children in B- and C-streams, who were top of the class, also had good self-concepts. 'I was the best in the class and I still am—I was sent up to Mr. D's class, but I didn't like it and after two days, I went down again. She (teacher) likes people who concentrate and do good work—she thinks I'm like that.'

One noticeable finding of the discussions was that a considerable number of lower ability children in non-streamed schools had poor self images and expressed shame at their not being clever. 'I'd like to begin all over again.' 'We're useless at school work.' In such cases, it appeared that these children were constantly being compared (at least they felt this) with brighter members of their class.

The pupil's self image, in terms of school work, will, one suspects, depend to a large extent on the teacher. Inadequate teaching methods can result in a poor self image, particularly when the pupil has been given tasks too difficult for him and been allowed to experience constant failure. Or frequent comparisons with pupils of superior ability will result in the 'slower' ones feeling inferior and of less personal worth than the brighter ones in the class.

Importance of school work

For most children, 'doing well at school' was important and failure resulted in a depressingly poor self image. So that 'if I got everything wrong, I'd revise every night.' 'When I get my sums wrong, I cry.' 'I used to cry at night when I got my work wrong or had done badly.'

For a few, however, school work was not important—perhaps because of past failures. One of the symptoms associated with this, was unruliness and antagonism to teachers and school.

'In our class, all those who don't like school muck about—yer get a rubber on the end of a ruler and flick it.'

'We melt the crayons down on the pipes.'

'We throw crayons across the room—paper planes, as well.'

'We'd do anything for a bit of fun in our class.'

'No teacher stays with us—the boys were terrible last year—they used to run behind the teacher and when she turned round they'd all run round again. We'd all be out of our places . . .'

Although, by no means, had all the 'duller' children become 'rebels' nor were all the 'rebels' 'dull'. The brighter children enjoyed the occasional 'bit of fun' too.

Construction of the Children's Attitude Scales

THE children's attitude scales were devised to test hypotheses arising from the exploratory research described in Appendix 3A. They were derived empirically and each is made up of a number of

TABLE 9.1: *Inter-correlation coefficients of the children's attitude scales (product moment)*

ATTITUDE SCALE		A	B	C	D	E	F	G	H	I	J
Academic self-image	A	—									
Anxiety	B	0·40	—								
Social adjustment	C	0·29	0·23	—							
Relationship with teacher	D	0·42	0·24	0·21	—						
Importance of doing well	E	0·26	0·02	0·12	0·36	—					
Attitude to school	F	0·20	0·15	0·09	0·39	0·44	—				
Interest in school work	G	0·25	0·16	0·13	0·43	0·45	0·71	—			
Conforming versus Non-conforming	H	0·13	0·09	0·00	0·36	0·37	0·37	0·38	—		
Attitude to class	I	0·09	0·01	0·12	0·36	0·36	0·40	0·43	0·25	—	
Other image of class	J	0·09	0·14	0·10	0·20	0·09	0·21	0·23	0·14	0·25	—

N=2,087.

statements made by children during the group discussions and selected after factor analysis and scalogram analysis. For each scale the aim was to achieve homogeneity of content and, where possible, a cumulative structure.

Procedure

The stages involved in the development of the scales were (i) group discussions, which have already been described, (ii) quantitative pilot trial, (iii) factor analysis and (iv) a second stage of fieldwork to develop the scales further.

The records of the group discussions provided a wealth of data about children's values and attitudes and how they viewed school life. Content analysis indicated a number of areas crucial to a study of this type. One-hundred statements were selected from the discussions to represent the range of opinion in each of these attitude areas. A questionnaire was drawn up and items were randomized throughout. After a preliminary screening, the questionnaire containing 73 statements was administered to 355 nine- to eleven-year-old children in twelve schools, six in the North and six in the South of England.

The resulting data were subjected to exploratory factor analysis. The main emphasis here was on the rotated solution. Following the intercorrelation of the items, a principal components factor analysis was obtained; eleven factors were extracted. These were rotated by the Varimax procedure to orthogonal simple structure. Seven interpretable factors were identified. By and large these confirmed the findings of the exploratory research. Although the factor analysis clarified the structure of the attitudes, it did not provide a completely satisfactory set of measuring instruments. Three of the attitude areas consisted of promising sub-sets of items but did not emerge as factors, apparently because the number of suitable items was inadequate. In order to develop instruments in all areas, a revised questionnaire was developed. The transcripts of the exploratory discussions were re-examined and statements which appeared to be related to these 'promising sub-sets' of items were selected. Advantage was also taken of the new questionnaire to improve the other seven areas and items with low loadings were rejected and replaced by other statements. A questionnaire, comprising 79 statements covering ten attitude areas, was developed and used. The attitude scales were constructed on the basis of the results of this second stage of fieldwork.

Approximately 2,300 third- and fourth-year children, in 28 schools, completed the revised questionnaire. Based on the responses of 400 of the boys and girls selected at random from the total sample, intercorrelations between the items hypothesized to form an attitude scale were obtained, and those items with a low overall level of correlation were rejected. The remaining items for each attitude area were then submitted to scalogram analysis. If the usual Guttman method (Guttman, 1950) proved unsatisfactory, the H-technique was tried (Stouffer *et al.*, 1952) and a modified type of Guttman scale was formed. The responses to items in three areas did not form a cumulative pattern and were therefore unsuitable for scalogram analysis; so factor scales were formed. The procedure for this was to carry out a centroid analysis (Harman, 1967) of the inter-item correlations and then to extract the first two factors. To test whether the correlation matrix could be accounted for by one general factor, a comparison of the size of the variance of these two factors was made. Vernon (1950) claims that a ratio of 4:1 (i.e. if the amount of variance explained by the first factor is four times as great as that explained by the second) is evidence of unidimensionality.

Internal consistency of the scales

The internal consistency of the attitude scales was determined by Cronbach's (1951) Alpha-coefficient. For the Guttman scales,

Internal consistency of the scales

ATTITUDE SCALE	COEFFICIENT OF REPRODUCIBILITY	ALPHACOEFFICIENT
A. Academic self-image (9 items)	Factor scale‡	0·88
B. Anxiety in class (7 items)	0·94†	0·80
C. Social adjustment (4 items)	0·90	0·58
D. Relationship with teacher (6 items)	0·92†	0·82
E. Importance of doing well (5 items)	Factor scale‡	0·77
F. Attitude to school (6 items)	0·95	0·89
G. Interest in school work (6 items)	0·95†	0·88
H. Conforming versus non-conforming pupil (5 items)	0·95	0·90
I. Attitude to class (8 items)	Factor scale‡	0·91
J. 'Other' image of class (6 items)	0·92	0·69

†Modified Guttman scale constructed by H-technique (Stouffer *et al.*, 1952).
‡Guttman scale not obtained.

coefficients of reproducibility were also calculated (Guttman, 1950). In all cases the Guttman scales were replicated satisfactorily on a further two samples of 100, and the reproducibility coefficients given in the table are based on the average obtained from three separate samples, drawn at random from the total set of pupils.

Support for the validity of these attitude scales comes from three sources (*a*) from the internal structure of the instruments, discussed above, (*b*) from the correlations of the different scales with other measures with which they would be presumed to be related, (*c*) from expected group differences, those predicted on theoretical grounds or on the basis of other workers' findings (Barker Lunn, 1969). For further details of scales, see Manual (Barker Lunn, unpublished, 1968).

The statements contained in the attitude questionnaire were as follows:—

1. If I missed a games lesson I should be disappointed.
2. I'm sorry when school is over for the day.
3. It's nice to fool about in class.
4. Teacher gets on well with me.
5. I get a lot of sums wrong.
6. When the teacher goes out of the room I play about.
7. I think I'm pretty good at school work.
8. School lessons are boring.
9. My class is nicest of all.
10. I have no one to play with at playtime.
11. I should like to be better at games than at school work.
12. I enjoy doing school tests.
13. We spend too much time doing arithmetic.
14. I'd rather be in my class than the other(s) for my age.
15. I sometimes think I'm no good at anything.
16. Other classes think we're nice in my class.
17. I think a lot of children of my age would like to be in my class.
18. My teacher thinks I'm clever.
19. I bet going out to work is better than school.
20. I shall be sorry to leave my class.
21. I'm scared to ask my teacher for help when I don't understand.
22. I have no friends I like very much in my class.
23. I enjoy reading.
24. I like people who get me into mischief.
25. I like doing hard sums.
26. Teacher is always nagging me.
27. School is boring.

28. I'm happy to be in the class I'm in now.
29. School work worries me.
30. I have a best friend in my class.
31. I feel scared when teacher asks me questions about my work.
32. Other children think we're very clever in my class.
33. When we have tests I get very good marks.
34. We have interesting lessons in school.
35. Children who can't do their schoolwork feel ashamed.
36. I dislike children who are noisy in class.
37. I hate being in the class I'm in now.
38. I like children who get into trouble.
39. Teacher is interested in me.
40. My class gets blamed for things we don't do.
41. Other classes like my class.
42. I should feel a little afraid if I got my spellings or sums wrong.
43. Our teacher treats us as if we're babies.
44. I think the other children in my class like me.
45. I'd prefer to be in another class.
46. School is fun.
47. I find a lot of school work difficult to understand.
48. I should like to be one of the cleverest pupils in the class.
49. I work and try very hard in school.
50. I'm very good at sums.
51. I don't always get on well with some of the children in my class.
52. I enjoy most school work.
53. Going to school is a waste of time.
54. I wish there were nicer children in my class.
55. My teacher is nice to me.
56. I'm useless at school work.
57. If I didn't understand something I should ask my teacher.
58. Teacher thinks I'm a trouble-maker.
59. Nobody cares about us in my class.
60. I should like to be very good at school work.
61. Other children make fun of my class.
62. I think my teacher likes me.
63. I'd like to get away from the children in my class.
64. I never play about during lessons.
65. When people ask what class I'm in I always feel happy to tell them.
66. I like school.
67. I don't seem to be able to do anything really well in school.
68. They are very friendly children in my class.

69. When we have reading, I often pretend to read.
70. It would bother me if I got my work wrong.
71. I like being in my class.
72. I would leave school tomorrow if I could.
73. I enjoy being asked questions by my teacher.
74. I like children who tell jokes in class.
75. Other classes think they're better than us.
76. I think nearly everyone in my class likes me.
77. I get told off by my teacher.
78. Doing well at school is most important to me.
79. At school they make you do things you don't want to do.

References

BARKER LUNN, J. C. (1968). 'Manual of instructions for use of children's attitude scales'. Unpublished. (NFER).

BARKER LUNN, J. C. (1969). 'The development of scales to measure junior school children's attitudes', *Brit. J. Educ. Psychol.*, 39, 1, 64-71.

CRONBACH, L. J. (1951). 'Coefficient-alpha and the internal structure of tests', *Psychometrika*, 16, 3, 297-334.

GUTTMAN, L. (1950). In: STOUFFER, S. A. *et al. Measurement and Prediction.* Princeton, New Jersey: Princeton University Press.

HARMAN, H. H. (1967). *Modern Factor Analysis.* (2nd ed.). Chicago, Illinois: Chicago University Press.

STOUFFER, S. A. *et al.* (1952). 'A technique for improving cumulative scales', *Publ. Opin. Quart.*, 16, 273-91.

VERNON, P. E. (1950). 'An application of factorial analysis to the study of test items', *Brit. J. Psychol. (Stat. Sec.)*, 3, 1-15.

Instruments Used to Assess Dependent and Independent Variables

Achievement/Ability tests

Reading tests A and B

Reading tests A and B, parallel versions, were used to assess the child's understanding of what he reads. Each test consisted of 48 items which were of the incomplete sentence type. The children had to select from five alternatives, which would best complete the sentence given. The items were arranged in order of difficulty and the tests were designed to be suitable for children aged seven to eleven. The time limit was 20 minutes. (See Table A4.1.)

English A and B

The two parallel versions of the English test consisted principally of tests of comprehension, but also there were items based on spelling and formal grammar (i.e. parts of speech, punctuation). The items were graded in difficulty, and the early questions were suitable for average seven-year-olds and the later ones more for pupils of eleven years. These were 'untimed' tests— a maximum of 50 minutes was allowed but most children were able to finish in 35-40 minutes. (See Table A4.1.)

Problem Arithmetic A and B

Each of the two parallel problem arithmetic tests was made up of 30 items, these being arranged in order of difficulty. The first ten items were read aloud so that children unable to read were not at a disadvantage.[1] The tests were suitable for children aged seven to eleven. The maximum time allowance was 50 minutes. Strictly speaking the tests were untimed and most of the children were expected to finish in 20–30 minutes. (See Table A4.1.)

[1] Trials had shown that children unable to read were unlikely to be able to answer correctly beyond the tenth item.

Mechanical Arithmetic A and B

These two parallel tests consisted of 44 items[1] and contained examples of the four processes—addition, subtraction, multiplication and division. Some of the items also involved knowledge of fractions, money and the more common weights and measures. The items were selected for children aged seven to eleven. They were, like the Problem and English tests, untimed; the maximum allowance was 50 minutes, whereas the time necessary for most children to complete the test was 30–40 minutes. (See Table A4.1.)

Concept Arithmetic

The aim of this test was to assess the child's knowledge and understanding of mathematics, placing less emphasis than the more conventional tests on computational skills. The test was made up of 56 items and was designed for children aged eight to eleven years. The first 12 questions were orally administered so that poor readers were not handicapped (see footnote to Problem Arithmetic). Again plenty of time was allowed, giving a maximum of 50 minutes, but most children were expected to finish in 30–40 minutes. (See Table A4.1.)

Primary Verbal

This test was designed to give a measure of the verbal ability of children aged eight to ten years. It consisted of 85 items. In order to familiarize the children with the type of question they would meet, a number of practice examples were given before the start of the test. The time allowed was 30 minutes. (See Table A4.1.)

Verbal/Non-Verbal

This test was made up of 80 questions; verbal and non-verbal items were presented alternatively. Six practice items, with the answers explained, were given before the start of the test. This test was constructed for upper juniors, nine-plus to eleven years. The time allowed was 30 minutes. (See Table A4.1.)

---

[1] In Year 1, there were only 35 items in the Mechanical Arithmetic tests and the scores of the 4th year pupils indicated that the test ceiling was too low for this age group. Another nine items were therefore added to the test. Of the Cohort 1 children in Year 1, less than one per cent scored 30 and 2 children out of approximately 7,000 scored more than 30.

TABLE A4.1: *Test Reliabilities (calculated by the Kuder-Richardson Formula 20)*

TEST	YEAR GROUP	VERSION A		VERSION B	
		Reliability	Reliability Sample Size	Reliability	Reliability Sample Size
Reading (48 items)	7+	0·942	99	0·942	104
	8+	0·949	96	0·927	102
	9+	0·945	100	0·929	106
	10+	0·943	98	0·929	108
English (64 items)	7+	0·960	88	0·966	100
	8+	0·966	82	0·971	102
	9+	0·957	86	0·968	110
	10+	0·965	86	0·960	110
Problem Arithmetic (30 items)	7+	0·877	100	0·904	94
	8+	0·903	98	0·921	98
	9+	0·916	98	0·917	100
	10+	0·914	100	0·931	106
Mechanical Arithmetic (35 items)	7+	0·890	94	0·883	100
Mechanical Arithmetic (44 items)	8+	0·931	100	0·911	100
	9+	0·938	100	0·937	100
	10+	0·942	100	0·946	100
Concept Arithmetic (56 items)	8+	0·935	94		
	9+	0·936	98		
	10+	0·956	98		
Primary Verbal I (85 items)	8+	0·971	330	ONE VERSION ONLY	
Verbal/Non-Verbal (80 items)	9+	0·929	253		
	10+	0·945	254		

Tests of divergent thinking

Free Writing S.A.

This test consisted of two essay items, each designed to stimulate the child's imagination and creative thinking. Parts 1 and 2 each contained four choices of topic. The titles for Part 1 were selected from those devised by E. P. Torrance (1962) for the Imaginative Stories Task of his Minnesota Tests of Creative Thinking. The Part 2 titles were brief story beginnings, selected from numerous suggestions put forward by members of the streaming research team, deliberately designed to avoid channelling the child's thoughts into any particular area, while at the same time providing a stimulus for an interesting story.

Twenty minutes were allowed for the Part 1 essay and more or less unlimited time for Part 2. This timing proved quite suitable in a trial run of the test. Very few instructions were given to the children, except that they should make their stories as interesting and original as possible and not worry too much about words they could not spell.

The tests were to be marked by a panel of three experienced teachers. It was decided to appoint a panel to carry out the marking since the combined judgement of several markers would, it was hoped, give a close approximation of the 'true' mark than the assessment of a single marker. The panel was selected from among six teachers, all of whom marked a sample of 150 essay scripts.

TABLE A4.2: *Inter-correlations between the six markers*

MARKER	A	B	C	D	E	F
A	—					
B	0·70	—				
C	0·72	0·77	—			
D	0·52	0·72	0·59	—		
E	0·64	0·73	0·72	0·62	—	
F	0·62	0·64	0·59	0·53	0·58	—

A briefing meeting was held to explain the purpose and aims of the test and to give marking instructions, stressing the need to reward imaginativeness and originality rather than technical perfection. The written instructions issued to markers were based on those devised by Wiseman (1949) in his work on essay marking. Marking was carried out using the quick impression method, and marks were awarded for originality of ideas rather than for a grammatically well-written but 'stereotyped' essay. Markers were instructed not to penalize mistakes in grammar, spelling and punctuation. A maximum of 10 marks was awarded to each essay, giving a total of 20 for the whole test.

Inter-correlations between the total scores awarded by these six markers were calculated (see Table A4.2) and the highest average inter-correlations were found to exist between markers B, C and E. However, marker E was unable to participate further in the project and marker A was chosen as having the next highest correlations with B and C. The final panel had the following inter-correlations:

TABLE A4.3: *Inter-correlations between the chosen markers*

MARKER	A	B	C
A	—		
B	0·70	—	
C	0·72	0·77	—

Average inter-correlation=0·73 (product moment)

These inter-correlations compare favourably with those of Wiseman's four-member marking panel in 1948 (average r=0·62) although they were slightly lower than those of his 1943 panel (average r=0·79).

The actual marking of the 2,350 sample[1] was carried out mostly during the summer holidays. No marks were entered on the test scripts themselves, but in a separate mark-booklet. The tests were split into 3 batches and rotated among the three teachers.

Free Writing S.A. 1967

The test took the same form as in 1966, although the essay topics were changed. The titles in Part 1 were again adapted from those used by E. P. Torrance. In Part 2 actual essay titles were given, as opposed to the story beginnings used in 1966, but as they were likewise designed to be stimulating to the child's imagination, it was not felt that the slightly different presentation was of importance.

[1] All the Cohort 1 children in 1966 completed the test. It was not possible, however, to mark all the essays (budgetary and time limitations) and a sample had to be drawn. It was decided to include those third year (Cohort 1) children from the 28 schools who had completed the Attitude Questionnaire (i.e. one half of the third-year children—approximately 1,000), plus a 1 in 3 random sample from all other schools.

The marking panel in 1967 consisted of two of the three teachers who had marked the 1966 essays. The slight loss in reliability resulting from reducing the marking panel to two, was not considered large enough to justify bringing in a third marker who had not previously been involved in the project. Marking instructions were identical to those issued the previous year. The correlation between the two markers on a sample of the 1967 tests was found to be 0·77 (product moment).

'*Divergent Thinking*' *test—Free writing S.B.*

Free Writing S.B. was designed as a test of 'creativity' or 'divergent thinking'. Most of the work on creativity has been carried out in the United States, and, in constructing this test, material from American instruments was drawn on to a large extent, notably tests devised by E. P. Torrance and J. P. Guilford.

Free Writing S.B. contained items deliberately designed to present a new and unfamiliar situation to the child. For example, some questions asked the child to list as many possible consequences as he could, of a situation quite removed from everyday experience, e.g.

'Write down all the things that might happen if a hole were bored through the earth.'

'Just suppose that everybody looked alike. Write down all the things that might happen because of this.'

Another type of item asked the child to write down as many possible unusual uses as he could of such mundane objects as a brick or a spoon.[1]

In another question a simple drawing of a toy dog was given and the child was asked to think of as many ways as possible of improving it to make it more fun to play with.

It is clear from these examples that items such as these have no single, correct answer; on the contrary, the child is asked to give as many, varied responses as he can within the time allowed. Each item on the test was strictly timed: two minutes was allowed for the majority of items.

The tests were marked for fluency, flexibility and originality, these being three of the factors scored by Torrance (1962) in the Minnesota Tests of Creative Thinking. Elaboration, the fourth factor examined by Torrance, was not scored.

---

[1] Item devised by Miss Anne Coghill. During construction of this test, discussions were held with Miss Coghill, whose Ph.D. work at Birkbeck College, University of London, included a similar test of creativity.

Fluency

The fluency score was obtained by adding up the total number of relevant responses to each item, one mark being awarded for each. A response was considered irrelevant if it bore no relation to the situation presented by the question.

Flexibility

The flexibility score was obtained by counting up the total number of *categories* into which the responses to each item fell, e.g. item 1 asked the child to list 'all the things which are round and can be eaten'. The responses 'apple, cherry, grape' would all come under the category 'fruit'. One mark was awarded for each category used, so these three responses together would gain one mark.

Originality

When scoring for originality each response was again evaluated separately. Each response gained a score of 0, 1 or 2 based on the frequency of occurrence of that response in a sample of 300 scripts. The marks were awarded as follows:

given by 5% or more of the sample $= 0$
given by 2%—4·99% of the sample $= 1$
given by less than 2% of sample $= 2$

A marking key was prepared in which all the accepted responses found in a 300 script sample were listed, item by item, and subdivided into categories. This was done by three independent judges. The originality score for each response was given alongside the response in the marking key. While this key contained a very full list of responses, it could not be expected to be exhaustive. A certain amount of discretion had to be employed in interpreting responses, and where queries arose these were discussed by markers and members of the research team.

An analysis was carried out on the results of a trial run of the test, and the following inter-item correlations were calculated:

TABLE A4.4: *Inter-correlations of items* (*phi coefficient*)
(*a*) *Fluency (number of responses given)*

		1	2	3	4	5a	5b	5c
round and can be eaten	1	—	0·48	0·64	0·48	0·40	0·60	0·36
consequences of invisible at will	2	0·48	—	0·44	0·36	0·40	0·52	0·36
consequences of hole in earth ...	3	0·64	0·44	—	0·52	0·48	0·68	0·60
consequences of birds/animals speaking	4	0·48	0·36	0·52	—	0·40	0·56	0·44
uses of a spoon	5a	0·40	0·40	0·48	0·40	—	0·60	0·52
uses of a brick	5b	0·60	0·52	0·68	0·56	0·60	—	0·56
uses of silver paper	5c	0·36	0·36	0·60	0·44	0·52	0·56	—

(*b*) *Flexibility (number of categories into which responses fall)*

		1	2	3	4	5a	5b	5c
round and can be eaten	1	—	0·40	0·36	0·12	0·32	0·44	0·28
consequences of invisible at will	2	0·40	—	0·56	0·48	0·56	0·56	0·44
consequences of hole in earth ...	3	0·36	0·56	—	0·40	0·56	0·72	0·36
consequences of birds/animals speaking	4	0·12	0·48	0·40	—	0·40	0·40	0·32
uses of a spoon	5a	0·32	0·56	0·56	0·40	—	0·60	0·44
uses of a brick	5b	0·44	0·56	0·72	0·40	0·60	—	0·52
uses of silver paper	5c	0·28	0·44	0·36	0·32	0·44	0·52	—

(*c*) *Fluency and Flexibility correlations*

$$\begin{array}{ll} \text{Item 1} & \varphi = 0·52 \\ 2 & \varphi = 0·68 \\ 3 & \varphi = 0·72 \\ 4 & \varphi = 0·64 \\ 5a & \varphi = 0·80 \\ 5b & \varphi = 0·80 \\ 5c & \varphi = 0·72 \end{array}$$

Free Writing S.B.—1967

In 1967 a second version of the Free Writing S.B. was constructed, similar in length and content to the 1966 test. Correlations of 0·77 on fluency and 0·66 on flexibility were obtained when the two versions of the test were tried out together.

The marking procedure in 1967 was identical to that employed in the previous year.

The inter-item correlations on the 1967 version of the test were as follows:

TABLE A4.5: *Inter-correlations of items (phi coefficient)* 1967

(*a*) *Fluency (number of responses given)*

		1	2	3	4a	4b	5	6
fit in matchbox	1	—	0·28	0·36	0·30	0·28	0·22	0·21
consequences of earth like springy rubber	2	0·28	—	0·33	0·26	0·36	0·30	0·33
consequences of everybody looking alike	3	0·36	0·33	—	0·19	0·35	0·26	0·23
uses of a toothbrush	4a	0·30	0·26	0·29	—	0·34	0·24	0·42
uses of a blanket	4b	0·28	0·36	0·35	0·34	—	0·33	0·32
improve toy dog	5	0·22	0·30	0·26	0·24	0·33	—	0·20
uses of tin-cans	6	0·21	0·33	0·23	0·42	0·32	0·20	—

(b) *Flexibility (number of categories into which responses fall)*

		1	2	3	4a	4b	5	6
fit in matchbox	1	—	0·28	0·16	0·25	0·27	0·26	0·15
consequences of earth like springy rubber	2	0·28	—	0·18	0·19	0·32	0·27	0·21
consequences of everybody looking alike	3	0·16	0·18	—	0·21	0·17	0·16	0·24
uses of a toothbrush	4a	0·25	0·19	0·21	—	0·44	0·20	0·22
uses of a blanket	4b	0·27	0·32	0·17	0·44	—	0·33	0·28
improve toy dog	5	0·26	0·27	0·16	0·20	0·33	—	0·24
uses of tin-cans	6	0·15	0·21	0·24	0·22	0·28	0·24	—

Interests questionnaire

Group discussions with children aged 9–11 years old revealed interests popular with this age group. Other 'interests' questionnaires were examined and a review of the literature on this subject was made. From this information a list of interests to be included in the final questionnaire were selected on *a priori* grounds for their creative content—in addition the same number of non-creative interests were included in the list. After completion of the questionnaires, a sub-sample of questionnaires of 400 boys and 400 girls was drawn. The responses of this sample were factor analysed.

Factor analysis (Promax solution—Hendrickson and White 1965, 1966) revealed nine first-order and three second-order factors. Two of the second-order factors were considered suitable as a basis for developing interest scales. Taking items from the latter with loadings of 0·50 and higher yielded two promising factors, both concerned with creative interests, one imaginative and the other logical. These have been named 'creative interests A' and 'logical/analytic interests B'. They are made up of the following interests:

Creative Interests A
writing stories
making up plays
making up poems
painting pictures
acting
playing musical instruments
reading poetry

Logical/Analytic Interests B
chess
doing science experiments
making models
reading encyclopaedias

The internal consistency of these scales determined by Cronbach's (1951) Alpha Coefficient was 0·70 and 0·63 respectively.

Sociometric data

The sociometric questionnaire provided information on the 'popularity' of a child and also identified those who were 'neglectees'. In 1964, the first year of the study, this took the form of a sociomatrix on which the teacher indicated the first and second choices of friends made by each child in the class. The instructions to the children were as follows:

'We have been asked by some people in London to help them with their work with children. They are interested in boys and girls like you and they want to find out more about children's friends.

'Now listen carefully. They want you to think who in this class is your very best friend. They also want you to think who in this class is your second best friend, that is, someone you like very much but not quite as much as your best friend. Your friends must be in this class and they can be either a boy or a girl. If you have only one friend and do not have another friend, then you only name one friend. If you have no friend in this class, then you need not choose anyone. Children who have no friends in this class can say whether they have a friend in the school.

'Now I am going to ask you to come out in turn and to tell me who is your very best friend and who is your second best friend, and I shall write them down.

'After we have done that, I shall send the list back to London and they can have a look at your choices—along with choices of other children in many other schools.'

For the 1966 administration, two new criteria were introduced: 'Who would you like to work with?' and 'Who would you like to play with?', and the number of choices on each criteria increased to three. In addition, the form of administration changed. Since the Cohort 1 children were at the end of their third junior school year it was assumed that the majority would be able to read, know the surnames of their friends, and be able to cope with the filling in of a simple form. So instead of a sociomatrix being completed by the teacher, each child completed an individual form. In this way, the teacher did not see the responses, and a possible source of bias was thus removed. Easier administration for the teachers also resulted.

Other pupil variables

Pupil Assessment—Questionnaire S.5

This questionnaire was designed to contain all data obtained each year on the individual pupil. It varied slightly from year to year.

Besides the variables already discussed, e.g. tests, attitude scores, etc. the questionnaire contained information in four other areas:

(*A*) Personal details
(*B*) Teacher-ratings of behaviour
(*C*) Teacher-ratings of achievement
(*D*) Participation in school activities

(*A*) *Personal details*

(i) Social Class. In the first year (1964) and fourth year (1967), information concerning the pupil's father's occupation was obtained and teachers were asked to categorize this according to the following (Registrar-General) groupings:

1 = Professional/Managerial occupations
2 = Clerical/Supervisory occupations
3 = Skilled Occupations (including farmers, shopkeepers)
4 = Semi-skilled occupations
5 = Unskilled occupations

They were told that it was left to the teacher's discretion as to how this information was obtained.[1] Details as to what method they had used for determining parental occupation were obtained and it was found that the vast majority had asked the pupils what their father did, had asked the parents, or had looked it up in the school records. Less than 3 per cent had based the rating solely on their own estimate.

(ii) Length of Infant Schooling. In year 1, teachers were asked to record the number of terms each child had spent in the infant school.

(iii) Physical Disabilities. In year 1, teachers were asked to record for each pupil any handicaps:

(*a*) hearing: child has difficulty in hearing or has to wear a hearing-aid.

(*b*) speech: child has speech impediment—stammering, stuttering, lisping, etc.

(*c*) vision: child has defective sight—short or long-sighted with or without spectacles, squints, colour blind.

---

[1] In 1964, detailed interviews were carried out by Government Social Survey with parents of children in four of the schools. This enabled a comparison to be made between the objective measure of socio-economic status (i.e. father's actual occupation as given to interviewers) and the teacher's ratings of social class. One-hundred and eighty-three (8+) pupils in twelve school classes were involved. The teachers' ratings were on a five-point scale and the information obtained from the interviewers were also graded into as many categories. The product moment correlation between the two measures was 0·60.

(*d*) other disabilities: physically under-developed for his/her age, any long-standing disabilities preventing the child from taking part in games, or bodily disfigurations.

(iv) Record of Absenteeism. Information was collected in years 2, 3 and 4 on the number of days the pupil had been absent throughout the school year.

(v) Change of Stream. In years 2, 3 and 4, teachers in streamed schools indicated whether a pupil had been promoted, demoted or was in the same stream as the previous year.

(*B*) *Teacher-ratings of behaviour.* The design of this part of the questionnaire was particularly influenced by the Bristol Adjustment guides of D. H. Stott (1963) and by instruments used by Eli Bower (1960).

Teachers were asked to 'rate each pupil's behaviour as you have observed and experienced it'. Each pupil was rated on a four-point scale on five isolated behaviour traits, namely:

		4	3	2	1
1	This pupil gets into fights or bullies other children	true most of the time (every day or more)	quite often (at least once a week)	sometimes (less than once a week)	seldom or never (less than once a term)
2	This pupil is 'picked on', teased and baited by other children	rating scale as above			
3	This pupil is withdrawn and plays and talks very little with other children	rating scale as above			
4	This pupil is disobedient and/or insolent in class	rating scale as above			
5	This pupil is a pleasure to have in the class	rating scale as above			

Each trait was on a separate page so that teachers completed all ratings for the class before proceeding to the next trait.

(*C*) *Teacher-ratings on school achievement*

(i) Attitude to School Work. Teachers, in years 2, 3 and 4 were asked to indicate for each child whether he was: a very hard worker; a hard worker; average; or poor or lazy worker.

(ii) Class Position in Reading. In years 2, 3 and 4 class teachers were asked for each child: 'How would you rate this pupil's performance in reading with respect to your present class?'

(*a*) One of the best pupils in reading (i.e. top 5, 6 or 7 pupils).

(*b*) Average in reading.

(*c*) One of the poorest pupils in reading (i.e. bottom 5, 6, or 7 pupils).

(iii) Class Position in Arithmetic. A similar rating was also obtained for arithmetic.

(iv) General Ability Rating. Teachers in all years made an assessment of each pupil's general ability on a five-point scale:

(*a*) Certain of a grammar school place or equivalent ability level

(*b*) Above average, possible grammar school place

(*c*) Average

(*d*) Below average and possibly backward

(*e*) Dull and definitely backward.

(*D*) *Participation in school activities.* Teachers were given a list of ten school activities and were asked to indicate for each pupil those in which he had participated.[1]

(*a*)   Took part in school dancing display

(*b*)   Took part in school play/opera

(*c*)   Member of school choir/orchestra/recorder group

(*d*)   Member of school football, netball or other team

(*e*)   Went on school holiday, i.e. away for two days or more

(*f*)   Went on school visit

(*g*)   Is a school prefect

(*h*)   Member of school club. e.g. stamp, chess, gardening

(*i*)   Has taken part in school morning prayers, e.g. read lesson

(*j*)   Contributed to school magazine

Pupil's participation ratio, relative to the whole school was defined as:

$$\frac{\text{number of school activities in which pupil has taken part} \times 100\%}{\text{total number of activities listed by Head}}$$

[1] This information was obtained in years 1 and 4 only.

Teacher variables

Three questionnaires covered information concerned with the teacher. These were based on the findings of the exploratory research (see Appendix 2). The teacher questionnaires were:

(*a*) Class Teacher Questionnaire (dealing with type of lesson, grouping within the class) (S.1.)
(*b*) Teachers' Personal Data—age, years' experience, etc. (S.2.)
(*c*) Teachers' Attitudes (S.3.)

(a) Class Teacher Questionnaire

'Traditional'/'progressive' scale construction. On the basis of the exploratory interviews with teachers a 'traditional'—'progressive' dimension in teaching was hypothesized. It was believed that every teacher would occupy a position along this continuum, his position being defined by the frequency with which he used lessons of the 'traditional' type (e.g. rote-learning, formal sums) or of the 'progressive' type (e.g. practical arithmetic, free activities).

From the interviews, 14 types of lesson were selected. These were listed on a questionnaire, together with six possible frequencies ranging from 'everyday' to 'less than once a term or never'. Teachers (N=1,000) were asked to indicate their frequency of using each type of lesson.

For the purposes of scoring, the types of lesson were divided into two categories: 'traditional' and 'progressive'. These were as follows:

'traditional'	*'progressive'*
(*a*) writing class-prepared compositions	(*h*) writing stories
(*b*) learning lists of spellings	(*i*) projects—where child does own research
(*c*) formal grammar	(*j*) nature study walks
(*d*) have tests, in any subject	(*k*) pupils working/helping each other in groups
(*e*) formal sums	(*l*) practical arithmetic
(*f*) problem sums	(*m*) free activity
(*g*) saying/learning tables by rote	(*n*) art lessons—child decides what to paint

The items designated 'traditional' were scored six for 'everyday', five for 'twice a week or more', down to one for 'less than once a term or never'. The 'progressive' items, however, were scored from one for 'everyday' to six for 'less than once a term or never'. The purpose of this scoring was to make possible a combined total score.

On the basis of the teachers' responses, item-analysis was carried out in order to reject items having a low correlation with the total score. It was carried out first with the 'traditional' items, then the 'progressive' and finally the two combined.

Item analysis led to the elimination of three items from each scale. These were (*d*), (*e*), (*f*) and (*h*), (*j*), (*n*).

Two criteria were used in the analysis:

(i) Firstly, items were tested for a difference of two points between the mean score of the top 25 per cent (i.e. teachers with the highest scores on 'traditional' items) and the bottom 25 per cent—the presence of this difference indicated an item of good discrimination.

(ii) Secondly, for each item, the mean scores of the top and bottom 25 per cent were compared and tested for statistically significant differences (for further details, see Edwards, 1957).

All items were in fact acceptable on the basis of the second criterion. But those rejected failed on the other, having a mean difference of less than two between the top and bottom 25 per cent. However, the criteria used were very exacting: all the items did make some contribution to the total scores and there could be a case for not rejecting any items.

Item analysis showed that combining the items to form a single scale 'traditional'—'progressive' was unsatisfactory. So the two were kept quite separate and scores were obtained on a 'non-traditional'—'traditional' scale (i.e. writing class prepared compositions, learning lists of spellings, formal grammar, saying/learning tables by rote) and on a 'progressive'—'non-progressive' scale (i.e. projects, pupils working and helping each other in groups, practical arithmetic, free activity).[1]

---

[1] Kerlinger (1958) also found it more meaningful to have two dimensions—traditional—non-traditional; progressive—non-progressive.

Grouping within the class.   The categories of 'grouping within the class' listed in the Class Teacher Questionnaire were also derived from the exploratory research.   It seemed that teachers often used different types of grouping for different subjects.   Often they felt that grouping by attainment was necessary for reading and for arithmetic; many teachers in non-streamed schools were particularly conscious of this need, though some teachers in streamed schools also used this method in order to subdivide their streamed classes into even smaller ranges of attainment.   Many teachers made use of class lessons, particularly in English, History and Geography. Other teachers believed in the value of having groups working together within the class but they took care not to form groups on the basis of ability, because they did not wish to introduce 'streaming within the class'.

Two questions, one dealing with grouping and the other with seating-arrangements, covered this aspect of the study.

(b) Questionnaire S.3.—Teachers' Attitudes

Questionnaire S.3. studies *attitudes of teachers* towards seven aspects of teaching in junior schools.   This instrument was also derived from the exploratory research (see Appendix 2).   The interviews indicated a number of attitude areas which seemed fundamental to a study of streaming, e.g. attitudes towards streaming and non-streaming; towards bright children; towards backward children; towards the eleven-plus examination.   Other topics appeared to indicate more general social attitudes, e.g. attitudes towards punishment, permissive attitudes and authoritarian attitudes. After deciding the topics which were relevant to the streaming study, statements were collected which appeared to characterize particular attitude areas.   These were assembled in a questionnaire which was sent to a new sample of teachers who were asked to indicate their degree of agreement or disagreement with each statement.   The responses of these teachers were analysed by Guttman's method of scalogram analysis.   This led to the final version of the questionnaire. Guttman scales were formed in six of the attitude areas.   The responses to items in the area covering attitude to the less able child (scale K) did not form a cumulative pattern and therefore, being unsuitable for scalogram analysis, a factor scale was formed (see Appendix 3B).   The Table below gives the coefficient of reproductibility for the Guttman scales and the internal consistency, calculated by Cronbach's alpha-coefficient for scale K.

TABLE A4.6: *Reproducibilities of Guttman Scales for teachers'*
attitudes (Questionnaire S.3)

	TITLE	COEFFICIENT OF REPRODUCIBILITY†
Scale A	Permissive—non-permissive (5 items)	0·94
Scale B	Attitude to physical punishment (6 items)	0·95
Scale D	Attitude to 11+ selection (5 items)	0·95
Scale G	Attitude to noise in classroom (5 items)	0·93
Scale H	Attitude to streaming (6 items)	0·95
Scale I	Attitude to A-streams (5 items)	0·94
Scale K	Attitude to less able child (6 items)	0·70*

† These were calculated according to the formula proposed by Guttman (see
S. A. Stouffer, *et al.* [1950], *Measurement and Prediction*, p. 117) and are based
on two random samples of 100 teachers.
   * Factor scale: internal consistency calculated by Cronbach's alpha-coefficient.

Teachers' Attitudes—Questionnaire S.3
1. Streaming makes slow children feel inferior.
2. There is too much emphasis on cutting down noise in schools.
3. A-stream children have wider interests than other children, both
   inside and outside school.
4. I think a good slap in the right place at the right time does an
   awful lot of good.
5. Children in A-streams tend to become conceited about their
   abilities.
6. Teaching backward children is interesting.
7. Children must be taught to have decent manners.
8. I don't mind a resonably high working noise in my class.

9. Bright children should not be streamed off from the rest of their age group.
10. The 11+ exam is an entirely fair method of assessing a child's abilities.
11. Children in A-streams worry too much about marks.
12. Less able children can generally be relied upon to do a job faithfully.
13. Physical punishment does no good at all to any child.
14. Bright children deserve a special academic course in a separate school when they are 11 years old.
15. An occasional hard slap does children no harm.
16. I cannot stand fidgeting in class.
17. It is socially wrong to segregate children into streams.
18. I would find teaching the backward the least rewarding job in junior school.
19. The 11+ exam can prevent slackness in junior schools and this is a good thing.
20. Teachers should demand clean hands in school.
21. I would not allow talking in a class of 35 or more children.
22. The bright children will be neglected in non-streamed classes.
23. Less able children are often outstanding in art or drama.
24. Naturalness is more important than good manners in juniors.
25. I would enjoy the challenge of teaching less able children.
26. An 11+ exam is more fair than relying on record cards and teachers' assessments.
27. If children in my class are insolent, they have to be slapped.
28. Opportunities for self-expression through movement, painting and writing poetry are more important than concentrating on the 3 Rs.
29. In a streamed school, one gets far more done for the slow learner.
30. I'm quite prepared to spank bottoms for disobeying rules.
31. The majority of less able children have no interest in school.
32. The atmosphere in A-streams is too competitive.
33. Nothing worthwhile will be achieved by a class that talks while it works.
34. Non-streaming would be impossible with large classes of 40 or more.
35. Any examination that segregates children into separate schools at 11+ is undesirable.
36. Physical punishment is out of the question and completely unnecessary.
37. A quiet atmosphere is the one best suited for all school-work.

38. Without streaming, neither the bright nor the dull get the best from what the school could offer.
39. Slow children gain from a free-activity approach.
40. With non-streaming I would find it impossible to keep duller children occupied while bright children received attention.

Parental attitudes questionnaire

This instrument was intended to assess the educational and vocational aspirations of parents for their children. The questionnaire was administered on a postal basis, and brevity and simplicity were the prime considerations to try and ensure a high response rate. Questionnaires for each school were sent *en bloc* and distributed by the class teachers to the children.

References

Bower, E. M. (1960). *Early Identification of Emotionally Handicapped Children in School.* Oxford: Blackwell.

Cronbach, L. J. (1951). 'Coefficient-alpha and the internal structure of tests', *Psychometrika*, 16, 297-334.

Edwards, A. L. (1957). *Techniques of Attitude Scale Construction.* New York: Appleton-Century-Crofts.

Hendrickson, A. E. and White, P. O. (1964). 'Promax: A quick method for rotation to oblique simple structure', *Brit. J. Statist. Psychol.*, 17, 1, 65-70.

Hendrickson, A. E. and White, P. O. (1966). 'A method for the rotation of higher-order factors', *Brit. J. Math. Statist. Psychol.*, 19, 1, 97-103.

Kerlinger, F. N. (1958). 'Progressivism and traditionalism: Basic educational attitudes', *School. Rev.*, 66, 80-92.

Stott, D. H. (1963). *The Social Adjustment of Children: Manual to the Bristol Social Adjustment Guides.* (Rev. ed.). London: University of London Press.

Stouffer, S. A. *et al.* (1950). *Measurement and Prediction.* Princeton, New Jersey: Princeton University Press.

Torrance, E, P. (1962). *Education and the Creative Potential.* Minneapolis: University of Minnesota Press.

Wiseman, S. (1949). 'The marking of English composition in grammar school selection', *Brit. J. Educ. Psychol.*, XIX, III, 200-9.

Sample Details

DETAILS OF THE 72 SCHOOLS INVOLVED IN THE LONGITUDINAL STUDY

Criteria for matching schools

(a) *Type of school:* junior or junior with infant, urban or rural. All the schools were non-denominational and all were located in England. The results of matching on this criterion are shown in the table below.

TABLE A5.1: *Type of school*

	STREAMED SCHOOLS	NON-STREAMED SCHOOLS	TOTAL
Junior Urban	32	32	64
Junior Rural	1	1	2
Junior with Infants Urban	3	3	6
Total	36	36	72

(b) *Number of classes in the school.* All the schools had at least eight junior classes (i.e. at least 2-form entry). The two members of a matched pair could differ in size by a maximum of one class.

The 36 streamed schools had a total of 99 classes.

The 36 non-streamed schools had a total of 95 classes.

(c) *Average number of pupils per class.* Matched schools had approximately equal pupil/teacher ratios. A margin of $\pm$ 3 pupils was tolerated.

The average number of Cohort 1 pupils per class were:

In streamed schools 35·6 (standard deviation=7·9).

In non-streamed schools 34·8 (standard deviation=5·3).

The difference was not statistically significant (CR=1·65). The greater standard deviation in the streamed schools was due to the tendency for A-streams to be larger than C-streams.

(*d*) *Percentage of children in the local education authority who attended non-selective schools.* It was believed that the forces tending to make a school concentrate on 'preparing for the eleven-plus' might be related to the proportion of children admitted to selective schools. The schools were matched on this criterion, allowing a margin of ± 5 per cent.

On average, 66 per cent of the children in the LEAs controlling the streamed schools and 66 per cent in those controlling the non-streamed schools attended secondary modern schools (based on the figures provided by the Department of Education and Science, 1964).

(*e*) *Predominant socio-economic status of parents.* Final matching[1] of schools was made on the basis of information given by teachers in 1964, about the occupational group of each pupil's father. The information below is for the school as a whole.

TABLE A5.2: *Fathers' occupational group*

OCCUPATION	STREAMED SCHOOLS	NON-STREAMED SCHOOLS
Professional/Managerial	6%	5%
Clerical/Supervisory	12%	12%
Skilled Workers	36%	35%
Semi-Skilled Workers	32%	36%
Unskilled Workers	14%	12%
Total	100%	100%
Number of Schools	36	36

[1] Initial matching of schools (i.e. 50 pairs) on this criterion was based on survey data (Stage 1—see page 12) in which the heads in the sample of some 2,000 schools were asked to give an estimate of the percentage of parents in each of the five occupational categories.

Appendix Five

Details of the 28 school sample
Twenty-eight of the schools were studied more intensively and the
attitudes of their pupils and parents were assessed.

TABLE A5.3. *Details of the 28 school sample*

	NUMBER OF PUPILS IN 1966		NUMBER OF CLASSES PER YEAR GROUP		
	3rd year (Cohort 1)	4th year (Cohort 2)	2 classes	3 classes	4 classes
Streamed	592	568	6	7	1
Non-Streamed	572	579	6	7	1

	GEOGRAPHICAL AREA			TYPE OF SCHOOL	
	North	Midlands	South	Junior/ Urban	Junior and Infant/Urban
Streamed	3	6	5	13	1
Non-Streamed	3	8	3	13	1

	PARENTS' OCCUPATIONAL STATUS (Cohorts 1 and 2)					ELEVEN-PLUS SELECTION TEST	
	1	2	3	4	5	Yes	No
Streamed	10%	14%	30%	31%	15%	11	3
Non-Streamed	7%	13%	32%	34%	14%	10	4

TABLE A5.4: *Details of the cohort 1 children involved in the study of attitude change in the 28 schools*

BOYS

Type of school: Type of teacher:	ABOVE AVERAGE			AVERAGE			BELOW AVERAGE		
	Non-Streamed Type 1	*Non-Streamed Type 2*	*Streamed*	*Non-Streamed Type 1*	*Non-Streamed Type 2*	*Streamed*	*Non-Streamed Type 1*	*Non-Streamed Type 2*	*Streamed*
Social 1, 2	(13) 29%	(8) 32%	(45) 50%	(10) 14%	(6) 22%	(13) 18%	(4) 7%	(2) 6%	(4) 5%
Class: 3	(19) 42%	(11) 44%	(23) 25%	(25) 37%	(13) 46%	(28) 39%	(15) 26%	(4) 12%	(21) 27%
4, 5	(13) 29%	(6) 24%	(23) 25%	(34) 49%	(9) 32%	(31) 43%	(38) 67%	(28) 82%	(54) 68%
	100%	100%	100%	100%	100%	100%	100%	100%	100%
No. children	45	25	91	69	28	72	57	34	79

GIRLS

Type of school: Type of teacher:	ABOVE AVERAGE			AVERAGE			BELOW AVERAGE		
	Non-Streamed Type 1	*Non-Streamed Type 2*	*Streamed*	*Non-Streamed Type 1*	*Non-Streamed Type 2*	*Streamed*	*Non-Streamed Type 1*	*Non-Streamed Type 2*	*Streamed*
Social 1, 2	(17) 28%	(14) 56%	32%	(8) 15%	(2) 7%	(11) 13%	(4) 10%	—	(5) 10%
Class: 3	(26) 42%	(10) 40%	39%	(19) 35%	(12) 43%	(36) 41%	(11) 27%	(6) 26%	(13) 25%
4, 5	(19) 30%	(1) 4%	29%	(27) 50%	(14) 50%	(40) 46%	(25) 63%	(17) 74%	(34) 65%
	100%	100%	100%	100%	100%	100%	100%	100%	100%
No. children	62	25	111	54	28	87	40	23	52

TABLE A5.5: *Details of the cohorts 1 and 2 children involved in the study of attitude (scores) in the 28 schools*

BOYS

Type of school: Type of teacher:	ABOVE AVERAGE			AVERAGE			BELOW AVERAGE		
	Non-Streamed Type 1	Non-Streamed Type 2	Streamed	Non-Streamed Type 1	Non-Streamed Type 2	Streamed	Non-Streamed Type 1	Non-Streamed Type 2	Streamed
Social 1, 2	(26) 31%	(16) 33%	45%	17%	(14) 20%	21%	8%	(4) 5%	8%
Class: 3	(33) 39%	(18) 38%	29%	33%	(30) 41%	36%	27%	(19) 22%	29%
4, 5	(26) 30%	(14) 29%	26%	50%	(28) 39%	43%	65%	(62) 73%	63%
	100%	100%	100%	100%	100%	100%	100%	100%	100%
No. children	85	48	178	123	72	165	100	85	169

GIRLS

Type of school: Type of teacher:	ABOVE AVERAGE			AVERAGE			BELOW AVERAGE		
	Non-Streamed Type 1	Non-Streamed Type 2	Streamed	Non-Streamed Type 1	Non-Streamed Type 2	Streamed	Non-Streamed Type 1	Non-Streamed Type 2	Streamed
Social 1, 2	28%	(20) 33%	32%	16%	(9) 13%	12%	(8) 11%	(1) 2%	7%
Class: 3	39%	(24) 40%	39%	33%	(27) 38%	39%	(16) 23%	(14) 28%	28%
4, 5	33%	(16) 27%	29%	51%	(35) 49%	49%	(47) 66%	(36) 70%	65%
	100%	100%	100%	100%	100%	100%	100%	100%	100%
No. children	111	60	224	115	71	162	71	51	118

Tables not in the Text

TABLE 3.2: Number of years' teaching experience

No. of Years	TEACHERS							
	OF 7+ CHILDREN		OF 8+ CHILDREN		OF 9+ CHILDREN		OF 10 + CHILDREN	
	Streamed	Non-streamed	Streamed	Non-streamed	Streamed	Non-streamed	Streamed	Non-streamed
0–2	10%	21%	17%	27%	14%	17%	11%	9%
3–5	12%	32%	17%	22%	9%	19%	5%	9%
6–10	30%	17%	17%	15%	17%	17%	21%	16%
11–20	25%	19%	27%	25%	37%	31%	34%	44%
20 plus	23%	11%	22%	11%	23%	16%	29%	22%
	100%	100%	100%	100%	100%	100%	100%	100%
No. of teachers giving information	92	90	90	88	90	89	92	91

TABLE 3.3: *Age of headteachers in streamed and non-streamed schools*

AGE	STREAMED	NON-STREAMED
31–35	—	1 (3%)
36–40	—	3 (8%)
41–45	—	1 (3%)
46–50	2 (6%)	7 (19%)
51–55	12 (34%)	9 (25%)
56–60	19 (54%)	13 (36%)
61–65	2 (6%)	2 (6%)
	(100%)	(100%)
No. of heads giving information	35	36

TABLE 3.4: *Frequency of tests and of different types of arithmetic lessons in streamed and non-streamed schools over the four years*

	FORMAL SUMS		PROBLEM SUMS		PRACTICAL ARITHMETIC		TESTS IN ARITHMETIC OR ANY OTHER SUBJECT	
	Streamed	*Non-Streamed*	*Streamed*	*Non-Streamed*	*Streamed*	*Non-Streamed*	*Streamed*	*Non-Streamed*
Every day	36%	23%	24%	28%	9%	18%	1%	1%
Every 2–3 days	36%	39%	41%	39%	22%	26%	4%	2%
Once a week	17%	19%	23%	19%	30%	30%	25%	27%
Less than once a week but at least once a month	7%	11%	9%	9%	27%	21%	39%	26%
Less than once a month but at least once a term	2%	5%	1%	3%	7%	4%	26%	30%
Less than once a term or never	2%	3%	2%	2%	5%	1%	5%	14%
	100%	100%	100%	100%	100%	100%	100%	100%
No. of teachers giving information	365	358	363	359	364	358	363	358
Chi-square test	$\chi^2 = 22\cdot08$ $P < 0\cdot001$		Not significant		$\chi^2 = 25\cdot54$ $P < 0\cdot001$		$\chi^2 = 29\cdot15$ $P < 0\cdot001$	
Inference	Significant at 0·1% level. Streamed schools had formal sums more frequently		No difference in the frequency of problem sums		Significant at 0·1% level. Streamed schools had practical arithmetic less frequently		Significant at 0·1% level. Streamed schools had tests more frequently	

TABLE 3.5: *Frequency of writing stories and of comprehension exercises and punctuation lessons in streamed and non-streamed schools at 9+ and 10+*

	Writing Stories		Comprehension Exercises		Punctuation Lessons	
	Streamed	*Non-Streamed*	*Streamed*	*Non-Streamed*	*Streamed*	*Non-Streamed*
Every day	2%	3%	1%	1%	—	—
Every 2–3 days	10%	13%	15%	10%	3%	2%
Once a week	34%	26%	55%	50%	20%	17%
Less than once a week but at least once a month	40%	38%	19%	18%	47%	43%
Less than once a month but at least once a term	12%	17%	6%	7%	18%	22%
Less than once a term or never	2%	3%	4%	14%	12%	16%
	100%	100%	100%	100%	100%	100%
No. of teachers giving information	179	179	181	180	180	179
Chi-square test	Not significant		$\chi^2 = 13 \cdot 20$, $P < 0 \cdot 05$		Not significant	
Inference	No difference in the frequency of writing stories		Significant at the 5% level. Streamed schools had comprehension exercises more frequently		No difference in the frequency of punctuation lessons	

TABLE 4.5: *Method used for teaching English*

	7+		8+		9+		10+	
	Streamed	*Non-Streamed*	*Streamed*	*Non-Streamed*	*Streamed*	*Non-Streamed*	*Streamed*	*Non-Streamed*
Taught as a class	80%	40%	71%	37%	60%	31%	55%	18%
Mixed ability groups	5%	9%	1%	4%	—	4%	1%	4%
Similar ability groups	15%	39%	7%	15%	9%	16%	9%	24%
Individually	—	8%	2%	16%	1%	16%	2%	14%
Class + similar ability groups	—	—	9%	7%	8%	10%	11%	6%
Similar ability + individually	—	—	—	1%	—	—	—	2%
Class + individually	—	—	2%	2%	4%	7%	6%	4%
Other combinations	—	4%	8%	18%	18%	16%	16%	28%
	100%	100%	100%	100%	100%	100%	100%	100%
Number of teachers giving information	80	88	92	89	90	89	103	98

TABLE 4.6: *Method used for teaching Maths*

	7+		8+		9+		10+	
	Streamed	Non-Streamed	Streamed	Non-Streamed	Streamed	Non-Streamed	Streamed	Non-Streamed
Taught as a class	42%	10%	38%	13%	37%	9%	29%	2%
Mixed ability groups	3%	10%	2%	3%	1%	3%	7%	5%
Similar ability groups	53%	68%	23%	38%	20%	37%	16%	45%
Individually	1%	9%	7%	16%	9%	21%	8%	18%
Class + similar ability groups	—	—	9%	4%	11%	5%	9%	7%
Similar ability + individually	—	—	2%	3%	1%	6%	3%	7%
Class + individually	—	—	—	2%	3%	2%	—	2%
Other combinations	1%	3%	19%	21%	18%	17%	28%	14%
	100%	100%	100%	100%	100%	100%	100%	100%
Number of teachers giving information	89	88	92	90	90	89	103	86

Table 4.7: *Method used for teaching Reading*

	7+		8+		9+		10+	
	Streamed	Non-Streamed	Streamed	Non-Streamed	Streamed	Non-Streamed	Streamed	Non-Streamed
Taught as a class	5%	—	10%	1%	3%	—	10%	—
Mixed ability groups	9%	12%	4%	2%	5%	2%	6%	3%
Similar ability groups	74%	66%	52%	42%	41%	38%	30%	28%
Individually	7%	11%	19%	43%	21%	49%	6%	50%
Class + similar ability groups			3%	2%	3%	2%	12%	—
Similar ability + individually	—	—	3%	4%	16%	6%	10%	9%
Class + individually	—	—	—	—	2%	—	4%	—
Other combinations	5%	11%	9%	6%	9%	3%	22%	10%
	100%	100%	100%	100%	100%	100%	100%	100%
Number of teachers giving information	92	90	73	86	58	65	50	58
Reading no longer taught	—	—	20	4	32	24	46	39

TABLE 4.8: *Method used for teaching other subjects, e.g. History, Social Studies*

	7+		8+		9+		10+	
	Streamed	*Non-Streamed*	*Streamed*	*Non-Streamed*	*Streamed*	*Non-Streamed*	*Streamed*	*Non-Streamed*
Taught as a class	95%	80%	73%	53%	64%	56%	52%	32%
Mixed ability groups	3%	12%	—	13%	11%	17%	11%	16%
Similar ability groups	1%	1%	3%	—	1%	1%	3%	1%
Individually	—	—	3%	1%	—	5%	3%	7%
Class + similar ability groups	—	—	3%	5%	2%	2%	6%	1%
Similar ability + individually	—	—	—	—	—	—	—	—
Class + individually	—	—	1%	2%	1%	2%	3%	1%
Other combinations	1%	7%	17%	26%	21%	17%	22%	42%
	100%	100%	100%	100%	100%	100%	100%	100%
Number of teachers giving information	94	87	93	89	91	98	104	97

TABLE 4.9: *Criteria used for assigning children to seats*

CRITERION	8+		9+		10+	
	Streamed	*Non-Streamed*	*Streamed*	*Non-Streamed*	*Streamed*	*Non-Streamed*
Free choice	29%	25%	30%	31%	40%	47%
'Streamed' part of the time	52%	61%	51%	53%	39%	47%
'Streamed' all the time	19%	14%	19%	16%	21%	6%
	100%	100%	100%	100%	100%	100%
Number of teachers giving information	86	92	95	93	90	91

TABLE 4.10: *Sex of Type 1 and Type 2 teachers† in streamed and non-streamed schools*

| | STREAMED | | NON-STREAMED | |
	Type 1	*Type 2*	*Type 1*	*Type 2*
Male	54%	41%	41%	40%
Female	46%	59%	59%	60%
	100%	100%	100%	100%
Number of teachers giving information	46	231	140	130

†When follow-up children were 8+, 9+, 10+

TABLE 4.11: *Age of Type 1 and Type 2 teachers† in streamed and non-streamed schools*

AGE OF TEACHER	STREAMED		NON-STREAMED	
	Type 1	*Type 2*	*Type 1*	*Type 2*
under 25	20%	17%	25%	22%
25–30	17%	16%	18%	17%
31–35	17%	11%	14%	8%
36–45	29%	23%	26%	22%
46–55	15%	20%	12%	26%
56–65	2%	13%	5%	5%
	100%	100%	100%	100%
Number of teachers giving information	46	230	139	129

†When children were 8+, 9+, 10+

TABLE 4.12: *Number of years' experience of Type 1 and Type 2 teachers† in streamed and non-streamed schools*

NUMBER OF YEARS' EXPERIENCE	STREAMED		NON-STREAMED	
	Type 1	Type 2	Type 1	Type 2
0–5	26%	26%	39%	32%
6–10	24%	17%	20%	15%
11–20	41%	28%	29%	36%
20 plus	9%	29%	12%	17%
	100%	100%	100%	100%
Number of teachers giving information	46	230	137	129

†When follow-up children were 8+, 9+, 10+

345

TABLE 4.13: *Attitude of teachers† in non-streamed schools and their use of formal sums*

USE OF FORMAL SUMS	YOUNGER TEACHERS (45 YEARS AND UNDER)		OLDER TEACHERS (46 YEARS AND OVER)	
	Anti-Streaming‡	Undecided or Pro-Streaming	Anti-Streaming	Undecided or Pro-Streaming
Every day or every 2-3 days	49%	68%	16 (59%)	25 (60%)
Less than every 2-3 days but more than once a month	37%	27%	9 (33%)	14 (33%)
Less than once a month	14%	5%	2 (8%)	3 (7%)
	100%	100%	100%	100%
Number of teachers giving information	109	87	27	42
Chi-square test	$\chi^2 = 8 \cdot 22$; $P < 0 \cdot 05$		Not significant	

†When follow-up children were 8+, 9+, 10+.
‡Anti-streaming scored 4-7 and undecided or pro-streaming scored 0-3 on attitude to streaming scale—cutting points decided by Guttman's method of intensity analysis (Guttman and Suchman, 1947).[1]   'Intensity and a zero point for attitude analysis', *American Social Review*, 12, 57.
[1] Guttman, L. and Suchman, E. A. (1947).

TABLE 4.14: *Attitude of teachers† in non-streamed schools and their use of tests*

USE OF TESTS	YOUNGER TEACHERS (45 YEARS AND UNDER)		OLDER TEACHERS (46 YEARS AND OVER)	
	Anti-Streaming‡	Undecided or Pro-Streaming	Anti-Streaming	Undecided or Pro-Streaming
At least once a week	27%	33%	12 (44%)	15 (37%)
Less than once a week but at least once a term	52%	59%	10 (37%)	23 (56%)
Less than once a term or never	21%	8%	5 (19%)	3 (7%)
	100%	100%	100%	100%
Number of teachers giving information	109	87	27	41
Chi-square test	$\chi^2=6{\cdot}48$; $P<0{\cdot}05$		Not significant	

†When follow-up children were 8+, 9+, 10+.
‡Anti-streaming scored 4-7 and undecided or pro-streaming scored 0-3 on attitude to streaming scale—cutting points decided by Guttman's method of intensity analysis (see footnote p. 346).

TABLE 4.15: *Attitude of teachers† in non-streamed schools and their use of 'progressive lessons'*

USE OF PROGRESSIVE LESSONS	YOUNGER TEACHERS (45 YEARS AND UNDER)		OLDER TEACHERS (46 YEARS AND OVER)	
'Progressive' Score	*Anti-Streaming‡*	*Undecided or Pro-Streaming*	*Anti-Streaming*	*Undecided or Pro-Streaming*
4– 9 (progressive)	14%	48%	6 (15%)	9 (36%)
10–12	31%	25%	9 (22%)	9 (36%)
13–24 (non-progressive)	55%	27%	26 (63%)	7 (28%)
	100%	100%	100%	100%
Number of teachers giving information	87	108	41	25
Chi-square test	$\chi^2 = 27 \cdot 75; P < 0 \cdot 001$		$\chi^2 = 8 \cdot 14; P < 0 \cdot 05$	

†When follow-up children were 8+, 9+, 10+.
‡Anti-streaming scored 4-7 and undecided or pro-streaming scored 0-3 on attitude to streaming scale—cutting points decided by Guttman's method of intensity analysis.

TABLE 4.16: *Attitude of teachers† in non-streamed schools and their use of 'traditional lessons'*

Use of Traditional Lessons	Younger Teachers (45 years and under)		Older Teachers (46 years and over)	
'Traditional' Score	Anti-Streaming‡	Undecided or Pro-Streaming	Anti-Streaming	Undecided or Pro-Streaming
4–12 (non-traditional)	45%	60%	20 (49%)	13 (48%)
13–15	34%	24%	14 (34%)	7 (26%)
16–24 (traditional)	21%	16%	7 (17%)	7 (26%)
	100%	100%	100%	100%
Number of teachers giving information	86	106	41	27
Chi-square test	No significant difference		No significant difference	

†When follow-up children were 8+, 9+, 10+.
‡Anti-streaming scored 4-7 and undecided or pro-streaming scored 0-3 on attitude to streaming scale—cutting points decided by Guttman's method of intensity analysis.

349

TABLE 5.3a: *Reading performance of upper and lower social group boys at 10+ who were superior or above average at 7+*

PERFORMANCE AT 10+	UPPER SOCIAL GROUP†	LOWER SOCIAL GROUP
Superior or above average‡	81%	70%
Average	13%	23%
Below or far below average	6%	7%
	100%	100%
Number of boys	664	158
Chi-square test	$\chi^2 = 9 \cdot 19$; $P < 0 \cdot 01$	

TABLE 5.3b: *Reading performance of upper and lower social group boys at 10+ who were average at 7+*

PERFORMANCE AT 10+	UPPER SOCIAL GROUP†	LOWER SOCIAL GROUP
Superior or above average‡	48%	32%
Average	34%	35%
Below or far below average	18%	33%
	100%	100%
Number of boys	352	185
Chi-square test	$\chi^2 = 19 \cdot 62$; $P < 0 \cdot 001$	

TABLE 5.3c: *Reading performance of upper and lower social group boys at 10+ who were below or far below average at 7+*

PERFORMANCE AT 10+	UPPER SOCIAL GROUP†	LOWER SOCIAL GROUP
Superior or above average‡	13%	8%
Average	25%	16%
Below or far below average	62%	76%
	100%	100%
Number of boys	521	528
Chi-square test	$\chi^2 = 22.51$; $P < 0.001$	

†Upper social group: occupational groups 1, 2 and 3 (professional, clerical, skilled workers)
Lower social group: occupational groups 4 and 5 (semi- and unskilled workers).
‡Superior or above average represent the top two-fifths on the Reading Test
Average—middle fifth,
Below or far below average—the bottom two-fifths.

TABLE 5.3d: *Reading performance of upper and lower social group girls at 10 + who were superior or above average at 7 +*

PERFORMANCE AT 10 +	UPPER SOCIAL GROUP†	LOWER SOCIAL GROUP
Superior or above average‡	78%	66%
Average	15%	19%
Below or far below average	7%	15%
	100%	100%
Number of girls	697	231
Chi-square test	$\chi^2 = 18 \cdot 02; P < 0 \cdot 001$	

TABLE 5.3e: *Reading performance of upper and lower social group girls at 10 + who were average at 7 +*

PERFORMANCE AT 10 +	UPPER SOCIAL GROUP†	LOWER SOCIAL GROUP
Superior or above average‡	37%	24%
Average	31%	32%
Below or far below average	32%	44%
	100%	100%
Number of girls	358	196
Chi-square test	$\chi^2 = 12 \cdot 13; P < 0 \cdot 01$	

TABLE 5.3f: *Reading performance of upper and lower social group girls at 10+ who were below or far below average at 7+*

PERFORMANCE AT 10+	UPPER SOCIAL GROUP†	LOWER SOCIAL GROUP
Superior or above average‡	11%	4%
Average	20%	10%
Below or far below average	69%	86%
	100%	100%
Number of girls	383	400
Chi-square test	$\chi^2 = 33 \cdot 89$; $P < 0 \cdot 001$	

†Upper social group: occupational groups 1, 2 and 3 (professional, clerical, skilled workers)
Lower social group: occupational groups 4 and 5 (semi- and unskilled workers).
‡Superior or above average represent the top two-fifths on the Reading Test
Average—middle fifth,
Below or far below average—the bottom two-fifths.

TABLE 5.4a: *Teachers' ability ratings of pupils of upper and lower social class origin compared with objective ratings of pupils' ability based on English test scores*

Social class	BASED ON ENGLISH TEST SCORE											
	Above Average		Average		Below Average							
	Upper (123)	Lower (45)	Upper (123)	Lower (45)	Upper (123)	Lower (45)						
Teachers' ratings:												
Above average	74%	60%	19%	14%	1%	1%						
Average	25%	39%	69%	68%	34%	28%						
Below average	1%	1%	12%	18%	65%	71%						
	100%	100%	100%	100%	100%	100%						
Number of children	899	424	1,292	1,183	391	860						
Chi-square test	$\chi^2 = 30 \cdot 39$; $P < 0 \cdot 001$		$\chi^2 = 28 \cdot 07$; $P < 0 \cdot 001$		Not significant							

TABLE 5.4b: *Teachers' ability ratings of pupils of upper and lower social class origin compared with objective ratings of pupils' ability based on English test scores in non-streamed schools†*

	BASED ON ENGLISH TEST SCORE					
	Above Average		*Average*		*Below Average*	
Social class	Upper (123)	Lower (45)	Upper (123)	Lower (45)	Upper (123)	Lower (45)
Teachers' ratings:						
Above average	82%	64%	24%	17%	1%	1%
Average	18%	33%	64%	66%	35%	29%
Below average		3%	12%	17%	64%	70%
	100%	100%	100%	100%	100%	100%
Number of children	369	185	658	629	188	464
Chi-square test	$\chi^2 = 19{\cdot}78$; $P < 0{\cdot}001$		$\chi^2 = 12{\cdot}80$; $P < 0{\cdot}01$		Not significant	

†See Table 7.6, Chapter 7, for a comparison of teachers' ability ratings and pupils' English test scores in *streamed* schools.

T<small>ABLE</small> 5.5

1. The definitions of Initial Mean and Final Mean are:

T<small>EST</small>	I<small>NITIAL</small> M<small>EAN</small>	F<small>INAL</small> M<small>EAN</small>
Reading English Problem Arithmetic Mechanical Arithmetic }	1964	1967
Concept Verbal }	1965	1967
Non-Verbal	1966	1967

2. Significance has been indicated by the following convention:

— = non-significant differences in final adjusted means for streamed and non-streamed schools.

*N
**N } = Significant difference in final adjusted mean at { 5·0%, 1·0%, 0·1% } Non-Streamed greater
***N

*S
**S } = Significant difference in final adjusted mean at { 5·0%, 1·0%, 0·1% } Streamed greater
***S

TABLE 5.5a: *Table of initial and final means and adjusted final means*
A-Version Tests
Professional and Clerical

	Non-Streamed and Streamed	BELOW AVERAGE ABILITY						AVERAGE ABILITY					
		N	Age	Initial Mean	Final Mean	Adjusted Final Mean	Significance level	N	Age	Initial Mean	Final Mean	Adjusted Final Mean	Significance level
Boys													
Reading	NS	8	10:4·9	84·00	92·63	93·51	—	31	10:4·1	101·29	105·97	105·63	—
	S	12	10:5·2	88·08	97·58	96·99		35	10:5·4	100·57	103·60	103·90	
English	NS	9	10:5·6	87·22	90·67	92·37	—	31	10:5·9	101·77	104·58	104·32	—
	S	14	10:5·8	93·07	93·00	91·90		33	10:5·1	101·12	101·85	102·10	
Mechanical Arithmetic	NS	8	10:6·1	96·75	100·13	99·61	—	30	10:6·1	105·43	108·30	107·48	—
	S	11	10:6·0	95·82	95·73	96·10		34	10:5·4	103·00	103·38	104·11	
Problem Arithmetic	NS	8	10:6·1	94·63	96·88	94·39	N**	33	10:5·9	106·73	110·18	108·44	N*
	S	15	10:5·8	89·40	91·33	92·66		33	10:5·3	101·70	100·97	102·71	
Concept	NS	10	10:6·1	95·90	108·10	106·90	—	36	10:5·4	103·94	110·69	108·49	—
	S	14	10:5·6	91·21	96·00	96·86		37	10:5·4	98·38	105·49	107·62	
Verbal	NS	11	10:5·3	93·64	100·18	98·02	—	36	10:5·7	102·22	103·25	103·26	—
	S	16	10:5·6	89·06	89·13	90·62		37	10:5·4	102·24	100·76	100·75	
Non-Verbal	NS	12	10:5·8	102·00	101·50	96·53	—	36	10:5·7	106·47	108·06	106·79	—
	S	17	10:5·4	91·06	95·71	99·22		38	10:5·5	102·37	104·87	106·07	

continued

Table 5.5a continued

	Non-Streamed and Streamed	N	Age	Initial Mean	Final Mean	Adjusted Final Mean	Significance level
Boys				ABOVE AVERAGE ABILITY			
Reading	NS	28	10:5·5	118·46	116·32	116·94	—
	S	75	10:5·4	120·19	119·63	119·40	
English	NS	33	10:5·1	113·45	113·30	115·80	—
	S	75	10:5·5	120·75	115·40	114·30	
Mechanical Arithmetic	NS	29	10:5·3	106·03	114·76	118·83	N*
	S	73	10:5·5	117·41	115·38	113·77	
Problem Arithmetic	NS	33	10:5·1	113·15	115·45	117·71	—
	S	73	10:5·5	119·85	117·19	116·17	
Concept	NS	35	10:5·5	114·94	118·37	120·38	—
	S	77	10:5·4	119·61	119·97	119·05	
Verbal	NS	37	10:5·2	114·62	113·57	114·97	—
	S	75	10:5·4	119·16	116·09	115·40	
Non-Verbal	NS	39	10:5·3	113·82	114·44	115·29	—
	S	79	10:5·5	115·59	117·56	117·14	

continued

Table 5.5a continued

	Non-Streamed and Streamed	BELOW AVERAGE ABILITY						AVERAGE ABILITY						
		N	Age	Initial Mean	Final Mean	Adjusted Final Mean	Significance level	N	Age	Initial Mean	Final Mean	Adjusted Final Mean	Significance level
GIRLS													
Reading	NS	12	10:6·4	89·33	95·83	95·80	—	30	10:5·3	101·53	105·57	105·02	—
	S	13	10:6·4	89·23	93·62	93·65		24	10:5·3	100·33	103·25	103·94	
English	NS	12	10:4·9	87·83	93·08	94·83	—	34	10:5·2	103·29	104·26	104·81	—
	S	14	10:6·3	92·43	95·21	93·71		26	10:4·9	104·96	105·62	104·91	
Mechanical Arithmetic	NS	13	10:6·5	90·00	97·38	98·72	—	28	10:5·2	99·71	106·21	106·57	—
	S	13	10:6·6	93·85	96·69	95·34		25	10:4·9	100·72	105·16	104·76	
Problem Arithmetic	NS	11	10:5·2	88·45	88·55	90·08	—	31	10:5·4	98·35	105·84	106·07	—
	S	14	10:6·1	91·86	92·79	91·59		25	10:4·8	99·28	101·84	101·56	
Concept	NS	14	10:5·9	94·07	95·21	95·09	—	37	10:5·1	101·92	107·65	106·44	—
	S	14	10:6·6	93·71	98·36	98·48		29	10:4·8	98·69	104·03	105·57	
Verbal	NS	15	10:6·0	91·87	96·20	96·71	—	33	10:5·0	99·85	104·73	105·07	—
	S	15	10:6·3	93·33	94·73	94·22		30	10:4·7	101·40	105·00	104·63	
Non-Verbal	NS	15	10:6·0	96·07	98·80	98·82	—	36	10:4·8	104·75	106·14	105·29	—
	S	18	10:5·6	96·11	96·17	96·15		30	10:4·7	101·47	103·60	104·62	

continued

359

Table 5.5a continued

	Non-Streamed and Streamed	N	Age	Initial Mean	Final Mean	Adjusted Final Mean	Signif-icance level
ABOVE AVERAGE ABILITY							
GIRLS							
Reading	NS	43	10:6·5	118·19	118·12	117·74	—
	S	56	10:5·4	117·16	116·07	116·37	
English	NS	40	10:5·8	119·15	116·63	117·40	—
	S	59	10:5·7	121·54	118·17	117·66	
Mechanical Arithmetic	NS	44	10:6·0	110·25	116·00	118·78	N *
	S	56	10:5·9	117·75	116·34	114·16	
Problem Arithmetic	NS	44	10:5·8	112·20	115·14	115·99	—
	S	58	10:5·8	114·90	114·53	113·89	
Concept	NS	47	10:6·1	114·53	118·83	118·63	—
	S	61	10:6·0	113·92	117·61	117·76	
Verbal	NS	44	10:6·1	116·16	116·50	117·13	—
	S	58	10:6·1	118·03	120·53	120·06	
Non-Verbal	NS	48	10:6·0	113·56	117·54	118·59	—
	S	63	10:6·0	116·10	117·14	116·34	

TABLE 5.5b: *Table of initial and final means and adjusted final means*
A-Version Tests
Skilled Manual

Boys

	Non-Streamed and Streamed	BELOW AVERAGE ABILITY						AVERAGE ABILITY					
		N	Age	Initial Mean	Final Mean	Adjusted Final Mean	Significance level	N	Age	Initial Mean	Final Mean	Adjusted Final Mean	Significance level
Reading	NS	85	10:6·1	84·68	88·79	88·80	—	73	10:4·9	99·19	101·84	102·26	N*
	S	61	10:6·3	84·70	92·23	92·22		96	10:5·5	100·19	99·74	99·42	
English	NS	89	10:5·9	88·36	87·24	86·80	—	71	10:4·7	98·14	98·77	99·36	—
	S	63	10:6·0	86·46	88·19	88·81		93	10:5·5	99·73	98·22	97·77	
Mechanical Arithmetic	NS	92	10:5·8	88·54	92·57	93·40	—	68	10:4·8	98·24	100·85	101·53	—
	S	63	10:6·1	91·73	91·59	90·38		96	10:5·6	100·22	101·66	101·18	
Problem Arithmetic	NS	87	10:5·8	89·41	92·15	92·81	—	70	10:4·7	100·13	100·93	100·99	—
	S	61	10:6·1	91·97	92·62	91·69		88	10:5·6	100·31	101·39	101·34	
Concept	NS	86	10:6·0	90·05	95·16	94·15	—	81	10:4·9	98·04	103·58	103·10	—
	S	68	10:6·2	86·85	91·49	92·77		101	10:5·4	96·73	101·82	102·20	
Verbal	NS	91	10:5·9	87·00	89·13	88·55	—	75	10:4·7	96·48	100·16	99·73	—
	S	69	10:6·2	84·74	90·16	90·92		98	10:5·5	93·83	99·00	99·33	
Non-Verbal	NS	98	10:5·8	92·87	95·89	95·55	—	80	10:4·7	100·26	104·36	104·30	—
	S	76	10:6·1	91·57	93·30	93·74		104	10:5·6	100·08	102·06	102·10	

continued

Table 5.5b continued

	Non-Streamed and Streamed	N	Age	Initial Mean	Final Mean	Ad-justed Final Mean	Signif-icance level
				ABOVE AVERAGE ABILITY			
Boys							
Reading	NS	71	10:5·9	115·30	110·58	110·09	—
	S	77	10:5·0	113·97	111·06	111·52	
English	NS	72	10:5·9	111·13	109·78	110·40	—
	S	74	10:5·1	113·14	110·68	110·07	
Mechanical Arithmetic	NS	76	10:6·1	105·43	110·62	112·57	—
	S	78	10:5·0	111·23	111·91	110·01	
Problem Arithmetic	NS	75	10:6·0	109·87	110·97	111·57	—
	S	76	10:5·2	112·34	111·79	111·19	
Concept	NS	76	10:5·9	110·11	113·88	113·58	—
	S	78	10:5·3	109·29	114·60	114·88	
Verbal	NS	73	10:6·2	110·64	111·03	110·57	—
	S	78	10:5·1	108·69	111·26	111·70	
Non-Verbal	NS	78	10:6·1	110·04	112·47	112·02	—
	S	80	10:5·1	108·68	110·66	111·10	

continued

Table 5.5b continued

	Non-Streamed and Streamed	Below Average Ability						Average Ability					
		N	Age	Initial Mean	Final Mean	Adjusted Final Mean	Signif-icance level	N	Age	Initial Mean	Final Mean	Adjusted Final Mean	Signif-icance level
Girls													
Reading	NS	57	10:6·3	86·63	89·77	88·80	—	73	10:6·0	100·48	101·37	101·54	—
	S	38	10:5·1	83·66	86·34	87·78		87	10:6·1	100·76	100·09	99·94	
English	NS	57	10:6·3	89·81	90·28	89·58	—	80	10:5·7	102·39	102·79	102·43	—
	S	30	10:5·4	86·87	86·13	87·44		88	10:6·0	101·40	101·58	101·90	
Mechanical Arithmetic	NS	58	10:6·4	89·81	90·64	90·55	—	84	10:5·8	99·64	102·43	102·95	N *
	S	34	10:5·7	89·12	88·03	88·18		87	10:6·0	101·17	100·44	99·94	
Problem Arithmetic	NS	59	10:6·4	88·37	89·88	89·64	—	80	10:5·8	99·63	102·29	101·44	N *
	S	33	10:5·6	87·15	84·82	85·25		89	10:6·1	97·26	97·47	98·23	
Concept	NS	62	10:6·5	90·63	90·82	89·52	—	87	10:5·7	98·91	103·97	102·81	—
	S	35	10:5·2	85·69	85·06	87·37		93	10:6·0	96·04	100·34	101·43	
Verbal	NS	62	10:6·3	88·94	91·34	89·73	—	86	10:5·9	100·10	105·52	105·21	N **
	S	34	10:5·2	81·65	87·79	90·71		92	10:6·0	99·04	101·20	101·50	
Non-Verbal	NS	36	10:6·3	91·52	96·17	95·65	—	94	10:5·7	99·88	104·71	104·48	—
	S	101	10:5·3	88·53	91·44	92·38		96	10:5·9	99·21	102·47	102·69	

continued

363

Table 5.5b continued

	Non-Streamed and Streamed	N	Age	Initial Mean	Final Mean	Adjusted Final Mean	Signif-icance level
				ABOVE AVERAGE ABILITY			
GIRLS							
Reading	NS	74	10:5·1	113·92	112·11	112·76	N*
	S	79	10:5·5	115·76	110·49	109·88	
English	NS	76	10:5·0	112·28	111·51	113·13	—
	S	84	10:5·5	117·15	114·15	112·69	
Mechanical Arithmetic	NS	73	10:4·7	103·38	108·16	111·06	—
	S	82	10:5·5	113·66	110·79	108·21	
Problem Arithmetic	NS	75	10:5·0	105·84	105·87	107·06	—
	S	76	10:5·6	110·29	107·82	106·64	
Concept	NS	78	10:4·8	107·85	111·90	111·71	—
	S	92	10:5·6	107·32	112·08	112·24	
Verbal	NS	82	10:4·8	109·77	113·66	114·37	—
	S	88	10:5·6	111·52	112·85	112·19	
Non-Verbal	NS	84	10:5·6	107·23	111·19	111·82	—
	S	94	10:5·2	109·23	111·26	110·70	

TABLE 5.5c: *Table of initial and final means and adjusted final means*

A-Version Tests

Semi-skilled and Unskilled

	Non-Streamed and Streamed	BELOW AVERAGE ABILITY						AVERAGE ABILITY					
		N	Age	Initial Mean	Final Mean	Adjusted Final Mean	Significance level	N	Age	Initial Mean	Final Mean	Adjusted Final Mean	Significance level
Boys													
Reading	NS	103	10:5·3	82·69	86·50	86·76	—	65	10:5·7	99·52	97·14	97·12	—
	S	105	10:5·7	83·44	86·97	96·72		56	10:4·8	99·45	100·29	100·31	
English	NS	109	10:5·4	83·18	82·85	83·07	—	65	10:5·5	97·02	96·08	96·47	—
	S	109	10:5·6	83·90	83·92	83·70		61	10:4·7	98·03	97·97	97·55	
Mechanical Arithmetic	NS	107	10:5·2	84·99	87·51	88·59	—	63	10:5·7	94·75	95·65	97·37	—
	S	98	10:5·5	88·59	87·47	86·29		59	10:5·1	102·34	102·34	100·50	
Problem Arithmetic	NS	110	10:5·3	88·95	89·22	89·03	—	65	10:5·9	99·65	99·42	98·93	S**
	S	96	10:5·5	88·35	87·27	87·49		59	10:4·8	97·80	102·54	103·08	
Concept	NS	113	10:5·4	87·51	88·76	88·26	—	69	10:5·7	96·30	98·87	99·34	—
	S	115	10:5·5	86·11	87·56	88·06		63	10:4·7	97·67	101·90	101·38	
Verbal	NS	107	10:5·2	83·93	86·65	86·06	—	65	10:5·7	95·05	97·03	97·48	—
	S	110	10:5·5	81·95	85·77	86·34		62	10:4·7	96·73	98·56	98·09	
Non-Verbal	NS	118	10:5·3	91·63	92·92	92·03	—	72	10:5·6	97·85	101·50	102·45	—
	S	120	10:5·5	88·08	91·30	92·18		68	10:4·9	100·97	101·60	100·59	

continued

365

Table 5.5c continued

	Non-Streamed and Streamed	N	Age	Initial Mean	Final Mean	Adjusted Final Mean	Significance level
			ABOVE AVERAGE ABILITY				
Boys							
Reading	NS	22	10:6.8	118·00	115·36	113·06	—
	S	29	10:4.2	112·86	110·41	112·16	
English	NS	24	10:6.6	110·13	110·08	110·30	—
	S	31	10:4.0	110·81	108·84	108·67	
Mechanical Arithmetic	NS	23	10:6.4	104·22	104·91	107·42	—
	S	33	10:4.1	111·91	107·15	105·40	
Problem Arithmetic	NS	23	10:6.4	110·17	107·83	107·41	—
	S	30	10:4.1	108·70	108·50	108·82	
Concept	NS	23	10:6.0	105·35	110·65	111·68	—
	S	33	10:4.1	108·24	111·03	110·31	
Verbal	NS	24	10:6.6	108·33	116·08	116·33	N **
	S	31	10:4.0	109·42	109·68	109·49	
Non-Verbal	NS	26	10:6.4	110·88	110·65	109·48	—
	S	36	10:4.1	105·83	110·17	111·01	

continued

Table 5.5c continued

| Girls | Non-Streamed and Streamed | Below Average Ability | | | | | | Average Ability | | | | | |
		N	Age	Initial Mean	Final Mean	Adjusted Final Mean	Signif- icance level	N	Age	Initial Mean	Final Mean	Adjusted Final Mean	Signif- icance level
Reading	NS	67	10:5·1	84·18	86·79	86·51	—	71	10:5·5	99·80	98·90	98·74	—
	S	66	10:6·0	83·17	83·18	83·47		71	10:5·4	99·30	97·35	97·51	
English	NS	72	10:5·0	85·96	86·31	86·10	—	76	10:5·5	99·62	99·70	99·69	—
	S	67	10:6·0	85·33	84·64	84·86		73	10:5·3	99·60	99·71	99·72	
Mechanical Arithmetic	NS	72	10:5·3	85·32	88·04	89·08	N*	79	10:5·3	95·24	97·43	98·38	—
	S	65	10:6·2	89·51	86·69	85·54		71	10:5·5	99·31	100·11	99·06	
Problem Arithmetic	NS	73	10:5·3	86·27	86·22	86·25	N*	76	10:5·2	97·54	97·67	97·35	—
	S	66	10:6·0	86·39	82·62	82·59		73	10:5·5	96·18	96·33	96·66	
Concept	NS	79	10:5·0	86·37	87·65	86·97	—	87	10:5·5	95·63	98·02	97·92	—
	S	74	10:6·1	84·22	83·38	84·11		74	10:5·6	95·28	97·95	98·07	
Verbal	NS	82	10:5·2	85·13	89·54	88·48	—	86	10:5·5	98·36	99·43	98·92	—
	S	70	10:6·0	81·89	86·21	87·46		76	10:5·4	96·24	99·49	100·06	
Non-Verbal	NS	90	10:5·3	87·99	92·98	92·04	—	92	10:5·5	97·90	99·18	99·14	—
	S	78	10:6·0	84·83	89·19	90·27		78	10:5·3	97·77	98·82	98·87	

continued

Table 5.5c continued

	Non-Streamed and Streamed	N	Age	Initial Mean	Final Mean	Adjusted Final Mean	Significance level
			ABOVE AVERAGE ABILITY				
GIRLS							
Reading	NS	37	10:5·8	112·95	111·49	111·12	—
	S	48	10:4·0	112·23	107·94	108·22	
English	NS	38	10:5·8	113·55	112·95	112·24	—
	S	52	10:4·1	111·52	109·85	110·37	
Mechanical Arithmetic	NS	38	10:5·6	104·89	112·21	114·58	N***
	S	50	10:4·1	112·76	107·52	105·72	
Problem Arithmetic	NS	37	10:5·6	107·57	110·05	109·76	N**
	S	51	10:4·1	106·76	104·82	105·03	
Concept	NS	42	10:5·9	105·36	113·50	112·97	N*
	S	54	10:4·0	103·94	107·80	108·21	
Verbal	NS	42	10:5·8	107·45	112·98	113·28	N*
	S	51	10:3·8	108·27	109·49	109·25	
Non-Verbal	NS	44	10:5·8	106·59	111·82	110·44	—
	S	56	10:4·0	103·55	107·91	109·00	

TABLE 5.5d: Table of initial and final means and adjusted final means

B-Version tests

Professional and Clerical

	Non-Streamed and Streamed	Below Average Ability						Average Ability					
		N	Age	Initial Mean	Final Mean	Adjusted Final Mean	Significance level	N	Age	Initial Mean	Final Mean	Adjusted Final Mean	Significance level
Boys													
Reading	NS	12	10:6·2	87·58	97·08	94·60	—	40	10:5·5	101·15	105·65	105·49	—
	S	15	10:4·9	81·00	90·60	92·59	—	40	10:5·0	100·88	108·63	108·77	—
English	NS	12	10:6·2	88·67	94·08	91·87	—	41	10:5·6	100·39	101·78	102·43	—
	S	17	10:4·7	82·94	88·29	89·85	—	41	10:4·8	103·05	102·83	102·18	—
Mechanical Arithmetic	NS	12	10:6·2	96·08	95·17	91·72	—	41	10:5·5	102·12	105·27	106·23	—
	S	16	10:4·7	88·38	93·19	95·77	—	40	10:4·6	104·43	106·60	105·61	—
Problem Arithmetic	NS	13	10:5·8	93·08	92·77	90·98	—	41	10:5·5	103·80	102·46	102·85	—
	S	16	10:4·8	88·50	90·75	92·20	—	40	10:4·7	105·30	104·88	104·48	—
Concept	NS	13	10:5·8	92·46	94·69	94·13	—	44	10:5·6	103·61	110·18	110·99	—
	S	15	10:5·6	91·40	96·13	96·61	—	41	10:4·5	105·83	111·27	110·40	—
Verbal	NS	13	10:5·8	88·31	92·00	92·04	—	44	10:5·5	102·59	104·50	106·24	—
	S	15	10:5·2	88·47	89·53	89·49	—	45	10:4·5	106·49	106·51	104·80	—
Non-Verbal	NS	13	10:5·8	93·23	95·62	94·26	—	48	10:5·7	107·60	110·21	109·30	—
	S	16	10:4·9	89·94	95·19	96·28	—	45	10:4·5	104·93	110·64	111·61	—

continued

Table 5.5d continued

	Non-Streamed and Streamed	ABOVE AVERAGE ABILITY					
		N	Age	Initial Mean	Final Mean	Ad-justed Final Mean	Signif-icance level
Boys							
Reading	NS	41	10:5·9	117·54	115·32	115·30	S *
	S	67	10:5·3	117·49	119·90	119·92	
English	NS	40	10:6·0	111·45	110·85	112·10	—
	S	71	10:5·4	115·34	112·80	112·10	
Mechanical Arithmetic	NS	39	10:5·9	106·03	106·51	109·08	—
	S	63	10:5·4	112·87	114·70	113·10	
Problem Arithmetic	NS	40	10:5·8	108·43	108·77	110·80	—
	S	70	10:5·3	116·41	115·23	114·07	
Concept	NS	46	10:5·7	113·63	115·57	117·00	—
	S	67	10:5·5	118·00	120·28	119·29	
Verbal	NS	46	10:5·9	114·17	115·67	116·74	—
	S	71	10:5·5	117·21	115·89	115·20	
Non-Verbal	NS	54	10:5·6	113·07	117·35	118·22	—
	S	71	10:5·5	115·35	118·44	117·78	

continued

Table 5.5d continued

	Non-Streamed and Streamed	Below Average Ability						Average Ability					
		N	Age	Initial Mean	Final Mean	Adjusted Final Mean	Signif-icance level	N	Age	Initial Mean	Final Mean	Adjusted Final Mean	Signif-icance level
Girls													
Reading	NS	6	10:5·0	85·17	90·17	90·75	—	41	10:5·3	100·10	102·24	102·80	—
	S	12	10:7·6	87·00	92·75	92·46		30	10:5·4	102·27	104·37	103·60	
English	NS	6	10:3·8	85·50	93·50	95·34	—	42	10:5·3	103·21	106·19	106·72	—
	S	13	10:7·6	91·23	92·31	91·46		29	10:5·4	105·66	107·79	107·02	
Mechanical Arithmetic	NS	7	10:5·9	88·71	88·71	90·84	—	42	10:5·2	100·69	101·83	102·87	—
	S	13	10:7·6	94·23	96·00	94·85		31	10:5·1	104·52	108·71	107·31	
Problem Arithmetic	NS	7	10:4·3	95·86	87·29	87·19	—	41	10:5·3	98·73	99·39	99·84	—
	S	13	10:7·6	95·54	89·92	89·97		31	10:5·1	100·23	103·55	102·96	
Concept	NS	9	10:5·0	92·33	98·00	99·04	—	43	10:5·1	103·19	105·86	106·68	—
	S	13	10:7·5	95·15	98·54	97·82		31	10:5·5	105·52	108·35	107·20	
Verbal	NS	7	10:4·3	88·00	94·71	95·80	—	42	10:5·1	102·98	105·24	106·26	—
	S	13	10:7·6	91·08	95·38	94·79		33	10:5·4	107·36	108·91	107·62	
Non-Verbal	NS	9	10:5·0	97·78	97·78	96·52	—	44	10:5·3	103·23	106·20	106·71	—
	S	13	10:7·6	94·62	96·54	97·41		35	10:5·3	105·26	110·00	109·35	

continued

371

Table 5.5d continued

	Non-Streamed and Streamed	N	Age	ABOVE AVERAGE ABILITY Initial Mean	Final Mean	Ad-justed Final Mean	Signif-icance level
GIRLS							
Reading	NS	60	10:5·1	113·52	111·58	112·53	—
	S	54	10:5·3	116·17	115·52	114·46	
English	NS	59	10:5·0	115·78	114·10	115·20	—
	S	54	10:5·4	120·69	114·67	113·46	
Mechanical Arithmetic	NS	56	10:4·8	106·84	113·36	115·24	—
	S	51	10:5·3	114·02	117·22	115·15	
Problem Arithmetic	NS	60	10:5·0	110·33	109·90	109·98	—
	S	46	10:5·3	110·72	111·02	110·92	
Concept	NS	61	10:4·8	112·74	116·20	117·25	—
	S	54	10:5·6	116·59	120·70	119·52	
Verbal	NS	61	10:4·7	111·28	115·98	118·09	—
	S	55	10:5·5	118·93	117·38	115·04	
Non-Verbal	NS	61	10:4·9	110·08	114·51	116·24	—
	S	59	10:5·5	115·08	118·29	116·50	

TABLE 5.5e: *Table of initial and final means and adjusted final means*
B-Version Tests
Skilled Manual

| | Non-Streamed and Streamed | BELOW AVERAGE ABILITY | | | | | | AVERAGE ABILITY | | | | | | |
		N	Age	Initial Mean	Final Mean	Adjusted Final Mean	Significance level	N	Age	Initial Mean	Final Mean	Adjusted Final Mean	Significance level
Boys													
Reading	NS	108	10:5·6	84·87	90·61	90·85	—	101	10:5·4	99·29	102·03	101·97	—
	S	82	10:5·7	85·76	90·67	90·35		104	10:4·6	99·16	102·38	102·43	
English	NS	106	10:5·6	86·42	87·61	87·38	—	103	10:5·5	97·68	99·15	99·39	—
	S	79	10:5·7	85·56	88·37	88·67		107	10:4·5	98·42	99·57	99·34	
Mechanical Arithmetic	NS	106	10:5·5	89·40	91·68	91·97	—	109	10:5·5	97·67	99·01	99·71	—
	S	79	10:5·6	90·68	91·68	91·30		109	10:4·7	99·63	102·70	102·00	
Problem Arithmetic	NS	107	10:5·6	90·46	91·05	90·87	—	100	10:5·5	101·71	101·12	100·29	—
	S	82	10:5·7	89·74	89·35	89·59		108	10:4·5	99·14	101·29	102·07	
Concept	NS	114	10:5·5	90·76	93·47	93·17	—	112	10:5·3	100·36	104·62	104·89	—
	S	82	10:5·3	89·73	93·29	93·71		108	10:4·7	101·13	105·06	104·78	
Verbal	NS	109	10:5·4	87·20	89·66	89·51	—	113	10:5·4	99·93	101·57	102·08	—
	S	83	10:5·5	86·58	88·99	89·19		115	10:4·7	101·57	103·75	103·25	
Non-Verbal	NS	113	10:5·5	92·52	95·10	94·74	—	120	10:5·4	100·64	104·25	104·91	—
	S	88	10:5·5	91·08	94·48	94·94		122	10:4·7	102·71	106·96	106·32	

continued

373

Table 5.5e continued

	Non-Streamed and Streamed	N	Age	Initial Mean	Final Mean	Adjusted Final Mean	Significance level
ABOVE AVERAGE ABILITY							
Boys							
Reading	NS	79	10:5·2	114·71	111·61	111·49	—
	S	70	10:5·2	114·41	113·70	113·83	
English	NS	78	10:5·4	110·04	107·95	107·89	—
	S	73	10:5·0	109·81	107·95	108·01	
Mechanical Arithmetic	NS	79	10:5·1	104·97	105·52	106·30	—
	S	73	10:5·1	108·05	108·60	107·76	
Problem Arithmetic	NS	79	10:5·3	109·53	107·52	107·19	—
	S	70	10:5·3	108·33	108·39	108·77	
Concept	NS	79	10:5·0	109·92	114·22	114·64	—
	S	80	10:5·2	111·18	114·31	113·89	
Verbal	NS	80	10:5·1	110·75	109·98	110·06	—
	S	73	10:5·2	111·03	110·67	110·58	
Non-Verbal	NS	83	10:5·0	107·69	110·30	110·31	—
	S	83	10:5·2	107·72	112·35	112·34	

continued

Table 5.5e continued

	Non-Streamed and Streamed	BELOW AVERAGE ABILITY						AVERAGE ABILITY					
		N	Age	Initial Mean	Final Mean	Adjusted Final Mean	Significance level	N	Age	Initial Mean	Final Mean	Adjusted Final Mean	Significance level
GIRLS													
Reading	NS	57	10:6·0	85·79	90·25	90·08	—	95	10:5·6	99·72	100·26	100·04	—
	S	61	10:6·0	85·34	89·15	89·31		120	10:5·1	99·20	100·57	100·74	
English	NS	60	10:6·0	89·27	91·75	90·84	—	94	10:5·8	101·50	101·03	100·86	—
	S	59	10:6·2	86·88	89·49	90·41		120	10:5·1	101·03	101·84	101·98	
Mechanical Arithmetic	NS	63	10:5·9	88·68	92·25	92·84	—	97	10:5·8	97·53	99·63	100·82	—
	S	57	10:6·2	91·14	94·07	93·42		118	10:5·1	100·99	102·86	101·88	
Problem Arithmetic	NS	55	10:5·9	91·73	89·85	88·21	—	93	10:5·7	97·24	97·67	97·56	S *
	S	58	10:6·2	85·81	87·53	89·08		119	10:5·2	96·88	99·83	99·92	
Concept	NS	66	10:5·9	90·98	95·12	95·39	—	110	10:5·6	101·07	103·35	102·92	—
	S	64	10:6·1	91·64	92·67	92·40		127	10:5·3	99·94	102·91	103·28	
Verbal	NS	63	10:5·9	89·06	93·03	93·00	—	102	10:5·9	101·01	102·09	101·98	S *
	S	61	10:6·1	88·95	91·90	91·94		130	10:5·2	100·76	104·34	104·42	
Non-Verbal	NS	68	10:6·0	93·91	96·25	95·71	—	110	10:5·8	100·96	104·04	103·48	—
	S	64	10:6·1	92·00	96·42	96·99		135	10:5·2	99·22	104·13	104·58	

continued

Table 5.5e continued

	Non-Streamed and Streamed	N	Age	Initial Mean	Final Mean	Ad-justed Final Mean	Signif-icance level
				ABOVE AVERAGE ABILITY			
GIRLS							
Reading	NS	66	10:6·2	115·18	110·95	110·51	—
	S	86	10:5·2	114·19	110·88	111·21	
English	NS	63	10:5·8	115·25	110·79	110·50	—
	S	86	10:5·0	114·37	112·36	112·57	
Mechanical Arithmetic	NS	68	10:6·0	106·74	108·68	110·54	—
	S	83	10:4·9	112·37	113·14	111·61	
Problem Arithmetic	NS	60	10:6·0	107·07	104·93	105·71	—
	S	84	10:5·0	109·76	107·69	107·14	
Concept	NS	71	10:6·0	110·08	113·56	113·96	—
	S	84	10:5·1	111·19	114·15	113·81	
Verbal	NS	71	10:6·0	111·96	112·69	112·82	S**
	S	88	10:5·0	112·40	116·49	116·38	
Non-Verbal	NS	74	10:6·0	108·82	111·88	112·14	—
	S	93	10:5·1	109·57	114·33	114·12	

TABLE 5.5f: Table of initial and final means and adjusted final means
B-Version Tests
Semi-skilled and Unskilled

	Non-Streamed and Streamed	BELOW AVERAGE ABILITY						AVERAGE ABILITY					
		N	Age	Initial Mean	Final Mean	Adjusted Final Mean	Significance level	N	Age	Initial Mean	Final Mean	Adjusted Final Mean	Significance level
Boys													
Reading	NS	112	10:5:7	83·46	86·06	85·68	—	64	10:5:1	98·98	98·13	98·16	S**
	S	92	10:5:8	82·08	87·30	87·77		55	10:5:1	99·04	103·65	103·62	
English	NS	115	10:5:5	83·31	82·49	82·75	—	67	10:5:1	93·73	94·61	95·69	S*
	S	95	10:5:6	84·14	84·12	83·81		62	10:5:3	97·68	99·40	98·24	
Mechanical Arithmetic	NS	123	10:5:5	87·06	86·87	87·02	—	69	10:5:1	95·88	94·91	96·36	S*
	S	94	10:5:7	87·60	88·80	88·59		60	10:5:2	101·25	102·27	100·61	
Problem Arithmetic	NS	116	10:5:6	90·02	88·31	88·17	—	73	10:5:2	96·84	95·84	96·71	—
	S	94	10:5:6	89·48	86·89	87·07		63	10:5:4	100·13	100·30	99·29	
Concept	NS	123	10:5:4	89·10	90·45	89·66	—	73	10:5:3	98·55	101·56	101·91	—
	S	95	10:5:7	86·43	86·45	87·48		68	10:5:6	99·66	103·79	103·42	
Verbal	NS	127	10:5:4	84·57	87·17	87·57	—	74	10:5:2	96·39	97·61	99·16	S*
	S	100	10:5:6	86·30	86·11	85·60		68	10:5:3	100·37	103·44	101·76	
Non-Verbal	NS	133	10:5:3	89·71	92·62	92·24	—	76	10:5:1	97·57	101·47	102·73	—
	S	108	10:5:6	87·92	89·81	90·27		75	10:5:4	101·40	104·32	103·04	

continued

Table 5.5f continued

Non-Streamed and Streamed	N	Age	ABOVE AVERAGE ABILITY			
			Initial Mean	Final Mean	Ad-justed Final Mean	Signif-icance level
Boys						
Reading NS	18	10:6·1	113·44	106·78	107·78	—
S	39	10:6·2	115·03	111·62	111·16	—
English NS	18	10:6·1	104·89	104·17	106·59	—
S	41	10:6·1	109·78	107·54	106·48	—
Mechanical Arithmetic NS	17	10:6·0	99·06	98·59	102·50	S **
S	37	10:6·3	111·08	113·43	111·64	
Problem Arithmetic NS	16	10:5·5	105·75	99·63	101·64	S **
S	40	10:6·0	111·90	109·82	109·01	
Concept NS	17	10:5·7	103·65	109·18	112·31	—
S	39	10:6·2	110·97	114·90	113·54	
Verbal NS	18	10:6·1	104·83	108·11	111·50	—
S	41	10:6·1	110·98	110·95	109·46	
Non-Verbal NS	18	10:6·1	107·28	110·83	110·71	—
S	41	10:6·1	106·93	111·22	111·27	

continued

Table 5.5f continued

	Non-Streamed and Streamed	**Below Average Ability**						**Average Ability**					
		N	Age	Initial Mean	Final Mean	Ad-justed Final Mean	Signif-icance level	N	Age	Initial Mean	Final Mean	Ad-justed Final Mean	Signif-icance level
GIRLS													
Reading	NS	86	10:5·3	82·10	82·00	82·29	S*	63	10:5·2	99·78	98·08	97·83	—
	S	65	10:5·9	83·12	86·05	85·67		66	10:4·8	99·18	97·42	97·66	
English	NS	86	10:5·6	84·69	84·22	84·78	—	62	10:5·0	99·73	99·85	99·72	—
	S	66	10:5·7	86·39	86·18	85·45		56	10:4·9	99·30	99·52	99·67	
Mechanical Arithmetic	NS	94	10:5·2	83·49	83·56	84·82	—	62	10:5·2	94·92	96·44	97·66	—
	S	61	10:5·6	88·46	89·49	87·56		55	10:4·8	98·51	102·05	100·68	
Problem Arithmetic	NS	88	10:5·6	86·90	82·10	81·66	—	62	10:5·1	96·40	93·74	94·04	—
	S	67	10:5·6	85·07	84·18	84·76		59	10:4·9	97·54	96·54	96·22	
Concept	NS	90	10:5·3	86·73	86·36	86·36	—	69	10:5·3	99·93	100·09	99·90	—
	S	70	10:5·7	86·71	87·99	88·00		64	10:5·0	99·28	100·97	101·17	
Verbal	NS	96	10:5·2	84·88	87·90	87·81	—	67	10:5·5	98·51	101·18	101·93	—
	S	67	10:5·7	84·52	85·96	86·08		63	10:5·1	100·49	101·54	100·74	
Non-Verbal	NS	106	10:5·3	86·72	90·40	90·19	—	72	10:5·4	96·68	100·33	100·89	—
	S	72	10:5·7	85·81	86·79	87·10		69	10:5·1	98·64	100·70	100·12	

continued

379

Table 5.5f continued

	Non-Streamed and Streamed	N	Age	Initial Mean	Final Mean	Ad-justed Final Mean	Signif-icance level
				ABOVE AVERAGE ABILITY			
GIRLS							
Reading	NS	35	10:5·0	112·63	106·06	106·15	—
	S	34	10:5·3	112·94	108·94	108·84	
English	NS	32	10:5·1	110·75	109·69	109·79	—
	S	38	10:5·2	111·16	109·47	109·38	
Mechanical Arithmetic	NS	34	10:4·9	99·12	103·18	107·26	—
	S	37	10:5·0	111·32	110·08	106·33	
Problem Arithmetic	NS	33	10:5·0	101·39	99·70	101·72	—
	S	38	10:5·2	108·84	107·00	105·25	
Concept	NS	35	10:5·2	105·89	106·69	108·55	—
	S	39	10:5·2	111·28	112·36	110·69	
Verbal	NS	37	10:5·0	107·65	111·92	112·69	—
	S	36	10:5·8	110·72	112·33	111·53	
Non-Verbal	NS	37	10:5·0	104·51	107·86	109·40	—
	S	42	10:5·6	109·24	111·52	110·17	

TABLE 5.6: *Analysis of teacher type*

1. *Definition of Initial and Final Mean*

Test	Initial Mean	Final Mean
	1964	1967
Problem Arithmetic ⎫		
English ⎬		
Concept ⎫	1966	1967
Verbal ⎬		

2. *Significance levels*

— = **non-significant differences in final adjusted means.**

* = 5% ⎫

** = 1% ⎬ Level of the significant differences indicated between all *three* means (final adjusted).

*** = 0·1% ⎭

TABLE 5.6a: *Table of initial and final means and adjusted final means by teacher and school type*
Professional and Clerical

continued

Boys and Girls	Non-Streamed and Streamed by Teacher Type	Below Average Ability						Average Ability					
		N	Age	Initial Mean	Final Mean	Adjusted Final Mean	Significance level	N	Age	Initial Mean	Final Mean	Adjusted Final Mean	Significance level
A-Version English (1964-1967)	NS 1	9	10:5·3	84·78	88·78	91·80	—	33	10:6·0	103·39	105·33	104·72	—
	NS 2	14	10:5·2	89·79	94·36	94·29		35	10:5·1	101·37	103·20	104·13	
	S 2	30	10:5·6	91·03	92·81	91·97		62	10:5·1	102·85	103·56	103·36	
A-Version Problem (1964-1967)	NS 1	9	10:5·3	88·11	89·89	91·03	—	34	10:5·9	102·29	109·97	109·35	**
	NS 2	14	10:5·2	90·29	94·00	93·57		36	10:5·0	101·47	103·97	103·87	
	S 2	31	10:5·6	89·87	91·42	91·29		61	10:5·2	100·67	101·93	102·34	
B-Version English (1964-1967)	NS 1	12	10:4·8	85·67	88·50	89·19	—	44	10:5·4	98·43	102·55	104·81	—
	NS 2	11	10:4·5	93·91	96·82	93·19		42	10:5·8	105·40	105·62	104·23	
	S 2	28	10:4·2	84·82	89·32	90·45		65	10:5·1	103·97	105·02	104·38	
B-Version Problem (1964-1967)	NS 1	12	10:4·8	94·17	87·25	86·67	—	43	10:5·2	102·91	98·70	98·08	**
	NS 2	12	10:6·6	97·75	96·92	94·70		41	10:5·7	100·05	102·98	104·07	
	S 2	27	10:6·3	90·22	88·89	90·13		64	10:5·1	102·34	104·38	104·10	
Concept (1966-1967)	NS 1	30	10:4·5	95·03	94·20	95·07	—	99	10:5·1	107·72	108·37	107·06	—
	NS 2	15	10:7·8	103·53	106·33	100·12		67	10:5·8	105·33	108·88	109·63	
	S All	60	10:6·2	94·74	96·10	97·21		146	10:5·0	105·57	107·59	108·13	
Verbal (1966-1967)	NS 1	29	10:4·5	92·17	93·31	94·03	—	98	10:5·1	104·36	104·05	103·54	—
	NS 2	19	10:5·3	96·21	99·79	97·91		66	10:5·8	103·82	105·20	105·04	
	S All	64	10:5·8	92·92	92·23	92·47		147	10:5·0	102·94	105·35	105·76	

Table 5.6a continued

BOYS AND GIRLS	Non-Streamed and Streamed by Teacher Type	ABOVE AVERAGE ABILITY					
		N	Age	Initial Mean	Final Mean	Adjusted Final Mean	Significance level
A-Version English (1964-1967)	NS 1	43	10:6·0	116·28	114·33	115·91	—
	NS 2	38	10:4·7	115·00	114·34	116·59	
	S 2	145	10:5·7	121·30	116·58	115·52	
A-Version Problem (1964-1967)	NS 1	45	10:6·0	112·42	117·00	118·71	*
	NS 2	39	10:4·6	111·21	112·21	114·54	
	S 2	143	10:5·8	118·01	116·27	115·10	
B-Version English (1964-1967)	NS 1	54	10:5·9	113·13	112·76	114·33	—
	NS 2	60	10:5·1	115·98	113·07	113·27	
	S 2	114	10:5·4	118·17	113·89	113·04	
B-Version Problem (1964-1967)	NS 1	54	10:5·9	108·69	108·61	110·07	*
	NS 2	60	10:5·1	111·97	111·18	111·26	
	S 2	109	10:5·2	114·02	114·84	114·06	
Concept (1966-1967)	NS 1	109	10:5·5	116·91	116·86	117·75	—
	NS 2	95	10:5·2	114·89	116·76	119·03	
	S All	271	10:5·6	119·91	119·42	118·27	
Verbal (1966-1967)	NS 1	108	10:5·4	114·55	114·07	114·94	—
	NS 2	95	10:5·4	115·49	116·95	117·22	
	S All	272	10:5·6	116·63	117·29	116·85	

TABLE 5.6b: *Table of initial and final means and adjusted final means by teacher and school type*

Skilled Manual

BOYS AND GIRLS	Non-Streamed and Streamed by Teacher Type	BELOW AVERAGE ABILITY						AVERAGE ABILITY					
		N	Age	Initial Mean	Final Mean	Adjusted Final Mean	Significance level	N	Age	Initial Mean	Final Mean	Adjusted Final Mean	Significance level
A-Version English (1964-1967)	NS 1	55	10:6·2	89·29	87·58	86·70	—	60	10:5·1	100·63	101·37	101·33	—
	NS 2	103	10:6·2	88·66	88·15	87·66		100	10:5·3	100·18	100·17	100·44	
	S 2	116	10:5·9	86·48	87·59	88·44		202	10:5·8	100·75	100·13	100·01	
A-Version Problem (1964-1967)	NS 1	58	10:6·2	90·64	91·50	90·68	—	64	10:5·0	97·69	100·78	101·84	—
	NS 2	103	10:6·2	88·32	91·31	91·95		100	10:5·3	100·90	101·43	100·34	
	S 2	112	10:5·9	89·62	89·23	89·05		193	10:5·8	98·95	99·76	99·97	
B-Version English (1964-1967)	NS 1	96	10:5·9	88·13	90·20	89·22	—	128	10:5·7	98·87	100·36	100·71	—
	NS 2	86	10:5·6	86·65	87·86	87·92		88	10:5·6	100·47	99·82	99·10	
	S 2	137	10:5·8	85·83	88·69	89·33		210	10:4·7	99·27	100·93	101·01	
B-Version Problem (1964-1967)	NS 1	95	10:5·9	93·14	91·40	89·60	—	127	10:5·6	99·37	99·12	98·59	**
	NS 2	86	10:5·6	88·78	89·92	90·61		88	10:5·6	99·26	99·07	98·61	
	S 2	141	10:5·8	88·60	89·20	89·99		212	10:4·8	97·71	100·79	101·29	
Concept (1966-1967)	NS 1	201	10:4·0	92·82	93·73	92·31	—	252	10:5·7	102·38	103·43	102·87	—
	NS 2	141	10:5·7	90·64	93·19	93·54		158	10:5·0	102·23	103·92	103·48	
	S All	263	10:5·7	89·97	91·60	92·49		454	10:5·3	101·09	102·81	103·27	
Verbal (1966-1967)	NS 1	200	10:6·0	88·94	90·75	90·86	—	251	10:5·7	100·14	102·02	102·28	—
	NS 2	144	10:5·6	88·76	90·01	90·22		152	10:5·1	101·29	102·19	101·66	
	S All	264	10:5·8	89·45	89·89	89·69		457	10:5·3	100·48	102·35	102·38	

continued

Table 5.6b continued

BOYS AND GIRLS	Non-Streamed and Streamed by Teacher Type	ABOVE AVERAGE ABILITY					
		N	Age	Initial Mean	Final Mean	Adjusted Final Mean	Significance level
A-Version English (1964-1967)	NS 1	63	10:5·6	100·83	109·65	111·29	—
	NS 2	98	10:5·2	111·84	110·65	111·64	
	S 2	175	10:5·4	115·19	112·39	111·24	
A-Version Problem (1964-1967)	NS 1	68	10:5·6	107·75	108·81	109·75	—
	NS 2	98	10:5·3	107·79	107·91	108·82	
	S 2	168	10:5·4	111·30	109·84	108·92	
B-Version English (1964-1967)	NS 1	67	10:5·2	111·00	109·00	109·80	—
	NS 2	82	10:5·8	113·63	109·49	108·78	
	S 2	147	10:5·3	112·33	110·10	110·13	
B-Version Problem (1964-1967)	NS 1	67	10:5·2	107·42	105·28	106·06	—
	NS 2	81	10:5·9	109·70	107·79	107·33	
	S 2	144	10:5·4	109·06	108·17	108·06	
Concept (1966-1967)	NS 1	168	10:6·0	113·56	114·50	113·74	—
	NS 2	147	10:4·8	110·85	111·89	113·03	
	S All	354	10:5·3	112·64	113·73	113·62	
Verbal (1966-1967)	NS 1	167	10:5·9	111·00	111·87	112·04	—
	NS 2	152	10:4·9	110·43	112·01	112·54	
	S All	349	10:5·3	111·79	113·14	112·82	

TABLE 5.6c: *Table of initial and final means and adjusted final means by teacher and school type*
Semi-skilled and Unskilled

Boys and Girls	Non-Streamed and Streamed by Teacher Type	Below Average Ability						Average Ability					
		N	Age	Initial Mean	Final Mean	Adjusted Final Mean	Significance level	N	Age	Initial Mean	Final Mean	Adjusted Final Mean	Significance level
A-Version English (1964-1967)	NS 1	68	10:5·6	83·85	84·21	84·41	—	56	10:6·5	99·80	98·04	97·45	—
	NS 2	133	10:4·7	84·12	83·50	83·51		99	10:4·9	98·14	98·28	98·98	
	S 2	202	10:5·7	84·23	83·64	83·57		149	10:5·0	99·34	99·42	99·18	
A-Version Problem (1964-1967)	NS 1	75	10:5·8	89·72	88·37	86·98	*	56	10:6·5	99·79	99·34	98·27	—
	NS 2	132	10:4·7	86·16	87·04	87·91		102	10:5·0	97·43	97·39	97·46	
	S 2	189	10:5·7	87·61	85·34	85·29		146	10:5·1	96·82	99·38	99·74	
B-Version English (1964-1967)	NS 1	145	10:5·8	83·72	83·66	83·82	—	80	10:5·2	96·45	96·56	96·95	—
	NS 2	81	10:5·0	83·59	82·11	82·36		67	10:5·1	96·82	97·79	97·95	
	S 2	165	10:5·6	84·32	84·24	83·98		110	10:5·0	97·71	99·50	99·12	
B-Version Problem (1964-1967)	NS 1	147	10:5·8	88·65	85·67	85·34	—	82	10:5·2	97·68	95·00	94·79	**
	NS 2	80	10:5·0	88·32	85·15	85·02		65	10:5·3	95·22	94·28	95·39	
	S 2	166	10:5·5	87·51	85·14	85·50		111	10:5·0	98·23	98·94	98·43	
Concept (1966-1967)	NS 1	270	10:5·6	87·90	87·96	87·13	—	178	10:5·8	100·36	100·07	99·78	—
	NS 2	166	10:4·7	87·51	88·54	88·01		136	10:5·0	98·64	98·94	100·00	
	S All	382	10:5·7	85·77	86·24	87·06		288	10:5·2	100·39	101·16	100·85	
Verbal (1966-1967)	NS 1	279	10:5·6	85·05	87·41	87·88	(**)	181	10:5·8	96·14	98·57	100·02	—
	NS 2	166	10:4·7	86·97	87·54	86·96		131	10:4·9	98·56	98·89	98·68	
	S All	378	10:5·7	86·07	85·75	85·66		290	10:5·2	99·42	100·83	100·03	

continued

Table 5.6c continued

BOYS AND GIRLS	Non-Streamed and Streamed by Teacher Type	N	Age	Initial Mean	Final Mean	Ad-justed Final Mean	Signif-icance level
A-Version English (1964-1967)	NS 1	23	10:6·2	111·30	108·65	108·71	*
	NS 2	47	10:5·9	111·83	112·85	112·60	
	S 2	97	10:4·1	111·22	109·54	109·64	
A-Version Problem (1964-1967)	NS 1	23	10:6·2	107·61	108·22	108·25	—
	NS 2	47	10:5·9	106·98	108·23	108·63	
	S 2	94	10:4·1	108·02	106·51	106·30	
B-Version English (1964-1967)	NS 1	35	10:5·3	109·94	108·77	108·84	—
	NS 2	18	10:5·7	106·83	106·11	107·97	
	S 2	81	10:5·8	110·85	109·17	108·72	
B-Version Problem (1964-1967)	NS 1	34	10:5·1	103·00	100·29	102·48	**
	NS 2	17	10:5·4	103·29	100·53	102·57	
	S 2	82	10:5·8	110·24	108·99	107·66	
Concept (1966-1967)	NS 1	63	10:4·2	110·16	111·89	111·62	—
	NS 2	60	10:5·0	108·02	109·18	110·55	
	S All	173	10:4·8	110·31	111·21	110·83	
Verbal (1966-1967)	NS 1	64	10:6·3	109·66	112·59	112·65	—
	NS 2	61	10:5·0	110·31	112·46	112·11	
	S All	175	10:4·9	109·59	110·35	110·45	

ABOVE AVERAGE ABILITY

TABLE 5.7: *A comparison of test score variances in streamed and non-streamed schools*

	SAMPLE A				SAMPLE B			
	Total	5%	1%	No. of comparisons	Total	5%	1%	No. of comparisons
Overall	18	8	10	144	35	25	10	144
By social class:								
Professional/Clerical (1,2)	8	2	6	48	16	11	5	48
Skilled (3)	7	3	4	48	—	—	—	48
Semi & Unskilled (4,5)	3	3	—	48	19	14	5	48
By sex:								
Boys	11	4	7	72	23	16	7	72
Girls	7	4	3	72	12	9	3	72
By year:								
1967	2	1	1	42	7	4	3	42
1966	4	2	2	42	8	7	1	42
1965	8	3	5	36	15	9	6	36
1964	4	2	2	24	5	5	—	24

TABLE 5.7—*continued*

	SAMPLE A				SAMPLE B			
	Total	5%	1%	No. of comparisons	Total	5%	1%	No. of comparisons
Overall	18	8	10	144	35	25	10	144
By test:								
Reading	—	—	—	24	5	4	1	24
English	2	1	1	24	5	3	2	24
Mechanical	6	4	2	24	7	6	1	24
Problem	5	2	3	24	9	6	3	24
Concept	—	—	—	18	3	2	1	18
Verbal	3	—	3	18	5	3	2	18
Non-Verbal	2	1	1	12	1	1	—	12

The 144 comparisons of test score variances in streamed and non-streamed schools were obtained by considering each test administration separately for pupils classified into groups according to their sex and social class. The above table provides summary counts of the number of comparisons in which variances were found to be significantly larger in streamed schools. No cases were found in which variances were larger in non-streamed schools.

The total column in the table provides the number of comparisons significant at, at least, the 5% level. Two-tailed tests were used for these comparisons, and under a null hypothesis to be tested at the 5% level we should expect on average that 2½% of the comparisons will indicate that variances are larger in streamed schools. Thus, for any row of the above table we can calculate our expectation of the total number of significant results by taking 2½% of the final entry in the row (number of comparisons). For example, for the top line which reports 18 significant cases for Sample A and 35 significant cases for sample B, the expected frequency for either sample is 2½% of 144 which equals 3.6.

389

TABLE 6.4: *Change of score between 9+ and 10+ on the 'Divergent Thinking' Test and on the Free Writing Essays*

Type of School: Type of teacher:		Non-Streamed Type 1			Non-Streamed Type 2			Streamed		
		No. of Pupils + // −		Sign Test	No. of Pupils + // −		Sign Test	No. of Pupils + // −		Sign Test
Fluency	Boys	93 76 83		N.S.	60 86 73		N.S.	132 160 168		*(2·02)
	Girls	80 92 66		N.S.	57 69 60		N.S.	129 183 138		N.S.
Flexibility	Boys	92 77 83		N.S.	58 87 74		N.S.	124 161 175		**(2·89)
	Girls	91 81 66		N.S.	55 65 66		N.S.	136 167 147		N.S.
Originality	Boys	88 66 98		N.S.	75 74 70		N.S.	136 148 176		*(2·21)
	Girls	82 75 81		N.S.	46 62 78		**(2·78)	130 158 162		N.S.
Free Writing	Boys	78 90 79		N.S.	57 88 65		N.S.	141 164 118		N.S.
	Girls	84 85 61		N.S.	65 58 62		N.S.	140 171 124		N.S.

* = significant at 5% level
** = significant at 1% level
N.S. = non-significant

+ = obtained higher score
− = obtained lower score
// = obtained same score

TABLE 6.5: *'Conforming—Non-conforming' score of above average 'highly creative' children compared with other above average children†*

Score	BOYS		GIRLS	
	'Highly Creative'	*Other Above Average*	*'Highly Creative'*	*Other Above Average*
0 (Non-conforming)	6% (2)	3%	2% (1)	—
1	17% (6)	8%	7% (3)	6%
2	11% (4)	16%	12% (5)	10%
3	25% (9)	24%	27% (11)	24%
4	30% (11)	33%	10% (4)	39%
5 (Conforming)	11% (4)	16%	42% (17)	21%
Total	100%	100%	100%	100%
Number of children	36	123	41	173
Chi-square test	Non-significant		$\chi^2 = 14.70$; P < 0.01	

†Only a limited sample of children completed the attitude scales and this did not include all the 'highly creative' children.

TABLE 6.6: *'Social adjustment' of 'highly creative' children compared with other above average children†*

	Boys		Girls	
Score	*'Highly creative'*	*Other above average*	*'Highly creative'*	*Other above average*
0 (Poor social adjustment)	— (—)	3%	2% (1)	5%
1	8% (3)	11%	10% (4)	22%
2	28% (10)	22%	20% (8)	29%
3	33% (12)	40%	29% (12)	30%
4	20% (7)	20%	32% (13)	10%
5 (Good social adjustment)	11% (4)	4%	7% (3)	4%
Total	100%	100%	100%	100%
Number of children	36	124	41	171
Chi-square test	Non-significant		$\chi^2 = 15\cdot54$; P $<$ 0·01	

†Only a limited sample of children completed the attitude scales and this did not include all the 'highly creative' children.

TABLE 6.7: 'Self-image' of above average 'highly creative' children compared with other above average children†

Score	BOYS 'Highly Creative'	BOYS Other Above Average	GIRLS 'Highly Creative'	GIRLS Other Above Average
0 (Poor self-image)	—	—	—	—
1	—	2%	—	1%
2	—	4%	—	3%
3	—	10%	5% (2)	16%
4	9% (3)	33%	12% (5)	38%
5	26% (9)	22%	7% (3)	22%
6	14% (5)	16%	34% (14)	14%
7	11% (4)	8%	20% (8)	5%
8	17% (6)	5%	15% (6)	1%
9	23% (8)		7% (3)	
Total	100%	100%	100%	100%
Number of children	35	125	41	173
Chi-square test	$\chi^2 = 14.81$; $P < 0.05$		$\chi^2 = 22.11$; $P < 0.01$	

†Only a limited sample of children completed the attitude scales and this did not involve all the 'highly creative' children.

TABLE 6.8: *'Anxiety' scores of above average 'highly creative' children compared with other above average children†*

Score	BOYS		GIRLS	
	'Highly Creative'	*Other Above Average*	*'Highly Creative'*	*Other Above Average*
0 (Anxious)	— (—)	2%	10% (4)	3%
1	— (—)	7%	2% (1)	10%
2	22% (8)	23%	20% (8)	24%
3	19% (7)	25%	24% (10)	24%
4	39% (14)	25%	25% (10)	24%
5	19% (7)	16%	17% (7)	13%
6 (Non-anxious)	— (—)	2%	2% (1)	2%
Total	100%	100%	100%	100%
Number of children	36	122	41	173
Chi-square test	Non-significant		Non-significant	

†Only a limited sample of children completed the attitude scale and this did not include all the 'highly creative' children.

TABLE 7.19a: *Proportions of boys and girls in different streams at 7+*

	2-Stream Schools		3- or 4-Stream Schools	
	Boys	*Girls*	*Boys*	*Girls*
A-stream	48%	58%	30%	40%
B-stream	52%	42%	41%	39%
C/D-stream	—	—	29%	21%
	100%	100%	100%	100%
Number of children (N=2,804)	559	518	895	832

TABLE 7.19b: *Proportions of boys and girls in different streams at 10+* (Same children as above)

	2-Stream Schools		3- or 4-Stream Schools	
	Boys	*Girls*	*Boys*	*Girls*
A-stream	50%	56%	32%	41%
B-stream	50%	44%	40%	36%
C/D-stream	—	—	28%	23%
	100%	100%	100%	100%
Number of children (N=2,804)	635	576	819	774

TABLE 8.4a: *Comparison of scores of boys and girls on the 'Imaginative Interests' scale*

SCORE	BOYS	GIRLS
0	—	—
1	8%	1%
2	20%	4%
3	25%	13%
4	21%	25%
5	16%	30%
6	7%	20%
7 8 9	3%	7%
Total	100%	100%
No. children	1066	983
Chi-square test	$\chi^2 = 323 \cdot 02$; P $< 0 \cdot 001$	

TABLE 8.4b: *Comparison of scores of boys and girls on the 'Logical Interests' scale*

SCORE	BOYS	GIRLS
0	—	4%
1	1%	11%
2	6%	17%
3	8%	20%
4	14%	18%
5	19%	13%
6	20%	10%
7	16%	4%
8	16%	3%
9	—	—
Total	100%	100%
No. children	1064	983
Chi-square test	$\chi^2 = 419\cdot09$; P $< 0\cdot001$	

TABLE 8.5a: *Comparison of scores on the 'Imaginative Interests' scale of children of different ability levels*

BOYS

SCORE	ABOVE AVERAGE	AVERAGE	BELOW AVERAGE
0 ⎫ 1 ⎬	10%	9%	7%
2	23%	19%	18%
3	28%	25%	23%
4	18%	20%	24%
5	13%	17%	19%
6	5%	6%	8%
7 ⎫ 8 ⎬ 9 ⎭	3%	4%	1%
Total	100%	100%	100%
No. children	309	383	374
Chi-square test		Not significant	

TABLE 8.5b: *Comparison of scores on the 'Imaginative Interests' scale of children of different ability levels*

GIRLS

SCORE	ABOVE AVERAGE	AVERAGE	BELOW AVERAGE
0 } 1	2%	2%	—
2	4%	4%	5%
3	12%	14%	12%
4	29%	25%	19%
5	30%	30%	30%
6	17%	20%	23%
7 } 8 } 9	6%	5%	11%
Total	100%	100%	100%
No. children	304	372	307
Chi-square test	$\chi^2 = 23 \cdot 35$; $P < 0 \cdot 05$		

TABLE 8.5c: *Comparison of scores on the 'Logical Interests' scale of children of different ability levels*

BOYS

SCORE	ABOVE AVERAGE	AVERAGE	BELOW AVERAGE
0	—	1%	1%
1	—	2%	2%
2	4%	6%	7%
3	5%	10%	9%
4	13%	12%	17%
5	18%	17%	20%
6	22%	18%	21%
7	18%	17%	12%
8	20%	17%	11%
9	—	—	—
Total	100%	100%	100%
No. children	308	383	373
Chi-square test		$\chi^2 = 38 \cdot 89, P < 0 \cdot 001$	

TABLE 8.5d: *Comparison of scores on the 'Logical Interests' scale of children of different ability levels*

GIRLS

SCORE	ABOVE AVERAGE	AVERAGE	BELOW AVERAGE
0	2%	4%	5%
1	11%	10%	13%
2	15%	17%	19%
3	22%	20%	18%
4	14%	20%	20%
5	13%	12%	13%
6	13%	9%	8%
7	7%	4%	4%
8	3%	4%	3%
9	—	—	—
Total	100%	100%	100%
No. children	304	372	307
Chi-square test		$\chi^2 = 34 \cdot 57$, P $< 0 \cdot 01$	

TABLE 8.6: *Comparison of the reading interests of 9+ children in streamed and non-streamed schools as expressed by the percentage scoring '2' (like very much)*

BOYS

	Above Average		Average		Below Average	
	Streamed	Non-Streamed	Streamed	Non-Streamed	Streamed	Non-Streamed
Comics	67% (2)†	66% (2)	76% (1)	65% (1)	75% (1)	68% (1)
Adventure stories	70% (1)	68% (1)	58% (2)	53% (2)	59% (2)	45% (2)
Newspapers	29% (4)	36% (4)	18% (4)	34% (4)	16% (5)	27% (4)
Poetry	16% (5)	13% (5)	15% (5)	13% (5)	20% (4)	14% (5)
Encyclopaedias	57% (3)	59% (3)	48% (3)	51% (3)	43% (3)	28% (3)
Number of children	100	100	123	100	100	100

GIRLS

	Above Average		Average		Below Average	
	Streamed	Non-Streamed	Streamed	Non-Streamed	Streamed	Non-Streamed
Comics	61% (2)	64% (2)	74% (1)	69% (1)	70% (1)	71% (1)
Adventure stories	77% (1)	76% (1)	65% (2)	62% (2)	55% (2)	46% (2)
Newspapers	22% (5)	18% (5)	21% (5)	25% (5)	27% (4)	21% (4)
Poetry	28% (4)	20% (4)	35% (4)	42% (4)	50% (3)	42% (3)
Encyclopaedias	41% (3)	30% (3)	34% (3)	31% (3)	23% (5)	20% (5)
Number of children	166	159	113	106	113	103

†Figures in brackets indicate rank order of preference

TABLE 9.6: *Scores obtained by girls of average ability on the 'relationship with teacher' scale in the fourth year (Cohorts 1 and 2)*

TYPE OF SCHOOL	STREAMED	NON-STREAMED Type 1	NON-STREAMED Type 2
Attitude score:			
'Good' relationship (456)	23%	37%	(29) 42%
Medium relationship (23)	45%	37%	(31) 45%
Poor relationship (01)	32%	26%	(9) 13%
	100%	100%	100%
Number of children	158	113	69
Chi-square tests	†Streamed versus Type 1: $\chi^2 = 6\cdot06$, $P < 0\cdot05$ †Streamed versus Type 2: $\chi^2 = 12\cdot45$, $P < 0\cdot01$ ‡Non-Streamed Type 1 versus Type 2: not significant		

†all four comparisons in one direction (see Chapter 9, p. 113)
‡data obtained from four comparisons not in same direction ..

TABLE 9.7: *Number of pupils obtaining higher and lower scores on the 'relationship with teacher' attitude scale in the fourth year*

Type of school: Type of teacher:	Non-Streamed Type 1				Non-Streamed Type 2				Streamed			
Relationship with Teacher	No. of Pupils +	//	—	Sign Test	No. of Pupils +	//	—	Sign Test	No. of Pupils +	//	—	Sign Test
Above average boys	22	7	13	NS	9	6	7	NS	33	23	27	NS
Above average girls	34	15	14	**	12	3	8	NS	47	37	26	*
All Above Average	56	22	27	**	21	9	15	NS	80	60	53	*
Average boys	35	20	13	**	5	6	15	*	27	5	30	NS
Average girls	20	14	20	NS	19	4	9	NS	19	30	32	NS
Below average boys	26	15	16	NS	11	11	15	NS	26	20	32	NS
Below average girls	10	9	20	NS	10	4	8	NS	16	17	24	NS
All Average And Below Average	91	58	69	NS	45	25	47	NS	88	72	118	*
Overall	147	80	96	**	66	34	62	NS	168	132	171	NS

* = change in attitude significant at 5% level
** = change in attitude significant at 1% level
+ = obtained higher score
| = obtained lower score
// = obtained same score
NS = non-significant

404

TABLE 9.8a: *The 'academic self-image' of boys and girls of average ability in the fourth year (Cohorts 1 and 2)*

SELF-IMAGE SCORE	Boys			Girls		
	Non-Streamed Type 1	Non-Streamed Type 2	Streamed	Non-Streamed Type 1	Non-Streamed Type 2	Streamed
Poor (0–4)	20%	(25) 36%	26%	22%	(29) 42%	37%
Medium (5)	30%	(23) 33%	26%	45%	(24) 35%	39%
Good (6–9)	50%	(22) 31%	48%	33%	(16) 23%	24%
Total	100%	100%	100%	100%	100%	100%
Number of children	121	70	164	113	69	158
Chi-square tests		†Streamed versus Type 1: not significant ‡Type 1 versus Type 2: $\chi^2=7\cdot38$, $P<0\cdot05$			‡Streamed versus Type 1: $\chi^2=7\cdot57$, $P<0\cdot05$ ‡Type 1 versus Type 2: $\chi^2=8\cdot18$, $P<0\cdot05$	

†all four comparisons *not* in same direction.
‡all four comparisons in one direction (see Chapter 9, p. 119,).

TABLE 9.8b: *The 'academic self-image' of boys and girls of below average ability in the fourth year (Cohorts 1 and 2)*

SELF-IMAGE SCORE	BOYS			GIRLS		
	Non-Streamed Type 1	Non-Streamed Type 2	Streamed	Non-Streamed Type 1	Non-Streamed Type 2	Streamed
Poor (0–4)	49%	(50) 53%	36%	(39) 57%	(27) 48%	43%
Medium (5)	33%	(24) 25%	27%	(26) 38%	(19) 34%	36%
Good (6–9)	18%	(21) 22%	37%	(3) 5%	(10) 18%	21%
Total	100%	100%	100%	100%	100%	100%
Number of children	103	95	171	68	56	120
Chi-square tests	†Streamed versus Type 1: $\chi^2=11\cdot10, P<0\cdot01$ †Streamed versus Type 2: $\chi^2=8\cdot76, P<0\cdot05$			†Streamed versus Type 1: $\chi^2=9\cdot69, P<0\cdot01$ ‡Streamed versus Type 2: not significant		

†all four comparisons (see Chapter 9, p. 119) in one direction.
‡data obtained from four comparisons not in same direction.

TABLE 9.9: *Number of pupils obtaining higher and lower scores on the 'academic self-image' attitude scale in the fourth year*

Type of school: Type of teacher:	NON-STREAMED TYPE 1				NON-STREAMED TYPE 2				STREAMED			
ACADEMIC SELF-IMAGE	No. of Pupils			Sign Test	No. of Pupils			Sign Test	No. of Pupils			Sign Test
	+	//	−		+	//	−		+	//	−	
Above average boys	15	12	15	NS	6	9	7	NS	32	29	22	NS
Above average girls	31	19	13	*	10	6	7	NS	41	37	32	NS
All Above Average	46	31	28	*	16	15	14	NS	73	66	54	NS
Average boys	33	20	15	*	6	9	11	NS	27	10	25	NS
Average girls	25	18	11	*	10	11	11	NS	30	24	27	NS
Below average boys	17	15	25	NS	10	9	18	NS	40	20	19	**
Below average girls	13	12	14	NS	5	8	9	NS	19	17	21	NS
All Average And Below Average	88	65	65	NS	31	37	49	†	116	71	92	NS
Overall	134	96	93	**	47	52	63	NS	189	137	146	*

* = change in attitude significant at 5% level
** = change in attitude significant at 1% level
† = approaching significance at 5% level
NS = non-significant
+ = obtained higher score (more favourable 'academic self-image')
− = obtained lower score
// = obtained same score.

TABLE 9.10: *Anxiety scores of boys and girls of below average ability in the fourth year (Cohorts 1 and 2)*

	Boys			Girls		
	Non-Streamed Type 1	Non-Streamed Type 2	Streamed	Non-Streamed Type 1	Non-Streamed Type 2	Streamed
Anxious (01)	25%	(21) 22%	19%	(33) 48%	(17) 31%	34%
Medium (23)	58%	(55) 58%	49%	(31) 46%	(28) 51%	49%
Non-anxious (456)	17%	(19) 20%	32%	(4) 6%	(10) 18%	17%
Number of children	100% 103	100% 95	100% 171	100% 68	100% 55	100% 119
Chi-square tests	†Streamed versus Type 1: $\chi^2=7\cdot72$, $P<0\cdot05$ †Streamed versus Type 2: $\chi^2=4\cdot12$, $P<0\cdot20$			†Streamed versus Type 1: $\chi^2=6\cdot28$, $P<0\cdot05$ ‡Streamed versus Type 2: not significant		

†all four comparisons (see Chapter 9, p. 119) in one direction.
‡data obtained from four comparisons not in same direction.

TABLE 9.11: *Number of pupils obtaining higher and lower scores on the anxiety scale in the fourth year*

Type of school: Type of teacher:	NON-STREAMED TYPE 1				NON-STREAMED TYPE 2				STREAMED			
	No. of Pupils			Sign Test	No. of Pupils			Sign Test	No. of Pupils			Sign Test
ANXIETY	+	//	−		+	//	−		+	//	−	
Above average boys	21	11	10	NS	10	5	7	NS	23	29	21	NS
Above average girls	20	16	27	NS	9	7	7	NS	43	33	33	NS
All Above Average	41	27	37	NS	19	12	14	NS	66	62	64	NS
Average boys	29	20	19	NS	10	7	8	NS	25	10	27	NS
Average girls	28	18	8	**	12	8	12	NS	33	21	27	NS
Below average boys	25	13	19	NS	13	13	11	NS	36	19	22	NS
Below average girls	14	6	19	NS	10	5	7	NS	20	16	21	NS
All Average and Below Average	96	57	65	*	45	33	38	NS	114	66	97	NS
Overall	137	84	102	**	64	45	52	NS	180	128	161	NS

* = change in attitude significant at 5% level
** = change in attitude significant at 1% level
NS = non-significant
+ = obtained higher score (less anxious)
− = obtained lower score (more anxious)
// = obtained same score.

TABLE 9.12: *A comparison of pupils obtaining higher and lower scores on the social adjustment scale in the fourth year*

Type of school: Type of teacher:	NON-STREAMED TYPE 1				NON-STREAMED TYPE 2				STREAMED			
	No. of Pupils			Sign Test	No. of Pupils			Sign Test	No. of Pupils			Sign Test
SOCIAL ADJUSTMENT	+	//	—		+	//	—		+	//	—	
Above average boys	16	15	9	NS	7	8	7	NS	28	34	18	NS
Above average girls	37	14	12	***	12	7	4	NS	59	21	30	**
All Above Average	53	29	21	***	19	15	11	NS	87	55	48	**
Average boys	32	19	16	*	12	8	6	NS	31	13	18	NS
Average girls	34	10	10	***	21	9	2	***	38	26	16	**
Below average boys	31	11	15	*	14	10	13	NS	47	17	15	***
Below average girls	15	15	9	NS	10	10	2	*	26	19	12	*
All Average and Below Average	112	55	50	***	57	37	23	***	142	75	61	***
Overall	165	84	71	***	76	52	34	***	229	130	109	***

* = change in attitude significant at 5% level
** = change in attitude significant at 1% level
*** = change in attitude significant at 0·1% level
NS = non-significant
+ = obtained higher score (more socially adjusted)
— = obtained lower score
// = obtained same score.

TABLE 9.13: *Number of pupils obtaining higher and lower scores on the 'importance of doing well' scale in the fourth year*

Type of school: Type of teacher:	NON-STREAMED TYPE 1			NON-STREAMED TYPE 2			STREAMED		
IMPORTANCE OF DOING WELL	No. of Pupils + // −		Sign Test	No. of Pupils + // −		Sign Test	No. of Pupils + // −		Sign Test
Above average boys	17 12 13		NS	7 9 6		NS	44 25 14		***
Above average girls	19 28 16		NS	9 10 4		NS	25 52 33		NS
All Above Average	36 40 29		NS	16 19 10		NS	69 77 47		NS
Average boys	36 17 15		**	16 4 6		†	21 9 32		NS
Average girls	17 20 17		NS	8 14 10		NS	25 23 33		NS
Below average boys	31 9 17		†	16 4 17		NS	40 13 26		NS
Below average girls	15 12 12		NS	8 6 8		NS	21 12 24		NS
All Average and Below Average	99 58 61		**	48 28 41		NS	107 57 115		NS
Overall	135 98 90		**	64 47 51		NS	176 134 162		NS

* = change in attitude significant at 5% level
** = change in attitude significant at 1% level
*** = change in attitude significant at 0·1% level
† = approaching significance at 5% level
NS = non-significant
+ = obtained higher score (more important to do well)
− = obtained lower score (less important to do well)
// = obtained same score.

411

TABLE 9.14: *Number of pupils obtaining higher or lower scores on the 'attitude to school' and 'interest in school-work' scales in the fourth year*

Type of school: Type of teacher: ATTITUDE TO SCHOOL	NON-STREAMED TYPE 1				NON-STREAMED TYPE 2				STREAMED			
	No. of Pupils +	//	−	Sign Test	No. of Pupils +	//	−	Sign Test	No. of Pupils +	//	−	Sign Test
Above average boys	13	14	15	NS	9	7	6	NS	42	23	18	**
Above average girls	28	20	15	NS	10	7	6	NS	31	43	36	NS
All Above Average	41	34	38	NS	19	14	12	NS	73	66	54	NS
Average boys	36	14	18	*	10	7	9	NS	25	15	22	NS
Average girls	14	15	25	NS	11	13	8	NS	23	18	40	*
Below average boys	25	8	24	NS	16	7	14	NS	34	23	22	NS
Below average girls	11	13	15	NS	8	8	6	NS	13	19	25	†
All Average and Below Average	86	50	82	NS	45	35	37	NS	95	75	109	NS
Overall	127	84	112	NS	64	49	49	NS	168	141	163	NS

Table 9.14—continued

Type of school: Type of teacher:	NON-STREAMED TYPE 1				NON-STREAMED TYPE 2				STREAMED			
	No. of Pupils			Sign Test	No. of Pupils			Sign Test	No. of Pupils			Sign Test
INTEREST IN SCHOOL WORK	+	//	−		+	//	−		+	//	−	
Above average boys	10	19	13	NS	8	5	9	NS	36	26	21	NS†
Above average girls	25	19	19	NS	9	7	7	NS	26	46	38	NS
All Above Average	35	38	32	NS	17	12	16	NS	62	72	59	NS
Average boys	30	14	23	NS	13	4	9	NS	32	7	23	NS
Average girls	17	12	25	NS	11	14	7	NS	18	24	39	**
Below average boys	24	16	17	NS	9	8	20	NS	33	21	25	NS
Below average girls	7	16	16	NS	7	7	8	NS	16	16	25	NS
All Average and Below Average	78	58	81	NS	40	33	44	NS	99	68	112	NS
Overall	113	96	113	NS	57	45	60	NS	161	140	171	NS

*   = change in attitude significant at 5% level
** = change in attitude significant at 1% level
†   = approaching significance at 5% level
NS = non-significant
+   = obtained higher score
−   = obtained lower score
// = obtained same score.

TABLE 9.15a: *Scores obtained by boys of above average ability on the conforming/non-conforming scale in the fourth year (Cohorts 1 and 2)*

Type of School: Type of Teacher:		STREAMED	NON-STREAMED TYPE 1	NON-STREAMED TYPE 2
Low conforming score	(012)	30%	(31) 38%	(10) 20%
Medium	(3)	35%	(34) 41%	(15) 31%
High conforming	(45)	35%	(17) 21%	(24) 49%
Number of children		100% 169	100% 82	100% 49
Chi-square tests:		†Streamed versus Type 1: $\chi^2 = 5.29$, $P < 0.10$ †Streamed versus Type 2: $\chi^2 = 3.48$, $P < 0.20$ †Type 1 versus Type 2: $\chi^2 = 11.75$, $P < 0.01$		

TABLE 9.15b: *Scores obtained by boys of average ability on the conforming/non-conforming scale in the fourth year (Cohorts 1 and 2)*

Type of School: Type of Teacher:		NON-STREAMED TYPE 1	NON-STREAMED TYPE 2
Low conforming score	(012)	42%	(22) 31%
Medium	(3)	41%	(22) 31%
High conforming	(45)	17%	(27) 38%
Number of children		100% 121	100% 71
Chi-square test		†Type 1 versus Type 2: $\chi^2 = 10.21$, $P < 0.01$	

TABLE 9.15c: *Scores obtained by girls of below average ability on the conforming/non-conforming scale in the fourth year (Cohorts 1 and 2)*

Type of School: Type of Teacher:	STREAMED	NON-STREAMED TYPE 1		NON-STREAMED TYPE 2	
Low conforming score (012)	17%	(27)	40%	(14)	25%
Medium (3)	43%	(15)	22%	(17)	31%
High conforming (45)	40%	(26)	38%	(24)	44%
	100%		100%		100%
Number of children	120	68		55	
χhi-square tests	†Streamed versus Type 1: $\chi^2 = 14 \cdot 76$, $P < 0 \cdot 001$				
	†Type 1 versus Type 2: $\chi^2 = 2 \cdot 99$, $P < 0 \cdot 20$				
	‡Streamed versus Type 2: not significant				

†all four comparisons in one direction (see page 119)
‡data obtained from four comparisons *not* in same direction

TABLE 9.16: *Number of pupils obtaining higher and lower scores on the 'conforming versus non-conforming' scale in the fourth year*

Type of school: Type of teacher:	Non-Streamed Type 1			Non-Streamed Type 2			Streamed		
Conforming versus Non-Conforming	No. of Pupils + // −		Sign Test	No. of Pupils + // −		Sign Test	No. of Pupils + // −		Sign Test
Above average boys	10 14 18		NS	7 8 7		NS	22 22 37		NS
Above average girls	21 22 20		NS	10 5 8		NS	19 45 46		**
All Above Average	31 36 38		NS	17 13 15		NS	41 67 83		***
Average boys	26 20 22		NS	10 6 10		NS	15 13 34		*
Average girls	10 27 17		NS	4 11 17		*	13 31 37		**
Below average boys	18 18 21		NS	9 15 13		NS	27 34 18		NS
Below average girls	8 10 21		*	5 10 7		NS	15 19 23		NS
All Average and Below Average	52 75 81		*	28 42 47		NS	70 97 112		***
Overall	93 111 119		NS	45 55 62		NS	111 164 195		***

* = change in attitude significant at 5% level
** = change in attitude significant at 1% level
*** = change in attitude significant at 0·1% level
NS = non-significant
\+ = obtained higher score
− = obtained lower score
// = obtained same score

TABLE 9.17a: *Scores obtained by boys of below average ability on 'attitude to class' scale in fourth year (Cohorts 1 and 2)*

Type of school: Type of teacher:	STREAMED	NON-STREAMED TYPE 1	NON-STREAMED TYPE 2
Poor attitude (0–4) Medium (5, 6) Good attitude (7, 8)	28% 36% 36%	12% 25% 63%	(19) 20% (31) 33% (45) 47%
Number of children	100% 171	100% 103	100% 95
Chi-square tests:		†Streamed versus Type 1: $\chi^2 = 18{\cdot}84, P = 0{\cdot}001$ ‡Type 1 versus Type 2: $\chi^2 = 4{\cdot}84, P < 0{\cdot}10$ ‡Streamed versus Type 2: not significant	

† all four comparisons in one direction (see page 119)
‡ data obtained from four comparisons not in same direction

417

TABLE 9.17b: *Scores obtained by girls of average ability on 'attitude to class' scale in fourth year (Cohorts 1 and 2)*

Type of school: Type of teacher:			STREAMED	NON-STREAMED TYPE 1	NON-STREAMED TYPE 2	
Poor attitude	(0–4)		16%	9%	(4)	6%
Medium	(5, 6)		20%	14%	(15)	21%
Good attitude	(7, 8)		64%	77%	(51)	73%
Number of children			100% 157	100% 113	100% 70	
Chi-square tests:			†Streamed versus Type 1 : $\chi^2 = 5\cdot04, P < 0\cdot10$ †Streamed versus Type 2 : $\chi^2 = 4\cdot59, P < 0\cdot20$			

† all four comparisons in one direction (see page 119)

TABLE 9.18: *Number of pupils obtaining higher and lower scores on the 'attitude to class' scale in the fourth year*

Type of school: Type of teacher: ATTITUDE TO CLASS	NON-STREAMED TYPE 1				NON-STREAMED TYPE 2				STREAMED			
	No. of Pupils			Sign Test	No. of Pupils			Sign Test	No. of Pupils			Sign Test
	+	//	—		+	//	—		+	//	—	
Above average boys	17	12	13	NS	6	6	10	NS	26	39	18	NS
Above average girls	29	18	16	†	6	8	9	NS	37	44	29	NS
All Above Average	46	30	29	NS	12	14	19	NS	63	83	47	NS
Average boys	35	15	18	*	10	6	10	NS	26	13	23	NS
Average girls	16	24	14	NS	20	4	8	*	27	24	30	NS
Below average boys	32	13	11	**	12	12	13	NS	34	11	34	NS
Below average girls	20	5	14	NS	6	9	7	NS	18	17	20	NS
All Average and Below Average	103	57	57	**	48	31	38	NS	105	65	107	NS
Overall	149	87	86	***	60	45	57	NS	168	148	154	NS

* = change in attitude significant at 5% level
** = change in attitude significant at 1% level
*** = change in attitude significant at 0.1% level
† = approaching significance at 5% level
NS = non-significant
+ = obtained higher score
— = obtained lower score
// = obtained same score

TABLE 9.19: *Number of pupils obtaining higher and lower scores on the 'other image' scale in the fourth year*

Type of school: Type of teacher: 'OTHER IMAGE'	Non-Streamed Type 1				Non-Streamed Type 2				Streamed			
	No. of Pupils +	//	−	Sign Test	No. of Pupils +	//	−	Sign Test	No. of Pupils +	//	−	Sign Test
Above average boys	15	15	12	NS	8	5	9	NS	25	34	24	NS
Above average girls	28	16	19	NS	11	7	5	NS	33	33	44	NS
All Above Average	43	31	31	NS	19	12	14	NS	58	67	68	NS
Average boys	31	20	16	*	13	6	7	NS	23	13	26	NS
Average girls	14	22	18	NS	17	8	7	NS	18	28	35	*
Below average boys	25	14	18	NS	8	16	13	NS	22	24	33	NS
Below average girls	7	19	13	NS	4	12	6	NS	19	13	25	NS
All Average and Below Average	77	75	65	NS	42	42	33	NS	82	78	119	*
Overall	120	106	96	NS	61	54	47	NS	140	145	187	*

* = change in attitude significant at 5% level
NS = non-significant
\+ = obtained higher score
− = obtained lower score
// = obtained same score

TABLE 9.20a: *Change in attitude between the third and fourth year of children in the top or 'A' stream and those in the lower ability streams in streamed schools*

ATTITUDE	STREAM	POSITIVE	NEGATIVE	SIGN TEST
Relationship with teacher	Top	80	67	not significant
	Others	89	99	not significant
Academic self-image	Top	79	61	not significant
	Others	111	76	*significant at 5% (2·48)
Anxiety in the classroom	Top	76	79	not significant
	Others	102	81	not significant
Social adjustment—getting on well with others	Top	95	52	***significant at 0·1% (3·46)
	Others	139	54	***significant at 0·1% (6·04)
Importance of doing well	Top	84	59	*significant at 5% (2·01)
	Others	96	105	not significant
Attitude to school	Top	81	66	not significant
	Others	89	95	not significant
Interest in school work	Top	71	73	not significant
	Others	86	98	not significant
Conforming versus non-conforming	Top	48	84	**significant at 1% (3·05)
	Others	64	107	**significant at 1% (3·20)
Attitude to class	Top	67	53	not significant
	Others	100	104	not significant
'Other image' of class	Top	74	79	not significant
	Others	68	107	**significant at 1% (2·87)

Positive = obtained higher score.
Negative = obtained lower score.

TABLE 9.20b: *Change of attitude between the third and fourth year according to stream*

ATTITUDE	NO. STREAMS		POSITIVE	NEGATIVE	SIGN TEST
Relationship with teacher	2	A	40	37	not significant
		B	42	38	not significant
	3 or more	A	40	30	not significant
		B	30	28	not significant
		C	17	33	*Deterioration significant at 5% level
Academic self-image	2	A	38	35	not significant
		B	52	30	*Improvement significant at 5% level
	3 or more	A	41	26	not significant
		B	33	24	not significant
		C	26	22	not significant
Anxiety in the classroom	2	A	43	36	not significant
		B	49	26	*Improvement significant at 5% level
	3 or more	A	33	43	not significant
		B	29	27	not significant
		C	24	28	not significant
Social Adjustment	2	A	45	30	not significant
		B	61	28	**Improvement significant at 1% level
	3 or more	A	50	22	**Improvement significant at 1% level
		B	43	16	**Improvement significant at 1% level
		C	35	10	**Improvement significant at 1% level
Importance of doing well	2	A	44	33	not significant
		B	56	39	not significant
	3 or more	A	40	26	not significant
		B	25	28	not significant
		C	15	38	**Deterioration significant at 1% level

Table 9.20b—continued

Attitude	No. Streams		Positive	Negative	Sign Test
Attitude to school	2	A	40	37	not significant
		B	40	40	not significant
	3 or more	A	41	29	not significant
		B	26	32	not significant
		C	23	23	not significant
Interest in school work	2	A	34	39	not significant
		B	39	40	not significant
	3 or more	A	37	34	not significant
		B	27	30	not significant
		C	20	28	not significant
Conforming versus non-conforming	2	A	26	45	*More non-conforming significant at 5% level
		B	33	34	not significant
	3 or more	A	22	39	*More non-conforming significant at 5% level
		B	16	48	**More non-conforming significant at 1% level
		C	15	25	not significant
Attitude to class	2	A	36	30	not significant
		B	48	44	not significant
	3 or more	A	31	23	not significant
		B	36	20	*Improvement significant at 5% level
		C	16	30	*Deterioration significant at 5% level
'Other image' of class	2	A	44	45	not significant
		B	35	37	not significant
	3 or more	A	30	34	not significant
		B	13	40	**Deterioration significant at 1% level
		C	20	30	not significant

Note: 'C' includes all bottom streams of large schools, i.e. 3 streams or more

TABLE 9.21: *Pleasurability ratings given to pupils (Cohort 1) at 9+*

ABOVE AVERAGE BOYS

Rated Pleasurable	Streamed	Non-Streamed Type 1	Non-Streamed Type 2
Seldom or never 1	1%	3%	2%
2	9%	8%	6%
3	18%	16%	15%
Most of the time 4	72%	73%	77%
Total	100%	100%	100%
Number of pupils	372	191	152

Chi-square tests: Streamed versus Non-streamed Type 1: not significant
Streamed versus Non-streamed Type 2: not significant
Non-streamed Type 1 versus Type 2: not significant

AVERAGE BOYS

Rated Pleasurable	Streamed	Non-Streamed Type 1	Non-Streamed Type 2
Seldom or never 1	2%	5%	5%
2	18%	10%	18%
3	28%	23%	24%
Most of the time 4	52%	62%	53%
Total	100%	100%	100%
Number of pupils	683	324	326

Chi-square tests: Streamed versus Non-streamed Type 1: $\chi^2 = 20 \cdot 57$, $P < 0 \cdot 001$
Streamed versus Non-streamed Type 2: not significant
Non-streamed Type 1 versus Type 2: $\chi^2 = 9 \cdot 01$, $P < 0 \cdot 05$

Table 9.21 continued
BELOW AVERAGE BOYS

Rated Pleasurable	Streamed	Non-Streamed Type 1	Non-Streamed Type 2
Seldom or never 1	10%	5%	14%
2	29%	25%	29%
3	28%	38%	26%
Most of the time 4	33%	32%	31%
Total	100%	100%	100%
Number of pupils	370	201	192

Chi-square tests: Streamed versus Non-streamed Type 1: $\chi^2 = 8 \cdot 23$, $P < 0 \cdot 05$
Streamed versus Non-streamed Type 2: not significant
Non-streamed Type 1 versus Type 2: $\chi^2 = 13 \cdot 14$, $P < 0 \cdot 01$

ABOVE AVERAGE GIRLS

Rated Pleasurable	Streamed	Non-Streamed Type 1	Non-Streamed Type 2
Seldom or never 1	—	5%	—
2	2%	5%	4%
3	10%	8%	10%
Most of the time 4	88%	82%	86%
Total	100%	100%	100%
Number of pupils	382	218	192

Chi-square tests: Streamed versus Non-streamed Type 1: $\chi^2 = 16 \cdot 98$, $P < 0 \cdot 001$
Streamed versus Non-streamed Type 2: not significant
Non-streamed Type 1 versus Type 2: $\chi^2 = 6 \cdot 64$, $P < 0 \cdot 05$

continued

O

Table 9.21 *continued*
AVERAGE GIRLS

RATED PLEASURABLE		STREAMED	NON-STREAMED TYPE 1	NON-STREAMED TYPE 2
Seldom or never	1	2%	2%	2%
	2	9%	8%	6%
	3	18%	25%	24%
Most of the time	4	71%	65%	68%
Total		100%	100%	100%
Number of pupils		663	325	327
Chi-square tests:		Streamed versus Non-streamed Type 1: $\chi^2 = 8\cdot53$, $P < 0\cdot05$		
		Streamed versus Non-streamed Type 2: $\chi^2 = 8\cdot55$, $P < 0\cdot05$		
		Non-streamed Type 1 versus Type 2: not significant		

BELOW AVERAGE GIRLS

RATED PLEASURABLE		STREAMED	NON-STREAMED TYPE 1	NON-STREAMED TYPE 2
Seldom or never	1	6%	3%	3%
	2	22%	16%	22%
	3	25%	26%	34%
Most of the time	4	47%	55%	41%
Total		100%	100%	100%
Number of pupils		278	141	115
Chi-square tests:		Streamed versus Non-streamed Type 1: not significant		
		Streamed versus Non-streamed Type 2: not significant		
		Non-streamed Type 1 versus Type 2: not significant		

TABLE 10.2: *A comparison of mutual pairs in terms of the similarity of their social class (aged 9+)*

TYPE OF MUTUAL PAIR	STREAMED	NON-STREAMED	NON-STREAMED	
			Type 1	*Type 2*
Category 1	36%	36%	38%	31%
Category 2	45%	45%	44%	49%
Category 3	14%	17%	15%	20%
Category 4	4%	2%	3%	—
Category 5	1%	†	†	—
	100%	100%	100%	100%
Number of mutual pairs	559	590	402	188

† = less than 0·5%

TABLE 10.3: *A comparison of sociometric status of children in streamed and non-streamed schools and with different teacher types (aged 9+)*

	STREAMED VERSUS NON-STREAMED	STREAMED VERSUS TYPE 1	STREAMED VERSUS TYPE 2
Criterion 1: **Best Friend**			
Above average boys	No difference	No difference	No difference
Above average girls	No difference	No difference	No difference
Average boys	No difference	No difference	No difference
Average girls	No difference	No difference	No difference
Below average boys	No difference	No difference	No difference
Below average girls	No difference	No difference	$\chi^2 = 6\cdot70, P < 0\cdot05$ (Fewer 'neglectees', fewer 'stars' with Type 2)
Criterion 2: **Work with**			
Above average boys	$\chi^2 = 16\cdot78, P < 0\cdot001$ (More 'stars' and fewer 'neglectees' in non-streamed)	$\chi^2 = 8\cdot06, P < 0\cdot02$ (More 'stars' and fewer 'neglectees' with Type 1)	$\chi^2 = 14\cdot23, P < 0\cdot001$ (More 'stars' and fewer 'neglectees' with Type 2)
Above average girls	No difference	No difference	No difference
Average boys	No difference	No difference	No difference
Average girls	No difference	No difference	No difference
Below average boys	No difference	No difference	No difference
Below average girls	No difference	No difference	No difference
Criterion 3: **Play with**			
Above average boys	$\chi^2 = 7\cdot15, P < 0\cdot05$ (More 'stars' and fewer 'neglectees' in non-streamed)	No difference	No difference
Above average girls	No difference	No difference	No difference
Average boys	No difference	No difference	No difference
Average girls	No difference	No difference	No difference
Below average boys	No difference	No difference	No difference
Below average girls	No difference	No difference	No difference

TABLE 10.4: *A comparison of the sociometric status of different ability groups (i.e. above average/average/below average ability) within different types of school*

Type of school: Type of teacher:	STREAMED	NON-STREAMED TYPE 1	NON-STREAMED TYPE 2
Criterion 1: Best Friend			
Boys	No difference	No difference	No difference
Girls	No difference	No difference	No difference
Criterion 2: Work with			
Boys	No difference	$\chi^2 = 25 \cdot 40$, df$=4$, $P < 0 \cdot 001$†	$\chi^2 = 34 \cdot 62$, df$=4$, $P < 0 \cdot 001$†
Girls	$\chi^2 = 23 \cdot 54$, df$=4$, $P < 0 \cdot 001$†	$\chi^2 = 11 \cdot 19$, df$=4$, $P < 0 \cdot 05$†	$\chi^2 = 40 \cdot 98$, df$=4$, $P < 0 \cdot 001$†
Criterion 3: Play with			
Boys	No difference	No difference	$\chi^2 = 13 \cdot 36$, df$=4$, $P < 0 \cdot 01$†
Girls	No difference	No difference	No difference

†Statistical significance indicates that more 'stars' and fewer 'neglectees' are among the above average and fewer 'stars' and more 'neglectees' among the below average

TABLE 10.5: *Change in sociometric status between the third and fourth year in streamed schools and in non-streamed schools with different teacher-types*

Type of School: Type of teacher: Number of children making change	STREAMED			NON-STREAMED TYPE 1			NON-STREAMED TYPE 2		
	+ve	−ve	Sign test	+ve	−ve	Sign test	+ve	−ve	Sign test
Criterion 1: Best Friend									
Boys Above average	97	89	NS	27	52	**	42	37	NS
Average	84	126	**	48	53	NS	51	50	NS
Below average	79	96	NS	49	48	NS	34	54	*
Girls Above average	80	91	NS	38	48	NS	28	34	NS
Average	88	97	NS	52	55	NS	46	50	NS
Below average	86	53	**	37	43	NS	34	33	NS
Criterion 2: Work with									
Boys Above average	116	109	NS	35	48	NS	41	40	NS
Average	86	132	**	56	59	NS	48	47	NS
Below average	83	98	NS	49	51	NS	41	52	NS
Girls Above average	75	103	*	44	58	NS	34	31	NS
Average	92	108	NS	67	49	NS	48	48	NS
Below average	83	71	NS	35	43	NS	32	26	NS
Criterion 3: Play with									
Boys Above average	101	117	NS	31	56	**	40	43	NS
Average	79	134	**	47	62	NS	51	55	NS
Below average	81	93	NS	52	62	NS	38	53	NS
Girls Above average	78	82	NS	44	47	NS	27	28	NS
Average	89	108	NS	53	62	NS	57	47	NS
Below Average	68	76	NS	36	39	NS	37	32	NS

NS = not significant
*   = change significant beyond 5% level
** = change significant beyond 1% level

−ve = decreased in sociometric status
+ve = increased in sociometric status

TABLE 10.6: *A comparison of the proportions of 'stars', 'neglectees' and medium status children in streamed and non-streamed schools and with different teacher-types*

Type of school: Type of teacher:	STREAMED	NON-STREAMED TYPE 1	NON-STREAMED TYPE 2
Best Friend—Boys			
neglectees	9%	11%	9%
medium status	86%	84%	86%
stars	5%	5%	5%
	100%	100%	100%
Number of children	1,305	538	709
Chi-square test	Difference not statistically significant		
Best Friend—Girls			
neglectees	7%	7%	6%
medium status	90%	88%	91%
stars	3%	5%	3%
	100%	100%	100%
Number of children	1,176	501	652
Chi-square test	Difference not statistically significant		
Work with—Boys			
neglectees	9%	9%	9%
medium status	86%	85%	86%
stars	5%	6%	5%
	100%	100%	100%
Number of children	1,305	538	709
Chi-square test	Difference not statistically significant		

Table 10.6—*continued*

Type of school: Type of teacher:	Streamed	Non-Streamed Type 1	Non-Streamed Type 2
Work with—Girls			
neglectees	8%	8%	7%
medium status	88%	88%	89%
stars	4%	4%	4%
	100%	100%	100%
Number of children	1,176	501	652
Chi-square test	Difference not statistically significant		
Play with—Boys			
neglectees	11%	11%	11%
medium status	84%	83%	84%
stars	5%	6%	5%
	100%	100%	100%
Number of children	1,305	538	709
Chi-square test	Difference not statistically significant		
Play with—Girls			
neglectees	7%	10%	7%
medium status	90%	87%	91%
stars	3%	3%	2%
	100%	100%	100%
Number of children	1,176	501	652
Chi-square test	Difference not statistically significant		

TABLE 10.7a: *A comparison of the class position of 'neglectees' in streamed and non-streamed schools*

Type of School: Type of Teacher:	STREAMED	NON-STREAMED TYPE 1	NON-STREAMED TYPE 2
Best Friend (neglectees) Top of class Middle Bottom of class	12% 57% 31% 100%	14% 50% 36% 100%	13% 44% 43% 100%
Number of children	257	153	121
Chi-square tests	Streamed versus Type 1: Difference not statistically significant Streamed versus Type 2: $\chi^2 = 6 \cdot 43$, $P < 0 \cdot 05$		
Work with (neglectees) Top of class Middle Bottom of class	9% 57% 34% 100%	7% 52% 41% 100%	10% 37% 53% 100%
Number of children	285	129	120
Chi-square tests:	Streamed versus Type 1: Difference not statistically significant Streamed versus Type 2: $\chi^2 = 15 \cdot 29$, $P < 0 \cdot 001$		
Play with (neglectees) Top of class Middle Bottom of class	13% 62% 25% 100%	18% 51% 31% 100%	13% 41% 46% 100%
Number of children	298	162	137
Chi-square tests:	Streamed versus Type 1: Difference not statistically significant Streamed versus Type 2: $\chi^2 = 19 \cdot 74$, $P < 0 \cdot 001$		

TABLE 10.7b: *A comparison of the class position of 'stars' in streamed and non-streamed schools*

Type of School: Type of Teacher:	STREAMED		NON-STREAMED TYPE 1		NON-STREAMED TYPE 2	
Best Friend (stars)						
Top of class	(30)	34%	(15)	36%	(15)	31%
Middle	(50)	58%	(22)	54%	(33)	69%
Bottom of class	(7)	8%	(4)	10%	(—)	—
		100%		100%		100%
Number of children	87		41		48	
Chi-square tests:	Streamed versus Type 1: Difference not statistically significant					
	Streamed versus Type 2: Difference not statistically significant					
Work with (stars)						
Top of class		52%	(33)	65%	(29)	57%
Middle		43%	(18)	35%	(22)	43%
Bottom of class		5%	(—)	—	(—)	—
		100%		100%		100%
Number of children	100		51		51	
Chi-square tests:	Streamed versus Type 1: Difference not statistically significant					
	Streamed versus Type 2: Difference not statistically significant					
Play with (stars)						
Top of class	(30)	38%	(20)	36%	(19)	42%
Middle	(40)	50%	(32)	57%	(26)	58%
Bottom of class	(10)	12%	(4)	7%	(—)	—
		100%		100%		100%
Number of children	80		56		45	
Chi-square tests:	Streamed versus Type 1: Difference not statistically significant					
	Streamed versus Type 2: Difference not statistically significant					

TABLE 10.8a: *A comparison of the social class of 'neglectees' in streamed and non-streamed schools*

Type of School: *Type of Teacher:*	STREAMED	NON-STREAMED TYPE 1	NON-STREAMED TYPE 2
Best Friend (neglectees) Social class† 1	3%	5%	1%
2	8%	11%	16%
3	39%	36%	37%
4	32%	30%	28%
5	18%	18%	18%
	100%	100%	100%
Number of children	259	151	120
Chi-square tests:	Streamed versus Type 1: Difference not significant Streamed versus Type 2: Difference not significant		
Work with (neglectees) Social class 1	3%	3%	1%
2	8%	7%	8%
3	44%	40%	34%
4	28%	30%	31%
5	17%	20%	26%
	100%	100%	100%
Number of children	292	134	104
Chi-square tests:	Streamed versus Type 1: Difference not significant Streamed versus Type 2: Difference not significant		

435

Table 10.8a—*continued*

Play with (neglectees) Social class			
1	2%	6%	3%
2	11%	10%	12%
3	39%	34%	36%
4	32%	32%	31%
5	16%	18%	18%
	100%	100%	100%
Number of children	305	163	116
Chi-square tests:	Streamed versus Type 1: Difference not significant Streamed versus Type 2: Difference not significant		

† For details of Social class, see Appendix 4.

TABLE 10.8b: *A comparison of the social class of 'stars' in streamed and non-streamed schools*

Type of School: Type of Teacher:	STREAMED	NON-STREAMED TYPE 1	NON-STREAMED TYPE 2
Best Friend (stars) **Social class†** 1	(7) 8%	(4) 10%	(6) 13%
2	(6) 7%	(6) 15%	(5) 10%
3	(44) 50%	(15) 36%	(25) 52%
4	(26) 29%	(14) 34%	(10) 21%
5	(5) 6%	(2) 5%	(2) 4%
	100%	100%	100%
Number of children	88	41	48
Chi-square tests:	Streamed versus Type 1: **Difference not significant** Streamed versus Type 2: **Difference not significant**		
Work with (stars) **Social class** 1	7%	(8) 16%	(10) 23%
2	13%	(15) 30%	(7) 16%
3	45%	(16) 32%	(15) 35%
4	26%	(10) 20%	(11) 26%
5	9%	(1) 2%	—
	100%	100%	100%
Number of children	106	50	43
Chi-square tests:	Streamed versus Type 1: $\chi^2 = 12\cdot79, P < 0\cdot05$ Streamed versus Type 2: $\chi^2 = 9\cdot28, P < 0\cdot05$		

Table 10.8b—continued

Play with (stars) Social class				
1	(5)	6%	(4)	7.5%
2	(8)	10%	(6)	11%
3	(40)	49%	(18)	34%
4	(22)	27%	(21)	40%
5	(7)	8%	(4)	7.5%
		100%		100%
Number of children	82		53	

(2)	4%	
(9)	20%	
(23)	51%	
(11)	25%	
	—	
	100%	
45		

Chi-square tests: Streamed versus Type 1: Difference not significant
Streamed versus Type 2: Difference not significant

† For details of Social class, see Appendix 4.

TABLE 10.9a: *A comparison of the pleasurability ratings of 'neglectees' in streamed and non-streamed schools*

Type of school: Type of Teacher:	STREAMED	NON-STREAMED TYPE 1	NON-STREAMED TYPE 2
Best Friend (neglectees) Pleasurable—seldom or never 1 2 3 most of time 4	5% 16% 21% 58% 100%	11% 15% 27% 47% 100%	12% 20% 18% 50% 100%
Number of children	258	160	121
Chi-square tests:	Streamed versus Type 1: $\chi^2=9 \cdot 33, P < 0 \cdot 05$ Streamed versus Type 2: $\chi^2=8 \cdot 93, P < 0 \cdot 05$		
Work with (neglectees) Pleasurable—seldom or never 1 2 3 most of time 4	6% 19% 23% 52% 100%	9% 18% 29% 44% 100%	17% 28% 22% 33% 100%
Number of children	289	134	105
Chi-square tests:	Streamed versus Type 1: Difference not significant Streamed versus Type 2: $\chi^2=20 \cdot 43, P < 0 \cdot 001$		

Table 10.9a—continued

Play with (neglectees)			
Pleasurable—seldom or never 1	6%	6%	9%
2	17%	13%	21%
3	21%	24%	21%
most of time 4	56%	57%	49%
	100%	100%	100%
Number of children	300	165	117

Chi-square tests: Streamed versus Type 1: Difference not significant
Streamed versus Type 2: Difference not significant

TABLE 10.9b: *A comparison of the pleasurability ratings of 'stars' in streamed and non-streamed schools*

Type of school: Type of Teacher:	Streamed		Non-Streamed Type 1		Non-Streamed Type 2	
Best Friend (stars)						
Pleasurable—seldom or never 1	(1)	1%	(1)	2%	(—)	—
2	(15)	17%	(2)	5%	(4)	8%
3	(14)	16%	(10)	24%	(9)	19%
most of time 4	(57)	66%	(29)	69%	(35)	73%
		100%		100%		100%
Number of children	87		42		48	
Chi-square tests:	Streamed versus Type 1: Difference not significant Streamed versus Type 2: Difference not significant					
Work with (stars)						
Pleasurable—seldom or never 1		—	(—)	—	(1)	2%
2		5%	(3)	6%	(2)	5%
3		10%	(7)	14%	(8)	18%
most of time 4		85%	(41)	80%	(32)	75%
		100%		100%		100%
Number of children	103		51		43	
Chi-square tests:	Streamed versus Type 1: Difference not significant Streamed versus Type 2: Difference not significant					

441

Table 10.9b—continued

Play with (stars)					
Pleasurable—seldom or never	1	(1)	1%	(2)	4%	(—)	—
	2	(8)	10%	(3)	6%	(5)	11%
	3	(22)	27%	(10)	19%	(11)	24%
most of time	4	(50)	62%	(38)	71%	(29)	65%
			100%		100%		100%
Number of children		81		53		45	
Chi-square tests:		Streamed versus Type 1: Difference not significant					
		Streamed versus Type 2: Difference not significant					

442

TABLE 10.10: *A comparison of the behaviour ratings of 'neglectees' and medium status children; also of 'stars' and medium status children on the best friend criterion*

	Fights or Bullies	Picked on or Teased	Withdrawn	Disobedient
Neglectees Medium status Chi-square test:	8% (N= 539) 4% (N=4626) $\chi^2 = 16.89$ $P < 0.001$ with 1df More neglectees fight or bully	7% (N= 536) 2% (N=4616) $\chi^2 = 36.05$ $P < 0.001$ with 1df More neglectees picked on or teased	8% (N= 531) 3% (N=4543) $\chi^2 = 25.55$ $P < 0.001$ with 1df More neglectees withdrawn	10% (N= 539) 5% (N=4628) $\chi^2 = 21.36$ $P < 0.001$ with 1df More neglectees disobedient
Stars Medium status Chi-square test:	5% (N= 177) 4% (N=4626) Not significant	†(N=177) 2% (N=4614) Not significant	†(N= 177) 3% (N=4543) $\chi^2 = 4.49$ $P < 0.05$ with 1df Fewer stars withdrawn	6% (N= 177) 5% (N=4628) Not significant

† = less than 0·5%.

TABLE 10.11a: *A comparison of the social adjustment of 'neglectees' and medium status children; also of 'stars' and medium status children*

	NEGLECTEES	MEDIUM STATUS	STARS
Social Adjustment scores:			
Poor 0	(3) 3%	3%	(1) 3%
1	(21) 25%	14%	(4) 12%
2	(26) 31%	22%	(4) 12%
3	(23) 27%	34%	(9) 26%
4	(8) 9%	20%	(9) 26%
Good 5	(4) 5%	7%	(7) 21%
	100%	100%	100%
Number of children	85	884	34
Chi-square tests:	Neglectees versus Medium Status: $\chi^2 = 14 \cdot 49$, $P < 0 \cdot 05$ Stars versus Medium Status: Difference not significant		

444

TABLE 10.11b: *A comparison of the social adjustment of 'neglectees' in streamed and non-streamed schools*

Type of school: Type of teacher:	STREAMED	NON-STREAMED TYPE 1	NON-STREAMED TYPE 2
Social Adjustment scores:			
Poor 0	(2) 6%	(—) —	(1) 5·3%
1	(11) 32%	(6) 19%	(4) 21%
2	(9) 26%	(9) 28%	(8) 42%
3	(7) 21%	(12) 38%	(4) 21%
4	(4) 12%	(3) 9%	(1) 5·3%
Good 5	(1) 3%	(2) 6%	(1) 5·3%
	100%	100%	100%
Number of children	34	32	19
Chi-square test:	Streamed versus Type 1: Difference not significant Streamed versus Type 2: Difference not significant		

445

TABLE 10.11c: *A comparison of the social adjustment of 'stars' in streamed and non-streamed schools*

Type of school: Type of teacher:	STREAMED	NON-STREAMED TYPE 1	NON-STREAMED TYPE 2
Social Adjustment scores:			
Poor 0	(1)	(–)	(–)
1	(1)	(3)	(1)
2	(2)	(1)	(1)
3	(6)	(3)	(1)
4	(4)	(4)	(1)
Good 5	(2)	(4)	(–)
Number of children	16	15	3
Chi-square tests:	Streamed versus Type 1: Difference not significant Streamed versus Type 2: Difference not significant		

TABLE 10.12a: *A comparison of the participation ratio of 'neglectees' and medium status children; also of 'stars' and medium status children*

Participation ratio percentage:	NEGLECTEES	MEDIUM STATUS	STARS
0– 9	17%	10%	3%
10– 19	10%	8%	6%
20– 29	20%	16%	8%
30– 39	10%	12%	6%
40– 49	10%	10%	8%
50– 59	12%	15%	17%
60– 69	11%	14%	22%
70– 79	4%	5%	12%
80– 89	4%	7%	11%
90–100	2%	3%	7%
	100%	100%	100%
Number of children	541	4,605	175
Chi-square tests:	Neglectees versus medium status: $\chi^2 = 37 \cdot 53$, $P < 0 \cdot 001$ Stars versus medium status: $\chi^2 = 53 \cdot 74$, $P < 0 \cdot 001$		

TABLE 10.12b: *A comparison of the participation ratio of 'neglectees' in streamed and non-streamed schools*

Type of school: Type of teacher:	STREAMED	NON-STREAMED TYPE 1	NON-STREAMED TYPE 2
Participation ratio percentage:			
0– 19	34%	12·5%	31%
20– 39	25%	33%	33%
40– 59	22%	28%	17%
60– 79	14%	17·5%	14%
80–100	5%	9%	5%
	100%	100%	100%
Number of children	258	160	121
Chi-square tests:	Streamed versus Type 1: $\chi^2 = 23{\cdot}02$, $P < 0{\cdot}01$ Streamed versus Type 2: Difference not significant		

448

TABLE 10.12c: *A comparison of the participation ratio of 'stars' in streamed and non-streamed schools*

Type of school: Type of teacher:	STREAMED	NON-STREAMED TYPE 1	NON-STREAMED TYPE 2
Participation ratio percentage:			
0– 19	(7) 8%	(3) 7%	(7) 15%
20– 39	(9) 10%	(6) 15%	(10) 21%
40– 59	(26) 30%	(10) 24%	(7) 15%
60– 79	(28) 32%	(17) 42%	(14) 30%
80–100	(17) 20%	(5) 12%	(9) 19%
	100%	100%	100%
Number of children	87	41	47
Chi-square tests:	Streamed versus Type 1: Difference not significant Streamed versus Type 2: Difference not significant		

TABLE 11.2: *Participation ratio scores of children at 7+ in streamed and non-streamed schools*

ABOVE AVERAGE

PARTICIPATION RATIO	BOYS		GIRLS	
	Streamed	Non-Streamed	Streamed	Non-Streamed
0— 9	67%	58%	65%	47%
10—19	18%	18%	17%	22%
20—29	11%	13%	14%	17%
30—39	1%	4%	2%	7%
40—49	3%	5%	2%	6%
50—59+	0%	2%	0%	1%
Total	100%	100%	100%	100%
No. of children	362	410	424	510
Chi-square test	$\chi^2 = 15 \cdot 20, P < 0 \cdot 01$		$\chi^2 = 41 \cdot 10, P < 0 \cdot 001$	

TABLE 11.2—*continued*

AVERAGE

PARTICIPATION RATIO	Boys		Girls	
	Streamed	*Non-Streamed*	*Streamed*	*Non-Streamed*
0— 9	76%	56%	72%	56%
10—19	14%	27%	12%	27%
20—29	8%	12%	13%	13%
30—39	0%	3%	1%	2%
40—49	2%	2%	2%	2%
50—59+	0%	0%	0%	0%
Total	100%	100%	100%	100%
No. of children	651	664	620	605
Chi-square test	$\chi^2 = 66.52, P < 0.001$		$\chi^2 = 50.88, P < 0.001$	

continued

451

TABLE 11.2—*continued*

BELOW AVERAGE

PARTICIPATION RATIO	BOYS		GIRLS	
	Streamed	*Non-Streamed*	*Streamed*	*Non-Streamed*
0— 9	88%	67%	80%	64%
10—19	6%	20%	14%	21%
20—29	6%	11%	6%	13%
30—39	0%	1%	0%	2%
40—49	0%	1%	0%	0%
50—59+	0%	0%	0%	0%
Total	100%	100%	100%	100%
No. of children	503	463	321	290
Chi-square test	$\chi^2 = 66{\cdot}13$, $P < 0{\cdot}001$		$\chi^2 = 22{\cdot}35$, $P < 0{\cdot}001$	

TABLE 11.3: *Participation ratio scores at 10+ of boys and girls of each social class and ability level in streamed and non-streamed schools*

BOYS

ABOVE AVERAGE

PARTICIPATION RATIO	SOCIAL CLASS 1-2†		SOCIAL CLASS 3		SOCIAL CLASS 4-5	
	Streamed	Non-Streamed	Streamed	Non-Streamed	Streamed	Non-Streamed
0— 9	4%	0%	7%	4%	19%	5%
10— 19	4%	4%	4%	3%	5%	13%
20— 29	14%	11%	17%	16%	13%	16%
30— 39	6%	6%	11%	13%	11%	9%
40— 49	9%	7%	14%	18%	9%	12%
50— 59	20%	18%	15%	12%	14%	13%
60— 69	21%	22%	16%	15%	13%	19%
70— 79	7%	12%	5%	7%	8%	8%
80— 89	7%	13%	7%	9%	1%	4%
90—100	8%	7%	4%	3%	7%	1%
Total	100%	100%	100%	100%	100%	100%
No. of children	168	114	188	144	126	85

Note: For results of chi-square tests, see Table 11.4, page 459

†See Appendix 4

continued

Table 11.3—continued

AVERAGE

BOYS

PARTICIPATION RATIO	SOCIAL CLASS 1-2†		SOCIAL CLASS 3		SOCIAL CLASS 4-5	
	Streamed	Non-Streamed	Streamed	Non-Streamed	Streamed	Non-Streamed
0— 9	6%	3%	18%	5%	25%	4%
10—19	12%	1%	7%	7%	8%	9%
20—29	27%	14%	16%	17%	16%	23%
30—39	12%	13%	12%	12%	14%	13%
40—49	6%	11%	8%	14%	4%	16%
50—59	17%	15%	16%	16%	18%	13%
60—69	13%	25%	10%	6%	7%	15%
70—79	0%	4%	7%	6%	3%	5%
80—89	6%	8%	4%	3%	3%	2%
90—100	2%	6%	2%	4%	2%	0%
Total	100%	100%	100%	100%	100%	100%
No. of children	52	72	182	189	180	168

Note: For results of chi-square tests, see Table 11.4, page 459

†See Appendix 4

TABLE 11.3—*continued*

BELOW AVERAGE

BOYS

PARTICIPATION RATIO	SOCIAL CLASS 1-2†		SOCIAL CLASS 3		SOCIAL CLASS 4-5	
	Streamed	Non-Streamed	Streamed	Non-Streamed	Streamed	Non-Streamed
0— 9	11%	0%	22%	10%	29%	11%
10— 19	14%	13%	13%	10%	16%	13%
20— 29	32%	29%	20%	21%	17%	29%
30— 39	11%	7%	16%	15%	14%	14%
40— 49	11%	16%	7%	10%	6%	8%
50— 59	7%	16%	8%	16%	11%	14%
60— 69	14%	19%	10%	11%	4%	8%
70— 79	0%	0%	1%	2%	2%	3%
80— 89	0%	7%	2%	3%	0%	0%
90—100	0%	3%	1%	2%	1%	0%
Total	100%	100%	100%	100%	100%	100%
No. of children	28	31	149	173	238	260

Note: For results of chi-square tests, see Table 11.4, page 459

†See Appendix 4

continued

TABLE 11.3—*continued*

GIRLS

ABOVE AVERAGE

PARTICIPATION RATIO	SOCIAL CLASS 1-2†		SOCIAL CLASS 3		SOCIAL CLASS 4-5	
	Streamed	*Non-Streamed*	*Streamed*	*Non-Streamed*	*Streamed*	*Non-Streamed*
0— 9	3%	2%	3%	3%	13%	2%
10— 19	2%	2%	6%	3%	5%	6%
20— 29	9%	5%	13%	14%	8%	14%
30— 39	2%	8%	5%	5%	10%	8%
40— 49	11%	14%	11%	11%	7%	13%
50— 59	15%	12%	16%	14%	21%	18%
60— 69	12%	16%	25%	16%	18%	11%
70— 79	12%	11%	2%	11%	9%	9%
80— 89	21%	20%	13%	17%	7%	15%
90—100	13%	10%	6%	6%	2%	4%
Total	100%	100%	100%	100%	100%	100%
No. of children	120	119	177	145	101	95

Note: For results of chi-square tests, see Table 11.4, page 459

†See Appendix 4

TABLE 11.3—*continued*

AVERAGE

GIRLS

PARTICIPATION RATIO	SOCIAL CLASS 1-2†		SOCIAL CLASS 3		SOCIAL CLASS 4-5	
	Streamed	*Non-Streamed*	*Streamed*	*Non-Streamed*	*Streamed*	*Non-Streamed*
0— 9	2%	1%	9%	5%	17%	5%
10— 19	3%	4%	6%	9%	7%	8%
20— 29	17%	8%	13%	17%	10%	15%
30— 39	10%	5%	11%	9%	12%	8%
40— 49	10%	12%	10%	7%	8%	10%
50— 59	9%	16%	11%	14%	19%	13%
60— 69	24%	27%	16%	20%	12%	21%
70— 79	8%	5%	8%	8%	5%	5%
80— 89	12%	16%	12%	8%	7%	10%
90—100	5%	6%	4%	3%	3%	5%
Total	100%	100%	100%	100%	100%	100%
No. of children	59	81	158	169	172	150

Note: For results of chi-square tests, see Table 11.4, page 459

†See Appendix 4

continued

TABLE 11.3—*continued*

GIRLS

BELOW AVERAGE

PARTICIPATION RATIO	SOCIAL CLASS 1-2†		SOCIAL CLASS 3		SOCIAL CLASS 4-5	
	Streamed	*Non-Streamed*	*Streamed*	*Non-Streamed*	*Streamed*	*Non-Streamed*
0— 9	3%	3%	24%	7%	28%	11%
10—19	13%	3%	12%	10%	15%	8%
20—29	13%	25%	14%	16%	18%	27%
30—39	14%	11%	15%	13%	9%	15%
40—49	24%	14%	7%	13%	6%	8%
50—59	13%	11%	14%	19%	13%	9%
60—69	7%	11%	8%	13%	7%	12%
70—79	7%	11%	2%	6%	3%	7%
80—89	3%	11%	3%	2%	1%	2%
90—100	3%	0%	1%	1%	0%	1%
Total	100%	100%	100%	100%	100%	100%
No. of children	30	28	153	133	241	256

Note: For results of chi-square tests, see Table 11.4, page 459

†See Appendix 4

TABLE 11.4: *Significant differences in participation level at 10+ of children in streamed and non-streamed schools, using the chi-square test*

SOCIAL CLASS		ABOVE AVERAGE		AVERAGE		BELOW AVERAGE	
		χ^2 value	Significance level	χ^2 value	Significance level	χ^2 value	Significance level
BOYS	1, 2	10·54	NS	14·30	NS	3·06	NS
	3	4·51	NS	20·99	*	13·87	NS
	4, 5	14·99	NS	48·63	***	36·41	***
All social classes		22·32	**	66·96	***	48·49	***
GIRLS	1, 2	8·80	NS	7·00	NS	3·74	NS
	3	17·17	*	8·36	NS	22·44	**
	4, 5	16·64	NS	21·04	*	40·94	***
All social classes		16·15	NS	21·51	*	56·33	***

   * = significant at 5% level
  ** = significant at 1% level
*** = significant at 0·1% level
  NS = not significant

In all cases differences were in favour of non-streamed schools

459

TABLE 11.5: *Comparison of the numbers of 'low', 'medium' and 'high' participants in streamed and non-streamed schools*

BOYS

	ABOVE AVERAGE†		AVERAGE		BELOW AVERAGE	
	Streamed	*Non-Streamed*	*Streamed*	*Non-Streamed*	*Streamed*	*Non-Streamed*
Low‡	9%	6%	25%	14%	39%	19%
MEDIUM	65%	69%	68%	75%	60%	79%
HIGH	26%	25%	7%	11%	1%	2%
Total	100%	100%	100%	100%	100%	100%
No. of children	373	337	683	646	468	489

GIRLS

	ABOVE AVERAGE		AVERAGE		BELOW AVERAGE	
	Streamed	*Non-Streamed*	*Streamed*	*Non-Streamed*	*Streamed*	*Non-Streamed*
Low	5%	3%	22%	13%	43%	24%
MEDIUM	62%	61%	65%	72%	54%	69%
HIGH	33%	36%	13%	15%	3%	7%
Total	100%	100%	100%	100%	100%	100%
No. of children	382	410	664	651	328	257

† Teachers' ability ratings

‡ Low=0—19; Medium=20—69; High=70—100

TABLE 11.6: *Comparison of the participation ratio scores of children at the top or bottom of their class† in streamed and non-streamed schools*

BOYS

Class Position	Top		Bottom	
Participation Ratio Scores	*Streamed*	*Non-Streamed*	*Streamed*	*Non-Streamed*
High‡	16%	23%	5%	2%
Medium	64%	71%	57%	72%
Low	20%	6%	38%	26%
Total	100%	100%	100%	100%
No. of children	316	287	274	308
Chi-square test	$\chi^2 = 26 \cdot 02, P < 0 \cdot 001$		$\chi^2 = 16 \cdot 53, P < 0 \cdot 001$	

GIRLS

Class Position	Top		Bottom	
Participation Ratio Scores	*Streamed*	*Non-Streamed*	*Streamed*	*Non-Streamed*
High	34%	32%	9%	7%
Medium	51%	63%	57%	70%
Low	15%	5%	34%	23%
Total	100%	100%	100%	100%
No. of children	254	295	259	271
Chi-square test	$\chi^2 = 17 \cdot 93, P < 0 \cdot 001$		$\chi^2 = 10 \cdot 05, P < 0 \cdot 01$	

† As rated by their teachers on arithmetic
‡ Low=0—19; Medium=20—69; High=70—100

TABLE 11.7: *Participation ratio scores of children regarded by teachers as pleasurable and unpleasurable† in streamed and non-streamed schools*

BOYS

PARTICIPATION	PLEASURABLE		NON-PLEASURABLE	
	Streamed	Non-Streamed	Streamed	Non-Streamed
HIGH‡	11%	13%	7%	7%
MEDIUM	65%	75%	55%	68%
LOW	24%	12%	38%	25%
Total	100%	100%	100%	100%
No. of children	1,106	1,077	322	298
Chi-square test	$\chi^2 = 53.77, P < 0.001$		$\chi^2 = 12.71, P < 0.01$	

GIRLS

PARTICIPATION	PLEASURABLE		NON-PLEASURABLE	
	Streamed	Non-Streamed	Streamed	Non-Streamed
HIGH	19%	20%	7%	15%
MEDIUM	60%	69%	57%	61%
LOW	21%	11%	36%	24%
Total	100%	100%	100%	100%
No. of children	1,160	1,175	162	145
Chi-square test	$\chi^2 = 48.64, P < 0.001$		$\chi^2 = 8.33, P < 0.05$	

† Those rated 3-4 were treated as pleasurable, those rated 1, 2 were unpleasurable, see Appendix 4
‡ Low = 0—19; Medium = 20—69; High = 70—100

TABLE 11.8: *Participation ratio scores of children in streamed and non-streamed schools who were and were not considered by their teachers as prone to fighting*

BOYS

PARTICIPATION	STREAMED		NON-STREAMED	
	Prone to fighting	*Not prone to fighting*	*Prone to fighting*	*Not prone to fighting*
High†	5%	11%	8%	12%
Medium	53%	63%	71%	74%
Low	42%	26%	21%	14%
Total	100%	100%	100%	100%
No. of children	101	1,327	95	1,279
Chi-square test	$\chi^2 = 12\cdot43, P < 0\cdot005$		Not Significant	

GIRLS

PARTICIPATION	STREAMED		NON-STREAMED	
	Prone to fighting	*Not prone to fighting*	*Prone to fighting*	*Not prone to fighting*
High	10%	17%	14%	20%
Medium	67%	60%	74%	68%
Low	23%	23%	12%	12%
Total	100%	100%	100%	100%
No. of children	30	1,292	35	1,284
Chi-square test	Not significant		Not significant	

†Low=0—19; Medium=20—69; High=70—100

TABLE 11.9: *Participation ratio scores of children in streamed and non-streamed schools who were considered by their teachers as withdrawn and not withdrawn*

BOYS

PARTICIPATION	STREAMED		NON-STREAMED	
	Withdrawn	*Not withdrawn*	*Withdrawn*	*Not withdrawn*
High†	0%	10%	0%	12%
Medium	53%	63%	68%	73%
Low	47%	27%	32%	15%
Total	100%	100%	100%	100%
No. of children	62	1,346	50	1,290
Chi-square test	$\chi^2 = 15\cdot61$, $P < 0\cdot001$		$\chi^2 = 15\cdot93$, $P < 0\cdot001$	

GIRLS

PARTICIPATION	STREAMED		NON-STREAMED	
	Withdrawn	*Not withdrawn*	*Withdrawn*	*Not withdrawn*
High	7%	17%	7%	20%
Medium	52%	60%	65%	68%
Low	41%	23%	28%	12%
Total	100%	100%	100%	100%
No. of children	42	1,280	46	1,246
Chi-square test	$\chi^2 = 8\cdot61$, $P < 0\cdot05$		$\chi^2 = 14\cdot30$, $P < 0\cdot001$	

†Low=0—19; Medium=20—69; High=70—100

TABLE 12.6a: *Choice of secondary school of parents with children of similar ability levels in streamed and non-streamed schools*

ABOVE AVERAGE

| | HIGHER SOCIAL CLASS† | | | | LOWER SOCIAL CLASS | | | |
| | BOYS | | GIRLS | | BOYS | | GIRLS | |
	Streamed	Non-Streamed	Streamed	Non-Streamed	Streamed	Non-Streamed	Streamed	Non-Streamed
Secondary Modern	1%	2%	3%	3%	10%	11%	11%	19%
Comprehensive	8%	9%	9%	14%	4%	22%	8%	16%
Technical	8%	8%	7%	1%	10%	11%	13%	10%
Grammar	83%‡	81%‡	81%‡	82%‡	76%‡	56%‡	68%‡	55%‡
	100%	100%	100%	100%	100%	100%	100%	100%
Number of parents giving information	190	171	215	210	59	75	79	106

†Social class categories are based on teachers' ratings of father's occupation. The higher social class group includes professional/managerial, clerical and skilled workers, whilst the lower social class group consists of semi-skilled and unskilled workers. For details, see Appendix 4.
‡Most popular choice.

continued

465

TABLE 12.6a—*continued*

AVERAGE

| | HIGHER SOCIAL CLASS† | | | | LOWER SOCIAL CLASS | | | |
| | BOYS | | GIRLS | | BOYS | | GIRLS | |
	Streamed	*Non-Streamed*	*Streamed*	*Non-Streamed*	*Streamed*	*Non-Streamed*	*Streamed*	*Non-Streamed*
Secondary Modern	17%	12%	23%	18%	27%‡	23%	40%‡	33%‡
Comprehensive	24%	24%	31%	30%	24%	24%	20%	28%
Technical	20%	19%	8%	9%	24%	20%	12%	7%
Grammar	39%‡	45%‡	38%‡	43%‡	25%	33%‡	28%	32%
	100%	100%	100%	100%	100%	100%	100%	100%
Number of parents giving information	231	177	208	179	204	208	218	169

†Social class categories are based on teachers' ratings of father's occupation. The higher social class group includes professional/managerial, clerical and skilled workers, whilst the lower social class group consists of semi-skilled and unskilled workers. For details, see Appendix 4.
‡Most popular choice.

TABLE 12.6a—*continued*

BELOW AVERAGE

	HIGHER SOCIAL CLASS†				LOWER SOCIAL CLASS			
	BOYS		GIRLS		BOYS		GIRLS	
	Streamed	*Non-Streamed*	*Streamed*	*Non-Streamed*	*Streamed*	*Non-Streamed*	*Streamed*	*Non-Streamed*
Secondary Modern	31%‡	23%	40%‡	18%	58%‡	38%‡	63%‡	48%‡
Comprehensive	28%	21%	33%	38%‡	17%	25%	9%	27%
Technical	27%	25%	11%	9%	15%	17%	15%	10%
Grammar	14%	31%‡	16%	35%	10%	20%	13%	15%
	100%	100%	100%	100%	100%	100%	100%	100%
Number of parents giving information	78	84	57	56	124	122	115	101

†Social class categories are based on teachers' ratings of father's occupation. The higher social class group includes professional/managerial, clerical and skilled workers, whilst the lower social class group consists of semi-skilled and unskilled workers. For details, see Appendix 4.
‡Most popular choice.

TABLE 12.6b: *A comparison of the percentage of parents in streamed and non-streamed schools preferring grammar school versus other types of secondary school*

	HIGHER SOCIAL CLASS		LOWER SOCIAL CLASS	
	Boys	*Girls*	*Boys*	*Girls*
Above Average	NS†	NS	$\chi^2 = 5 \cdot 10, P < 0 \cdot 05$	NS
Average	NS	NS	NS	NS
Below Average	$\chi^2 = 5 \cdot 59, P < 0 \cdot 05$	$\chi^2 = 4 \cdot 88, P < 0 \cdot 05$	$\chi^2 = 3 \cdot 98, P < 0 \cdot 05$	NS

†NS = non-significant

467

TABLE 12.7: *Choice of leaving age of parents with children of similar ability levels in streamed and non-streamed schools*

ABOVE AVERAGE

| | HIGHER SOCIAL CLASS† | | | | LOWER SOCIAL CLASS | | | |
| | BOYS | | GIRLS | | BOYS | | GIRLS | |
	Streamed	Non-Streamed	Streamed	Non-Streamed	Streamed	Non-Streamed	Streamed	Non-Streamed
15	3%	2%	2%	3%	7%	8%	7%	15%
16	9%	11%	12%	23%	12%	35%	33%	39%
17+	88%	87%	86%	74%	81%	57%	60%	46%
	100%	100%	100%	100%	100%	100%	100%	100%
Number of parents giving information	195	169	214	209	59	75	83	106
Chi-square test	NS		$\chi^2 = 8{\cdot}89,\ P < 0{\cdot}05$		$\chi^2 = 9{\cdot}84,\ P < 0{\cdot}01$		NS	

†Social class categories are based on teachers' ratings of father's occupation. The higher social class group includes professional/managerial, clerical and skilled workers, whilst the lower social class group consists of semi-skilled and unskilled workers. For details, see Appendix 4.

TABLE 12.7—continued

AVERAGE

| | HIGHER SOCIAL CLASS† | | | | LOWER SOCIAL CLASS | | | |
| | BOYS | | GIRLS | | BOYS | | GIRLS | |
	Streamed	Non-Streamed	Streamed	Non-Streamed	Streamed	Non-Streamed	Streamed	Non-Streamed
15	14%	8%	18%	17%	34%	34%	37%	37%
16	32%	35%	41%	45%	37%	41%	38%	41%
17+	54%	57%	41%	38%	29%	25%	25%	22%
	100%	100%	100%	100%	100%	100%	100%	100%
Number of parents giving information	234	171	210	178	200	212	216	179
Chi-square test	NS		NS		NS		NS	

†Social class categories are based on teachers' ratings of father's occupation. The higher social class group includes professional/managerial, clerical and skilled workers, whilst the lower social class group consists of semi-skilled and unskilled workers. For details, see Appendix 4.

continued

TABLE 12.7—*continued*

BELOW AVERAGE

| | HIGHER SOCIAL CLASS† | | | | LOWER SOCIAL CLASS | | | |
| | BOYS | | GIRLS | | BOYS | | GIRLS | |
	Streamed	*Non-Streamed*	*Streamed*	*Non-Streamed*	*Streamed*	*Non-Streamed*	*Streamed*	*Non-Streamed*
15	27%	15%	34%	18%	51%	42%	48%	53%
16	40%	38%	50%	50%	36%	45%	39%	37%
17+	33%	47%	16%	32%	13%	13%	13%	10%
	100%	100%	100%	100%	100%	100%	100%	100%
Number of parents giving information	75	82	58	56	124	120	113	112
Chi-square test	NS		$\chi^2 = 6 \cdot 32, P < 0 \cdot 05$		NS		NS	

†Social class categories are based on teachers' ratings of father's occupation. The higher social class group includes professional/managerial, clerical and skilled workers, whilst the lower social class group consists of semi-skilled and unskilled workers. For details, see Appendix 4.

470

TABLE 12.8: *Further training desired by parents with children of similar ability levels in streamed and non-streamed schools*

ABOVE AVERAGE

| | HIGHER SOCIAL CLASS† | | | | LOWER SOCIAL CLASS | | | |
| | BOYS | | GIRLS | | BOYS | | GIRLS | |
	Streamed	Non-Streamed	Streamed	Non-Streamed	Streamed	Non-Streamed	Streamed	Non-Streamed
None	0%	0%	3%	1%	2%	1%	3%	4%
Apprenticeship	7%	10%	2%	4%	33%	31%	9%	16%
Technical College—1 year	3%	4%	11%	21%	2%	7%	32%	33%
Technical College—2 years	10%	14%	6%	7%	10%	17%	9%	10%
University/College—3 years	80%‡	72%‡	78%‡	67%‡	53%‡	44%‡	47%‡	37%‡
	100%	100%	100%	100%	100%	100%	100%	100%
Number of parents giving information	191	166	210	206	58	71	78	101
Chi-square test	NS		χ² = 11·29, P < 0·05		NS		NS	

†Social class categories are based on teachers' ratings of father's occupation. The higher social class group includes professional/managerial, clerical and skilled workers, whilst the lower social class group consists of semi-skilled and unskilled workers. For details, see Appendix 4.
‡Most popular choice.

continued

TABLE 12.8—continued

AVERAGE

| | HIGHER SOCIAL CLASS† | | | | LOWER SOCIAL CLASS | | | |
| | BOYS | | GIRLS | | BOYS | | GIRLS | |
	Streamed	Non-Streamed	Streamed	Non-Streamed	Streamed	Non-Streamed	Streamed	Non-Streamed
None	0%	0%	8%	5%	2%	3%	12%	9%
Apprenticeship	34%‡	34%‡	17%	18%	60%‡	63%‡	19%	33%
Technical College—1 year	9%	10%	39%‡	39%‡	3%	8%	40%‡	37%‡
Technical College—2 years	27%	28%	11%	15%	24%	13%	13%	7%
University/College—3 years	30%	28%	25%	23%	11%	13%	16%	14%
	100%	100%	100%	100%	100%	100%	100%	100%
Number of parents giving information	227	172	206	175	200	210	211	163
Chi-square test	NS		NS		$\chi^2 = 12 \cdot 22$, $P < 0 \cdot 05$		$\chi^2 = 11 \cdot 39$, $P < 0 \cdot 05$	

†Social class categories are based on teachers' ratings of father's occupation. The higher social class group includes professional/managerial, clerical and skilled workers, whilst the lower social class group consists of semi-skilled and unskilled workers. For details, see Appendix 4.

‡Most popular choice.

TABLE 12.8—*continued*

BELOW AVERAGE

	HIGHER SOCIAL CLASS†				LOWER SOCIAL CLASS			
	BOYS		GIRLS		BOYS		GIRLS	
	Streamed	*Non-Streamed*	*Streamed*	*Non-Streamed*	*Streamed*	*Non-Streamed*	*Streamed*	*Non-Streamed*
None	4%	3%	6%	2%	9%	5%	22%	20%
Apprenticeship	53%‡	44%‡	26%	33%	72%‡	72%‡	33%‡	53%‡
Technical College—1 year	5%	10%	46%‡	37%‡	6%	4%	33%‡	17%
Technical College—2 years	30%	17%	8%	13%	9%	11%	6%	6%
University/College—3 years	8%	26%	14%	15%	4%	8%	6%	4%
	100%	100%	100%	100%	100%	100%	100%	100%
Number of parents giving information	76	81	50	54	116	119	108	97
Chi-square test	$\chi^2 = 11 \cdot 40$, $P < 0 \cdot 01$		NS		NS		$\chi^2 = 14 \cdot 52$, $P < 0 \cdot 01$	

†Social class categories are based on teachers' ratings of father's occupation. The higher social class group includes professional/managerial, clerical and skilled workers, whilst the lower social class group consists of semi-skilled and unskilled workers. For details, see Appendix 4.
‡Most popular choice.

473

TABLE 13.2: *The most popular occupational aspirations*

	Boys		Girls	
	Streamed	Non-Streamed	Streamed	Non-Streamed
Above Average				
Footballer / Teacher	17% (1)	22% (1)	25% (1)	23% (1)
Air pilot / Nurse	12% (2)	10% (2)	12% (2)	15% (2)
Forces	10% (3)	9% (3)		
Average				
Footballer / Secretarial/Office	22% (1)	30% (1)	21% (1)	10% (3)
Forces / Hairdresser	8% (2)	11% (2)	19% (2)	16% (1)
Teacher			7% (3)	12% (2)
Below Average				
Footballer / Hairdresser	19% (1)	29% (1)	23% (1)	22% (1)
Forces / Nurse	8%	11%	16% (2)	19% (2)
Engineer/Mechanic / Secretarial/Office	13% (2)	8% (2)	12% (3)	11% (3)

Note: Numbers in brackets refer to rank order

TABLES 16.1—16.6: *A comparison of results obtained with streaming and non-streaming in the three schools involved in the Dynamics of Change Study*

TABLE 16.1: *School A*

ENGLISH

at age 8+
By social class

	SOCIAL CLASSES 1—3		SOCIAL CLASSES 4 + 5	
	Streamed	Non-Streamed	Streamed	Non-Streamed
N	17	40	90	44
Mean	95·59	96·75	96·27	88·14
SD	15·95	14·05	17·78	12·33
Significance	Not significant		$t = 3·08$ ($P < 0·01$)	
Inference	—		Streamed organization better	

at age 9+
By social class

	SOCIAL CLASSES 1—3		SOCIAL CLASSES 4 + 5	
	Streamed	Non-Streamed	Streamed	Non-Streamed
N	14	35	86	58
Mean	99·07	103·74	95·92	91·95
SD	13·09	13·41	13·36	12·38
Significance	Not significant		Not significant	

TABLE 16.2: *School A*   PROBLEM ARITHMETIC

at age 8+
By social class

	SOCIAL CLASSES 1—3		SOCIAL CLASSES 4 + 5	
	Streamed	Non-Streamed	Streamed	Non-Streamed
N	18	40	94	46
Mean	99·94	99·63	95·71	88·85
SD	16·96	11·04	16·96	11·99
Significance	Not significant		$t = 3·28$ ($P < 0·002$)	
Inference	—		Streamed organization better	

at age 9+
By social class

	SOCIAL CLASSES 1—3		SOCIAL CLASSES 4 + 5	
	Streamed	Non-Streamed	Streamed	Non-Streamed
N	14	35	82	59
Mean	101·14	103·06	99·45	95·36
SD	19·20	5·96	16·32	13·54
Significance	Not significant		Not significant	

476

Table 16.3: *School B* — ENGLISH

at age 8+
By social class

	Social Classes 1—3		Social Classes 4 + 5	
	Streamed	*Non-Streamed*	*Streamed*	*Non-Streamed*
N	32	41	23	15
Mean	105·063	102·17	92·739	97·333
SD	15·76	12·23	8·436	16·75
Significance	Not significant		Not significant	

at age 9+
By social class

	Social Classes 1—3		Social Classes 4 + 5	
	Streamed	*Non-Streamed*	*Streamed*	*Non-Streamed*
N	28	37	21	17
Mean	103·429	105·919	86·905	102·765
SD	16·08	11·44	17·28	9·512
Significance	Not significant		$t = 3·587$ ($P < 0·002$)	
Inference	—		Non-Streamed organization better	

TABLE 16.4: *School B*   PROBLEM ARITHMETIC

at age 8+
By social class

	Social Classes 1—3		Social Classes 4 + 5	
	Streamed	Non-Streamed	Streamed	Non-Streamed
N	32	40	23	15
Mean	115·063	102·850	99·438	100·20
SD	12·65	12·84	12·23	17·42
Significance	$t = 4·044$ ($P < 0·001$)		Not significant	
Inference	Streamed organization better		—	

at age 9+
By social class

	Social Classes 1—3		Social Classes 4 + 5	
	Streamed	Non-Streamed	Streamed	Non-Streamed
N	28	37	21	19
Mean	105·857	107·649	90·252	103·632
SD	9·809	9·803	18·99	11·98
Significance	Not significant		$t = 2·691$ ($P < 0·02$)	
Inference	—		Non-Streamed organization better	

TABLE 16.5: *School C* ENGLISH

at age 8+
By social class

	SOCIAL CLASSES 1—3		SOCIAL CLASSES 4 + 5	
	Streamed	*Non-Streamed*	*Streamed*	*Non-Streamed*
N	40	28	42	60
Mean	101·15	98·214	88·048	95·20
SD	9·705	22·54	18·38	11·22
Significance	Not significant		$t = 2\cdot246$ ($P < 0\cdot05$)	
Inference	—		Non-Streamed organization better	

at age 9+
By social class

	SOCIAL CLASSES 1—3		SOCIAL CLASSES 4 + 5	
	Streamed	*Non-Streamed*	*Streamed*	*Non-Streamed*
N	28	24	54	49
Mean	98·321	98·583	92·148	93·878
SD	14·24	13·61	12·14	14·60
Significance	Not significant		Not significant	

TABLE 16.6: *School C*   PROBLEM ARITHMETIC

at age 8+
By social class

	SOCIAL CLASSES 1—3		SOCIAL CLASSES 4 + 5	
	Streamed	*Non-Streamed*	*Streamed*	*Non-Streamed*
N	39	30	43	60
Mean	99·974	99·867	90·837	96·80
SD	11·79	12·08	12·99	15·39
Significance	Not significant		$t = 2·126$ ($P < 0·05$)	
Inference	—		Non-Streamed organization better	

at age 9+
By social class

	SOCIAL CLASSES 1—3		SOCIAL CLASSES 4 + 5	
	Streamed	*Non-Streamed*	*Streamed*	*Non-Streamed*
N	27	25	55	52
Mean	101·778	101·88	96·546	97·346
SD	10·18	4·37	8·526	13·80
Significance	Not significant		Not significant	

Factor Analysis of Data Concerned with School Achievement, Pupil Behaviour and Teacher Attitudes

THE purpose of the factor analysis in this inquiry was to test hypotheses arising from the exploratory interviews with teachers (see Appendix 2) and also to structure and summarize the variables measured in the cross-sectional study. The major hypotheses to be tested were: (a) that there is an underlying personality dimension which determines a teacher's attitudes, teaching method and mode of discipline, (b) that teachers attribute desirable personality traits to those pupils with the highest intelligence and attainment.

Based on the cross-sectional study data (see Chapter 1) two separate factor analyses were carried out, one for the seven and one for the ten-plus age group. Fifty-one variables were included in the seven-plus analysis and an additional six in the ten-plus analysis. Product moment correlations were computed separately for each age group. The two resulting matrices were factor-analysed using the principal components method and eleven and twelve factors were extracted from the seven and ten-plus age groups, respectively. These accounted for 52 per cent of the variance in the seven-plus and 53 per cent in the ten-plus analysis. An oblique rotated solution was then computed by the Promax procedure (Hendrickson and White, 1964).

Four interpretable first-order Promax factors were obtained for the seven-plus, and three were obtained for the ten-plus age group analysis. Also two second-order Promax factors were obtained for both age groups.

The first Factor, A, was identified as school success versus failure. Variables having the highest loadings are shown in Table A7A.1.

All the variables having high loadings (i.e. greater than 0·40) were concerned with academic performance except social class, which nevertheless appeared to exert a marked influence on school performance. The picture at ten-plus was much sharper than at seven-plus with higher loadings on nearly all variables. One variable of considerable interest was the item 'chosen to participate

481

TABLE A7A.1: FACTOR A: *School success versus school failure*

VARIABLE DESCRIPTION	7+ LOADINGS	10+ LOADINGS
High versus low Reading test score	0·81	0·86
High versus low English test score	0·85	0·93
High versus low Mechanical test score	0·76	0·83
High versus low Problem test score	0·79	0·88
High versus low Primary Verbal score	test not given	0·92
High versus low Verbal reasoning score	test not given	0·90
High versus low Non-verbal score	test not given	0·78
High versus low ability rating by teacher	0·80	0·81
Middle class versus working class	0·48	0·44
High versus low participation	0·10	0·39

in school activities' which had a very low loading at 7+ (0·10) but a rather higher loading (0·39) at 10+. This was probably due to the fact that school activities are more the province of the ten than the seven year old child. (For details of school activities, see Appendix 4). Thus poor school work at ten-plus was associated with little talent, for games, drama, music—at least in the mind of the teacher.

Factor B was identified as desirable versus undesirable pupil and the highest loadings were as follows:

TABLE A7A.2: FACTOR B: *Desirable versus undesirable pupil*

VARIABLE DESCRIPTION	7+ LOADINGS	10+ LOADINGS
Seldom fights versus always fights†	0·81	0·76
Seldom teased or picked on versus frequently teased	0·58	0·61
Obedient versus disobedient	0·85	0·79
Pleasurable versus non-pleasurable to have in class	0·75	0·73
Well-adjusted versus maladjusted	0·89	0·92
Not withdrawn versus withdrawn	0·10	0·25

†All based on the teacher's ratings

All the variables loading on Factor B were based on teacher ratings. Two of the ratings—those on pleasurability and disobedience—were a 'measure' of teacher-pupil interaction; the others a 'measure' of peer-interaction as perceived by the teacher.

Teachers were asked to rate the pupils on five behaviour traits: frequency of fighting and bullying; whether the child was teased or picked on by other children; whether he was disobedient; whether he was withdrawn and played little with other children; and whether he was a pleasure to have in the class. Ratings were made on a four point scale, ranging from behaviour exhibited frequently to not at all. All pupils in the class were rated on one trait before the class teacher proceeded to the next. A well-adjusted versus maladjusted score was obtained on the basis of these five ratings.

It is interesting to note that all these traits with the exception of 'withdrawn' loaded highly on this factor: that is to say that a child exhibiting one characteristic tended to have similar ratings on the others as well.

The third factor, *Factor C*, was concerned with teacher attitudes, and markedly different results were obtained from the two analyses. With the seven-plus analysis two factors were extracted: one was identified as teacher attitude and one as teaching method (Factor D). With the ten-plus analysis only one factor was extracted and identified as teacher attitude (Factor C). The highest loadings on Factor C are given in Table A7A.3.

Factor D emerged from the seven-plus age analysis only. This can be described as teaching method—progressive versus traditional. The factor loadings are given in the table below. This factor does more than clarify the structure of the items concerned with teaching method; it also gives a clear indication of the different teaching methods in streamed and non-streamed schools at seven-plus.

Different factors emerged from the two analyses probably because of the meaning of traditionalism and progressiveness, as used in this study. The lesson that is considered appropriate at seven-plus or ten-plus is not necessarily so at the other age. A high traditional lessons score could be interpreted as learning the basic skills in a formal way. By inspecting the correlation matrix on page 487 it can be seen that at seven-plus the association between traditionalism and permissiveness is virtually zero—thus even permissive teachers may feel the need for daily rote learning, but by the time a child reaches the fourth year of the junior school, teachers feel that there should be less need for this drill. The correlation matrix (see page 487)

483

shows that the teacher who made frequent use of 'traditional' lessons at ten-plus tended to be non-permissive in outlook. Also it shows that a high traditional score obtained by teachers of ten-year-olds is associated with certain attitudes such as pro eleven-plus selection, belief in streaming, etc.

TABLE A7A.3: FACTOR C: *'Child-centred' versus 'knowledge-centred'* teacher

VARIABLE DESCRIPTION	7+ LOADINGS	10+ LOADINGS
Permissive versus non-permissive attitude	0·65	0·69
Unfavourable versus favourable attitude to physical punishment	0·59	0·64
Disapproval versus approval of eleven-plus selection test	0·72	0·75
High versus low tolerance of noise in classroom	0·69	0·67
Approval versus disapproval of non-streaming	0·71	0·65
Unfavourable versus favourable attitude to A-stream children	0·74	0·58
Frequent versus infrequent use of 'progressive' lessons	0·06	0·49
Infrequent versus frequent use of 'traditional' lessons	0·02	0·55

What has been said of the traditional scale was equally true of the progressive scale. At seven-plus it appeared to be a measure of teaching method, but at ten-plus, progressive score seemed to be very much influenced by teacher attitude. Inspection of the correlations at seven-plus (see page 487) indicates that the relationship between progressiveness and teacher attitudes, although significant, was relatively small. A possible explanation for the smaller relationship with teachers of younger children is that the use of apparatus (e.g.

Dienes, Cuisenaire) and consequent group work is becoming increasingly popular with lower juniors and is introduced by the school rather than being *chosen* by the individual teacher, thus blurring any natural connection between attitudes and choice of method.

TABLE A7A.4: FACTOR D: *'Progressive' versus 'traditional' teaching method*

VARIABLE DESCRIPTION	7+ LOADINGS
Infrequent versus frequent use of 'traditional' lessons	0·67
Frequent versus infrequent use of 'progressive' lessons	0·61
Infrequent versus daily practice of formal sums	0·50
Non-streamed versus streamed schools	0·61

Second order factors

Since Factors A and B were positively correlated, in the seven-plus analysis ($r = 0·18$) and in the ten-plus analysis ($r = 0·23$), and Factors C and D were also ($r = 0·24$), it was possible to factor analyse the correlations so as to obtain higher order or second order factors.[1] Rotation of the primary factors resulted in two interpretable second order factors. Put simply, first order Factors C and D made up higher order Factor I and Factors A and B made up the other higher order Factor II.

The second-order Factor I gives a clear pen-portrait of the characteristics of streamed and non-streamed schools. In both the 7+ and 10+ analyses, 'type of school' had the highest loading (see Table A7A.5). From the table it can be seen that teachers in streamed schools tended to hold contrasting attitudes and use different teaching approaches from those in non-streamed schools (for a further discussion, see Chapter 3). The product moment correlations between these variables are given in Table A7A.6.

[1] For further details see Hendrickson, A. E. and White, P. O. (1966).

TABLE A7A.5: FACTOR I: *The essential characteristics of the streamed and non-streamed school*

VARIABLE DESCRIPTION	7+ LOADINGS	10+ LOADINGS
Streamed versus non-streamed school	0·74	0·79
Teachers believed in streaming versus non-streaming	0·62	0·69
Teachers had favourable versus unfavourable attitude to A-stream child	0·52	0·62
Frequent versus infrequent use of 'traditional' lessons	0·53	0·36
Infrequent versus frequent use of 'progressive' lessons	0·34	0·53
Teachers approved versus disapproved of eleven-plus selection test	0·40	0·45
Low versus high tolerance of noise in the classroom	0·49	0·51
'Non-permissive' versus 'permissive' attitude to children	0·33	0·54
Teachers approved versus disapproved of physical punishment	0·33	0·44
Frequent versus infrequent practice of formal sums	0·42	0·01
Frequent versus infrequent tests	0·40	0·03

The other second order factor, Factor II, revealed an association between adjustment and school work. That there is a clear link between maladjustment and poor school work or backwardness is shown by the variables loading on this factor, though cause and effect here is difficult to disentangle.

TABLE A7A.6: *Product Moment Correlations of items loading on Factor I*

		1	2	3	4	5	6	7	8	9	10	11
Streamed school	1	—										
Pro streaming	2	0·45 0·51	—									
Pro A-stream children	3	0·27 0·37	0·58 0·57	—								
Frequent 'traditional' lessons	4	0·35 0·26	0·21 0·28	0·12 0·24	—							
Infrequent 'progressive' lessons	5	0·27 0·36	0·11 0·36	0·09 0·38	0·37 0·10	—						
Pro eleven-plus test	6	0·15 0·20	0·48 0·44	0·42 0·41	0·19 0·28	0·08 0·26	—					
Low tolerance of noise	7	0·26 0·25	0·37 0·45	0·31 0·36	0·13 0·22	0·07 0·31	0·31 0·36	—				
'Non-permissive'	8	0·12 0·32	0·29 0·34	0·28 0·32	0·01 0·33	0·05 0·15	0·34 0·33	0·39 0·43	—			
Pro physical punishment	9	0·11 0·19	0·48 0·30	0·27 0·27	0·10 0·18	0·14 0·15	0·23 0·37	0·34 0·34	0·31 0·47	—		
Daily formal sums	10	0·24 0·01	0·01 0·07	0·01 0·05	0·31 0·18	0·33 0·11	0·03 0·10	0·05 0·11	0·11 0·06	0·05 0·11	—	
Frequent tests	11	0·19 0·03	0·14 0·00	0·19 0·03	0·25 0·12	0·08 0·06	0·02 0·01	0·17 0·01	0·10 0·08	0·12 0·05	0·25 0·08	—

Note: Upper figures indicate correlations at seven-plus, lower figures at ten-plus

TABLE A7A.7: FACTOR II: *Desirable versus undesirable pupil*

VARIABLE DESCRIPTION	7+ LOADINGS	10+ LOADINGS
High versus low English test score	0·71	0·65
High versus low Verbal Reasoning score	test not given	0·64
Well adjusted versus maladjusted relative to class	0·63	0·64
High versus low Primary Verbal score	test not given	0·61
High versus low Reading score	0·67	0·58
High versus poor ability rating by teacher	0·66	0·56
High versus low Problem Arithmetic score	0·62	0·59
High versus low Mechanical Arithmetic score	0·59	0·57
Pleasurable versus non-pleasurable in class	0·61	0·54
High versus low Non-Verbal test score	test not given	0·55
Obedient versus disobedient	0·58	0·54
Seldom versus frequently teased or picked on	0·43	0·49
Middle class versus working class	0·41	0·34
Chosen versus never chosen to participate in school activities	0·28	0·43

Inspection of the correlation matrix (Table A7A.8) shows that the pleasurability of a child at seven-plus, as seen by the teacher, seemed to depend very much on his ability (r=0·60). This drops considerably at ten-plus (r=0·24). It would appear that the traits on which the teacher was asked to rate each child were by no means independent. The child with a low ability and who performed badly in class was also attributed with other undesirable personality traits.

TABLE A7A.8: *Product moment correlations of items loading on Factor II*

		1	2	3	4	5	6	7	8	9	10	11	12	13	14	15
High Reading score	1	—														
High English score	2	0·80 0·81	—													
High Mechanical Arithmetic score	3	0·58 0·60	0·67 0·70	—												
High Problem Arithmetic score	4	0·63 0·67	0·69 0·74	0·74 0·82	—											
High ability rating	5	0·66 0·63	0·70 0·69	0·56 0·63	0·60 0·69	—										
High Primary Verbal score	6	†0·79	†0·86	†0·68	†0·75	†0·64	—									
High Verbal Reasoning score	7	†0·71	†0·80	†0·68	†0·73	†0·68	†0·80	—								
High Non-Verbal score	8	†0·55	†0·62	†0·61	†0·66	†0·58	†0·65	†0·77	—							

continued

TABLE A7A.8—*continued*

		1	2	3	4	5	6	7	8	9	10	11	12	13	14	15
Well adjusted	9	0·18 0·14	0·19 0·18	0·18 0·16	0·16 0·15	0·21 0·19	† 0·16	† 0·17	† 0·17	—						
Pleasurable	10	0·23 0·19	0·25 0·23	0·22 0·21	0·21 0·20	0·60 0·24	† 0·20	† 0·21	† 0·19	0·67 0·66	—					
Obedient	11	0·15 0·11	0·17 0·14	0·15 0·12	0·11 0·11	0·16 0·15	† 0·12	† 0·14	† 0·13	0·69 0·67	0·60 0·55	—				
Seldom fights	12	0·13 0·13	0·16 0·17	0·12 0·14	0·07 0·12	0·12 0·14	† 0·15	† 0·16	† 0·15	0·63 0·63	0·46 0·48	0·64 0·56	—			
Seldom teased	13	0·13 0·10	0·14 0·12	0·14 0·10	0·12 0·09	0·13 0·11	† 0·11	† 0·12	† 0·09	0·53 0·52	0·30 0·28	0·35 0·30	0·36 0·36	—		
Chosen for school activities	14	0·17 0·32	0·16 0·36	0·09 0·34	0·15 0·36	0·15 0·38	† 0·35	† 0·35	† 0·29	0·15 0·14	0·11 0·14	0·08 0·10	0·04 0·09	0·09 0·10	—	
Middle class	15	0·33 0·35	0·35 0·35	0·29 0·31	0·29 0·33	0·31 0·34	† 0·35	† 0·36	† 0·31	0·09 0·09	0·12 0·11	0·06 0·06	0·07 0·10	0·05 0·09	0·08 0·21	—

Note: Upper figures indicate correlations at seven-plus, lower figures at ten-plus
†Test not given at seven-plus

Conclusion

Both of the hypotheses that the factor analysis set out to test were confirmed. The first order Factor C and the second order Factor I provided evidence for an underlying dimension which determines a teacher's attitudes, teaching method and mode of discipline—although the age of the children being taught influences the choice of teaching method (i.e. frequency of traditional and progressive lessons) and this tends to blur the connection. Factor II provided evidence for the second hypothesis: that teachers associate desirable personality traits with high attainment level.

Reference

HENDRICKSON, A. E. and WHITE, P.O. (1966). 'A method for the rotation of higher-order factors', *Brit. J. Statist. Psychol.*, 19, 1, 97-103.

Q*

Classification of Teachers

THE results of the factor analysis confirmed the findings of the exploratory interviews that there were differences between streamed and non-streamed schools, and that at least two approaches or educational philosophies could be distinguished. The acceptance of a particular philosophy seemed to depend just as much on the teacher as on the type of school in which he taught.

The results also indicated that a straight comparison between one type of school and the other was out of the question, and that statistical adjustments for teacher differences would have to be made, otherwise they could well mask the true effects of type of organization. But when one is dealing with, say, as many as ten to fifteen characteristics of teachers, such adjustments would become extremely complex. It was therefore decided to classify teachers according to their attitudes and teaching methods. The process for doing this is usually referred to as profile analysis, a generic term for methods concerned with grouping persons.

The classification procedure[1] was based on ten key variables[2] and, in order to minimize redundancy those included were not too highly correlated.[3]

Teachers were classified according to their scores on the following:

    (1) seating or degree of streaming within the class

    (2) 'traditional' lessons

---

[1] See 'Users' Guide to the CEIR Cluster Analysis Program', Scientific Control Systems Ltd., January 1968.

[2] The classification was based on data obtained from the longitudinal study. Most of the instruments have already been described in the factor analysis section but there were two additional ones. One was a scale measuring attitude towards backward children and the other measured the degree of streaming within the class; they were found to be related to the attitudes and teaching methods already described.

[3] For this reason the two variables measuring attitude towards A-stream children and towards eleven-plus selection were omitted because of their relatively high correlation with attitude towards streaming.

(3) 'progressive' lessons

(4) frequency of tests

(5) frequency of formal sums

(6) permissiveness

(7) attitude to physical punishment

(8) attitude to noise and talking in class

(9) attitude to streaming

(10) attitude to the backward child.

Two analyses were carried out, one for teachers of upper juniors and another for teachers of lower juniors since it was known that the age of the children taught was related to the score a teacher obtained on some of the above variables, for example, on the traditional and progressive lessons scales. The results obtained were similar for both age groups.

The problem involved the clustering of teachers on the basis of the ten characteristics listed above. The maximum number of clusters was stated in advance and although nine were taken, interpretation began at the seven-cluster solution. In order to make the process used as clear as possible, only the solution for one group of teachers is given in Figure 10. The figure gives the results obtained for teachers of upper juniors. The top line in Figure 10 is the seven-cluster solution. Seven clusters of teachers have been identified and those in each cluster can be said to be more similar to each other, in terms of their scores on the ten characteristics, than they are to other teachers in the total sample.

For each of the ten characteristics the program yielded means and standard deviations for each of the clusters and also for the total sample. Only the defining characteristics of each cluster are given in the figure, these being based on the mean—a characteristic was used as a definer when its mean score was greater than half a standard deviation above or below the mean of the total sample (asterisked ones were approaching this value). Teachers in cluster A of the seven-cluster solution were significantly different from the total sample in terms of their non-traditionalism (i.e. made infrequent use of traditional lessons) and also in terms of their permissiveness and belief in non-streaming. For the characteristics of the other clusters see Figure 10.

The mean scores of the ten characteristics of teachers in Clusters A and B in the two-cluster solution are given below.[1]

TABLE A7B.1: *The mean scores on the ten characteristics of teachers in Cluster A (Type 1) and Cluster B (Type 2) in streamed and non-streamed schools*

		CLUSTER A (TYPE 1)	CLUSTER B (TYPE 2)
1. Seating or degree of streaming within the class	(range 0–5)	3·8	3·1
2. 'Traditional' lessons	(range 6–0)†	1·9	2·9
3. 'Progressive' lessons	(range 6–0)†	1·8	3·1
4. Frequency of tests	(range 6–1)	2·6	3·1
5. Frequency of formal lessons	(range 6–1)	4·0	5·0
6. Permissiveness	(range 0–5)	3·5	2·6
7. Attitude to physical punishment	(range 0–7)	3·1	1·8
8. Attitude to noise and talking	(range 0–5)	3·3	2·0
9. Attitude to streaming	(range 0–7)	4·2	1·8
10. Attitude to backward child‡	(range 0–8)†	5·5	5·2
Number of teachers of 8+, 9+ and 10+ children		186	361

† The range for 'traditional', 'progressive' and 'attitude to backward child' represents the coded and not the actual score, the former being the one used in the classification process.

‡ Information on this attitude was obtained only from teachers taking the follow-up children when they were 9+ and 10+. The instrument had not been constructed in time and was not available for those teachers responsible for the children when 8+.

With the exception of 'attitude to backward child', all the mean scores of Clusters A and B were significantly different.

After the seven-cluster solution, the program yielded a six-cluster solution which was based on a re-grouping of the teachers according to their scores on the ten characteristics. Figure 10 illustrates the movement of teachers in the formation of six instead of seven groups. Most of the shrinkage appears to have come about through the merging of clusters C and E in the seven-cluster solution, both having shared the defining characteristic of streaming through seating arrangements.

[1] For further details, see Chapter 4.

Details are given in the figure of the five, four, three and two-cluster solutions.

Having obtained a number of solutions which solution does one take? One answer to this is that it depends on the desired homogeneity of the clusters, but a more practical one is that it depends on the problem and the size of the sample. Obviously much information is lost in the higher order (two-cluster) solutions but on the other hand, unless one proposes to replicate, there is not much point in considering clusters or groups made up of small numbers. One problem in this research was to find a reasonable number of teachers of each 'type' both in streamed and non-streamed schools teaching comparable age groups. To keep the numbers reasonably large, it was decided to use the two-cluster solution for the analysis.

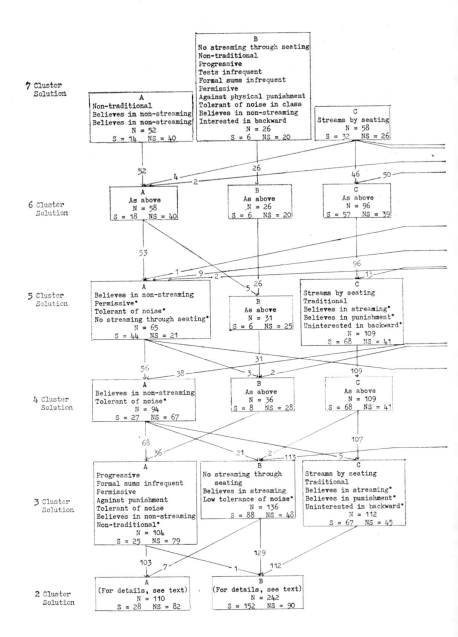

7 Cluster Solution

A
Non-traditional
Believes in non-streaming
Believes in non-streaming
N = 52
S = 14   NS = 40

B
No streaming through seating
Non-traditional
Progressive
Tests infrequent
Formal sums infrequent
Permissive
Against physical punishment
Tolerant of noise in class
Believes in non-streaming
Interested in backward
N = 26
S = 6   NS = 20

C
Streams by seating
N = 58
S = 32   NS = 26

52   4   2   26   46   50

6 Cluster Solution

A
As above
N = 58
S = 18   NS = 40

B
As above
N = 26
S = 6   NS = 20

C
As above
N = 96
S = 57   NS = 39

53   96

1   9   2   5   26   13

5 Cluster Solution

A
Believes in non-streaming
Permissive*
Tolerant of noise*
No streaming through seating*
N = 65
S = 44   NS = 21

B
As above
N = 31
S = 6   NS = 25

C
Streams by seating
Traditional
Believes in streaming*
Believes in punishment*
Uninterested in backward*
N = 109
S = 68   NS = 41

55   38   31   3   2   109

4 Cluster Solution

A
Believes in non-streaming
Tolerant of noise*
N = 94
S = 27   NS = 67

B
As above
N = 36
S = 8   NS = 28

C
As above
N = 109
S = 68   NS = 41

68   36   21   2   113   107   5

3 Cluster Solution

A
Progressive
Formal sums infrequent
Permissive
Against punishment
Tolerant of noise
Believes in non-streaming
Non-traditional*
N = 104
S = 25   NS = 79

B
No streaming through
seating
Believes in streaming
Low tolerance of noise*
N = 136
S = 88   NS = 48

C
Streams by seating
Traditional
Believes in streaming*
Believes in punishment*
Uninterested in backward*
N = 112
S = 67   NS = 45

103   7   1   129   112

2 Cluster Solution

A
(For details, see text)
N = 110
S = 28   NS = 82

B
(For details, see text)
N = 242
S = 152   NS = 90

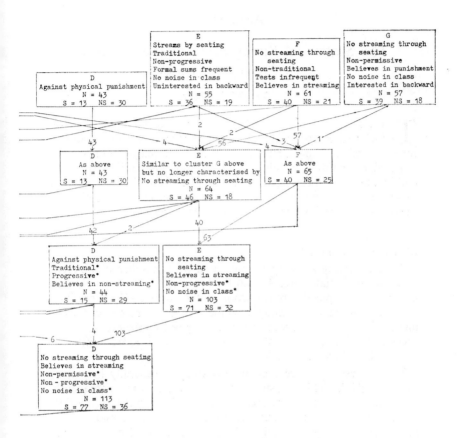

FIGURE 10: *Classification of teachers according to their attitudes and teaching methods*

N = Number of teachers
S = Number of Streamed teachers
NS = Number of Non-streamed teachers
* = Approaching definer value.

497

The Statistical Background to the Analysis of Progress Scores[1]

By JILL M. TARRYER

THE analyses reported in Chapter 5 probe a series of hypotheses which relate to the relative academic progress of children attending streamed and non-streamed schools. These analyses were carried out under conditions which held constant (1) the ability level of the child and (2) the social class of his parents. Three levels of each of these variables were used, full definitions of which have been given in the text together with a description of the test procedure.

Measures of progress

Academic progress may be measured by a number of different functions of initial score, X, and final score, Y. The most obvious measure, a simple difference score of the form X-Y, suffers from two well-known disadvantages, namely that difference scores are unreliable and also that some difficulty may be experienced when it is necessary to interpret 'gains' which have been derived from different levels of initial score.

The progress measure used in this study is generally known as 'residual gain'. This measure is the one which is most frequently recommended in the literature. It may be interpreted as the difference between observed and predicted final score. Residual gain may be expressed symbolically as Y-bX, where X and Y have the same meaning as above and b is the estimated linear regression coefficient of Y on X based on combined within-groups sums of squares and products.

An exploratory analysis of 8+ and 9+ data

One advantage of a longitudinal study is that typical data become available at a relatively early date. It was evident that a preliminary analysis of the 8+ and 9+ results would be of particular advantage

---

[1] See Chapter 5.

in the present study, and a series of correlation and regression analyses were carried out with the following aims in view.

(1) To study the relationships between pupil attributes and academic attainment.

(2) To study the relationships between pupil attributes and academic progress.

(3) To simulate the main analysis, thereby identifying any likely technical problems.

In order to minimize any disruptive effects arising from school and teacher oriented variables, these exploratory analyses were based on pooled within-class correlations. The children were first split into above average, average and below average ability groups according to their 8+ standardized scores on the four basic attainment tests. The children from streamed and non-streamed schools were then studied separately at each of the ability levels, but where appropriate combined results over all three ability groups were considered. In addition, the streamed classes were subdivided into top, middle and bottom streams so that behaviour within streams could also be investigated.[1]

At each level of ability the regression phases of these analyses sought to express either observed standardized scores at 9+, or observed progress scores from 8+ to 9+, in terms of five pupil attributes, sex, age, social class, amount of absence from school and pleasurability rating. In streamed schools a variable based on whether the child had recently changed stream was also included.

The within class correlations between 8+ and 9+ score have been set out in Table A8.1 for each ability level. This shows that when correlations are based on children of comparable ability, the correlations obtained for streamed and non-streamed classes were very similar. Moreover correlations obtained from the ability level most appropriate to a given stream were also of the same order.

The regression analysis indicated that, in addition to ability level, social class should be controlled in the main analysis and also that, contrary to some expectations, it would not be necessary to control age in cases where progress measures were of prime interest.

---

[1] 'Top' streams were A-streams in all schools.

'Middle' streams were B-streams in 3-, 4- and 5-stream schools and C-streams in 4- and 5-stream schools.

'Bottom' streams were B-streams in 2-stream schools, C-streams in 3-stream schools and D- and E-streams in 4- and 5-stream schools.

TABLE A8.1: *Correlations between 8+ and 9+ scores based on within class variation*

SCHOOL ORGANIZATION	TEST NAME	CHILDREN OF BELOW AVERAGE ABILITY	CHILDREN OF AVERAGE ABILITY	CHILDREN OF ABOVE AVERAGE ABILITY
Children in Streamed Classes	Reading	0·63	0·43	0·57
	English	0·72	0·56	0·69
	Mechanical Arithmetic	0·58	0·47	0·57
	Problem Arithmetic	0·56	0·48	0·62
	Concept Arithmetic	0·45	0·46	0·62
Children in Non-Streamed Classes	Reading	0·66	0·52	0·59
	English	0·74	0·64	0·72
	Mechanical Arithmetic	0·52	0·54	0·56
	Problem Arithmetic	0·55	0·48	0·61
	Concept Arithmetic	0·56	0·55	0·70
Sample Sizes: Streamed Classes		711	547	893
Non-Streamed Classes		795	693	607

Note: For the exploratory analysis, ability groups were defined according to standardized scores on the four basic attainment tests, i.e. reading, English, problem and mechanical arithmetic

The analysis of covariance and its relationship to residual gain

The correlation coefficients which were obtained in the exploratory study indicated that the analysis of covariance would be an acceptable technique for assessing academic progress.

Covariance analysis is a method of adjusting criterion variables for the effects of related variables, usually known as covariates, which have not been controlled by the experimental design. In the present context the variable which requires adjustment is the final score, Y, and the covariate is the initial score, X.

The general technique lies in estimating the combined within-group regression coefficient of criterion score on covariate, using this to adjust the criterion scores from each experimental group and then comparing the adjusted criterion scores by analysis of variance.

An essential requirement of this method is that regression coefficients of criterion score on covariate do not differ significantly from one experimental group to another, and it is usual for this underlying assumption of homogeneity of regression to be tested during the course of the covariance calculations.

Appendix Eight

The connection between the analysis of covariance and the concept of residual gain is quite easily demonstrated. Suppose X, Y and b have the same meaning as on page 498, that $\bar{X}$ and $\bar{Y}$ are means of X, Y in the total sample and that subscripts p and q refer to statistics from the two experimental groups, which are to be compared. An application of the analysis of covariance would provide the following expression for the difference between the two adjusted means.

$$[(\bar{Y}_p - \bar{Y}) - b(\bar{X}_p - \bar{X})] - [(\bar{Y}_q - \bar{Y}) - b(\bar{X}_q - \bar{X})]$$

On rearrangement this gives the difference between the mean residual gains from the two samples,

$$\text{i.e. } (\bar{Y}_p - b\bar{X}_p) - (\bar{Y}_q - b\bar{X}_q).$$

The main analysis comparing academic progress in streamed and non-streamed schools

The results of the main analysis are set out in symbolic form in Table 5.1 in the text, and also in greater detail in Tables 5.5a–f in Appendix 6.

The thirty-six groups of pupils which were analysed separately were defined according to the set of tests worked (A/B version), the sex of pupil (boy/girl), and the social class of the pupil (12/3/45)[1] and ability level of pupil (above average, average and below average in terms of the Reading Test score at 7+. See Chapter 5). The pupils were classified by ability primarily because it was felt that different effects might be observed at different ability levels, but, in addition, such a classification was found to be necessary in order to increase the probability of finding homogeneous regression relationships in streamed and non-streamed schools. (See page 500).

Certain differences in the behaviour of the three ability groups were to be expected on account of regression effects (that is the tendency for the scores of a segmented distribution to 'regress' towards the mean on subsequent measurements). This phenomenon arises because any extreme errors of measurement which are inherent in the segmented variables are unlikely to operate in the same direction on further observations. Thus we would expect observed means for below average ability children to increase slightly over the period of the experiment and those for above average children to decrease slightly. These effects should be approximately equal in streamed and non-streamed schools.

[1] For details of the social class definitions see Appendix 4.

Another artefact of segmentation is that standard deviations within ability groups appear to increase over the four year period. This was found to be the case and, as expected, this trend was most marked for the Reading tests on which the ability groups were defined.

There were altogether seven tests and up to four periods of time over which progress could be measured. This resulted in 818 covariance analyses which were carried out on the Orion computer at Rothamsted Experimental Station. The program was written in such a way that all stages of the covariance procedure were calculated, even in cases where the hypothesis of homogeneous regression relationships in streamed and non-streamed schools was rejected.

When this hypothesis of homogeneity is rejected the justification for applying a common adjustment to the means from streamed and non-streamed schools is removed. Thus extreme caution should be exercised whenever interpretations are given to significant differences between adjusted means which have arisen under such tenuous circumstances. Such results have been included in Table 5.1 for the sake of completeness, but have been placed in brackets to draw attention to the fact that the hypothesis of a common regression relationship was suspect.

The complete results of the analysis are far too bulky to be included in the present report. Tables 5.5a–f of Appendix 6 provide further details of progress over the longest time span which was available for each test. These details include sample size, initial mean, final mean, adjusted final mean and mean age (fourth year) for each group of children analysed. The unadjusted initial mean and the unadjusted final mean do not incorporate the usual age-allowances and mean ages should be taken into account when comparing *unadjusted* means from different experimental groups. This procedure was adopted because the exploratory analysis had revealed that age was not associated with progress score. It should be stressed, however, that age was taken into account when children were allocated to ability groups.

The analysis of progress within teacher-type

The second series of covariance analyses compared the academic progress of three groups of children, those taught by Type 1 teachers in non-streamed schools, those taught by Type 2 teachers in non-streamed schools and those taught by all teachers in streamed schools.

The results of boys and girls were combined for this analysis because a further subdivision of the experimental groups would reduce sample sizes to an unacceptable level.

This pooling of the sexes might have biased the outcome of the analysis of progress within teacher-type. A restricted series of co-variance analyses confirmed the expectation that girls make better progress in English and boys make better progress in Problem Arithmetic over the duration of their primary course. Furthermore, an inspection of the relative frequencies of boys and girls in the various experimental groups revealed that, in one or two cases, significant differences in progress score might be attributed to an uneven balance of the sexes between streamed and non-streamed schools rather than to type of teacher or to school type.

In particular, relatively more boys of above average ability and social class 1/2 and also of above average ability and social class 4/5 were found in both A and B samples of streamed schools. Thus it might be expected that pupils from streamed schools in these experimental groups would make better progress in Problem Arithmetic and pupils from non-streamed schools would make better progress in English. An opposite situation arises in B version schools for below average ability children of social class 3. In this instance pupils from non-streamed schools would be expected to make better progress in Problem Arithmetic and pupils from streamed schools to make better progress in English.

Index